ORATIONS

THOMAS HUGHES

ORATIONS

FROM HOMER TO
WILLIAM MCKINLEY

EDITED BY

MAYO W. HAZELTINE, A.M.

ILLUSTRATED

IN TWENTY-FIVE VOLUMES

VOL. XIX

NEW YORK

P. F. COLLIER AND SON

MCMII

CONTENTS

VOLUME NINETEEN

ORATIONS

ANDREW

JOHN ALBION ANDREW, a prominent American statesman and orator, was born in Windham, Maine, May 31, 1818, and educated at Bowdoin College. After studying law he was admitted to the bar in 1840, and for twenty years practised his profession in Boston. He took a lively interest in politics, often making political addresses in support of the Whig party, to which he then belonged; and his action as counsel in several fugitive slave cases brought him into prominence as an ardent opponent of slavery. In 1858 he was elected to the State senate and in 1860 was chosen governor of Massachusetts by the Republicans. He promptly seconded the war measures of Lincoln's administration and in a week after the President had called for troops, on April 15, 1861, Governor Andrew had dispatched five regiments to Washington. He was four times reelected to the governorship, holding the office until January, 1866, when he declined further nomination. During the Civil War he delivered many eloquent and patriotic addresses. He was a man of great executive ability and flawless integrity, and as an orator was both forcible and eloquent. He was prominent as a conservative member of the Unitarian body and presided over the first national Unitarian convention in 1865. He died in Boston, October 30, 1867.

THE EVE OF WAR

FROM ADDRESS TO THE LEGISLATURE OF MASSACHUSETTS, JANUARY 5, 1861

THE constitutional choice to the presidency of a citizen who adheres to the original principles of the fathers of the country, is the happy result of the recent national election. But by events which have since transpired in the southern States it appears that a large, influential, and energetic body of men in that section of the country, who control the action of at least the State of South Carolina, desire to resist, if necessary, by force of arms, this peaceful and constitutional triumph of republican principles, to which they ought in honor and loyalty to yield a generous acquiescence.

Forgetful of the traditions of their ancestors they seem determined to live in peace under no government which shall not concede to them the privilege not only of enslaving their fellow beings within their own dominion, but also of transporting them at their pleasure into the national territory, or from State to State absolutely without restriction, and of retaining them as slaves wheresoever within the national limits they themselves may please to sojourn.

It is the recommendation of President Buchanan in his recent annual message, that by means of constitutional amendments to be initiated by Congress or in a national convention, concessions shall be made for the satisfaction of this extraordinary demand. This is a subject which I commend to your immediate but deliberate consideration, and I shall be happy to concur with what I hope will be the unanimous sentiment of the legislature, in a declaration of the opinion of Massachusetts with reference to the state of the Union and the suggestions of the federal Executive.

If Massachusetts, either by voice or vote, can properly do anything to avert from those misguided men the miserable consequences which threaten to succeed their violent action —the pecuniary disturbances and the civil commotions which must necessarily occur within their own borders if they persist in their career, her voice and vote should not be withheld. Not the least deplorable result of the action of South Carolina I apprehend will be the insecurity to life and property which will result throughout the whole South from fear of servile insurrection. Wherever slavery exists, we have the authority of Jefferson for believing that, in his own words, " the hour of emancipation is advancing in the march of time; it will come; and whether brought on by the generous energy of our own minds, or by the bloody process of St. Domingo, is a leaf of our history not turned over."

The enslaved negro population of the South is not destitute of intelligence nor devoid of that sentiment of resistance to tyranny which naturally inspires the oppressed to seek for freedom. If as appears probable it shall once conceive from the present march of events that it has no hope of emancipation from any generous exertion of the minds of its masters a resort to that process will be only the logical impulse of human nature. That God may be pleased to overrule the folly of man so as to avert so dreadful a calamity must be the prayer of every American; but in my judgment it lies at the end of the road which South Carolina invites her sister States upon the Gulf of Mexico to enter.

I have searched the position of Massachusetts with all the disinterested patriotism which I could command for the performance of that duty, and I find nothing by which I can reproach her with responsibility for such results if they shall come to pass; but I invite you to a similar examination.

The truth of history compels me to declare that one chief source of the difficulty which we are called to encounter lies in the incessant misrepresentation of the principles, purposes, and methods of the people who compose the majority in the free States by superserviceable individuals, who undertake to monopolize friendship for the people of the slaveholding States; and candor requires me to add that they profess a friendship the largest part of which might be analyzed into dislike of their political opponents.

I have for twenty years past been a constant and careful observer of public men and affairs; and for twelve years, at least, I have been intimately aware of the private as well as the public declarations and conduct of the representative men in almost every town and village of the Commonwealth. I think I may claim also some intimacy with the great body of the people of Massachusetts of whatsoever party. This period has been one of extraordinary and intense political interest. The tenderest sentiments, the deepest convictions, the warmest emotions have all been stirred by the course of public affairs. Bitter disappointments, the keenest sense of injustice, the consciousness of subjection to most flagrant wrong have fallen to the lot of our people.

The Fugitive Slave Bill of 1850 with its merciless severity and the ostentatious indignity with which it was executed; the repeal of the Missouri restriction upon the extension of slavery over national territory; the violent means adopted to prevent emigrants from this Commonwealth from participating in the settlement of Kansas; the invasion of that Territory by men armed with the plunder from national arsenals; the imposition of fraudulent legislatures upon a people temporarily subjugated by ruffianism and unprotected by a federal executive which also forbade them to protect themselves; the indiscriminate pillage, fire, and slaughter to which peaceable settlers were subjected without cause or excuse; the repeated exertions of the national administration in conspiracy with the enemies of freedom and good government, to impose and enforce upon Kansas a constitution sanctioning slavery; the attempt to withdraw the discussion of political questions from the people themselves and to confine it to a conclave of judges; the assault upon free speech in Congress by a murderous attack upon a senator in his seat for opinions expressed in debate and for the manner of their expression; the indifference of positive approval with which this attempt to overthrow representative institutions was treated throughout a large portion of the country; the prostitution of all the powers of the government and the bending of all its energy to propagate a certain interest for the benefit of a few speculators in lands, negroes, and politics, and to discourage the free labor of the toiling masses of the people; the menaces of violence and war against the constitution and the Union with which our arguments and our constitutional resistance have been met; these all are but a part of the record of the last ten years of American political history, which is burned into the memory of the people of Massachusetts.

And yet during all the excitement of this period, inflamed by the heats of repeated presidential elections, I have never known a single Massachusetts Republican to abandon his loyalty, surrender his faith, or seal up his heart against the good hopes and kind affections which every devoted citizen ought to entertain for every section of his country. During all this maladministration of the national government, the people of Massachusetts have never wavered from their faith in its principles or their loyalty to its organization.

Looking forward to the long ages of the future; building always, in their own minds, for countless generations yet to come; they have endured, and are willing still cheerfully and hopefully to endure, much wrong and more misconception, because they trust in the blood inherited from heroic ancestors; in the principles of constitutional liberty; in the theory of democratic institutions; in the honest purpose of the intelligent masses of the people everywhere; in the capacity of truth and right ultimately to reach and control the minds of men; in an undying affection for their whole country, its memories, traditions, and hopes; and above all in the good Providence of God.

It was at a great cost that our fathers established their independence and erected this Union of States—which exists under the form of a national government, unquestionable as to its authority to act on all persons and all things within the sphere of its jurisdiction and the range of its granted powers. It needs ask permission from no one to fulfil its functions or to perpetuate its existence. It has no right nor power to abdicate; nor to expel a State, or any portion of the people of any State, from the benefits of its protection; nor to permit their revolt against the duties of a common citizenship.

By the incurring of national debts, by the granting of pensions, patents, and copyrights, by the issue of commissions establishing a tenure of office not terminable at the pleasure of the appointing power, by the purchase and the conquest of territory erected into additional States, by the improvement of harbors and rivers and the construction of military roads, by the settlement of wildernesses and the development of their resources under the national patronage, by the investment of vast sums of money in buildings for the transaction of public business, in light-houses, navy-yards, fortifications, vessels of war, and their equipment, by the assumption of obligations under treaties with Indian tribes and foreign powers, the people of the United States have paid and are paying a continuing consideration for the existence of this national government in all its sovereign territorial integrity.

All the people of all the States are interlocked and interlaced in a vast web of mutual interests, rights, and obligations as various and as precious as are the characteristics of that wonderful civilization in which they participate. And this Union, through whatever throes or crises it may pass, cannot expire except with the annihilation of the people.

Come what may I believe that Massachusetts will do her duty. She will stand by the incoming national administration as she has stood by the past ones; because her people will forever stand by their country. The records of her revolutionary history declare her capacity and her will to expend money, sympathy, and men to sustain the common cause. More than half the soldiers of the Revolution were furnished by New England; and Massachusetts alone contributed more men to the federal armies than were enlisted in all the southern States. She is willing to make the same sacrifices again if need be in the same cause; and her capacity to do so has increased in proportion with the increase in her wealth and population.

The echoes of the thunder of her revolutionary battlefields have not yet died away upon the ears of her sons, and the vows and prayers of her early patriots still whisper their inspiration. The people of Massachusetts will in any event abide by her plighted faith. She agreed to the constitution of the United States. It is the charter of the Union, it is the record of the contract, and the written evidence of rights intended to be secured to the States and to the people.

History shows that never at any one time is there more than one grand issue on trial under a popular government before the great tribunal of the people. A reactionary movement against the doctrines and traditions of liberty handed down from the beginning precipitated the trial in the elections of 1856 of an issue made up upon the relation of slavery to the territorial possessions of the nation, and the right of the people to manage those possessions so as to protect themselves, preserve their liberties, strengthen the Union, promote the common happiness and welfare, and best develop the resources of the lands within exclusive federal jurisdiction.

By the conduct and manifest designs of the leaders of that same reactionary movement the same issue was kept open and presented to the country in a form still more intense, and a popular verdict demanded in the elections of 1860. So far as that issue can be settled by a popular election of President of the United States, its settlement is for the present complete. In the next national election it may again be presented and the grand issue of 1860 be repeated in 1864, should the people of the country be of opinion that any duty or practical advantage remains dependent on the possible result of a new trial. Meanwhile other duties command our immediate care. There is now no issue before the people touching their political relations to slavery in the Territories. The policy of the national government in that regard is determined for the next four years; but instead of preparing for a rehearing and an endeavor to reverse the verdict at the end of that period, that party of reaction has now engaged in an effort to abolish the tribunal and overthrow the authority of the people themselves. And the single question now presented to the nation is this: " Shall a reactionary spirit, unfriendly to liberty, be permitted to subvert democratic republican government organized under constitutional forms? "

Upon this issue, over the heads of all mere politicians and partisans, in behalf of the Commonwealth of Massachusetts I appeal directly to the warm hearts and clear heads of the great masses of the people. The men who own and till the soil, who drive the mills, and hammer out their own iron and leather on their own anvils and lapstones, and they who, whether in the city or the country, reap the rewards of enterprising industry and skill in the varied pursuits of business, are honest, intelligent, patriotic, independent, and brave. They know that simple defeat in an election is no cause for the disruption of a government. They know that those who declare that they will not live peaceably within the Union do not mean to live peaceably out of it. They know that the people of all sections have a right which they intend to maintain, of free access from the interior to both oceans, and from Canada to the Gulf of Mexico, and of the free use of all the lakes and rivers and highways of commerce, north, south, east, or west. They know that the Union means peace and unfettered commercial intercourse from sea to sea and from shore to shore; that it secures us all against the unfriendly presence or possible dictation of any foreign power, and commands respect for our flag and security for our trade.

And they do not intend, nor will they ever consent to be excluded from these rights which they have so long enjoyed, nor to abandon the prospect of the benefits which humanity claims for itself by means of their continued enjoyment in the future. Neither will they consent that the continent shall be overrun by the victims of a remorseless cupidity, and the elements of civil danger increased by the barbarizing influences which accompany the African slave trade.

Inspired by the same ideas and emotions which commanded the fraternization of Jackson and Webster on another great occasion of public danger, the people of Massachusetts, confiding in the patriotism of their brethren in other States, accept this issue and respond in the words of Jackson: "The Federal Union, it must be preserved!"

IN HONOR OF PATRIOT HEROES

AT COMMEMORATION EXERCISES HELD IN CAMBRIDGE,
JULY 21, 1865

MR. PRESIDENT,—Not an alumnus or scholar of Harvard College, I could hardly persuade myself of the propriety of my position upon the platform to-day; and yet the relation which I have borne these last four years to so many of the sons of Harvard, and to the soldier-sons of Massachusetts, forbade me to deny myself the honor of the meeting. And now that I rise to speak a few words of allusion to those who are not here, so many are the struggling memories and contending fancies that rush thick upon the heart, that I hardly know whether I address myself to the dim shadows and dusky reminiscences that have passed away, or to the more palpable forms of this real presence; and if there were words of human speech fit to portray their history, to speak their praise, or to deck their graves, those words, alas! they are not mine. They spring not from human lips; they are not born from oral speech. But there are testimonies more potent, more impressive, more electric than the human voice, and they are here to-day, in that cloud of living witnesses who have come back laden with glory from the fields where their comrades fell. Let them speak! Let the hero of Gettysburg by his presence speak! Of the ten sons of Harvard who left their fair young forms upon that gory field, let the young Murat of Harvard, the hero of twenty fights, by his presence speak! Let all these brave men, whatever uniform they wear, from that of the humble private to the more ambitious regalia of the commander,—they who saw their brethren go down at Gettysburg, and bite the dust at Fredericksburg, beneath the wall, or sink below the stream,—let them speak? At Ball's Bluff, where many a young life was lost in the Potomac or on the Virginia shore, at Chancellorsville, on the James river, in front of Petersburg, down along the shore of North Carolina, up the rivers of South Carolina, up the Savannah, on the Gulf, before New Orleans, all the way up the Mississippi river, wherever on land or sea, on field or deck, our flag was borne, whether in victory or defeat, there stood the sons of Massachusetts and of Harvard College.

Your president has alluded to some of the statistics of the sons of Harvard. I have already mentioned the fact that ten fell at Gettysburg; seven also fell at Antietam; five at Fredericksburg; five at Cedar Mountain; three at Chancellorsville; three at Bull Run; three in the Wilderness, and three at Fort Wagner. I need not detain you with the statistics of other engagements where your brothers fell; but every arm of the service, military and naval, was represented from your college; every rank, from major-general to private, was represented from your college,—represented in life and in death,—from Wadsworth, the major-general of the class of 1828, who fell in the Wilderness, to Emerson, the private of the class of 1861, who fell at Chancellorsville. So also upon the sea, from the rear-admiral to the lieutenant, you find also there the sons of Harvard College.

My eye has fallen this afternoon upon at least two field officers, to say nothing of others who during the first seven days of the war marched either to the rescue of the national capital or to the deliverance of the key of the Potomac River—Fortress Monroe. And I ought not to omit, as the thought occurs to me in speaking, especial reference to that

Middlesex regiment, the Fifth Massachusetts militia, commanded by a graduate of Harvard College, who after their three months of duty had expired by voluntary election chose to remain to fight out the battle of Bull Run. And I know not that the history of the war records an instance of a single man who ever retired to the rear while the battle was going on, and he capable of service.

But not merely at the beginning and through the major part of the conflict, but down to its very close, your brethren remained, and two of your young brethren, Sumner Paine and Cabot Russell, who would have graduated in the class of the present year, laid down their lives in separate battles, one of them falling at Gettysburg and the other by the side of Colonel Shaw at Fort Wagner.

Nor did they win their honors in Massachusetts or New England regiments alone. Colonel Porter from New York fell at Cold Harbor; Colonel Peabody from Missouri fell at Pittsburg Landing; and not to delay you with the list of less conspicuous names, I beg your scrutiny of the catalogue laid before you,—to this record and roll of your honored sons,— as a testimony of the wide diffusiveness of the patriotism and military heroism exhibited by the sons of your honored university. I allude to it because it illustrates the wide range of influence which belongs to this ancient and revered seminary of learning.

Nor is any particular class of the people of New England or of the other States, who in their own persons or in the persons of their sons have resorted here for the purposes of learning, been found alone in these works of war more than in the other ways of patriotic duty; but from every class and employment and interest of human society they have rushed to the service of their country. The sacred profession as

well as the other learned professions has been amply represented; and I count it to be one of the crowning glories of
the intellectual culture and intelligence in which properly
you may take pride, that throughout the whole army of the
Union the medical staff of Massachusetts stands pre-eminently and confessedly by universal consent the first. The
first chaplain who laid down his life in the war was Arthur
Fuller, your own brother of the Sixteenth Massachusetts,
who, musket in hand, fell in front of Fredericksburg. All
ages, too,—all ages of your alumni have been represented.
It might easily have been true, were you to compare the
ages without reference to the relationship of the men in the
volunteer service or the regular service, on land or sea, that
son and father and grandfather had been fighting at the
same time on the same field and in defence of the same flag.

All the old historic names, or nearly all, which in former
times have illustrated the fame of New England and the
memories of the college, have been found upon the rosters
of our volunteer regiments. I hardly know whether I ought
to trust myself from mere recollection, to speak of half a
dozen of them, since there are so many dozens who with equal
honor ought to be remembered. But five names represented
each by two brothers, whose lives consecrated to their
country were at last laid a forfeit upon its altar need not be
omitted. The family of Revere offered two brothers who
gave their lives upon the field of battle; the name of Lowell
two more,—two brothers slain in the conflict; the name of
Abbott two more,—two brothers who from the field of battle
ascended to immortality; the family of Dwight two more,—
two brothers; the family of Stevens two more,—two brothers;
and I speak no more than the simplicity of truth when I declare to you that if you will but look over the catalogue of

your college and compare the list of names with the more honorable names in all that has distinguished the public service, the science, the patriotism, the literary culture of New England, you will find them all represented in this sternest duty of modern patriotism.

There have been no nobler acts of specific personal heroism than those which have been performed by your own alumni. I see the name of one upon that immortal role of fame,—one not widely known, not destined by military rank to illustrious homage in the great hereafter, but one nobler than whom neither Lacedæmonian nor American patriotism ever knew. I mean Sergeant Brown of the Nineteenth Massachusetts, who after he was smitten with death on the field of Antietam refused to give up the colors of which he was the bearer, but with one desperate, determined rush in front of his lines, with the volcanic energy of his patriotic nature, just as his heart struggled with the throes of death, he stuck the staff of the flag deep into the earth, and falling lay there and died by its side, its ample folds waving aloft. I know no instance of more perfect, of more heroic gentility bespeaking a noble nature than the act performed by one captain of the Second Massachusetts, whose name I would not dare, in this connection, before this company and in his presence to speak; who, standing by the side of Lieutenant-Colonel Savage, one of the noblest of the sons of Massachusetts, of the boys of Harvard, fatally wounded, not believed by the enemy to be worth the saving, refused to surrender to the enemy until he had wrung from them the pledge that they would, in capturing him, save also his comrade and bear him back to the nearest hospital; declaring that if they did not, single-handed and alone, he would fight it out and sell his life at the dearest cost.

Your graduates, your fellow students, associated in their

family histories, not only with the patriotism of Massachusetts and of New England, but of the whole country, were associated not only at the beginning of the war, but at an early period with the volunteer militia of the Commonwealth. It occurs to me that there was one who bore a name not less honored than any other in western Massachusetts,—I mean Major William Sedgwick,—who was himself a lineal descendent of that Captain Robert Sedgwick who was the first commander of the ancient and honorable artillery of Massachusetts.

Therefore, when you trace yourselves back in the persons of your comrades through the public service of the country, either in peace or in war,—whether you trace yourselves back through the military service in time of war, but through that of the militia in time of peace, preparing for war,—whether you seek for illustrations of fidelity in camp or whether you seek for more striking and brilliant illustrations of bravery on the field, you find men who may be safely counted among the most conspicuous. All over the country in all parts of the great field,—not only in the Army of the Potomac, not only in the Army of Virginia, not only in the Army of North Carolina, but in all the Western armies, under whatever commander, whether Fremont, or Halleck, or Sherman, or Banks, or Grant,—you have found the sons of your own institution. As I sat down this morning I wrote off from the catalogue a few names, most of them the least conspicuous, because the least conspicuous would be the most truly illustrative just to show how far you have extended, and how wisely your soldier-boys have spread themselves over this vast theatre of war. Surgeon Wheelwright fell on the lower Mississippi; Lieutenant Ripley in Arkansas; Private Goodrich at Vicksburg; Lieutenant Leavitt at White

Stone Hill, Dacotah; Paymaster Bowman at New Orleans; Lieutenant Burrage at Lookout Mountain; Lieutenant Haven at Baton Rouge; and Private Tucker at Port Hudson.

But time would fail me were I to venture upon these illusions or illustrations personal to any men. The work of the war is almost over. The hardships of these many campaigns have been nobly borne. The record of your heroism and valor upon the field has been made complete. God grant the present generation of men may not be called on to repeat the struggle! But the work of manhood and of duty is not complete; and I hold it a higher praise to this great and venerable institution of thought and of learning, that while she has been through the war among the foremost in the front ranks of patriotism in carrying forward the flag of our country upon the field, she is to-day the foremost in the front ranks of liberal thought, of progressive politics, of scientific and honest philosophy in America. And when I heard commencement day, the repeated testimonies of the coming prophets of the Harvard of 1865, I knew so rapidly has history been made within the last twenty years that the fulfilment of the prophecies will not be later than 1875. I am not one of those who are impatient for the visible progress of events; for well I know that wherever there is the prophet, and the truth behind him, there must follow as a part of the necessary providence of God in the order of human events, the historic fulfilment. You may build your monumental walls,—I applaud the loving purpose that would pile high in the air magnificent structures of eternal granite, piercing the sky and standing upon the solid base of earth immortal as the Pyramids, to preserve in indestructible, visible form the history of your patriotic brethren who now sleep beneath the dust; but there is a monument more enduring than brass;

there is a record more lasting and immortal than the page of
history or the songs of poets—the grateful memory of mankind. The memory of mankind shall preserve their names
when all monumental structures shall have sunk beneath the
dust that covers us. You can make a monument that shall
keep in remembrance not only your brethren, but yourselves,
by making mankind your debtors by the fidelity with which
you adhere to the truth and the doctrines for which they died.
From ten thousand homes all over this broad, fair land, proud
hearts, grateful hearts and tearful eyes remember them.
For ten thousand ages, if you are faithful to their work, they
and you shall be remembered, and the graves they fill shall
be the door through which you and they shall enter immortality.

But I must not detain you upon this theme. They
sleep well, and you remember fondly,

> " So sleep the brave who sink to rest
> With all their country's wishes blest.
> When Spring, with dewy fingers cold,
> Returns to deck their hallowed mold,
> It there shall dress a sweeter sod
> Than fancy's feet have ever trod.
> By fairy hands their knell is rung,
> By forms unseen their dirge is sung;
> There Honor comes, a pilgrim gray,
> To bless the turf that wraps their clay,
> And Freedom shall awhile repair,
> To dwell a weeping hermit there."

ON THE RETURN OF THE BATTLE FLAGS

[Major-General Couch, upon delivering the flags of the hundred Massachusetts regiments and batteries, December 22, 1865, addressed the governor in the following words:

" May it please your Excelleney: We have come here to-day as the
representatives of the army of volunteers furnished by Massachusetts for
the suppression of the rebellion, bringing these colors in order to return
them to the State which intrusted them to our keeping. You must, however, pardon us if we give them up with profound regret—for these tat-

tered shreds forcibly remind us of long and fatiguing marches, cold
bivouacs, and many hard-fought battles. The rents in their folds, the
battle-stains on their escutcheons, the blood of our comrades that has
sanctified the soil of a hundred fields, attest the sacrifices that have
been made, the courage and constancy shown, that the nation might live.
It is, sir, a peculiar satisfaction and pleasure to us that you, who have
been an honor to the State and nation, from your marked patriotism and
fidelity throughout the war, and have been identified with every organization before you, are now here to receive back, as the State custodian
of her precious relics, these emblems of the devotion of her sons. May
it please your Excellency, the colors of the Massachusetts volunteers are
returned to the State."

The governor replied:]

GENERAL,—This pageant, so full of pathos and of
glory, forms the concluding scene in the long series
of visible actions and events in which Massachusetts
has borne a part for the overthrow of rebellion and the
vindication of the Union.

These banners return to the government of the Commonwealth through welcome hands. Borne, one by one, out of
this Capitol during more than four years of civil war as the
symbols of the nation and the Commonwealth, under which
the battalions of Massachusetts departed to the field,—they
come back again, borne hither by surviving representatives
of the same heroic regiments and companies to which they
were intrusted.

At the hands, General, of yourself, the ranking officer of
the volunteers of the Commonwealth (one of the earliest
who accepted a regimental command under appointment of
the governor of Massachusetts)—and of this grand column
of scarred and heroic veterans who guard them home, they
are returned with honors becoming relics so venerable, soldiers so brave, and citizens so beloved.

Proud memories of many a field; sweet memories alike of
valor and friendship; sad memories of fraternal strife; tender
memories of our fallen brothers and sons, whose dying eyes
looked last upon their flaming folds; grand memories of

heroic virtues sublimed by grief; exultant memories of the great and final victory of our country, our Union, and the righteous cause; thankful memories of a deliverance wrought out for human nature itself, unexampled by any former achievement of arms—immortal memories with immortal honors blended, twine around these splintered staves, weave themselves along the warp and woof of these familiar flags, war-worn, begrimed, and baptized with blood. Let " the brave heart, the trusty heart, the deep, unfathomable heart," in words of more than mortal eloquence, uttered though unexpressed, speak the emotions of grateful veneration for which these lips of mine are alike too feeble and unworthy.

General, I accept these relics in behalf of the people and the government. They will be preserved and cherished amid all the vicissitudes of the future as mementoes of brave men and noble actions.

VALEDICTORY ADDRESS

DELIVERED TO THE TWO BRANCHES OF THE LEGISLATURE ON RETIRING FROM OFFICE, JANUARY 5, 1866

GENTLEMEN OF THE SENATE AND THE HOUSE OF REPRESENTATIVES,—The people of Massachusetts have vindicated alike their intelligence, their patriotism, their will, and their power; both in the cultivation of the arts of peace, and in the prosecution of just and unavoidable war. At the end of five years of executive administration I appear before a convention of the two Houses of her general court in the execution of a final duty.

For nearly all that period the Commonwealth as a loyal

State of the American Union has been occupied within her sphere of co-operation in helping to maintain by arms the power of the nation, the liberties of the people, and the rights of human nature.

Having contributed to the army and the navy—including regulars, volunteers, seamen, and marines, men of all arms and officers of all grades and of the various terms of service— an aggregate of 159,165 men; and having expended for the war out of her own treasury $27,705,109,—besides the expenditures of her cities and towns she has maintained by the unfailing energy and economy of her sons and daughters her industry and thrift even in the waste of war. She has paid promptly, and in gold, all interest on her bonds,—including the old and the new,—guarding her faith and honor with every public creditor, while still fighting the public enemy; and now at last in retiring from her service I confess the satisfaction of having first seen all of her regiments and batteries (save two battalions) returned and mustered out of the army; and of leaving her treasury provided for by the fortunate and profitable negotiation of all the permanent loan needed or foreseen—with her financial credit maintained at home and abroad, her public securities unsurpassed, if even equalled, in value in the money market of the world by those of any State or of the nation.

I have already had the honor to lay before the general court, by special message to the Senate, a statement of all affairs which demand my own official communication. And it only remains for me to transfer at the appropriate moment the cares, the honors, and the responsibilities of office to the hands of that eminent and patriotic citizen on whose public experience and ability the Commonwealth so justly relies.

But perhaps before descending for the last time from this

venerable seat, I may be indulged in some allusion to the broad field of thought and statesmanship to which the war itself has conducted us. As I leave the Temple where, humbled by my unworthiness, I have stood so long like a priest of Israel sprinkling the blood of the holy sacrifice on the altar—I would fain contemplate the solemn and manly duties which remain to us who survive the slain, in honor of their memory and in obedience to God.

The nation having been ousted by armed rebellion of its just possession and the exercise of its constitutional juris-diction over the territory of the rebel States, has now at last by the suppression of the rebellion (accomplished by the vic-tories of the national arms over those of the rebels) regained possession and restored its own rightful sway.

The rebels had overthrown the loyal State governments. They had made war against the Union. The government of each rebel State had not only withdrawn its allegiance, but had given in its adhesion to another, namely, the Con-federate government,—a government not only injurious by its very creation, but hostile to and in arms against the Union, asserting and exercising belligerent rights both on land and sea, and seeking alliances with foreign nations, even demanding the armed intervention of neutral powers.

The pretensions of this " Confederacy " were maintained for some four years in one of the most extensive, persistent, and bloody wars of history. To overcome it and maintain the rights and the very existence of the Union, our national government was compelled to keep on foot one of the most stupendous military establishments the world has ever known. And probably the same amount of force, naval and military, was never organized and involved in any national controversy.

On both sides there was war, with all its incidents, all its claims, its rights and its results.

The States in rebellion tried, under the lead of their new Confederacy, to conquer the Union; but in the attempt they were themselves conquered.

They did not revert by their rebellion nor by our conquest into "Territories." They did not commit suicide. But they rebelled, they went to war; and they were conquered.

A "Territory" of the United States is a possession or dependency of the United States having none of the distinctive constitutional attributes of a State. A Territory might be in rebellion; but not thereby cease to be a Territory. It would be properly described as a Territory in rebellion. Neither does a State in rebellion cease to be a State. It would be correctly described, a State in rebellion. And it would be subject to the proper consequences of rebellion both direct and incidental,—among which may be that of military government or supervision by the nation, determinable only by the nation at its own just discretion in the due exercise of the rights of war. The power to put an end to its life is not an attribute of a State of our Union. Nor can the Union put an end to its own life, save by an alteration of the national constitution, or by suffering such defeat in war as to bring it under the jurisdiction of a conqueror. The nation has a vested interest in the life of the individual State. The States have a vested interest in the life of the Union. I do not perceive, therefore, how a State has the power by its own action alone, without the co-operation of the Union, to destroy the continuity of its corporate life. Nor do I perceive how the national Union can by its own action, without the action or omission of the States, destroy the continuity of its own corporate life. It seems to me that the stream of life flows through both State and nation from a double source; which is a distinguishing element of its vital power. Eccentricity of motion is not death; nor is abnormal action organic change.

The position of the rebel States is fixed by the constitution, and by the laws or rights of war. If they had conquered the Union they might have become independent, or whatever else it might have been stipulated they should become by the terms of an ultimate treaty of peace. But being conquered they failed in becoming independent, and they failed in accomplishing anything but their own conquest. They were still States,—though belligerents conquered. But they had lost their loyal organization as States, lost their present possession of their political and representative power in the Union. Under the constitution they have no means nor power of their own to regain it. But the exigency is provided for by that clause in the federal constitution in which the federal government guarantees a republican form of government to every State. The regular and formal method would be therefore for the national government to provide specifically for their reorganization.

The right and duty, however, of the general government under the circumstances of their present case is not the single one of reorganizing these disorganized States. The war imposed rights and duties peculiar to itself, and to the relations and the results of war. The first duty of the nation is to regain its own power. It has already made a great advance in the direction of its power.

If ours were a despotic government it might even now be thought that it had already accomplished the re-establishment of its power as a government. But ours being a republican and a popular government, it cannot be affirmed that the proper power of the government is restored until a peaceful, loyal and faithful state of mind gains a sufficient ascendancy in the rebel and belligerent States, to enable the Union and loyal citizens everywhere to repose alike on the purpose and the ability of their people in point of numbers and capacity, to assert, maintain, and conduct State governments, republican in form, loyal in sentiment and character, with safety to themselves and to the national whole. If the people, or too large a portion of the people of a given rebel State are not willing and able to do this, then the state of war still exists, or at least a condition consequent upon and incidental thereto exists, which only the exercise on our part f belligerent rights, or some of their incidents can meet or an cure. The rights of war must continue until the objects of the war have been accomplished and the nation recognizes the return of a state of peace. It is absolutely necessary then for the Union government to prescribe some reasonable test of loyalty to the people of the States in rebellion. It is necessary to require of them conformity to those arrangements which the war has rendered or proved to be necessary to the public peace and necessary as securities for the future. As the conquering party, the national government has the right to govern these belligerent States meanwhile, at its own wise and conscientious discretion, subject: 1st. To the demands of natural justice, humanity, and the usages of civilized nations. 2d. To its duty under the constitution, to guarantee republican governments to the States.

But there is no arbiter, save the people of the United States, between the government of the Union and those States. Therefore the precise things to be done, the precise way to do them, the precise steps to be taken, their order, progress, and direction, are all within the discretion of the national government, in the exercise, both of its belligerent and its more strictly constitutional functions,—exercising them according to its own wise, prudent, and just discretion. Its duty is not only to restore those States, but also to make sure of a lasting peace of its own ultimate safety and the permanent establishment of the rights of all its subjects. To this end I venture the opinion that the government of the United States ought to require the people of those States to reform their constitutions:

1. Guaranteeing to the people of color, now the wards of the nation, their civil rights as men and women on an equality with the white population by amendments irrepealable in terms.

2. Regulating the elective franchise according to certain laws of universal application, and not by rules merely arbitrary, capricious, and personal.

3. Annulling the ordinances of secession.

4. Disaffirming the rebel debt, and

5. To ratify the anti-slavery amendment of the United States constitution by their legislatures.

And I would have all these questions save the fifth—the disposition of which is regulated by the federal constitution— put to the vote of the people themselves. We should neither be satisfied with the action of the conventions which have been held nor with what is termed the " loyal vote." We want the popular vote. And the rebel vote is better than the loyal vote if on the right side. If it is not on the right side, then I fear those States are incapable at present of reorganization; the proper power of the Union government is not restored; the people of those States are not yet prepared to assume their original functions with safety to the Union;

and the state of war still exists; for they are contumacious and disobedient to the just demands of the Union, disowning the just conditions precedent to reorganization.

We are desirous of their reorganization and to end the use of the war power. But I am confident we cannot reorganize political society with any proper security: 1. Unless we let in the people to a co-operation, and not merely an arbitrarily selected portion of them. 2. Unless we give those who are, by their intelligence and character, the natural leaders of the people, and who surely will lead them by-and-by, an opportunity to lead them now.

I am aware that it has been a favorite dogma in many quarters, " No rebel voters." But it is impossible in certain States to have any voting by white men if only " loyal men "—that is, those who continued so during the rebellion— are permitted to vote. This proposition is so clear that the President adopted the expedient of assuming that those who had not risen above certain civil or military grades in the rebel public service, and who had neither inherited nor earned more than a certain amount of property, should be deemed and taken to be sufficiently harmless to be intrusted with the suffrage in the work of reorganization. Although there is some reason for assuming that the less conspicuous and less wealthy classes of men had less to do than their more towering neighbors in conducting the State into the rebellion and through it—still I do not imagine that either wealth or conspicuous position, which are only the accidents of men, or at most only external incidents, affect the substance of their characters. I think the poorer and less significant men who voted or fought for Southern independence had quite as little love for the Yankees, quite as much prejudice against the Abolitionists, quite as much contempt for the colored man, and quite as much disloyalty at heart as their more powerful neighbors.

The true question is now not of past disloyalty but of present loyal purpose. We need not try to disguise the fact that we have passed through a great popular revolution. Everybody in the rebel States was disloyal with exceptions too few and too far between to comprise a loyal force sufficient to constitute the State, even now that the armies of the rebellion are overthrown. Do not let us deceive ourselves. The truth is the public opinion of the white race in the South was in favor of the rebellion. The colored people sympathized with the Union cause. To the extent of their intelligence they understood that the success of the South meant their continued slavery; that an easy success of the North meant leaving slavery just where we found it; that the war meant, if it lasted long enough—their emancipation. The whites went to war and supported the war because they hoped to succeed in it; since they wanted or thought they wanted separation from the Union, or Southern independence. There were then three great interests—there were the Southern whites, who as a body wished for what they called Southern independence; the Southern blacks who desired emancipation; the people of the " loyal States " who desired to maintain the constitutional rights and the territorial integrity of the nation. Some of us in the North had a strong hope, which by the favor of God has not been disappointed, out of our defence of the Union to accomplish the deliverance of our fellow men in bondage. But the loyal idea included emancipation, not for its own sake but for the sake of the Union—if the Union could be saved or served by it. There were many men in the South—besides those known as loyal—who did not like to incur the responsibility of war against the Union; or who did not think the opportune moment had arrived to fight the North; or in whose hearts there was "a divided allegiance." But they were not the positive men. They were with very few exceptions not the leading minds, the courageous men, the impressive and powerful characters,—they were not the young and active men. And when the decisive hour came they went to the wall. No matter what they thought or how they felt about it; they could not stand, or they would not stand—certainly they did not stand against the storm. The revolution either converted them or swept them off their feet. Their own sons volunteered. They became involved in all the work and in all the consequences of the war. The Southern people— as a people—fought, toiled, endured, and persevered, with a courage, a unanimity, and a persistency not outdone by any people in any revolution. There was never an acre of territory abandoned to the Union while it could be held by arms. There was never a rebel regiment surrendered to the Union arms until resistance was overcome by force; or a surrender was compelled by the stress of battle or of military strategy. The people of the South, men and women, soldiers and civilians, volunteers and conscripts, in the army and at home followed the fortunes of the rebellion and obeyed its leaders so long as it had any fortunes or any leaders. Their young men marched up to the cannon's mouth a thousand times where they were mowed down like grain by the reapers when the harvest is ripe. Some men had the faculty and the faith in the rebel cause to become its leaders. The others had the faculty and faith to follow them.

All honor to the loyal few! But I do not regard the distinction between loyal and disloyal persons of the white race residing in the South during the rebellion as being for present purposes a practical distinction. It is even doubtful whether the comparatively loyal few (with certain prominent and honorable exceptions), can be well discriminated from the disloyal mass. And since the President finds himself obliged to let in the great mass of the disloyal by the very terms of his proclamation of amnesty to a participation in the business of reorganizing the rebel States, I am obliged also to confess that I think to make one rule for the richer and higher rebels and another rule for the poorer and more lowly rebels is impolitic and unphilosophical. I find evidence in the granting of pardons that such also is the opinion of the President.

When the day arrives which must surely come, when an amnesty, substantially universal, shall be proclaimed, the leading minds of the South, who by temporary policy and artificial rules had been for the while disfranchised, will resume their influence and their sway. The capacity of leadership is a gift, not a device. They whose courage, talents, and will entitle them to lead, will lead. And these men—not then estopped by their own consent or participation in the business of reorganization—may not be slow to question the validity of great public transactions enacted during their own disfranchisement. If it is asked in reply, "What can they do?" and "What can come of their discontent?" I answer, that while I do not know just what they can do nor what may come of it, neither do I know what they may not attempt nor what they may not accomplish. I only know that we ought to demand and to secure the co-operation of the strongest and ablest minds and the natural leaders of opinion in the South. If we cannot gain their support of the just measures needful for the work of safe reorganization, reorganization will be delusive and full of danger.

Why not try them? They are the most hopeful subjects to deal with in the very nature of the case. They have the brain and the experience and the education to enable them to understand the exigencies of the present situation. They have the courage as well as the skill to lead the people in the direction their judgments point, in spite of their own and the popular prejudice. Weaker men, those of less experience, who have less hold on the public confidence are comparatively powerless. Is it consistent with reason and our knowledge of human nature to believe the masses of Southern men able to face about, to turn their backs on those they have trusted and followed, and to adopt the lead of those who have no magnetic hold on their hearts or minds? Reorganization in the South demands the aid of men of great moral courage, who can renounce their own past opinions and do it boldly; who can comprehend what the work is and what are the logical consequences of the new situation; men who have interests urging them to rise to the height of the occasion. They are not the strong men from whom weak, vacillating counsels come; nor are they the great men from whom come counsels born of prejudices and follies, having their root in an institution they know to be dead and buried beyond the hope of resurrection.

Has it never occurred to us all that we are now proposing the most wonderful and unprecedented of human transactions? The conquering government at the close of a great war is about restoring to the conquered rebels not only their local governments in the States, but their representative share in the general government of the country! They are, in their States, to govern themselves as they did before the rebellion. The conquered rebels are in the Union to help govern and control the conquering loyalists! These being the privileges which they are to enjoy when reorganization becomes complete, I declare that I know not any safeguard, precaution, or act of prudence, which wise statesmanship might not recognize to be reasonable and just. If we have no right to demand guarantees for the future; if we have no right to insist upon significant acts of loyal submission from the rebel leaders themselves; if we have no right to demand the positive popular vote in favor of the guarantees we need; if we may not stipulate for the recognition of the just rights of the slaves, whom, in the act of suppressing the rebellion, we converted from slaves into freemen, then I declare that we had no right to emancipate the slaves nor to suppress the rebellion.

It may be asked: Why not demand the suffrage for colored men in season for their vote in the business of reorganization? My answer is—I assume that the colored men are in favor of those measures which the Union needs to have adopted. But it would be idle to reorganize those States by the colored vote. If the popular vote of the white race is not to be had in favor of the guarantees justly required, then I am in favor of holding on—just where we now are. I am not in favor of a surrender of the present rights of the Union to a struggle between a white minority aided by the freedmen on one hand, against a majority of the white race on the other. I would not consent, having rescued those States by arms from secession and rebellion, to turn them over to anarchy and chaos. I have however no doubt— none whatever—of our right to stipulate for colored suffrage. The question is one of statesmanship, not a question of constitutional limitation.

If it is urged that the suffrage question is one peculiarly for the States, I reply: so also that of the abolition of slavery ordinarily would have been. But we are not now deciding what a loyal State acting in its constitutional sphere, and in its normal relations to the Union, may do; but what a rebel, belligerent, conquered State must do in order to be reorganized and to get back into those relations. And in deciding this I must repeat that we are to be governed only by justice, humanity, the public safety, and our duty to reorganize those conquered, belligerent States, as we can and when we can, consistently therewith.

In dealing with those States, with a view to fulfilling the national guarantee of a republican form of government, it is plain, since the nation is called upon to reorganize government, where no loyal republican State government is in existence, that it must of absolute necessity deal directly with the people themselves. If a State government were menaced and in danger of subversion, then the nation would be called upon to aid the existing government of the State in sustaining itself against the impending danger. But the present case is a different one. The State government was subverted in each rebel State more than four years ago. The State in its corporate capacity went into rebellion; and as long as it had the power waged and maintained against the nation rebellious war. There is no government in them to deal with. But there are the people. It is to the people we must go. It is through their people alone, and it is in their primary capacity alone as people, unorganized and without a government, that the nation is capable now of dealing with them at all. And therefore the government of the nation is obliged, by the sheer necessity of the case, to know who are the people of the State, in the sense of the national constitution, in order to know how to reach them. Congress, discerning new people, with new rights, and new duties and new interests (of the nation itself even) springing from them, may rightfully stipulate in their behalf. If Congress perceives that it cannot fulfil its guarantee to all the people of a State, without such a stipulation, then it not only may, but it ought to, require and secure it. The guarantee is one concerning all, not merely a part of the people. And, though the government of a State might be of republican form, and yet not enfranchise its colored citizens; still the substance and equity of the guarantee would be violated, if, in addition to their non-enfranchisement, the colored people should be compelled to share the burdens of a State government, the benefits of which would enure to other classes,— to their own exclusion. A republican form of government is not of necessity just and good. Nor is another form, of necessity, unjust and bad. A monarch may be humane, thoughtful, and just to every class and to every man. A republic may be inhumane, regardless of, and unjust to some of its subjects. Our national government and most of the State governments were so, to those whom they treated as slaves, or whose servitude they aggravated by their legislation in the interest of slavery. The nation cannot hereafter pretend that it has kept its promise and fulfilled its guarantee, when it shall have only organized governments of republican form, unless it can look all the people in the face and declare that it has kept its promise with them all. The voting class alone, those who possessed the franchise under the State constitutions, were not the people. They never were the people. They are not now. They were simply the trustees of a certain power for the benefit of all the people, and not merely for their own advantage. The nation does not fulfil its guarantee by dealing with them alone. It may deal through them with the people. It may accept their action as satisfactory in its discretion. But no matter who may be the agents through whom the nation reaches and deals with the people, that guaranty of the national constitution is fatally violated unless the nation secures to all the people of those disorganized States the substantial benefits and advantages of a " government." We cannot hide behind a word. We cannot be content with the form. The substance bargained for is a " government." The form is also bargained for, but that is only an incident. The people, and all the people alike, must have and enjoy the benefits and advantages of a government for the common good, the just and equal protection of each and all.

But what of the policy of the President? I am not able to consider his future policy. It is undisclosed. He seems to me to have left to Congress alone the questions controlling the conditions on which the rebel States shall resume their representative power in the federal government. It was not incumbent on the President to do otherwise. He naturally leaves the duty of theoretical reasoning to those whose responsibility it is to reach the just, practical conclusion. Thus far the President has simply used according to his proper discretion the power of commander-in-chief. What method he should observe was a question of discretion; in the absence of any positive law, to be answered by himself. He might have assumed, in the absence of positive law, during the process of reorganization, purely military methods. Had that been needful it would have been appropriate. If not necessary, then it would have been unjust and injurious. It is not just to oppress even an enemy merely because we have the power. In a case like the present it would be extremely impolitic and injurious to the nation itself. Bear in mind, ours is not a conquest by barbarians, nor by despots;

but by Christians and republicans. The commander-in-chief was bound to govern with a view to promoting the true restoration of the power of the Union, as I attempted to describe it in the beginning of this address, not merely with a view to the present, immediate control of the daily conduct of the people. He deemed it wise therefore to resort to the democratic principle, to use the analogies of republicanism and of constitutional liberty. He had the power to govern through magistrates under military or under civil titles. He could employ the agencies of popular and of representative assemblies. Their authority has its source, however, in his own war powers as commander-in-chief. If the peace of society, the rights of the government and of all its subjects are duly maintained, then the method may justify itself by its success as well as its intention. If he has assisted the people to reorganize their legislatures and to re-establish the machinery of local State government; though his method may be less regular than if an act of Congress had prescribed it, still it has permitted the people to feel their way back into the works and ways of loyalty, to exhibit their temper of mind and to " show their hands." Was it not better for the cause of free government, of civil liberty, to incur the risk of error in that direction than of error in the opposite one? It has proved that the national government is not drunk with power; that its four years' exercise of the dangerous rights of war has not affected its brain. It has shown that the danger of despotic centralism or of central despotism is safely over.

Meanwhile, notwithstanding the transmission of the seals to State magistrates chosen by vote in the States themselves; notwithstanding the inauguration, in fact, of local legislatures, the powers of war remain. The commander-in-chief has not abdicated. His generals continue in the field. They still exercise military functions, according to the belligerent rights of the nation. What the commander-in-chief may hereafter do, whether less or more, depends I presume in great measure on what the people of the rebel States may do or forbear doing. I assume that, until the executive and legislative departments of the national government shall have reached the united conclusion that the objects of the war have been fully accomplished, the national declaration of peace is not and cannot be made.

The proceedings already had are only certain acts in the great drama of reorganization. They do not go for nothing; they were not unnecessary; nor do I approach them with criticism. But they are not the whole drama. Other acts are required for its completion. What they shall be depends in part on the wisdom of Congress to determine.

The doctrine of the President that—in the steps preliminary to reorganizing a State which is not and has not been theoretically cut off from the Union—he must recognize its own organic law antecedent to the rebellion, need not be contested. I adhere quite as strictly as he to the logical consequences of that doctrine. I agree that the rebel States ought to come back again into the exercise of their State functions and the enjoyment of their representative power,—by the action and by the votes of the same class of persons, namely, the same body of voters or tenants of political rights and privileges, by the votes, action or submission of whom, those States were carried into the rebellion.

But yet it may be at the same time needful and proper, in the sense of wise statesmanship, to require of them the amplification of certain privileges, the recognition of certain rights, the establishment of certain institutions, the redistribution even of political power—to be by them accorded and executed through constitutional amendments or otherwise—as elements of acceptable reorganization; and as necessary to the readjustment of political society in harmony with the new relations, and the new basis of universal freedom, resulting from the rebellion itself. If these things are found to be required by wise statesmanship, then the right to exact them, as conditions of restoring those States to the enjoyment of their normal functions, is to be found just where the nation found the right to crush the rebellion and the incidental right of emancipating slaves.

Now, distinctions between men as to their rights, purely arbitrary, and not founded in reason nor in the nature of things, are not wise, statesmanlike nor "republican," in the constitutional sense. If they ever are wise and statesmanlike they become so only where oligarchies, privileged orders, and hereditary aristocracies are wise and expedient.

There are two kinds of republican government however known to political science, namely: aristocratic republics and democratic republics, or those in which the government resides with a few persons or with a privileged body, and those in which it is the government of the people. I cannot doubt that nearly all men are prepared to admit that our governments—both State and national—are constitutionally democratic, representative republics. That theory of government is expressly set forth in the Declaration of Independence. The popular theory of government is again declared in the preamble to the federal constitution. The federal government is elaborately constructed according to the theory of popular and representative government and against the aristocratic theory in its distinguishing features. And in divers places the federal constitution in set terms presupposes the democratic and representative character of the governments of the States; for examples, by assuming that they have legislatures, that their legislatures are composed of more than one body, and by aiming to prevent even all appearance of aristocratic form, by prohibiting the States from granting any title of nobility. In his recent message to Congress President Johnson affirms "the great distinguishing principle of the recognition of the rights of man" as the fundamental idea in all our governments. "The American system," he adds in the same paragraph, "rests on the assertion of the equal right of every man to life, liberty, and the pursuit of happiness, to freedom of conscience, to the culture and exercise of all his faculties."

But is it pretended that the idea of a government of the people and for the people in the American sense is inclusive of the white race only or is exclusive of men of African descent? On what ground can the position rest?

The citizenship of free men of color, even in those States where no provision of law seemed to include them in the category of voters, has been frequently demonstrated, not only as a legal right but as a right asserted and enjoyed.

Nay more; both under the confederation and in the time of the adoption of the constitution of the United States all free native-born inhabitants of the States of New Hampshire, Massachusetts, New York, New Jersey, and North Carolina, though descended from African slaves, were not only citizens of those States but such of them as had the other necessary qualifications possessed the franchise of electors on equal terms with other citizens. And even Virginia declares in her ancient Bill of Rights, "that all men having sufficient evidence of permanent common interest with and attachment to the community have the right of suffrage." Wherever free colored men were recognized as free citizens or subjects but were nevertheless not fully enfranchised, I think the explanation is found, not in the fact of their mere color nor of their antecedent servitude, but in the idea of their possible lapse into servitude again—of which condition their color was a badge and a continuing presumption. The policy of some States seems to have demanded that slavery should be the prevailing condition of all their inhabitants of African descent. In those States the possession of freedom by a colored man has therefore been treated as if that condition was only exceptional and transient. But wherever the policy and legislation of a State were originally dictated by men who saw through the confusion of ideas occasioned by the presence of slavery, there we are enabled to discern the evidence of an unclouded purpose (with which the American mind always intended to be consistent), namely: The maintenance of equality between free citizens concerning civil rights and the distribution of privileges, according to capacity and desert, and not according to the accidents of birth. And now that slavery has been rendered forever impossible within any State or Territory of the Union by framing the great natural law of universal freedom into the organic law of the Union, all the ancient disabilities which slavery had made apparently attendant on African descent must disappear.

Whatever may be the rules regulating the distribution of political power among free citizens in the organization of such a republican government as that guaranteed by the national constitution, descent in either the evidence of right nor the ground of disfranchisement.

The selection of a fraction or class of the great body of freemen in the civil State to be permanently invested with its entire political power (selected by mere human predestination irrespective of merit),—that power to be incommunicable to the freemen of another class—the two classes, of rulers and ruled, governors and governed, to be determined by the accident of birth, and all the consequences of that accident to descend by generation to their children,—seems to me to be the establishment of an hereditary aristocracy of birth, the creation of a privileged order, inconsistent both with the substance and the essential form of American republicanism, unstatesmanlike, and unwise; and (in the rebel States) in every sense dangerous and unjust.

To demand a certain qualification of intelligence is eminently safe and consists with the interests and rights of all. It is as reasonable as to require a certain maturity of age. They who are the representatives of the political power of society, acting not only for themselves but also for the women and children, who, too, belong to it; representing the interests of the wives, mothers, sisters, daughters, infant sons, and the posterity of us all, ought to constitute an audience reasonably competent to hear.   And since the congregation of American voters is numbered by millions, and covers a continent it cannot hear with its ears all that it needs to know; but must learn intelligently much that it needs to know through the printed page and by means of its eyes.   The protection of the mass of men against the deceptions of local demagogues and against their own prejudices hereafter—as well as the common safety—calls for the requirement of the capacity to read the mother tongue as a condition of coming for the first time to the ballot-box.   Let this be required at the South and immediately the whole Southern community will be aroused to the absolute necessity of demanding free schools and popular education.   These are more than all things else to be coveted, both for the preservation of public liberty and for the temporal salvation of the toiling masses of our own Saxon and Norman blood, whom alike with the African slave the oppression of ages has involved in a common disaster.

I think the wisest and most intelligent persons in the South are not ignorant of the importance of raising the standard of intelligence among voters; nor of extending the right to vote so as to include those who are of competent intellect notwithstanding the recent disability of color. There is evidence that they are not unwilling to act consistently with the understanding, example, and constitutional precedents of the fathers of the Republic; consistently with the ancient practice of the States, coeval with the organic law of the nation established by the very men who made that law, who used and adopted the very phrase, " a republican form of government," of the meaning of which their own practice was a contemporary interpretation. But if the conquering power of the nation, if the victorious arm of the Union is paralyzed; if the federal government, standing behind the ramparts of defensive war, wielding its weapons both of offence in the hour of struggle and of diplomacy in the hour of triumph, is utterly powerless to stipulate for the execution of this condition; then I confess I do not know how the best and wisest in the South will be enabled, deserted and alone, to stand up on its behalf against the jealousy of ignorance and the traditions of prejudice.

If the measures I have attempted to delineate are found to be impracticable then Congress has still the right to refuse to the rebel States readmission to the enjoyment of their representative power until amendments to the federal constitution shall have been obtained adequate to the exigency. Nor can the people of the rebel States object to the delay. They voluntarily withdrew from Congress; they themselves elected the attitude of disunion. They broke the agreements of the constitution: not we. They chose their own time, opportunity, and occasion to make war on the nation and to repudiate the Union. They certainly cannot now dictate to us the time nor the terms. Again I repeat the just discretion of the nation — exercised in good faith toward all — must govern.

The federal Union was formed first of all "to establish justice." "Justice" in the language of statesmen and of jurists has had a definition for more than two thousand years, exact, perfect, and well understood.

It is found in the Institutes of Justinian,—

"Constans et perpetua voluntas, jus suum cuique tribuendi."[1]

I believe I have shown that under our federal constitution,—

1. All the people of the rebel States must share in the benefits to be derived from the execution of the national guarantee of republican governments.

2. That our "republican form of government" demands "the maintenance of equality between free citizens concerning civil rights in the distribution of privileges according to capacity and desert and not according to the accidents of birth."

3. That people "of African descent" not less than people of the white race are included within the category of free subjects and citizens of the United States.

4. That, in the distribution of political power under our form of government, "descent is neither the evidence of right nor the ground of disfranchisement," so that

---

[1] "The constant and perpetual will to secure to every man his own right."

5. The disfranchisement of free citizens for the cause of "descent" or for any reason other than lawful disqualification, as by non-residence, immaturity, crime, or want of intelligence, violates their constitutional rights.

6. That in executing our national guarantee of republican government to the people of the rebel States, we must secure the constitutional, civic liberties and franchises of all the people.

7. That we have no right to omit to secure to the new citizens, made free by the Union, in war, their equality of rights before the law, and their franchises of every sort— including the electoral franchise—according to laws and regulations, of universal, and not of unequal and capricious application.

We have no right to evade our own duty. We must not, by substituting a new basis for the apportionment of representatives in Congress, give up the just rights of these citizens. Increasing the proportion of the political power of the loyal States, at the expense of the disloyal States, by adopting their relative numbers of legal voters, instead of their relative populations—while it might punish some States for not according the suffrage to colored men—would not be justice to the colored citizen. For justice demands, "for every man his own right."

Will it be said that, by such means, we shall strengthen our own power in the loyal States, to protect the colored people in the South? If we will not yield to them justice now, on what ground do we expect grace to give them "protection" hereafter?

You will have compromised for a consideration—paid in an increase of your own political power—your right to urge their voluntary enfranchisement on the white men of the

South.   You will have bribed all the elements of political
selfishness, in the whole country, to combine against negro
enfranchisement.   The States of the rebellion will have no
less power than ever in the Senate.   And the men who hold
the privilege of electing representatives to the lower house,
will retain their privilege.   For the sake of doubling the
delegation from South Carolina, do you suppose the
monopoly of choosing three members would be surrendered
by the whites, giving to the colored men the chance to choose
six?   Nay:—Would the monopolists gain anything by according the suffrage to the colored man; if they could themselves only retain the power to dictate three representatives,
and the colored people should dictate the selection of the
other three?

The scheme to substitute legal voters, instead of population, as the basis of representation in Congress, will prove a
delusion and a snare.   By diminishing the representative
power of the Southern States, in favor of other States, you
will not increase Southern love for the Union.   Nor, while
Connecticut and Wisconsin refuse the suffrage to men of
color, will you be able to convince the South that your amendment was dictated by political principle, and not by political
cupidity.   You will not diminish any honest apprehension
at extending the suffrage, but you will inflame every prejudice, and aggravate discontent.   Meanwhile the disfranchised freedman, hated by some because he is black,
contemned by some because he has been a slave, feared by
some because of the antagonisms of society, is condemned
to the condition of a hopeless pariah of a merciless civilization.   In the community, he is not of it.   He neither belongs
to a master nor to society.   Bodily present in the midst of
the society composing the State, he adds nothing to its weight

in the political balance of the nation; and therefore, he stands in the way, occupies the room and takes the place, which might be enjoyed as opportunities by a white immigrant, who would contribute by his presence to its representative power. Your policy would inflame animosity and aggravate oppression, for at least the lifetime of a generation, before it would open the door to enfranchisement.

Civil society is not an aggregation of individuals. According to the order of nature and the divine economy it is an aggregation of families.

The adult males of the family vote because the welfare of the women and children of the family is identical with theirs; and it is intrusted to their affection and fidelity, whether at the ballot-box or on the battle-field. But, while the voting men of a given community represent the welfare of its women and children, they do not represent that of another community. The men, women, and children of Massachusetts are alike concerned in the ideas and interests of Massachusetts. But the very theory of representation implies that the ideas and interests of one State are not identical with those of another. On what ground, then, can a State on the Pacific or the Ohio gain preponderance in Congress over New Jersey or Massachusetts by reason of its greater number of males, while it may have even a less number of people? The halls of legislation are the arenas of debate, not of muscular prowess. The intelligence, the opinions, the wishes, and the influence of women, social and domestic, stand for something—for much—in the public affairs of civilized and refined society. I deny the just right of the government to banish woman from the count. She may not vote, but she thinks; she persuades her husband; she instructs her son. And through them at least she has a right to be heard in the government. Her existence and the existence of her children are to be considered in the State.

No matter who changes, let Massachusetts at least stand by all the fundamental principles of free, constitutional, republican government.

The President is the tribune of the people. Let him be chosen directly by the popular election. The Senate represents the reserved rights and the equality of the States. Let the senators continue to be chosen by the legislatures of the States. The House represents the opinions, interests, and the equality of the people of each and every State. Let the people of the respective States elect their representatives, in numbers proportional to the numbers of their people. And let the legal qualifications of the voters, in the election of President, Vice-President, and representatives in Congress, be fixed by a uniform, equal, democratic, constitutional rule, of universal application. Let this franchise be enjoyed " according to capacity and desert, and not according to the accidents of birth."

Congress may, and ought to, initiate an amendment granting the right to vote for President, Vice-President and representatives in Congress, to colored men, in all the States, being citizens and able to read, who would by the laws of the States where they reside, be competent to vote if they were white. Without disfranchising existing voters, it should apply the qualification to white men also. And the amendment ought to leave the election of President and Vice-President directly in the hands of the people, without the intervention of electoral colleges. Then the poorest, humblest, and most despised men, being citizens and competent to read, and thus competent, with reasonable intelligence, to represent others, would find audience through the ballot-box.

The President, who is the grand tribune of all the people, and the direct delegates of the people in the popular branch of the national legislature, would feel their influence. This amendment would give efficiency to the one already adopted, abolishing slavery throughout the Union. The two amendments taken together would practically accomplish or enable Congress to fulfil the whole duty of the nation to those who are now its dependent wards.

I am satisfied that the mass of thinking men at the South accept the present condition of things in good faith; and I am also satisfied that with the support of a firm policy from the President and Congress in aid of the efforts of their good faith, and with the help of a conciliatory and generous disposition on the part of the North—especially on the part of those States most identified with the plan of emancipation— the measures needed for permanent and universal welfare can surely be obtained. There ought now to be a vigorous prosecution of the peace,—just as vigorous as our recent prosecution of the war. We ought to extend our hands with cordial good will to meet the proffered hands of the South; demanding no attitude of humiliation from any; inflicting no acts of humiliation upon any; respecting the feelings of the conquered—notwithstanding the question of right and wrong between the parties belligerent. We ought, by all the means and instrumentalities of peace, and by all the thrifty methods of industry; by all the recreative agencies of education and religion to help rebuild the waste places and restore order, society, prosperity. Without industry and business there can be no progress. In their absence civilized man even recedes toward barbarism. Let Massachusetts bear in mind the not unnatural suspicion which the past has engendered. I trust she is able, filled with emotions of boundless joy and gratitude to Almighty God who has given such victory and such honor to the right, to exercise faith in his goodness without vain glory, and to exercise charity without weakness toward those who have held the attitude of her enemies.

The offence of war has met its appropriate punishment by the hand of war.

In this hour of triumph, honor and religion alike forbid one act, one word of vengeance or resentment. Patriotism and Christianity unite the arguments of earthly welfare, and the motives of heavenly inspiration to persuade us to put off all jealousy and all fear, and to move forward as citizens and as men in the work of social and economic reorganization—each one doing with his might whatever his hand findeth to do.

We might wish it were possible for Massachusetts justly to avoid her part in the work of political reorganization. But in spite of whatever misunderstanding of her purpose or character she must abide her destiny. She is a part of the nation. The nation for its own ends and its own advantage, as a measure of war, took out of the hands of the masters their slaves. It holds them therefore in its hands as freedmen. It must place them somewhere. It must dispose of them somehow. It cannot delegate the trust. It has no right to drop them, to desert them. For by its own voluntary act it assumed their guardianship and all its attendant responsibilities before the present generation, and all the coming generations of mankind. I know not how well, nor how ill, they might be treated by the people of the States where they reside. I only know that there is a point beyond which the nation has no right to incur any hazard. And while the fidelity of the nation need not abridge the humanity of the

States, on the other hand our confidence in those States cannot be pleaded before the bar of God, nor of history in defence of any neglect of our own duty.

Let their people remember that Massachusetts has never deceived them. To her ideas of duty and her theory of the government she has been faithful. If they were ever misled or betrayed by others into the snare of attempted secession and the risks of war, her trumpet at least gave no uncertain sound. She has fulfilled her engagements in the past and she intends to fulfil them in the future. She knows that the reorganization of the States in rebellion carries with it consequences which come home to the firesides and the consciences of her own children. For as citizens of the Union they become liable to assume the defence of those governments when reorganized, against every menace, whether of foreign invasion or of domestic violence. Her bayonets may be invoked to put down insurgents of whatever color; and whatever the cause, whether rightful or wrongful, which may have moved their discontent. And when they are called for they will march. If she were capable of evading her duty now she would be capable of violating her obligations hereafter. If she is anxious to prevent grave errors, it is because she appreciates, from her past experience, the danger of admitting such errors into the structure of government. She is watchful against them now, because in the sincere fidelity of her purpose she is made keenly alive to the duties of the present, by contemplating the inevitable responsibilities of the future.

In sympathy with the heart and hope of the nation, she will abide by her faith. Undisturbed by the impatient, undismayed by delay, "with malice toward none, with charity for all; with firmness in the right, as God gives us to see the right," she will persevere. Impartial, democratic, constitutional liberty is invincible. The rights of human nature are sacred; maintained by confessors, and heroes, and martyrs; reposing on the sure foundation of the commandments of God.

> " Through plots and counterplots;
> Through gain and loss; through glory and disgrace;
> Along the plains where passionate Discord rears
> Eternal Babel; still the holy stream
> Of human happiness glides on!
>
> .   .   .   .
>   There is One above
> Sways the harmonious mystery of the world."

Gentlemen, for all the favors, unmerited and unmeasured, which I have enjoyed from the people of Massachusetts; from the councillors, magistrates, and officers by whom I have been surrounded in the government; and from the members of five successive legislatures, there is no return in my power to render but the sincere acknowledgments of a grateful heart.

RUSKIN

JOHN RUSKIN, a distinguished English art critic, lecturer, and writer, the son of a wealthy wine-merchant of Scotch descent, was born in London, February 8, 1819. He was privately fitted for Oxford, where he became a gentleman commoner of Christ College, graduating in 1842. He studied painting under Copley, Fielding, and Harding and in 1843 brought out the first volume of his " Modern Painters " in which he argued strenuously to prove that artists of his own time, and especially Turner, were superior to the old masters. During seventeen years he elaborated this theme and the last volume appeared in 1860, the work having grown into a complete treatise on the principles of art. It met with much hostility from conservative critics, but no one could fail to recognize the brilliancy and vigor of his style, and his views have undeniably revolutionized English art. In 1849 appeared " The Seven Lamps of Architecture " and in 1851-53 " The Stones of Venice," both illustrated by Ruskin himself and designed to set up a loftier ideal of domestic architecture. In 1858 he was Honorary Student of Christ College; in 1867 Rede Lecturer (at Cambridge) and from 1870 to 1879 he was Slade Professor of Art, being re-elected in 1883. During all those years he was indefatigable in his publications, the titles including " The King of the Golden River " (1851); " The Two Paths " (1854); " Lectures on Architecture and Painting " (1854); " Harbors of England " (1856); " Munera Pulveris " (1862-63); " Sesame and Lilies " (1865); " Ethics of the Dust " (1866); " Crown of Wild Olive " (1866); and a dozen other titles. In 1891 he republished a volume of his privately issued poems with original drawings. For several years " Fors Clavigera " appeared at irregular intervals, and the eight volumes contain nearly a hundred letters to the workmen and laborers of England on a great variety of artistic and economical subjects. A large part of his immense fortune he gave away during his lifetime, founding a mastership of drawing at Oxford, a museum at Walkley (now at Sheffield), and the St. George's Guild. He died at Brantwood, January 20, 1900, universally honored for his unselfish life and lofty conception of character and conduct. Few men have had more influence or exerted their powers for nobler ends.

LECTURE ON THE GREEK MYTHS OF STORM

GIVEN IN UNIVERSITY COLLEGE, LONDON, MARCH 9, 1869

I WILL not ask your pardon for endeavoring to interest you in the subject of Greek mythology; but I must ask your permission to approach it in a temper differing from that in which it is frequently treated. We cannot justly interpret the religion of any people unless we are pre-

pared to admit that we ourselves, as well as they, are liable
to error in matters of faith, and that the convictions of others,
however singular, may in some points have been well
founded, while our own, however reasonable, may in some
particulars be mistaken. You must forgive me, therefore,
for not always distinctively calling the creeds of the past
" superstition," and the creeds of the present day " religion;"
as well as for assuming that a faith now confessed may sometimes be superficial, and that a faith long forgotten may once
have been sincere. It is the task of the Divine to condemn
the errors of antiquity, and of the philologists to account for
them; I will only pray you to read with patience and human
sympathy the thoughts of men who lived without blame in
a darkness they could not dispel; and to remember that whatever charge of folly may justly attach to the saying, " There
is no God," the folly is prouder, deeper, and less pardonable
in saying, " There is no God but for me."

2. A myth, in its simplest definition, is a story with a
meaning attached to it other than it seems to have at first;
and the fact that it has such a meaning is generally marked
by some of its circumstances being extraordinary, or, in the
common use of the word, unnatural. Thus if I tell you that
Hercules killed a water-serpent in the lake of Lerna, and if
I mean, and you understand, nothing more than that fact,
the story, whether true or false, is not a myth. But if by
telling you this I mean that Hercules purified the stagnation
of many streams from deadly miasmata, my story, however
simple, is a true myth; only, as if I left it in that simplicity
you would probably look for nothing beyond, it will be wise
in me to surprise your attention by adding some singular
circumstance; for instance, that the water-snake had several
heads which revived as fast as they were killed, and which

poisoned even the foot that trod upon them as they slept. And in proportion to the fulness of intended meaning I shall probably multiply and refine upon these improbabilities; as, suppose if, instead of desiring only to tell you that Hercules purified a marsh, I wished you to understand that he contended with the venom and vapor of envy and evil ambition, whether in other men's souls or in his own, and choked that malaria only by supreme toil,—I might tell you that this serpent was formed by the goddess whose pride was in the trial of Hercules; and that its place of abode was by a palm-tree; and that for every head of it that was cut off two rose up with renewed life; and that the hero found at last he could not kill the creature at all by cutting its heads off or crushing them, but only by burning them down; and that the midmost of them could not be killed even that way, but had to be buried alive. Only in proportion as I mean more, I shall certainly appear more absurd in my statement; and at last when I get unendurably significant, all practical persons will agree that I was talking mere nonsense from the beginning and never meant anything at all.

3. It is just possible however also that the story-teller may all along have meant nothing but what he said; and that, incredible as the events may appear, he himself literally believed—and expected you also to believe—all this about Hercules, without any latent moral or history whatever. And it is very necessary in reading traditions of this kind to determine first of all whether you are listening to a simple person who is relating what at all events he believes to be true (and may therefore possibly have been so to some extent), or to a reserved philosopher, who is veiling a theory of the universe under the grotesque of a fairy tale. It is, in general, more likely that the first supposition should be the

right one: simple and credulous persons are, perhaps fortunately, more common than philosophers; and it is of the highest importance that you should take their innocent testimony as it was meant, and not efface under the graceful explanation which your cultivated ingenuity may suggest, either the evidence their story may contain (such as it is worth) of an extraordinary event having really taken place, or the unquestionable light which it will cast upon the character of the person by whom it was frankly believed. And to deal with Greek religion honestly you must at once understand that this literal belief was, in the mind of the general people, as deeply rooted as ours in the legends of our own sacred book; and that a basis of unmiraculous event was as little suspected, and an explanatory symbolism as rarely traced by them as by us.

You must therefore observe that I deeply degrade the position which such a myth as that just referred to occupied in the Greek mind by comparing it (for fear of offending you) to our story of St. George and the Dragon. Still the analogy is perfect in minor respects; and though it fails to give you any notion of the vitally religious earnestness of the Greek faith it will exactly illustrate the manner in which faith laid hold of its objects.

4. This story of Hercules and the Hydra, then, was to the general Greek mind, in its best days, a tale about a real hero and a real monster. Not one in a thousand knew anything of the way in which the story had arisen, any more than the English peasant generally is aware of the plebeian original of St. George, or supposes that there were once alive in the world, with sharp teeth and claws, real and very ugly flying dragons. On the other hand, few persons traced any moral or symbolical meaning in the story, and the average Greek

was as far from imagining any interpretation like that I have just given you as an average Englishman is from seeing in St. George the Red Cross Knight of Spenser, or in the Dragon the spirit of infidelity. But for all that there was a certain undercurrent of consciousness in all minds that the figures meant more than they at first showed; and according to each man's own faculties of sentiment he judged and read them; just as a Knight of the Garter reads more in the jewel on his collar than the George and Dragon of a public-house expresses to the host or to his customers. Thus to the mean person the myth always meant little; to the noble person, much; and the greater their familiarity with it the more contemptible it became to one and the more sacred to the other, until vulgar commentators explained it entirely away, while Virgil made it the crowning glory of his choral hymn to Hercules.

> "Around thee, powerless to infect thy soul,
> Rose, in his crested crowd, the Lerna worm."

> " Non te rationis egentem
> Lernæus turbâ capitum circumstetit anguis."

And although, in any special toil of the hero's life, the moral interpretation was rarely with definiteness attached to its event, yet in the whole course of the life, not only a symbolical meaning, but the warrant for the existence of a real spiritual power, was apprehended of all men. Hercules was no dead hero, to be remembered only as a victor over monsters of the past—harmless now as slain. He was the perpetual type and mirror of heroism and its present and living aid against every ravenous form of human trial and pain.

5. But if we seek to know more than this and to ascertain the manner in which the story first crystallized into its shape, we shall find ourselves led back generally to one or other of two sources,—either to actual historical events, represented

by the fancy under figures personifying them; or else to natural phenomena similarly endowed with life by the imaginative power usually more or less under the influence of terror. The historical myths we must leave the masters of history to follow; they and the events they record being yet involved in great, though attractive and penetrable mystery. But the stars, and hills, and storms are with us now, as they were with others of old; and it only needs that we look at them with the earnestness of those childish eyes to understand the first words spoken of them by the children of men, and then, in all the most beautiful and enduring myths we shall find not only a literal story of a real person, not only a parallel imagery of moral principle, but an underlying worship of natural phenomena out of which both have sprung and in which both forever remain rooted. Thus, from the real sun rising and setting,—from the real atmosphere, calm in its dominion of unfading blue and fierce in the descent of tempest,—the Greek forms first the idea of two entirely personal and corporeal gods, whose limbs are clothed in divine flesh, and whose brows are crowned with divine beauty; yet so real that the quiver rattles at their shoulder and the chariot bends beneath their weight. And on the other hand, collaterally with these corporeal images, and never for one instant separated from them, he conceives also two omnipresent spiritual influences, of which one illuminates as the sun with a constant fire, whatever in humanity is skilful and wise; and the other, like the living air, breathes the calm of heavenly fortitude and strength of righteous anger into every human breast that is pure and brave.

6. Now, therefore, in nearly every myth of importance and certainly in every one of those of which I shall speak to-night, you have to discern these three structural parts,—

the root and the two branches: the root, in physical existence,
sun, or sky, or cloud, or sea; then the personal incarnation
of that becoming a trusted and companionable deity with
whom you may walk hand in hand, as a child with its brother
or its sister; and lastly, the moral significance of the image
which is in all the great myths eternally and beneficently
true.

7. The great myths; that is to say, myths made by great
people. For the first plain fact about myth-making is one
which has been most strangely lost sight of,—that you cannot
make a myth unless you have something to make it of. You
cannot tell a secret which you don't know. If the myth is
about the sky it must have been made by somebody who had
looked at the sky. If the myth is about justice and fortitude
it must have been made by some one who knew what it was
to be just or patient. According to the quantity of understanding in the person will be the quantity of significance in
his fable; and the myth of a simple and ignorant race must
necessarily mean little, because a simple and ignorant race
have little to mean. So the great question in reading a
story is always, not what wild hunter dreamed, or what childish race first dreaded it; but what wise man first perfectly
told, and what strong people first perfectly lived by it. And
the real meaning of any myth is that which it has at the
noblest age of the nation among whom it is current. The
farther back you pierce the less significance you will find,
until you come to the first narrow thought, which indeed
contains the germ of the accomplished tradition; but only as
the seed contains the flower. As the intelligence and passion
of the race develop, they cling to and nourish their beloved
and sacred legend; leaf by leaf it expands under the touch
of more pure affections and more delicate imagination until

at last the perfect fable burgeons out into symmetry of milky stem and honeyed bell.

8. But through whatever changes it may pass, remember that our right reading of it is wholly dependent on the materials we have in our own minds for an intelligent answering sympathy. If it first arose among a people who dwelt under stainless skies and measured their journeys by ascending and declining stars, we certainly cannot read their story if we have never seen anything above us in the day but smoke, nor anything around us in the night but candles. If the tale goes on to change clouds or planets into living creatures,—to invest them with fair forms and inflame them with mighty passions,—we can only understand the story of the human-hearted things in so far as we ourselves take pleasure in the perfectness of visible form, or can sympathize by an effort of imagination with the strange people who had other loves than that of wealth and other interests than those of commerce. And, lastly, if the myth complete itself to the fulfilled thoughts of the nation by attributing to the gods whom they have carved out of their fantasy continual presence with their own souls, and their every effort for good is finally guided by the sense of the companionship, the praise and the pure will of immortals, we shall be able to follow them into this last circle of their faith only in the degree in which the better parts of our own beings have been also stirred by the aspects of nature or strengthened by her laws. It may be easy to prove that the ascent of Apollo in his chariot signifies nothing but the rising of the sun. But what does the sunrise itself signify to us? If only languid return to frivolous amusement or fruitless labor, it will indeed not be easy for us to conceive the power, over a Greek of the name of Apollo. But if for us also, as for the Greek, the sunrise

means daily restoration to the sense of passionate gladness and of perfect life; if it means the thrilling of new strength through every nerve,—the shedding over us of a better peace than the peace of night in the power of the dawn,—and the purging of evil vision and fear by the baptism of its dew; if the sun itself is an influence to us also of spiritual good, and becomes thus in reality, not in imagination to us also, a spiritual power,—we may then soon over-pass the narrow limit of conception which kept that power impersonal and rise with the Greek to the thought of an angel who rejoiced as a strong man to run his course, whose voice calling to life and to labor rang round the earth, and whose going forth was to the ends of heaven.

9. The time then at which I shall take up for you, as well as I can decipher it, the traditions of the gods of Greece, shall be near the beginning of its central and formed faith,—about 500 B.C.—a faith of which the character is perfectly represented by Pindar and Æschylus, who are both of them outspokenly religious and entirely sincere men; while we may always look back to find the less developed thought of the preceding epoch given by Homer in a more occult, subtle, half-instinctive and involuntary way.

10. Now, at that culminating period of the Greek religion we find under one governing Lord of all things, four subordinate elemental forces and four spiritual powers living in them and commanding them. The elements are of course the well-known four of the ancient world,—the earth, the waters, the fire, and the air; and the living powers of them are Demeter, the Latin Ceres; Poseidon, the Latin Neptune; Apollo, who has retained always his Greek name; and Athena, the Latin Minerva. Each of these are descended from, or changed from more ancient, and therefore more mystic deities of the

earth and heaven and of a finer element of æther supposed
to be beyond the heavens;[1] but at this time we find the four
quite definite both in their kingdoms and in their personali-
ties. They are the rulers of the earth that we tread upon and
the air that we breathe; and are with us as closely, in their
vivid humanity as the dust that they animate and the winds
that they bridle. I shall briefly define for you the range of
their separate dominions, and then follow as far as we have
time, the most interesting of the legends which relate to the
queen of the air.

11. The rule of the first spirit, Demeter, the earth mother,
is over the earth, first as the origin of all life,—the dust from
whence we were taken; secondly, as the receiver of all things
back at last into silence,—" Dust thou art, and unto dust
shalt thou return." And therefore, as the most tender image
of this appearing and fading life, in the birth and fall of
flowers, her daughter Proserpine plays in the fields of Sicily,
and thence is torn away into darkness and becomes the Queen
of Fate,—not merely of death but of the gloom which closes
over and ends, not beauty only, but sin, and chiefly of sins
the sin against the life she gave; so that she is in her highest
power, Persephone, the avenger and purifier of blood—" The
voice of thy brother's blood cries to me *out of the ground.*"
Then, side by side with this queen of the earth, we find a
demigod of agriculture by the plough—the lord of grain, or
of the thing ground by the mill. And it is a singular proof
of the simplicity of Greek character at this noble time, that
of all representations left to us of their deities by their art,
few are so frequent and none perhaps so beautiful as the
symbol of this spirit of agriculture.

---

[1]And by modern science now also asserted, and with probability argued,
to exist.

12. Then the dominant spirit of the element water is Neptune, but subordinate to him are myriads of other water spirits, of whom Nereus is the chief, with Palæmon, and Leucothea, the " white lady " of the sea; and Thetis, and nymphs innumerable who like her, could " suffer a sea change," while the river deities had each independent power, according to the preciousness of their streams to the cities fed by them,—the " fountain Arethuse, and thou, honored flood, smooth sliding Mincius, crowned with vocal reeds." And spiritually this king of the water is lord of the strength and daily flow of human life: he gives it material force and victory, which is the meaning of the dedication of the hair as the sign of the strength of life to the river or the native land.

13. Demeter, then, over the earth, and its giving and receiving of life. Neptune over the waters, and the flow and force of life,—always among the Greeks typified by the horse, which was to them as a crested sea-wave, animated and bridled. Then the third element, fire, has set over it two powers: over earthly fire, the assistant of human labor, is set Hephæstus, lord of all labor, in which is the flush and the sweat of the brow; and over heavenly fire, the source of day, is set Apollo, the spirit of all kindling, purifying, and illuminating intellectual wisdom: each of these gods having also their subordinate or associated powers,—servant, or sister, or companion muse.

14. Then, lastly, we come to the myth which is to be our subject of closer inquiry,—the story of Athena and of the deities subordinate to her. This great goddess, the Neith of the Egyptians, the Athena or Athenaia of the Greeks, and with broken power, half usurped by Mars, the Minerva of the Latins, is, physically, the queen of the air, having su-

preme power over both its blessing of calm and wrath of
storm; and, spiritually, she is the queen of the breath of
man, first of the bodily breathing which is life to his blood
and strength to his arm in battle; and then of the mental
breathing, or inspiration, which is his moral health and
habitual wisdom; wisdom of conduct and of the heart, as
opposed to the wisdom of imagination and the brain; moral,
as distinct from intellectual; inspired, as distinct from illuminated.

15. By a singular and fortunate, though I believe wholly
accidental, coincidence, the heart-virtue of which she is the
spirit was separated by the ancients into four divisions, which
have since obtained acceptance from all men as rightly dis-
cerned, and have received, as if from the quarters of the
four winds of which Athena is the natural queen, the name
of " cardinal " virtues: namely, Prudence (the right-seeing
and foreseeing of events through darkness); Justice (the
righteous bestowal of favor and of indignation); Fortitude
(patience under trial by pain); and Temperance (patience
under trial by pleasure). With respect to these four virtues
the attributes of Athena are all distinct. In her prudence, or
sight in darkness, she is " Glaukopis," "owl-eyed." In her
justice, which is the dominant virtue she wears two robes,
one of light and one of darkness; the robe of light, saffron-
color, or the color of the daybreak, falls to her feet, covering
her wholly with favor and love,—the calm of the sky in
blessing; it is embroidered along its edge with her victory
over the giants (the troublous powers of the earth), and the
likeness of it was woven yearly by the Athenian maidens and
carried to the temple of their own Athena,—not to the
Parthenon, that was the temple of all the world's Athena,—
but this they carried to the temple of their own only one who

loved them and stayed with them always. Then her robe
of indignation is worn on her breast and left arm only,
fringed with fatal serpents, and fastened with Gorgonian
cold, turning men to stone; physically, the lightning and the
hail of chastisement by storm. Then in her fortitude she
wears the crested and unstooping helmet;[1] and lastly, in her
temperance, she is the queen of maidenhood—stainless as the
air of heaven.

16. But all these virtues mass themselves in the Greek mind
into the two main ones,—of Justice, or noble passion, and
Fortitude, or noble patience; and of these, the chief powers
of Athena, the Greeks had divinely written for them, and for
all men after them, two mighty songs,—one, of the Menis,[2]
Mens, passion or zeal of Athena, breathed into a mortal
whose name is " Ache of heart," and whose short life is only
the incarnate brooding and burst of storm; and the other is
of the foresight and fortitude of Athena, maintained by her
in the heart of a mortal whose name is given to him from a
longer grief, Odysseus, the full-of-sorrow, the much-endur-
ing, and the long-suffering.

17. The minor expressions by the Greeks in word, in
symbol, and in religious service, of this faith, are so many
and so beautiful that I hope some day to gather at least a
few of them into a separate body of evidence respecting the
power of Athena and its relations to the ethical conception
of the Homeric poems, or, rather, to their ethical nature;
for they are not conceived didactically, but are didactic in

---

[1] I am compelled, for clearness' sake, to mark only one meaning at a
time. Athena's helmet is sometimes a mask, sometimes a sign of anger,
sometimes of the highest light of æther; but I cannot speak of all this
at once.

[2] This first word of the Iliad, Menis, afterwards passes into the Latin
Mens; is the root of the Latin name for Athena, " Minerva," and so of
the English " mind."

their essence, as all good art is. There is an increasing in-
sensibility to this character and even an open denial of it
among us now which is one of the most curious errors of
modernism,—the peculiar and judicial blindness of an age
which, having long practised art and poetry for the sake of
pleasure only, has become incapable of reading their language when they were both didactic; and also having been
itself accustomed to a professedly didactic teaching, which
yet for private interests studiously avoids collision with every
prevalent vice of its day (and specially with avarice), has become equally dead to the intensely ethical conceptions of a
race which habitually divided all men into two broad classes
of worthy or worthless,—good, and good for nothing. And
even the celebrated passage of Horace about the Iliad is now
misread or disbelieved, as if it was impossible that the Iliad
could be instructive because it is not like a sermon. Horace
does not say that it is like a sermon, and would have been
still less likely to say so if he ever had had the advantage of
hearing a sermon. " I have been reading that story of Troy
again " (thus he writes to a noble youth of Rome whom he
cared for) " quietly at Præneste while you have been busy
at Rome; and truly I think that what is base and what is
noble, and what useful and useless, may be better learned
from that than from all Chrysippus' and Crantor's talk put
together." Which is profoundly true, not of the Iliad only,
but of all other great art whatsoever; for all pieces of such
art are didactic in the purest way, indirectly and occultly, so
that, first, you shall only be bettered by them if you are already hard at work in bettering yourself; and when you *are*
bettered by them it shall be partly with a general acceptance
of their influence, so constant and subtile that you shall be
no more conscious of it than of the healthy digestion of food;

and partly by a gift of unexpected truth, which you shall
only find by slow mining for it,—which is withheld on purpose and close-locked, that you may not get it till you have
forged the key of it in a furnace of your own heating.   And
this withholding of their meaning is continual and confessed in the great poets.   Thus Pindar says of himself:
"There is many an arrow in my quiver full of speech to the
wise, but for the many they need interpreters." And
neither Pindar, nor Æschylus, nor Hesiod, nor Homer, nor
any of the greater poets or teachers of any nation or time
ever spoke but with intentional reservation; nay, beyond this
there is often a meaning which they themselves cannot interpret,—which it may be for ages long after them to interpret,—in what they said, so far as it recorded true
imaginative vision.   For all the greatest myths have been
seen by the men who tell them, involuntarily and passively,—
seen by them with as great distinctness (and in some respects,
though not in all, under conditions as far beyond the control
of their will) as a dream sent to any of us by night when we
dream clearest; and it is this veracity of vision that could
not be refused, and of moral that could not be foreseen,
which in modern historical inquiry has been left wholly out
of account; being indeed the thing which no merely historical
investigator can understand, or even believe; for it belongs
exclusively to the creative or artistic group of men, and can
only be interpreted by those of their race who themselves in
some measure also see visions and dream dreams.

So that you may obtain a more truthful idea of the nature
of Greek religion and legend from the poems of Keats, and
the nearly as beautiful, and in general grasp of subject, far
more powerful recent work of Morris than from frigid
scholarship, however extensive.   Not that the poet's impres-

RUSKIN

sions or renderings of things are wholly true, but their truth
is vital, not formal. They are like sketches from the life by
Reynolds or Gainsborough, which may be demonstrably in-
accurate or imaginary in many traits and indistinct in others,
yet will be in the deepest sense like and true; while the work
of historical analysis is too often weak with loss through the
very labor of its miniature touches, or useless in clumsy and
vapid veracity of externals and complacent security of having done all that is required for the portrait when it has
measured the breadth of the forehead and the length of the
nose.

18. The first of requirements, then, for the right reading
of myths is the understanding of the nature of all true vision
by noble persons; namely, that it is founded on constant
laws common to all human nature; that it perceives, however
darkly, things which are for all ages true; that we can only
understand it so far as we have some perception of the same
truth; and that its fulness is developed and manifested more
and more by the reverberation of it from minds of the same
mirror-temper, in succeeding ages. You will understand
Homer better by seeing his reflection in Dante, as you may
trace new forms and softer colors in a hillside redoubled by
a lake.

I shall be able partly to show you, even to-night, how much
in the Homeric vision of Athena has been made clearer by
the advance of time, being thus essentially and eternally
true; but I must in the outset indicate the relation to that
central thought of the imagery of the inferior deities of
storm.

19. And first I will take the myth of Æolus (the " sage
Hippotades " of Milton) as it is delivered pure by Homer
from the early times.

Why do you suppose Milton calls him " sage "? One does not usually think of the winds as very thoughtful or deliberate powers. But hear Homer: " Then we came to the Æolian island, and there dwelt Æolus Hippotades, dear to the deathless gods; there he dwelt in a floating island, and round it was a wall of brass that could not be broken; and the smooth rock of it ran up sheer. To whom twelve children were born in the sacred chambers,—six daughters and six strong sons; and they dwell forever with their beloved father and their mother, strict in duty; and with them are laid up a thousand benefits; and the misty house around them rings with fluting all the day long." Now, you are to note first in this description the wall of brass and the sheer rock. You will find throughout the fables of the tempest-group that the brazen wall and precipice (occurring in another myth as the brazen tower of Danaë) are always connected with the idea of the towering cloud lighted by the sun, here truly described as a floating island. Secondly, you hear that all treasures were laid up in them; therefore you know this Æolus is lord of the beneficent winds (" he bringeth the wind out of his treasuries "); and presently afterward Homer calls him the " steward " of the winds, the master of the store-house of them. And this idea of gifts and preciousness in the winds of heaven is carried out in the well-known sequel of the fable: Æolus gives them to Ulysses, all but one, bound in leathern bags with a glittering cord of silver, and so like bags of treasure that the sailors think they are so and open them to see. And when Ulysses is thus driven back to Æolus and prays him again to help him, note the deliberate words of the king's refusal: " Did I not," he says, " send thee on thy way heartily that thou mightest reach thy country, thy home, and whatever is dear to thee? It is not

lawful for me again to send forth favorably on his journey
a man hated by the happy gods." This idea of the
beneficence of Æolus remains to the latest times, though
Virgil by adopting the vulgar change of the cloud island into
Lipari, has lost it a little; but even when it is finally explained away by Diodorus, Æolus is still a kind-hearted
monarch who lived on the coast of Sorrento, invented the
use of sails, and established a system of storm-signals.

20. Another beneficent storm-power, Boreas, occupies an
important place in early legend and a singularly principal
one in art; and I wish I could read to you a passage of Plato
about the legend of Boreas and Oreithyia,[1] and the breeze
and shade of the Ilissus—notwithstanding its severe reflection upon persons who waste their time on mythological
studies; but I must go on at once to the fable with which you
are all generally familiar, that of the Harpies.

This is always connected with that of Boreas or the north
wind, because the two sons of Boreas are enemies of the
Harpies and drive them away into frantic flight. The myth
in its first literal form means only the battle between the
fair north wind and the foul south one: the two Harpies,
" Stormswift " and " Swiftfoot," are the sisters of the rainbow; that is to say, they are the broken drifts of the showery
south wind, and the clear north wind drives them back; but
they quickly take a deeper and more malignant significance.
You know the short, violent, spiral gusts that lift the dust
before coming rain: the Harpies get identified first with these
and then with more violent whirlwinds, and so they are
called " Harpies," " the Snatchers," and are thought of as
entirely destructive; their manner of destroying being two-

---

[1] Translated by Max Müller in the opening of his essay on " Comparative Mythology."—" Chips from a German Workshop," vol. ii.

fold—by snatching away and by defiling and polluting. This is a month in which you may really see a small Harpy at her work almost whenever you choose. The first time that there is threatening of rain after two or three days of fine weather leave your window well open to the street and some books or papers on the table, and if you do not in a little while know what the Harpies mean, and how they snatch, and how they defile, I'll give up my Greek myths.

21. That is the physical meaning. It is now easy to find the mental one. You must all have felt the expression of ignoble anger in those fitful gusts of sudden storm. There is a sense of provocation and apparent bitterness of purpose in their thin and senseless fury, wholly different from the nobler anger of the greater tempests. Also, they seem useless and unnatural, and the Greek thinks of them always as vile in malice, and opposed, therefore, to the sons of Boreas, who are kindly winds that fill sails and wave harvests,—full of bracing health and happy impulses. From this lower and merely malicious temper the Harpies rise into a greater terror, always associated with their whirling motion, which is indeed indicative of the most destructive winds; and they are thus related to the nobler tempests, as Charybdis to the sea; they are devouring and desolating, merciless, making all things disappear that come in their grasp; and so, spiritually, they are the gusts of vexatious, fretful, lawless passion, vain and overshadowing, discontented and lamenting, meagre and insane—spirits of wasted energy, and wandering disease, and unappeased famine, and unsatisfied hope. So you have on the one side the winds of prosperity and health, on the other of ruin and sickness. Understand that, once, deeply— any who have ever known the weariness of vain desires, the pitiful, unconquerable, coiling and recoiling and self-involved

returns of some sickening famine and thirst of heart—and you will know what was in the sound of the Harpy Celæno's shriek from her rock; and why in the seventh circle of the " Inferno " the Harpies make their nests in the warped branches of the trees that are the souls of suicides.

22. Now you must always be prepared to read Greek legends as you trace threads through figures on a silken damask: the same thread runs through the web, but it makes part of different figures. Joined with other colors you hardly recognize it, and in different lights it is dark or light. Thus the Greek fables blend and cross curiously in different directions till they knit themselves into an arabesque where sometimes you cannot tell black from purple nor blue from emerald, they being all the truer for this because the truths of emotion they represent are interwoven in the same way, but all the more difficult to read and to explain in any order. Thus the Harpies, as they represent vain desire, are connected with the Sirens, who are the spirits of constant desire; so that it is difficult sometimes in early art to know which are meant, both being represented alike as birds with women's heads; only the Sirens are the great constant desires—the infinite sicknesses of heart—which rightly placed give life, and wrongly placed waste it away; so that there are two groups of Sirens, one noble and saving, as the other is fatal. But there are no animating or saving Harpies; their nature is always vexing and full of weariness, and thus they are curiously connected with the whole group of legends about Tantalus.

23. We all know what it is to be tantalized; but we do not often think of asking what Tantalus was tantalized for,— what he had done to be forever kept hungry in sight of food.

Well, he had not been condemned to this merely for being a glutton. By Dante the same punishment is assigned to simple gluttony to purge it away; but the sins of Tantalus were of a much wider and more mysterious kind. There are four great sins attributed to him: one, stealing the food of the gods to give it to men; another, sacrificing his son to feed the gods themselves (it may remind you for a moment of what I was telling you of the earthly character of Demeter, that while the other gods all refuse, she, dreaming about her lost daughter, eats part of the shoulder of Pelops before she knows what she is doing); another sin is telling the secrets of the gods; and only the fourth—stealing the golden dog of Pandareos—is connected with gluttony. The special sense of this myth is marked by Pandareos receiving the happy privilege of never being troubled with indigestion; the dog in general, however, mythically represents all utterly senseless and carnal desires, mainly that of gluttony; and in the mythic sense of Hades—that is to say, so far as it represents spiritual ruin in this life, and not a literal hell—the dog Cerberus as its gatekeeper, with this special marking of his character of sensual passion that he fawns on all those who descend, but rages against all who would return (the Vergilian *facilis descensus* being a later recognition of this mythic character of Hades); the last labor of Hercules is the dragging him up to the light; and in some sort he represents the voracity or devouring of Hades itself; and the mediæval representation of the mouth of hell perpetuates the same thought. Then also the power of evil passion is partly associated with the red and scorching light of Sirius, as opposed to the pure light of the sun: he is the dog-star of ruin; and hence the continual Homeric dwelling upon him and comparison of the flame of anger to his swarthy light; only in his scorching it is thirst, not hunger, over which he rules physically; so that the fable of Icarius, his first master, corresponds among the Greeks to the legend of the drunkenness of Noah.

The story of Actæon, the raging death of Hecuba, and the tradition of the white dog which ate part of Hercules' first sacrifice, and so gave name to the Cynosarges, are all various phases of the same thought,—the Greek notion of the dog being throughout confused between its serviceable fidelity, its watchfulness, its foul voracity, shamelessness, and deadly madness while with the curious reversal or recoil of the meaning which attaches itself to nearly every great myth—and which we shall presently see notably exemplified in the relations of the serpent to Athena—the dog becomes in philosophy a type of severity and abstinence.

24. It would carry us too far aside were I to tell you the story of Pandareos' dog—or rather of Jupiter's dog, for Pandareos was its guardian only; all that bears in our present purpose is that the guardian of this golden dog had three daughters, one of whom was subject to the power of the Sirens and is turned into the nightingale; and the other two were subject to the power of the Harpies and this was what happened to them: They were very beautiful and they were beloved by the gods in their youth, and all the great goddesses were anxious to bring them up rightly. Of all types of young ladies' education there is nothing so splendid as that of the younger daughters of Pandareos. They have literally the four greatest goddesses for their governesses. Athena teaches them domestic accomplishments, how to weave and sew, and the like; Artemis teaches them to hold themselves up straight; Hera, how to behave proudly and oppressively to company; and Aphrodite, delightful gov-

erness, feeds them with cakes and honey all day long. All goes well until just the time when they are going to be brought out; then there is a great dispute whom they are to marry, and in the midst of it they are carried off by the Harpies, given by them to be slaves to the Furies, and never seen more. But of course there is nothing in Greek myths; and one never heard of such things as vain desires and empty hopes and clouded passions defiling and snatching away the souls of maidens in a London season.

I have no time to trace for you any more Harpy legends, though they are full of the most curious interest; but I may confirm for you my interpretation of this one and prove its importance in the Greek mind by noting that Polygnotus painted these maidens in his great religious series of paintings at Delphi, crowned with flowers and playing at dice; and that Penelope remembers them in her last fit of despair, just before the return of Ulysses, and prays bitterly that she may be snatched away at once into nothingness by the Harpies, like Pandareos' daughters, rather than be tormented longer by her deferred hope and anguish of disappointed love.

25. I have hitherto spoken only of deities of the winds. We pass now to a far more important group, the deities of cloud. Both of these are subordinate to the ruling power of the air, as the demigods of the fountains and minor seas are to the great deep; but as the cloud-firmament detaches itself more from the air and has a wider range of ministry than the minor streams and seas, the highest cloud-diety, Hermes, has a rank more equal with Athena than Nereus or Proteus with Neptune; and there is greater difficulty in tracing his character, because his physical dominion over the clouds can of course be asserted only where clouds are, and therefore

scarcely at all in Egypt;[1] so that the changes which Hermes undergoes in becoming a Greek from an Egyptian and Phœnician god are greater than in any other case of adopted tradition. In Egypt Hermes is a deity of historical record and a conductor of the dead to judgment; the Greeks take away much of this historical function, assigning it to the Muses; but in investing him with the physical power over clouds they give him that which the Muses disdain,—the power of concealment and of theft. The snatching away by the Harpies is with brute force; but the snatching away by the clouds is connected with the thought of hiding and of making things seem to be what they are not; so that Hermes is the god of lying, as he is of mist; and yet with this ignoble function of making things vanish and disappear is connected the remnant of his grand Egyptian authority of leading away souls in the cloud of death (the actual dimness of sight caused by mortal wounds physically suggesting the darkness and descent of clouds and continually being so described in the Iliad); while the sense of the need of guidance on the untrodden road follows necessarily. You cannot but remember how this thought of cloud guidance and cloud-receiving of souls at death has been elsewhere ratified.

26. Without following that higher clue I will pass to the lovely group of myths connected with the birth of Hermes on the Greek mountains. You know that the valley of Sparta is one of the noblest mountain ravines in the world, and that the western flank of it is formed by an unbroken chain of

---

[1] I believe that the conclusions of recent scholarship are generally opposed to the Herodotean ideas of any direct acceptance by the Greeks of Egyptian myths: and very certainly Greek art is developed by giving the veracity and simplicity of real life to Eastern savage grotesque, and not by softening the severity of pure Egyptian design. But it is of no consequence whether one conception was, or was not, in this case, derived from the other; my object is only to mark the essential differences between them.

crags, forty miles long, rising, opposite Sparta, to a height
of 8,000 feet, and known as the chain of Taygetus. Now,
the nymph from whom that mountain ridge is named was
the mother of Lacedæmon; therefore the mythic ancestress
of the Spartan race. She is the nymph Taygeta, and one of
the seven stars of spring; one of those Pleiades of whom is
the question to Job,—" Canst thou bind the sweet influences
of Pleiades, or loose the bands of Orion?" " The sweet influences of Pleiades," of the stars of spring,—nowhere sweeter
than among the pine-clad slopes of the hills of Sparta and
Arcadia, when the snows of their higher summits, beneath
the sunshine of April, fell into fountains and rose into
clouds; and in every ravine was a newly awakened voice of
waters,—soft increase of whisper among its sacred stones;
and on every crag its forming and fading veil of radiant
cloud; temple above temple, of the divine marble that no
tool can pollute nor ruin undermine. And therefore beyond
this central valley, this great Greek vase of Arcadia, on the
" hollow " mountain, Cyllene, or " pregnant " mountain,
called also " cold," because there the vapors rest,[1] and born
of the eldest of those stars of spring, that Maia, from whom
your own month of May has its name, bringing to you, in the
green of her garlands and the white of her hawthorn, the
unrecognized symbols of the pastures and the wreathed snows
of Arcadia, where long ago she was queen of stars; there,
first cradled and wrapt in swaddling-clothes; then raised, in
a moment of surprise into his wandering power,—is born
the shepherd of the clouds, winged-footed and deceiving,—
blinding the eyes of Argus,—escaping from the grasp of
Apollo—restless messenger between the highest sky and top-

---

[1] On the altar of Hermes on its summit, as on that of the Lacinian Hera,
no wind ever stirred the ashes. By those altars the Gods of Heaven
were appeased and all their storms at rest.

most earth,—" the herald Mercury new lighted on a heaven-kissing hill."

27. Now it will be wholly impossible at present to trace for you any of the minor Greek expressions of this thought except only that Mercury, as the cloud-shepherd is especially called Eriophoros, the woolbearer. You will recollect the name from the common woolly rush " eriophorum " which has a cloud of silky seed; and note also that he wears distinctively the flap cap, *petasos,* named from a word meaning " to expand;" which shaded from the sun and is worn on journeys. You have the epithet of mountains " cloud-capped " as an established form with every poet, and the Mont Pilot of Lucerne is named from a Latin word signifying specially a woollen cap; but Mercury has, besides, a general Homeric epithet, curiously and intensely concentrated in meaning, " the profitable or serviceable by wool."[1] that is to say, by shepherd wealth; hence, " pecuniarily," rich or serviceable, and so he passes at last into a general mercantile deity; while yet the cloud sense of the wool is retained by Homer always, so that he gives him this epithet when it would otherwise have been quite meaningless (in Iliad, xxiv, 440), when he drives Priam's chariot and breathes force into his horses precisely as we shall find Athena drive Diomed; and yet the serviceable and profitable sense—and something also of gentle and soothing character in the mere wool-softness, as used for dress and religious rites—is retained also in the epithet, and thus the gentle and serviceable Hermes is opposed to the deceitful one.

---

[1] I am convinced that the ἐρι in ἐριούνιος is not intensitive, but retained from ἔριον ; but even if I am wrong in thinking this, the mistake is of no consequence with respect to the general force of the term as meaning the profitableness of Hermes. Athena's epithet of ἀγελεία has a parallel significance.

28. In connection with this driving of Priam's chariot remember that as Autolycus is the son of Hermes the deceiver, Myrtilus (the Auriga of the Stars) is the son of Hermes the guide. The name Hermes itself means impulse; and he is especially the shepherd of the flocks of the sky, in driving, or guiding, or stealing them; and yet his great name, Argeiphontes, not only—as in different passages of the olden poets—means " Shining White," which is said of him as being himself the silver cloud lighted by the sun; but " Argus-Killer," the killer of brightness which is said of him as he veils the sky, and especially the stars, which are the eyes of Argus; or, literally, eyes of brightness, which Juno, who is with Jupiter, part of the type of highest heaven, keeps in her peacock's train. We know that this interpretation is right, from a passage in which Euripides describes the shield of Hippomedon, which bore for its sign, " Argus the all-seeing, covered with eyes; open toward the rising of the stars, and closed toward their setting."

And thus Hermes becomes the spirit of the movement of the sky or firmament; not merely the fast flying of the transitory cloud, but the great motion of the heavens and stars themselves. Thus in his highest power he corresponds to the *primo mobile* of the later Italian philosophy, and in his simplest is the guide of all mysterious and cloudy movement and of all successful subtleties. Perhaps the prettiest minor recognition of his character is when, on the night foray of Ulysses and Diomed, Ulysses wears the helmet stolen by Autolycus, the son of Hermes.

29. The position in the Greek mind of Hermes as the lord of cloud is however more mystic and ideal than that of any other deity just on account of the constant and real presence of the cloud itself under different forms, giving rise

to all kinds of minor fables. The play of the Greek imagination in this direction is so wide and complex that I cannot
even give you an outline of its range in my present limits.
There is first a great series of storm-legends connected with
the family of the historic Æolus centralized by the story
of Athamas, with his two wives, "the Cloud" and the
"White Goddess," ending in that of Phrixus and Helle, and
of the golden fleece (which is only the cloud-burden of
Hermes Eriophoros). With this there is the fate of Sal-
moneus and the destruction of Glaucus by his own horses;
all these minor myths of storm concentrating themselves
darkly into the legend of Bellerophon and the Chimæra, in
which there is an under-story about the vain subduing of
passion and treachery and the end of life in fading melancholy,—which I hope not many of you could understand even
were I to show it you (the merely physical meaning of the
Chimæra is the cloud of volcanic lightning connected wholly
with earth-fire, but resembling the heavenly cloud in its
height and its thunder). Finally, in the Æolic group there
is the legend of Sisyphus, which I mean to work out thoroughly by itself; its root is in the position of Corinth as ruling
the isthmus and the two seas—the Corinthian Acropolis, two
thousand feet high, being the centre of the crossing currents
of the winds and of the commerce of Greece. Therefore
Athena and the fountain-cloud Pegasus are more closely connected with Corinth than even with Athens in their material,
though not in their moral, power; and Sisyphus founds the
Isthmian games in connection with a melancholy story about
the sea gods; but he himself is κέρδωτος ἀνδρῶν, the most
"gaining" and subtle of men, who having the key of the
Isthmus, becomes the type of transit, transfer, or trade, as
such, and of the apparent gain from it, which is not gain;

and this is the real meaning of his punishment in hell—
eternal toil and recoil (the modern idol of capital being, indeed, the stone of Sisyphus with a vengeance, crushing in
its recoil). But throughout the old ideas of the cloud power
and cloud feebleness,—the deceit of its hiding,—and the
emptiness of its banishing,—the Autolycus enchantment of
making black seem white,—and the disappointed fury of
Ixion (taking shadow for power), mingle in the moral meaning of this and its collateral legends; and give an aspect at
last not only of foolish cunning, but of impiety or literal
" idolatry," " imagination worship," to the dreams of avarice
and injustice, until this notion of atheism and insolent blindness becomes principal; and the " Clouds " of Aristophanes,
with the personified " just " and " unjust " sayings in the
latter part of the play, foreshadow almost feature by feature
in all that they were written to mock and to chastise, the
worst elements of the impious "δῖνος" and tumult in men's
thoughts which have followed on their avarice in the present
day, making them alike forsake the laws of their ancient
gods and misapprehend or reject the true words of their existing teachers.

30. All this we have from the legends of the historic
Æolus only; but besides these there is the beautiful story
of Semele, the mother of Bacchus. She is the cloud with
the strength of the vine in its bosom, consumed by the light
which matures the fruit; the melting away of the cloud
into the clear air at the fringe of its edges being exquisitely
rendered by Pindar's epithet for her, Semele, " with the
stretched-out hair " ταυυέθειρα). Then there is the entire tradition of the Danaides and of the tower of
Danaë and golden shower; the birth of Perseus connecting
this legend with that of the Gorgons and Graiæ, who are the

true clouds of thunderous and ruinous tempest. I must in
passing mark for you that the form of the sword or sickle
of Perseus, with which he kills Medusa, is another image
of the whirling Harpy vortex and belongs especially to the
sword of destruction or annihilation; whence it is given to
the two angels who gather for destruction the evil harvest
and evil vintage of the earth (Rev. xiv, 15). I will collect
afterward and complete what I have already written respecting the Pegasean and Gorgonian legends, noting here only
what is necessary to explain the central myth of Athena herself, who represents the ambient air, which included all
cloud, and rain, and dew, and darkness, and peace, and wrath
of heaven. Let me now try to give you, however briefly,
some distinct idea of the several agencies of this great goddess.

31. I. She is the air giving life and health to all animals.

II. She is the air giving vegetative power to the earth.

III. She is the air giving motion to the sea and rendering navigation possible.

IV. She is the air nourishing artificial light, torch or
lamp light; as opposed to that of the sun on one
hand and of consuming fire on the other.

V. She is the air conveying vibration of sound.

I will give you instances of her agency in all these functions.

32. First and chiefly she is air as the spirit of life, giving
vitality to the blood. Her psychic relation to the vital force
in matter lies deeper, and we will examine it afterward; but
a great number of the most interesting passages in Homer
regard her as flying over the earth in local and transitory
strength, simply and merely the goddess of fresh air.

It is curious that the British city which has somewhat

saucily styled itself the Modern Athens is indeed more under her especial tutelage and favor in this respect than perhaps any other town in the island. Athena is first simply what in the Modern Athens you so practically find her, the breeze of the mountain and the sea; and wherever she comes there is purification and health and power. The sea-beach round this isle of ours is the frieze of our Parthenon; every wave that breaks on it thunders with Athena's voice; nay, whenever you throw your window wide open in the morning you let in Athena as wisdom and fresh air at the same instant; and whenever you draw a pure, long, full breath of right heaven you take Athena into your heart through your blood, and with the blood into the thoughts of your brain.

Now, this giving of strength by the air, observe, is mechanical as well as chemical. You cannot strike a good blow but with your chest full; and in hand-to-hand fighting it is not the muscle that fails first, it is the breath; the longest-breathed will, on the average, be the victor,—not the strongest. Note how Shakespeare always leans on this. Of Mortimer, in " changing hardiment with great Glendower ":

> " Three times they breathed, and three times did they drink,
> Upon agreement, of swift Severn's flood."

And again, Hotspur, sending challenge to Prince Harry:

> " That none might draw short breath to-day
> But I am Harry Monmouth."

Again, of Hamlet, before he receives his wound:

> " He's fat, and scant of breath."

Again, Orlando in the wrestling:

> " Yes; I beseech your grace
> I am not yet well breathed."

Now, of all the people that ever lived the Greeks knew best what breath meant, both in exercise and in battle, and therefore the queen of the air becomes to them at once the queen of bodily strength in war; not mere brutal muscular strength,—that belongs to Ares,—but the strength of young lives passed in pure air and swift exercise,—Camilla's virginal force that " flies o'er the unbending corn and skims along the main."

33. Now I will rapidly give you two or three instances of her direct agency in this function. First when she wants to make Penelope bright and beautiful and to do away with the signs of her waiting and her grief. " Then Athena thought of another thing; she laid her into deep sleep, and loosed all her limbs, and made her taller, and made her smoother, and fatter, and whiter than sawn ivory; and breathed ambrosial brightness over her face; and so she left her and went up to heaven." Fresh air and sound sleep at night, young ladies! You see you may have Athena for lady's maid whenever you choose. Next, hark how she gives strength to Achilles when he is broken with fasting and grief. Jupiter pities him and says to her " ' Daughter mine, are you forsaking your own soldier, and don't you care for Achilles any more? See how hungry and weak he is,—go and feed him with ambrosia.' So he urged the eager Athena; and she leaped down out of heaven like a harpy falcon, shrill-voiced; and she poured nectar and ambrosia, full of delight, into the breast of Achilles that his limbs might not fail with famine; then she returned to the solid dome of her strong father." And then comes the great passage about Achilles arming—for which we have no time. But here is again Athena giving strength to the whole Greek army. She came as a falcon to Achilles, straight at him, a sudden drift of breeze; but to the army she must come widely, she sweeps around them all. "As when Jupiter

spreads the purple rainbow over heaven, portending battle
or cold storm, so Athena, wrapping herself round with a
purple cloud, stooped to the Greek soldiers and raised up
each of them." Note that purple, in Homer's use of it,
nearly always means "fiery," "full of light." It is the
light of the rainbow not the color of it which Homer means
you to think of.

34. But the most curious passage of all, and fullest of
meaning, is when she gives strength to Menelaus, that he
may stand unwearied against Hector. He prays to her:
"And blue-eyed Athena was glad that he prayed to her first;
and she gave him strength in his shoulders and in his limbs,
and she gave him the courage "—of what animal do you suppose? Had it been Neptune or Mars they would have given
him the courage of a bull or a lion; but Athena gives him
the courage of the most fearless in attack of all creatures,
small or great, and very small it is, but wholly incapable of
terror,—she gives him the courage of a fly.

35. Now this simile of Homer's is one of the best instances
I can give you of the way in which great writers seize truths
unconsciously which are for all time. It is only recent science which has completely shown the perfectness of this
minute symbol of the power of Athena; proving that the insect's flight and breath are co-ordinated; that its wings are
actually forcing-pumps, of which the stroke compels the
thoracic respiration; and that it thus breathes and flies simul-
taneously by the action of the same muscles, so that respiration is carried on most vigorously during flight, "while the
air-vessels, supplied by many pairs of lungs instead of one,
traverse the organs of flight in far greater numbers than the
capillary blood-vessels of our own system, and give enormous
and untiring muscular power, a rapidity of action measured

by thousands of strokes in the minute and an endurance by miles and hours of flight."

Homer could not have known this; neither that the buzzing of the fly was produced, as in a wind instrument, by a constant current of air through the trachea. But he had seen and doubtless meant us to remember the marvellous strength and swiftness of the insect's flight (the glance of the swallow itself is clumsy and slow compared to the darting of common house-flies at play); he probably attributed its murmur to the wings, but in this also there was a type of what we shall presently find recognized in the name of Pallas,—the vibratory power of the air to convey sound, while, as a purifying creature, the fly holds its place beside the old symbol of Athena in Egypt, the vulture; and as a venomous and tormenting creature has more than the strength of the serpent in proportion to its size, being thus entirely representative of the influence of the air both in purification and pestilence; and its courage is so notable that, strangely enough, forgetting Homer's simile, I happened to take the fly for an expression of the audacity of freedom in speaking of quite another subject. Whether it should be called courage or mere mechanical instinct may be questioned, but assuredly no other animal exposed to continual danger is so absolutely without sign of fear.

36. You will perhaps have still patience to hear two instances, not of the communication as strength, but of the personal agency of Athena as the air. When she comes down to help Diomed against Ares she does not come to fight instead of him, but she takes his charioteer's place.

> " She snatched the reins, she lashed with all her force,
> And full on Mars impelled the foaming horse."

Ares is the first to cast his spear; then—note this—Pope says:

> " Pallas opposed her hand, and caused to glance,
> Far from the car, the strong immortal lance."

She does not oppose her hand in the Greek—the wind could not meet the lance straight— she catches it in her hand and throws it off. There is no instance in which a lance is so parried by a mortal hand in all the Iliad, and it is exactly the way the wind would parry it, catching it and turning it aside. If there are any good rifle-shots here they know something about Athena's parrying; and in old times the English masters of feathered artillery knew more yet. Compare also the turning of Hector's lance from Achilles: Iliad, xx, 439.

37. The last instance I will give you is as lovely as it is subtle. Throughout the Iliad Athena is herself the will or Menis of Achilles. If he is to be calmed it is she who calms him; if angered it is she who inflames him. In the first quarrel with Atreides, when he stands at pause with the great sword half drawn, "Athena came from heaven and stood behind him and caught him by the yellow hair." Another god would have stayed his hand upon the hilt but Athena only lifts his hair. "And he turned and knew her and her dreadful eyes shone upon him." There is an exquisite tenderness in this laying her hand upon his hair, for it is the talisman of his life, vowed to his own Thessalian river if he ever returned to its shore, and cast upon Petroclus' pile, so ordaining that there should be no return.

38. Secondly, Athena is the air giving vegetative impulse to the earth. She is the wind and the rain, and yet more the pure air itself, getting at the earth fresh turned by spade or plough, and above all feeding the fresh leaves; for though

the Greeks knew nothing about carbonic acid they did know that trees fed on the air.

Now note first in this the myth of the air getting at ploughed ground. You know I told you the Lord of all labor by which man lived was Hephæstus; therefore Athena adopts a child of his and of the earth,—Erichthonius,—literally, "the tearer up of the ground," who is the head (though not in direct line) of the kings of Attica; and having adopted him she gives him to be brought up by the three nymphs of the dew. Of these, Aglauros, the dweller in the fields, is the envy or malice of the earth; she answers nearly to the envy of Cain, the tiller of the ground, against his shepherd brother, in her own envy against her two sisters, Herse, the cloud dew, who is the beloved of the shepherd Mercury; and Pandrosos, the diffused dew, or dew of heaven. Literally, you have in this myth the words of the blessing of Esau: "Thy dwelling shall be of the fatness of the earth and of the dew of heaven from above." Aglauros is for her envy turned into a black stone; and hers is one of the voices—the other being that of Cain—which haunts the circle of envy in the Purgatory:

"Io sono Aglauro, chi divenne sasso."

But to her two sisters, with Erichthonius (or the hero Erectheus), is built the most sacred temple of Athena in Athens; the temple to their own dearest Athena—to her and to the dew together; so that it was divided into two parts: one the temple of Athena of the city, and the other that of the dew. And this expression of her power as the air bringing the dew to the hill pastures, in the central temple of the central city of the heathen, dominant over the future intellectual world, is, of all the facts connected with her worship as the spirit of life, perhaps the most important. I have no time now to trace for you the hundredth part of the different ways in which it bears both upon natural beauty and on the best order and happiness of men's lives. I hope to follow out some of these trains of thought in gathering together what I have to say about field herbage; but I must say briefly here that the great sign to the Greeks of the coming of spring in the pastures, was not, as with us, in the primrose, but in the various flowers of the asphodel tribe (of which I will give you some separate account presently); therefore it is that the earth answers with crocus flame to the cloud on Ida; and the power of Athena in eternal life is written by the light of the asphodel on the Elysian fields.

But further, Athena is the air, not only to the lilies of the field but to the leaves of the forest. We saw before the reason why Hermes is said to be the son of Maia, the eldest of the sister stars of spring. Those stars are called not only Pleiades, but Vergiliæ, from a word mingling the ideas of the turning or returning of springtime with the outpouring of rain. The mother of Vergil bearing the name of Maia, Vergil himself received his name from the seven stars; and he in forming first the mind of Dante, and through him that of Chaucer (besides whatever special minor influence came from the Pastorals and Georgics) became the fountain-head of all the best literary power connected with the love of vegetative nature among civilized races of men. Take the fact for what it is worth; still it is a strange seal of coincidence in word and in reality, upon the Greek dream of the power over human life, and its purest thoughts in the stars of spring. But the first syllable of the name of Vergil has relation also to another group of words of which the English ones, virtue and virgin, bring down the force to modern days. It is a group containing mainly the idea of " spring," or increase of life in vegetation—the rising of the new branch of the tree out of the bud and of the new leaf out of the ground. It involves secondarily the idea of greenness and of strength, but primarily that of living increase of a new rod from a stock, stem, or root (" There shall come forth a rod out of the stem of Jesse "); and chiefly the stem of certain plants—either of the rose tribe, as in the budding of the almond rod of Aaron; or of the olive tribe, which has triple significance in this symbolism, from the use of its oil for sacred anointing, for strength in the gymnasium and for light. Hence in numberless divided and reflected ways it is connected with the power of Hercules and Athena : Hercules plants the wild olive, for its shade, on the course of Olympia, and it thenceforward gives the Olympic crown of consummate honor and rest; while the prize at the Panathenaic games is a vase of its oil (meaning encouragement to continuance of effort); and from the paintings on these Panathenaic vases we get the most precious clue to the entire character of Athena. Then to express its propagation by slips, the trees from which the oil was to be taken were called " Moriai," trees of division (being all descendants of the sacred one in the Erechtheum). And thus in one direction we get to the " children like olive plants round about thy table " and the olive-grafting of St. Paul; while the use of the oil for anointing gives chief name to the rod itself of the stem of Jesse, and to all those who were by that name signed for his disciples first in Antioch. Remember further since that name was first given the influence of the symbol, both in extreme unction and in consecration of priests and kings to their " divine right;" and think, if you can reach with any grasp of thought, what the influence on the earth has been of those twisted branches whose leaves give gray bloom to the hill-sides under every breeze that blows from the midland sea. But above and beyond all, think how strange it is that the chief agonia of humanity and the chief giving of strength from heaven for its fulfilment should have been under its night shadow in Palestine.

39. Thirdly, Athena is the air in its power over the sea.

On the earliest Panathenaic vase known—the " Burgon " vase in the British museum—Athena has a dolphin on her shield. The dolphin has two principal meanings in Greek symbolism. It means first the sea; secondarily the ascending and descending course of any of the heavenly bodies from one sea horizon to another—the dolphins' arching rise and replunge (in a summer evening, out of calm sea, their black backs roll round with exactly the slow motion of a water-wheel; but I do not know how far Aristotle's exaggerated account of their leaping or their swiftness has any foundation) being taken as a type of the emergence of the sun or stars from the sea in the east and plunging beneath in the west. Hence, Apollo, when in his personal power he crosses the sea leading his Cretan colonists to Pytho, takes the form of a dolphin, becomes Apollo Delphinius and names the founded colony " Delphi." The lovely drawing of the Delphic Apollo on the hydria of the Vatican (Le Normand and De Witte, vol. ii, p. 6) gives the entire conception of this myth. Again, the beautiful coins of Tarentum represent Taras coming to found the city, riding on a dolphin, whose leaps and plunges have partly the rage of the sea in them and partly the spring of the horse, because the splendid riding of the Tarentines had made their name proverbial in Magna Græcia. The story of Arion is a collateral fragment of the same thought; and again, the plunge, before their

transformation, of the ships of Æneas.   Then this idea of
career upon or conquest of the sea—either by the creatures
themselves or by dolphin-like ships (compare the Merlin
prophecy,

> " They shall ride
> Over ocean wide
> With hempen bridle and horse of tree ")

—connects itself with the thought of undulation and of the
wave-power in the sea itself, which is always expressed by
the serpentine bodies either of the sea-gods or of the sea-
horse; and when Athena carries, as she does often in later
work, a serpent for her shield-sign it is not so much the
repetition of her own ægis-snakes as the further expression
of her power over the sea-wave; which, finally, Vergil gives
in its perfect unity with her own anger in the approach of
the serpents against Laocoön from the sea; and then finally,
when her own storm-power is fully put forth on the ocean
also, and the madness of the ægis-snake is given to the wave-
snake, the sea-wave becomes the devouring hound at the
waist of Scylla, and Athena takes Scylla for her helmet-crest;
while yet her beneficent and essential power on the ocean, in
making navigation possible, is commemorated in the Panathenaic festival by her peplus being carried to the Erechtheum suspended from the mast of a ship.

In Plate cxv of vol. ii, Le Normand, are given two sides
of a vase, which in rude and childish way assembles most of
the principal thoughts regarding Athena in this relation.   In
the first the sunrise is represented by the ascending chariot
of Apollo, foreshortened; the light is supposed to blind the
eyes, and no face of the god is seen (Turner, in the Ulysses
and Polyphemus sunrise, loses the form of the god in light,
giving the chariot-horses only; rendering in his own manner
after 2,200 years of various fall and revival of the arts pre-

cisely the same thought as the old Greek potter). He ascends out of the sea; but the sea itself has not yet caught the light. In the second design Athena as the morning breeze and Hermes as the morning cloud fly over the sea before the sun. Hermes turns back his head; his face is unseen in the cloud, as Apollo's in the light; the grotesque appearance of an animal's face is only the cloud-phantasm modifying a frequent form of the hair of Hermes beneath the back of his cap. Under the morning breeze the dolphins leap from the rippled sea and their sides catch the light.

The coins of the Lucanian Heracleia give a fair representation of the helmed Athena, as imagined in later Greek art, with the embossed Scylla.

40. Fourthly, Athena is the air nourishing artificial light —unconsuming fire. Therefore a lamp was always kept burning in the Erechtheum; and the torch-race belongs chiefly to her festival, of which the meaning is to show the danger of the perishing of the light even by excess of the air that nourishes it; and so that the race is not to the swift, but to the wise. The household use of her constant light is symbolized in the lovely passage in the Odyssey where Ulysses and his son move the armor while the servants are shut in their chambers and there is no one to hold torches for them; but Athena herself " having a golden lamp fills all the rooms with light. Her presence in war-strength with her favorite heroes is always shown by the " unwearied " fire hovering on their helmets and shields; and the image gradually becomes constant and accepted, both for the maintenance of household watchfulness, as in the parable of the ten virgins, or as the symbol of direct inspiration, in the rushing wind and divided flames of Pentecost; but together with this thought of unconsuming and constant fire there is

always mingled in the Greek mind the sense of the consuming by excess, as of the flame by the air, so also of the inspired creature by its own fire (thus, again, " the zeal of thine house hath eaten me up "—" my zeal hath consumed me, because of thine enemies," and the like); and especially Athena has this aspect toward the truly sensual and bodily strength; so that to Ares, who is himself insane and consuming, the opposite wisdom seems to be insane and consuming: "All we the other gods have thee against us, O Jove! when we would give grace to men; for thou hast begotten the maid without a mind—the mischievous creature, the doer of unseemly evil. All we obey thee and are ruled by thee. Her only thou wilt not resist in anything she says or does, because thou didst bear her—consuming child as she is."

41. Lastly, Athena is the air conveying vibration of sound.

In all the loveliest representations in central Greek art of the birth of Athena, Apollo stands close to the sitting Jupiter, singing with a deep, quiet joyfulness to his lyre. The sun is always thought of as the master of time and rhythm, and as the origin of the composing and inventive discovery of melody; but the air, as the actual element and substance of the voice, the prolonging and sustaining power of it, and the symbol of its moral passion. Whatever in music is measured and designed belongs therefore to Apollo and the Muses; whatever is impulsive and passionate, to Athena; hence her constant strength a voice or cry (as when she aids the shout of Achilles) curiously opposed to the dumbness of Demeter. The Apolline lyre, therefore, is not so much the instrument producing sound as its measurer and divider by length or tension of string into given notes; and I believe it is, in a double connection with its office as a measurer of time or motion and its relation to the transit of the sun in the sky, that Hermes forms it from the tortoise-shell, which is the image of the dappled concave of the cloudy sky. Thenceforward all the limiting or restraining modes of music belong to the Muses; but the passionate music is wind music, as in the Doric flute. Then, when this inspired music becomes degraded in its passion, it sinks into the pipe of Pan and the double pipe of Marsyas and is then rejected by Athena. The myth which represents her doing so is that she invented the double pipe from hearing the hiss of the Gorgonian serpents; but when she played upon it, chancing to see her face reflected in water, she saw that it was distorted, whereupon she threw down the flute which Marsyas found. Then the strife of Apollo and Marsyas represents the enduring contest between music in which the words and thought lead, and the lyre measures or melodizes them (which Pindar means when he calls his hymns " kings over the lyre "), and music in which the words are lost and the wind or impulse leads,—generally, therefore, between intellectual and brutal or meaningless music. Therefore, when Apollo prevails, he flays Marsyas, taking the limit and external bond of his shape from him, which is death, without touching the mere muscular strength, yet shameful and dreadful in dissolution.

42. And the opposition of these two kinds of sound is continually dwelt upon by the Greek philosophers, the real fact at the root of all their teaching being this, that true music is the natural expression of a lofty passion for a right cause; that in proportion to the kingliness and force of any personality the expression either of its joy or suffering becomes measured, chastened, calm, and capable of interpretation only by the majesty of ordered, beautiful, and worded sound. Exactly in proportion to the degree in which we become nar-

row in the cause and conception of our passions, incontinent
in the utterance of them, feeble of perseverance in them,
sullied or shameful in the indulgence of them, their expression by musical sound becomes broken, mean, fatuitous, and
at last impossible; the measured waves of the air of heaven
will not lend themselves to expression of ultimate vice, it
must be forever sunk into discordance or silence. And
since, as before stated, every work of right art has a tendency to reproduce the ethical state which first developed
it, this, which of all the arts is most directly ethical in origin,
is also the most direct in power of discipline; the first, the
simplest, the most effective of all instruments of moral instruction; while in the failure and betrayal of its functions
it becomes the subtlest aid of moral degradation. Music is
thus in her health the teacher of perfect order and is the
voice of obedience of angels and the companion of the course
of the spheres of heaven; and in her depravity she is also
the teacher of perfect disorder and disobedience and the
" Gloria in Excelsis " becomes the " Marseillaise." In the
third section of this volume I reprint two chapters from
another essay of mine (" The Cestus of Aglaia "), on modesty
or measure, and on liberty, containing further reference to
music in her two powers; and I do this now because, among
the many monstrous and misbegotten fantasies which are the
spawn of modern license, perhaps the most impishly opposite
to the truth is the conception of music which has rendered
possible the writing by educated persons, and more strangely
yet, the tolerant criticism, of such words as these: " This so
persuasive art is the only one that has no didactic efficacy,
that engenders no emotions save such as are without issue on
the side of moral truth, that expresses nothing of God,
nothing of reason, nothing of human liberty." I will not

give the author's name; the passage is quoted in the " Westminster Review " for last January [1869].

43. I must also anticipate something of what I have to
say respecting the relation of the power of Athena to organic
life, so far as to note that her name, Pallas, probably refers
to the quivering or vibration of the air; and to its power,
whether as vital force or communicated wave, over every
kind of matter, in giving it vibratory movement; first, and
most intense, in the voice and throat of the bird, which is
the air incarnate; and so descending through the various
orders of animal life to the vibrating and semi-voluntary
murmur of the insect; and, lower still, to the hiss or quiver
of the tail of the half-lunged snake and deaf adder; all these,
nevertheless, being wholly under the rule of Athena as representing either breath or vital nervous power; and therefore,
also, in their simplicity the " oaten pipe and pastoral song,"
which belong to her dominion over the asphodel meadows
and breathe on their banks of violets.

Finally, is it not strange to think of the influence of this
one power of Pallas in vibration (we shall see a singular
mechanical energy of it presently in the serpent's motion),
in the voices of war and peace? How much of the repose,
how much of the wrath, folly, and misery of men, has literally depended on this one power of the air; on the sound of
trumpet and of the bell on the lark's song and the bee's
murmur!

44. Such is the general conception in the Greek mind of
the physical power of Athena. The spiritual power associated with it is of two kinds: first, she is the Spirit of Life
in material organism; not strength in the blood only, but
formative energy in the clay; and, secondly, she is inspired
and impulsive wisdom in human conduct and human art, giv-

ing the instinct of infallible decision and of faultless invention.

It is quite beyond the scope of my present purpose—and indeed will only be possible for me at all after marking the relative intention of the Apolline myths—to trace for you the Greek conception of Athena as the guide of moral passion. But I will at least endeavor on some near occasion to define some of the actual truths respecting the vital force in created organism and inventive fancy in the works of man, which are more or less expressed by the Greeks under the personality of Athena. You would perhaps hardly bear with me if I endeavored further to show you—what is nevertheless perfectly true—the analogy between the spiritual power of Athena in her gentle ministry, yet irresistible anger, with the ministry of another Spirit whom we also, holding for the universal power of life, are forbidden at our worst peril to quench or to grieve.

45. But I think to-night you should not let me close without requiring of me an answer on one vital point, namely, how far these imaginations of gods—which are vain to us— were vain to those who had no better trust? And what real belief the Greek had in these creations of his own spirit, practical and helpful to him in the sorrow of earth? I am able to answer you explicitly in this. The origin of his thoughts is often obscure, and we may err in endeavoring to account for their form of realization; but the effect of that realization on his life is not obscure at all. The Greek creed was of course different in its character, as our own creed is, according to the class of persons who held it. The common people's was quite literal, simple, and happy; their idea of Athena was as clear as a good Roman Catholic peasant's idea of the Madonna. In Athens itself the centre of thought and

refinement, Pisistratus obtained the reins of government through the ready belief of the populace that a beautiful woman, armed like Athena, was the goddess herself. Even at the close of the last century some of this simplicity remained among the inhabitants of the Greek islands; and when a pretty English lady first made her way into the grotto of Antiparos she was surrounded on her return by all the women of the neighboring village, believing her to be divine and praying her to heal them of their sicknesses.

46. Then, secondly, the creed of the upper classes was more refined and spiritual but quite as honest and even more forcible in its effect on the life. You might imagine that the employment of the artifice just referred to implied utter unbelief in the persons contriving it; but it really meant only that the more worldly of them would play with a popular faith for their own purposes, as doubly-minded persons have often done since, all the while sincerely holding the same ideas themselves in a more abstract form; while the good and unworldly men, the true Greek heroes, lived by their faith as firmly as St. Louis, or the Cid, or the Chevalier Bayard.

47. Then, thirdly, the faith of the poets and artists was necessarily less definite, being continually modified by the involuntary action of their own fancies, and by the necessity of presenting, in clear verbal or material form, things of which they had no authoritative knowledge. Their faith was in some respects like Dante's or Milton's: firm in general conception, but not able to vouch for every detail in the forms they gave it; but they went considerably farther, even in that minor sincerity, than subsequent poets, and strove with all their might to be as near the truth as they could. Pindar says, quite simply, " I cannot think so and so of the gods. It

must have been this way—it cannot have been that way—that the thing was done." And as late among the Latins as the days of Horace this sincerity remains. Horace is just as true and simple in his religion as Wordsworth; but all power of understanding any of the honest classic poets has been taken away from most English gentlemen by the mechanical drill in verse-writing at school. Throughout the whole of their lives afterward they never can get themselves quit of the notion that all verses were written as an exercise, and that Minerva was only a convenient word for the last of a hexameter and Jupiter for the last but one.

48. It is impossible that any notion can be more fallacious or more misleading in its consequences. All great song, from the first day when human lips contrived syllables, has been sincere song. With deliberate didactic purpose the tragedians —with pure and native passion the lyrists—fitted their perfect words to their dearest faiths. *Operosa parvus carmina fingo.* " I, little thing that I am, weave my laborious songs " as earnestly as the bee among the bells of thyme on the Matin mountains. Yes, and he dedicates his favorite pine to Diana, and he chants his autumnal hymn to the Faun that guards his fields, and he guides the noble youth and maids of Rome in their choir to Apollo, and he tells the farmer's little girl that the gods will love her though she has only a handful of salt and meal to give them—just as earnestly as ever English gentlemen taught Christian faith to English youth in England's truest days.

49. Then, lastly, the creed of the philosophers or sages varied according to the character and knowledge of each, their relative acquaintance with the secrets of natural science, their intellectual and sectarian egotism, and their mystic or monastic tendencies; for there is a classic as well as a medi-

æval monasticism. They end in losing the life of Greece in play upon words; but we owe to their early thought some of the soundest ethics and the foundation of the best practical laws yet known to mankind.

50. Such was the general vitality of the heathen creed in its strength. Of its direct influence on conduct, it is, as I said, impossible for me to speak now; only, remember always, in endeavoring to form a judgment of it, that what of good or right the heathens did they did looking for no reward. The purest forms of our own religion have always consisted in sacrificing less things to win greater, time to win eternity, the world to win the skies. The order, " Sell that thou hast," is not given without the promise, " Thou shalt have treasure in heaven;" and well for the modern Christian if he accepts the alternative as his Master left it, and does not practically read the command and promise thus: " Sell that thou hast in the best market and thou shalt have treasure in eternity also." But the poor Greeks of the great ages expected no reward from heaven but honor, and no reward from earth but rest; though when, on these conditions they patiently and proudly fulfilled their task of the granted day, an unreasoning instinct of an immortal benediction broke from their lips in song; and they, even they, had sometimes a prophet to tell them of a land " where there is sun alike by day and alike by night, where they shall need no more to trouble the earth by strength of hands for daily bread; but the ocean breezes blow around the blessed islands, and golden flowers burn on their bright trees forevermore."

LOWELL

JAMES RUSSELL LOWELL, a distinguished American wit, poet, essayist, and statesman, was born in Cambridge, Massachusetts, February 22, 1819, and graduated from Harvard College in 1838. In 1841 he published a volume, his first, of poems, entitled "A Year's Life," which showed some facility in versification but no great promise of genius. In 1843 he helped edit "The Pioneer." In 1846 at the outbreak of the Mexican war he published in the "Courier" a satiric poem in the Yankee dialect denouncing the pro-slavery party and out of this grew "The Biglow Papers" which, more than anything else of his, spread his fame wide. He threw himself heart and soul into the anti-slavery movement and wielded a great influence by his wit and caustic verses. Among his serious poems published in the forties may be mentioned "The Vision of Sir Launfal." His "Fable for Critics" pictured in dashing verse in a series of clever sketches a résumé of the abilities and faults of many of his contemporaries. In 1855 after an extended residence in Europe he was appointed professor of modern languages at Harvard. At the same time he edited the "Atlantic Monthly" and from 1863 until 1867 he was associate editor of the "North American Review." In 1865 he produced his "Commemoration Ode," which many critics consider to be the finest poem so far produced in America. In 1877 he was appointed United States minister to Spain and three years later was transferred to the Court of St. James, where he remained until 1885, winning great popularity by his geniality and tact. He died at Cambridge August 12, 1891. Among his best known prose works are "My Study Windows" and "Among my Books," "Democracy," a volume of his addresses made in England, "A Life of Hawthorne" (1890). His collected works are published in thirteen volumes.

ORATION AT THE 250TH ANNIVERSARY OF THE FOUNDING OF HARVARD COLLEGE

DELIVERED AT CAMBRIDGE, NOVEMBER 8, 1886

IT seems an odd anomaly that while respect for age and deference to its opinions have diminished, and are still sensibly diminishing among us, the relish of antiquity should be more pungent and the value set upon things merely because they are old should be greater in America than anywhere else. It is merely a sentimental relish, for ours is a new country in more senses than one, and like children when they are fancying themselves this or that, we have to play very hard in order to believe that we are old.

But we like the game none the worse and multiply our anniversaries with honest zeal, as if we increased our centuries by the number of events we could congratulate ourselves on having happened a hundred years ago. There is something of instinct in this, and it is a wholesome instinct if it serve to quicken our consciousness of the forces that are gathered by duration and continuity; if it teach us that, ride fast and far as we may, we carry the past on our crupper, as immovably seated there as the black care of the Roman poet. The generations of men are braided inextricably together, and the very trick of our gait may be countless generations older than we. . . .

Are we to suppose that these memories were less dear and gracious to the Puritan scholars at whose instigation this college was founded than to that other Puritan who sang in the dim religious light, the long-drawn aisles and fretted vaults, which these memories recalled? Doubtless all these things were present to their minds, but they were ready to forego them all for the sake of that truth whereof, as Milton says of himself, they were members incorporate.

The pitiful contrast which they must have felt between the carven sanctuaries of learning they had left behind and the wattled fold they were rearing here on the edge of the wilderness is to me more than tenderly—it is almost sublimely— pathetic. When I think of their unpliable strength of purpose, their fidelity to their ideal, their faith in God and in themselves, I am inclined to say, with Donne, that

    " We are scarce our fathers' shadows cast at noon."

Our past is well-nigh desolate of æsthetic stimulus. **We**

have none, or next to none, of these aids to the imagination, of these coigns of vantage for the tendrils of memory or affection. Not one of our older buildings is venerable or will ever become so. Time refuses to console them. They all look as though they meant business and nothing more. And it is precisely because this college meant business—business of the gravest import—and did that business as thoroughly as it might with no means that were not niggardly, except an abundant purpose to do its best, it is precisely for this that we have gathered to-day. We come back hither from the experiences of a richer life as the son who has prospered returns to the household of his youth, to find in its very homeliness a pulse, if not of deeper, certainly of fonder emotion than any splendor could stir. "Dear old mother," we say, "How charming you are in your plain cap and the drab silk that has been turned again since we saw you! You were constantly forced to remind us that you could not afford to give us this and that which some other boys had, but your discipline and diet were wholesome, and you sent us forth into the world with the sound constitutions and healthy appetites that are bred of simple fare."

It is good for us to commemorate this homespun past of ours; good in these days of reckless and swaggering prosperity, to remind ourselves how poor our fathers were, and that we celebrate them because for themselves and their children they chose wisdom and understanding and the things that are of God rather than any other riches. This is our Founders' Day, and we are come together to do honor to them all. First, to the Commonwealth, which laid our corner-stone; next, to the gentle and godly youth from whom we took our name—himself scarce more than a name—and with them to the countless throng of benefactors, rich and poor, who have built us up to what we are. We cannot do it better than in the familiar words:

" Let us now praise famous men and our fathers that begat us. The Lord hath wrought great glory by them through his great power from the beginning. Leaders of the people by their counsels, and, by their knowledge of learning, meet for the people; wise and eloquent in their instructions. There be of them that have left a name behind them that their praises might be reported. And some there be which have no memorial, who are perished as though they had never been. But these were merciful men whose righteousness hath not been forgotten. With their seed shall continually remain a good inheritance. Their seed standeth fast and their children for their sakes."

This 250th anniversary of our college is not remarkable as commemorating any venerable length of days. There is hardly a country in Europe that cannot show us universities that were older than ours now is when ours was but a grammar school with Eaton as master. Bologna, Paris, Oxford were already famous schools when Dante visited them six hundred years ago. We are ancient, it is true, on our own continent, ancient even as compared with several German universities more renowned than we. It is not, then, primarily the longevity of our alma mater upon which we are gathered here to congratulate her and each other.

Kant says, somewhere, that as the record of human transactions accumulate, the memory of man will have room only for those of supreme cosmopolitical importance. Can we claim for the birthday we are keeping a significance of so wide a bearing and so long a reach? If we may not do that, we may at least affirm, confidently, that the event it records and emphasizes is second in real import to none that has happened in this western hemisphere. The material growth of the colonies would have brought about their political separation from the mother country in the fulness of time, without that stain of blood which unhappily keeps its own memory green so long.

But the founding of the first English college here was what saved New England from becoming a mere geographical expression. It did more, for it ensured, and I believe was meant to ensure, our intellectual independence of the Old World. That independence has been long in coming, but it will come at last; and are not the names of the chiefest of those who have hastened its coming written on the roll of Harvard College?

I think this foundation of ours a quite unexampled thing. Surely never were the bases of such a structure as this has become, and was meant to be, laid by a community of men so poor, in circumstances so unprecedented, and under what seemed such sullen and averted stars. The colony was in danger of an Indian war, was in the throes of that Antinomian controversy which threatened its very existence, yet the leaders of opinion on both sides were united in the resolve that sound learning and an educated clergy should never cease from among them or their descendants in the Commonwealth they were building up.

In the midst of such fears and such tumults Harvard College was born; and not Marina herself had a more blusterous birth or a more chiding nativity. The prevision of those men must have been as clear as their faith was steadfast. Well they knew and had laid to heart the wise man's precept, "Take fast hold of instruction; let her not go, for she is thy life."

There can be little question that the action of the general court received its impulse and direction from the clergy, men of eminent qualities and of well-deserved authority. Among the Massachusetts Bay colonists the proportion of ministers trained at Oxford and Cambridge was surprisingly large, and if we may trust the evidence of contemporary secular literature, such men as Higginson, Cotton, Wilson, Norton, Shephard, Buikley, Davenport, to mention no more, were in learning, intelligence, and general accomplishment far above the average parson of the country and the church from which their consciences had driven them out.

The presence and influence of such men were of inestimable consequence to the fortunes of the colony.   If they were narrow, it was as the sword of righteousness was narrow. If they had but one idea it was as the leader of a forlorn hope had but one and can have no other—namely, to do the duty that is laid on him and ask no questions.

Our Puritan ancestors have been misrepresented and maligned by persons without imagination enough to make themselves contemporary with, and therefore able to understand, the men whose memories they strive to blacken.   That happy breed of men who both in church and state led our first emigration were children of the most splendid intellectual epoch that England has ever known.   They were the coevals of a generation which passed on, in scarcely a diminished radiance, the torch of life kindled in great Eliza's golden days.   Out of the new learning, the new ferment, alike religious and national, and the new discoveries with their suggestion of boundless possibility, the alembic of that age had distilled a potent elixir either inspiring or intoxicating, as the mind that imbibed it was strong or weak.

Are we to suppose that the lips of the founders of New England alone were unwetted by a drop of that stimulating draught?   That Milton was the only Puritan that had read Shakespeare and Ben Johnson and Beaumont and Fletcher?

I do not believe it, whoever may. Communities as well as men have a right to be judged by their best. We are justified in taking the elder Winthrop as a type of the leading emigrants, and the more we know him the more we learn to reverence his great qualities, whether of mind or character. The posterity of those earnest and single-minded men may have thrown the creed of their fathers into the waste basket, but their fidelity to it and to the duties they believed it to involve is the most precious and potent drop in their transmitted blood. It is especially noteworthy that they did not make a strait-waistcoat of this creed for their new college. The more I meditate upon them the more I am inclined to pardon the enthusiasm of our old historian when he said that God had sifted three kingdoms to plant New England.

The Massachusetts Bay colony itself also was then, and since, without a parallel. It was established by a commercial company whose members combined in themselves the two by no means incongruous elements, enthusiasm and business sagacity, the earthy ingredient, as in dynamite, holding in check its explosive partner, which yet could and did explode on sufficient concussion. They meant that their venture should be gainful, but at the same time believed that nothing could be longer profitable for the body wherein the soul found not also her advantage. They feared God, and kept their powder dry because they feared him, and meant that others should.

I think their most remarkable characteristic was their public spirit, and in nothing did they show both that and the wise forecast that gives it its best value more clearly than when they resolved to keep the higher education of youth in their own hands and under their own eye. This they provided for in the college. Eleven years later they established their system of public schools, where reading and writing should be taught. This they did partly, no doubt, to provide feeders for the more advanced schools, and so for the college, but even more, it may safely be inferred, because they had found that the policy to which their ends, rough-hew them as they might, must be shaped by the conditions under which they were forced to act, could be safe only in the hands of intelligent men, or, at worst, of men to whom they had given a chance to become such.

One is sometimes tempted to think that all learning is as repulsive to ingenuous youth as the multiplication table to Scott's little friend, Marjorie Fleming, though this is due in great part to mechanical methods of teaching.

" I am now going to tell you," she writes, " the horrible and wretched plague that my multiplication table gives me; you can't conceive it; the most devilish thing is eight times eight and seven times seven; it is what nature itself can't endure."

I know that I am approaching treacherous ashes which cover burning coals, but I must on. Is not Greek, nay, even Latin, yet more unendurable than poor Marjorie's task? How many boys have not sympathized with Heine in hating the Romans because they invented Latin grammar? And they were quite right, for we begin the study of languages at the wrong end, at the end which nature does not offer us, and are thoroughly tired of them before we arrive at them, if you will pardon the bull. But is that any reason for not studying them in the right way?

I am familiar with the arguments for making the study of Greek especially a matter of choice or chance. I admit their plausibility and the honesty of those who urge them. I should be willing, also, to admit that the study of the ancient languages without the hope or the prospect of going on to what they contain would be useful only as a form of intellectual gymnastics. Even so they would be as serviceable as the higher mathematics to most of us. But I think that a wise teacher should adapt his tasks to the highest and not the lowest capacities of the taught.

For those lower, also, they would not be wholly without profit. When there is a tedious sermon, says George Herbert,

     " God takes a text, and teacheth patience,"

not the least pregnant of lessons. One of the arguments against the compulsory study of Greek, namely, that it is wiser to give our time to modern languages and modern history than to dead languages and ancient history, involves, I think, a verbal fallacy. Only those languages can properly be called dead in which nothing living has been written. If the classic languages are dead they yet speak to us and with a clearer voice than that of any living tongue.

If their language is dead, yet the literature it enshrines is crammed with life as, perhaps, no other writing except Shakespeare's ever was or will be. It is as contemporary with to-day as with the ears it first enraptured, for it appeals not to the man of then or now, but to the entire round of human nature itself. Men are ephemeral or evanescent, but whatever badge the authentic soul of man has touched with her immortalizing finger, no matter how long ago, is still young and fair as it was to the world's gray father's. Oblivion looks in the face of the Grecian muse only to forget her purpose. Even for the mastering of our own tongue there is no expedient so truthful as translation out of another; how much more when that other is a language at once so precise and so flexible as the Greek! Greek literature is also the most fruitful comment on our own. Coleridge has told us with what profit he was made to study Shakespeare and Milton in conjunction with the Greek dramatists. It is no sentimental argument for this study that the most justly balanced, the most serene and the most fecundating minds since the revival of learning have been saturated with Greek literature. We know not whither other studies will lead us, especially if dissociated from this; we do not know to what summits, far above our lower region of turmoil, this has led, and what the many-sided outlook thence.

Will such studies make anachronisms of us? Unfit us for the duties and the business of to-day? I can recall no writer more truly modern than Montaigne, who was almost more at home in Athens and Rome than in Paris. Yet he was a thrifty manager of his estate and a most competent mayor of Bordeaux.

I remember passing once in London where demolition for a new thoroughfare was going on. Many houses left standing in the rear of those cleared away bore signs with the inscription "Ancient Lights." This was the protest of their owners against being built out by the new improvements from such glimpse of heaven as their fathers had, without adequate equivalent. I laid the moral to heart.

I am speaking of the college as it has always existed and still exists. In so far as it may be driven to put on the forms of the university—I do not mean the four faculties merely, but in the modern sense—we shall naturally find ourselves compelled to assume the method with the function. Some day we shall offer here a chance, at least, to acquire the *omne scibile*. I shall be glad, as shall we all, when the young American need no longer go abroad for any part of his training, though that may not be always a disadvantage, if Shakspeare was right in thinking that—

"Home-keeping youths have ever homely wits."

I should be still gladder if Harvard should be the place that offered the alternative. It seems more than ever probable that this will happen, and happen in our day.

And whenever this consummation is accomplished it will be due, more than to any and all others, to the able, energetic, and simple-minded man who has presided over the college during the trying period of transition, and who by a rare combination of eminent qualities, will carry that transition to its fulfilment without haste and without jar. "*Ohne Hast, ohne Rast.*" He more than any of his distinguished predecessors, has brought the university into closer and more telling relations with the national life in whatever that life has which is most distinctive, most excellent, and most hopeful.

But we still mainly occupy the position of a German gymnasium. Under existing circumstances therefore, and with the methods of teaching they enforce, I think that special and advanced courses should be pushed on, as the other professional courses are, into the post-graduate period. The opportunity would be greater because the number would be less, and the teaching not only more thorough but more vivifying through the more intimate relation of teacher and pupil. Under those conditions the voluntary system will not only be possible, but will come of itself, for every student will know what he wants and where he may get it, and learning will be loved as it should be, for its own sake as well as for what it gives.

The friends of university training can do nothing that

would forward it more than the founding of post-graduate fellowships and the building and endowing of a hall where the holders of them might be commensals, remembering that when Cardinal Wolsey built Christ Church at Oxford his first care was the kitchen. Nothing is so great a quickener of the faculties or so likely to prevent their being narrowed to a single groove as the frequent social commingling of men who are aiming at one goal by different paths: If you would have really great scholars, and our life offers no prize for such, it would be well if the university could offer them. I have often been struck with the many-sided versatility of the fellows of the English colleges who have kept their wits in training by continual fencing with one another.

During the first two centuries of her existence it may be affirmed that Harvard did sufficiently well the only work she was called on to do, perhaps the only work it was possible for her to do. She gave to Boston her scholarly impress, to the Commonwealth her scholastic impulse. To the clergy of her training was mainly intrusted the oversight of the public schools; these were, as I have said, though indirectly, feeders of the college, for their teaching was the plainest.

But if a boy in any country village showed uncommon parts the clergyman was sure to hear of it. He and the squire and the doctor, if there was one, talked it over and the boy was sure to be helped onward to college, for next to the five points of Calvinism, our ancestors believed in a college education; that is, in the best education that was to be had. The system, if system it should be called, was a good one, a practical application of the doctrine of natural selection. Ah! how the parents, nay, the whole family toiled and pinched that this boy might have the chance denied to them.

Mr. Matthew Arnold has told us that in contemporary

France, which seems doomed to try every theory of enlight-enment by which the fingers may be burned or the house set on fire, the children of the public schools are taught in answer to the question, " Who gives you all these fine things?" to say, " The State."

Ill fares the State in which the parental image is replaced by an abstraction. The answer of the boy of whom I have been speaking would have been in a spirit better for the State and for the hope of his own future life : " I owe them under God to my own industry, to the sacrifices of my father and mother and to the sympathy of good men." Nor was the boy's self-respect lessened, for the aid was given by loans to be repaid when possible. The times have changed, and it is no longer the ambition of a promising boy to go to college. They are taught to think that a common school education is good enough for all practical purposes; and so perhaps it is, but not for all ideal purposes. Our public schools teach too little or too much; too little, if education is to go no further; too many things if what is taught is to be taught thoroughly. And the more they seem to teach the less likely is education to go further, for it is one of the prime weaknesses of a de-mocracy to be satisfied with the second best if it appear to answer the purpose tolerably well, and to be cheaper—as it never is in the long run.

Harvard has done much, by raising its standard, to force upward that also of the preparatory schools. The leaven thus infused will, let us hope, filter gradually downward till it raise a ferment in the lower grades as well. What we need more than anything else is to increase the number of our highly cultivated men and thoroughly trained minds, for these, wherever they go, are sure to carry with them, consci-ously or not, the seeds of sounder thinking and of higher ideals. The only way in which our civilization can be maintained, even at the level it has reached; the only way in which that level can be made more general and be raised higher, is by bringing the influence of the more cultivated to bear with more energy and directness on the less cultivated and by opening more inlets to those indirect influences which make for refinement of mind and body.

Democracy must show its capacity for producing, not a higher average man, but the highest possible types of manhood in all its manifold varieties, or it is a failure. No matter what it does for the body, if it do not in some sort satisfy that inextinguishable passion of the soul for something that lifts life away from prose, from the common and the vulgar, it is a failure. Unless it know how to make itself gracious and winning, it is a failure. Has it done this? Is it doing this? Or trying to do it?

Not yet, I think, if one may judge by that commonplace of our newspapers that an American who stays long enough in Europe is sure to find his own country unendurable when he comes back. This is not true, if I may judge from some little experience, but it is interesting as implying a certain consciousness, which is of the most hopeful augury. But we must not be impatient; it is a far cry from the dwellers in caves to even such civilization as we have achieved. I am conscious that life has been trying to civilize me for now nearly seventy years with what seem to me very inadequate results. We cannot afford to wait but the race can. And when I speak of civilization I mean those things that tend to develop the moral forces of man and not merely to quicken his æsthetic sensibility, though there is often a nearer relation between the two than is popularly believed.

The tendency of a prosperous democracy—and hitherto

we have had little to do but prosper—is toward an overween-
ing confidence in itself and its home-made methods, an over-
estimate of material success and a corresponding indifference
to the things of the mind. The popular ideal of success
seems to be more than ever before the accumulation of riches.
I say "seems," for it may be only because the opportunities
are greater.

I am not ignorant that wealth is the great fertilizer of civilization and of the arts that beautify it. The very names of
civilization and politeness show that the refinement of manners which made the arts possible is the birth of cities where
wealth earliest accumulated because it found itself secure.
Wealth may be an excellent thing, for it means power, it
means leisure, it means liberty.

But these, divorced from culture, that is, from intelligent
purpose, become the very mockery of their own essence, not
goods but evils fatal to their possessor, and bring with them
like the Nibelung hoard a doom instead of a blessing. I am
saddened when I see our success as a nation measured by the
number of acres under tillage or of bushels of wheat ex-
ported, for the real value of a country must be weighed in
scales more delicately than the balance of trade. The gardens of Sicily are empty now, but the bees from all climes
still fetch honey from the tiny garden plot of Theocritus.
On a map of the world you may cover Judea with your thumb,
Athens with a finger tip, and neither of them figures in the
prices current, but they still lord it in the thought and action
of every civilized man. Did not Dante cover with his hood
all that was Italy six hundred years ago? And if we go back
a century, where was Germany unless in Weimar?

Material success is good but only as the necessary preliminary of better things. The measure of a nation's true suc-

cess is the amount it has contributed to the thought, the moral energy, the intellectual happiness, the spiritual hope and consolation of mankind.   There is no other, let our candidates flatter us as they may.   We still make a confusion between huge and great.   I know that I am repeating truisms but they are truisms that need to be repeated in season and out of season.

The most precious property of culture and of a college as its trustee is to maintain high ideals of life and its purpose, to keep trimmed and burning the lamps of that Pharos built by wiser than we which warps from the reefs and shallows of popular doctrine.   In proportion as there are more thoroughly cultivated persons in a community will the finer uses of prosperity be taught and the vulgar uses of it become disreputable.

And it is such persons that we are commissioned to send out with such consciousness of their fortunate vocation and such devotion to it as we may.   We are confronted with unexpected problems.   First of all is democracy, and that under conditions in great part novel, with its hitherto imperfectly tabulated results, whether we consider its effects upon national character, on popular thought, or on the functions of law and government.

We have to deal with a time when the belief seems to be spreading that truth not only can but should be settled by a show of hands rather than by a count of heads, and that one man is as good as another for all purposes—as indeed he is till a real man is needed; with a time when the press is more potent for good or for evil than ever any human agency was before, and yet is controlled more than ever before by its interests as a business than by its sense of duty as a teacher, giving news instead of intelligence; with a time when divers

and strange doctrines touching the greatest human interests
are allowed to run about unmuzzled in greater number and
variety than ever before since the Reformation passed into
its stage of putrefactive fermentation; with a time when the
idols of the market-place are more devoutly worshipped than
ever Diana of the Ephesians was; when the electric telegraph
by making public opinion simultaneous is also making it liable
to those delusions, panics, and gregarious impulses which
transform otherwise reasonable men into a mob, and when
above all the better mind of the country is said to be growing
more and more alienated from the highest of all sciences and
services, the government of it.

I have drawn up a dreary catalogue and the moral it points
is this—that the college in so far as it continues to be still a
college, as in great part it does and must, is and should be
limited by pre-existing conditions, and must consider first
what the more general objects of education are without
neglecting special aptitudes more than cannot be helped.

That more general purpose is, I take it, to set free, to supple
and train the faculties in such wise as shall make them most
effective for whatever task life may afterward set them, for
the duties of life rather than for its business, and to open
windows on every side of the mind where thickness of wall
does not prevent it. Let our aim be as hitherto to give a good
all-round education, fitted to cope with as many exigencies
of the day as possible. I had rather the college should turn
out one of Aristotle's four-square men, capable of holding
his own in whatever field he may be cast, than a score of lop-
sided ones developed abnormally in one direction.

Our scheme should be adapted to the wants of the majority
of undergraduates, to the objects that drew them hither, and
to such training as will make the most of them after they

come. Special aptitudes are sure to take care of themselves, but the latent possibilities of the average mind can only be discovered by experiment in many directions.

When I speak of the average mind I do not mean that the courses of study should be adapted to the average level of intelligence but to the highest, for in these matters it is wiser to grade upward than downward since the best is the only thing that is good enough. To keep the wing-footed down to the pace of the leaden-soled disheartens the one without in the least encouraging the other.

" Brains," says Machiavelli, are " of three generations, those that understand of themselves, those that understand when another shows them, and those that understand neither of themselves nor by the showing of others."

It is the first class that should set the stint; the second will get on better than if they had set it themselves, and the third will at least have the pleasure of seeing the others show their paces.

In the college proper I repeat, for it is the birthday of the college that we are celebrating, it is the college that we love and of which we are proud—let it continue to give such a training as will fit the rich to be trusted with riches and the poor to withstand the temptations of poverty. Give to history, give to political economy, the ample verge the times demand, but with no detriment to those liberal arts which have formed open-minded men and good citizens in the past nor have lost the skill to form them.

Let it be our hope to make a gentleman of every youth who is put under our charge, not a conventional gentleman but a man of culture, a man of intellectual resource, a man of public spirit, a man of refinement, with that good taste which is the conscience of the mind and that conscience which is the good taste of the soul. This we have tried to do in the past; this let us try to do in the future. We cannot do this for all at best; perhaps only for the few; but the influence for good of a highly trained intelligence and a harmoniously developed character is incalculable, for though it be subtle and gradual in its operation, it is as pervasive as it is subtle. There may be few of these—there must be few—but

> " That few is all the world which with a few
> Doth ever live and move and work and stirre."

They who, on a tiny clearing pared from the edge of the woods built here, most probably from the timber hewed from the trees they felled, our earliest hall, with the solitude of ocean behind them, the mystery of forest before them, and all about them a desolation, must surely (*si quis animis celestibis locus*) share our gladness and our gratitude at the splendid fulfilment of their vision. If we could have but preserved the humble roof which housed so great a future, Mr. Ruskin himself would almost have admitted that no castle or cathedral was ever richer in sacred associations, in pathos of the past and in moral significance.

They who reared it had the sublime presence of that courage which fears only God, and could say confidently, in the face of all discouragement and doubt, " He hath led us forth into a large place; because he delighted in me he hath delivered me." We cannot honor them too much; we can repay them only by showing, as occasions rise, that we do not undervalue the worth of their example.

Brethren of the alumni, it now becomes my duty to welcome in your name the guests who have come, some of them so far, to share our congratulations and hopes to-day. I cannot name them all and give to each his fitting phrase. Thrice welcome to them all, and as is fitting, first to those from abroad, representatives of illustrious universities that were old in usefulness and fame when ours was in its cradle, and next, to those of our own land from colleges and universities which, if not daughters of Harvard are young enough to be so, and are one with her in heart and hope. I said that I should single out none by name, but I should not represent you fitly if I gave no special greeting to the gentleman who brings the message of John Harvard's College Emmanuel. The welcome we give him could not be warmer than that which we offer to his colleagues, but we cannot help feeling that in pressing his hand our own instinctively closes a little more tightly as with a sense of nearer kindred. There is also one other name of which it would be indecorous not to make an exception. You all know that I can mean only the President of our country. His presence is a signal honor to us all, and to us all I may say a personal gratification. We have no politics here, but the sons of Harvard all belong to the party which admires courage, strength of purpose and fidelity to duty, and which respects, wherever he may be found, the—

"Justum et tenacem propositi virum,"[1]

who knows how to withstand the

"Civium ardor prava jubentium."[2]

He has left the helm of State to be with us here, and so long as it is intrusted to his hands we are sure that, should the storm come, he will say with Seneca's pilot, "O, Neptune, you may save me if you will; you may sink me if you will; but whatever happen, I shall keep my rudder true."

---

[1] The man who is upright and tenacious of his purpose.
[2] The evil zeal of clamorous citizens.

A PLEA FOR THE MODERN LANGUAGES

[An address delivered in Cambridge, Mass., at the Seventh Annual Convention of the Modern Language Association, December, 1889.]

THREE years ago I was one of those who gathered in the Sanders Theatre to commemorate the two hundred and fiftieth anniversary of a college founded to perpetuate living learning chiefly by the help of three dead languages, the Hebrew, the Greek, and the Latin. I have given them that order of precedence which they had in the minds of those our pious founders.

The Hebrew came first because they believed that it had been spoken by God himself, and that it would have been the common speech of mankind but for the judicial invention of the modern languages at Shinar. Greek came next because the New Testament was written in that tongue, and Latin last as the interpreter between scholars. Of the men who stood about that fateful cradle, swung from bough of the primeval forest, there were probably few who believed that a book written in any living language could itself live.

For nearly two hundred years no modern language was continuously and systematically taught here. In the latter half of the last century a stray Frenchman was caught now and then and kept as long as he could endure the baiting of his pupils. After failing as a teacher of his mother tongue, he commonly turned dancing-master, a calling which public opinion seems to have put on the same intellectual level with the other. Whatever haphazard teaching of French there may have been was, no doubt, for the benefit of those youth of the better classes who might go abroad after taking their degrees.

By hook or by crook some enthusiasts managed to learn German, but there was no official teacher before Dr. Follen, about sixty years ago. When at last a chair of French and Spanish was established here, it was rather with an eye to commerce than to culture. It indicates a very remarkable, and, I think, wholesome change in our way of looking at things that I should now be addressing a numerous society composed wholly of men engaged in teaching thoroughly and scientifically the very languages once deemed unworthy to be taught at all except as a social accomplishment or as a commercial subsidiary. There are now I believe as many teachers in that single department of Harvard College as sufficed for the entire undergraduate course when I took my first degree. And this change has taken place within two generations.

> *Τῶ δ' ἤδη δύο μὲν γενεαὶ μερόπων ἀνθρωπών*
> *Ἐθιαθ.*[1]

I make this familiar quotation for two reasons: because Chapman translates *μερόπων* " divers-languaged," which is apt for our occasion, and because it enables me to make an easier transition to what I am about to say, namely, that I rise to address you not without a certain feeling of embarrassment. For every man is, more or less consciously, the prisoner of his date, and I must confess that I was a great while in emancipating myself from the formula which prescribed the Greek and Latin classics as the canonical books of that infallible Church of Culture outside of which there could be no salvation, none, at least, that was orthodox. Indeed I am not sure that I have wholly emancipated myself even yet. The old phrases (for mere phrases they had mostly come to be)

---

[1] Already two generations of speaking men have passed away.

still sing in my ears with a pleasing if not a prevailing enchantment.

The traditions which had dictated this formula were of
long standing and of eminent respectability.   They dated
back to the *exemplaria Græca* of Horace.   For centuries the
languages which served men for all the occasions of private
life were put under a ban, and the revival of learning extended this outlawry to the literature, such as it was, that
had found vent through them.   Even the authors of that literature tacitly admitted the justice of such condemnation when
they used the word " Latin " as meaning language *par excellence*, just as the Newfoundlanders say " fish " when they
mean cod.

They could be witty, eloquent, pathetic, poetical, competent, in a word, to every demand of their daily lives, in their
mother tongue, as the Greeks and Romans had been in theirs
but all this would not do; what was so embalmed would not
keep.

All the prudent and forethoughtful among them accordingly were careful to put their thoughts and fancies, or what
with them supplied the place of these commodities, into Latin
as the one infallible pickle.   They forgot the salt, to be sure,
an ingredient which the author alone can furnish.   For it is
not the language in which a man writes, but what he has been
able to make that language say or sing, that resists decay.   Yet
men were naturally a great while in reaching this conviction.
They thought it was not good form, as the phrase is, to be
pleased with what, and what alone, really touched them home.
The reproach, *at vestri proavi*,[1] rang deterrent in their ears.
The author of " Partonopeus de Blois," it is true, plucks up
a proper spirit:

---

[1] Ah, but your ancestors!

> " Cil clerc dient que n'est pas sens
> Qu' escrive estoire d'antif tens,
> Quant je nes escris en latin,
> Et que je perc mon tans enfin;
> Cil le perdent qui ne font rien
> Moult plus que je ne fac le mien." [1]

And the sarcasm of the last couplet was more biting even than the author thought it. Those moderns who wrote in Latin truly *ne faiseient rien* for I cannot recollect any work of the kind that has in any sense survived as literature unless it be the " Epistolae Obscuroram Virorum " (whose Latin is a part of its humor) and a few short copies of verse, as they used, aptly enough, to be called.

You all remember du Bellay's eloquent protest, " I cannot sufficiently blame the foolish arrogance and temerity of some of our nation, who, being least of all Greeks or Latins, depreciate and reject with a more than stoic brow everything written in French, and I cannot sufficiently wonder at the strange opinion of some learned men who think our vernacular incapable of all good literature and erudition."

When this was said, Montaigne was already sixteen years old and, not to speak of the great mass of verse and prose then dormant in manuscript, France had produced in Rabelais a great humorist and strangely open-eyed thinker, and in Villon, a poet who had written at least one immortal poem which still touches us with that painless sense of the *lachrymœ rerum* so consoling in poetry and the burthen of which

> " Ou sont les neiges d'antan? " [2]

falters and fades away in the ear like the last stroke of Beauty's passing bell. I must not let you forget that du Bel-

---

[1] These pedants declare that there is no sense in writing the history of ancient times unless I write in Latin and that I am in fact wasting my time. Such men waste their time doing nothing far more than I waste mine.

[2] "Where are the snows of yore?"

lay had formed himself on the classics, and that he insists on the assiduous study of them. " Devour them," he says, " not in order to imitate, but to turn them into blood and nutriment." And surely this always has been and always will be their true use.

It was not long before the living languages justified their right to exist by producing a living literature, but as the knowledge of Greek and Latin was the exclusive privilege of a class, that class naturally made an obstinate defence of its vested rights. Nor was it less natural that men like Bacon, who felt that he was speaking to the civilized world, and lesser men who fancied themselves charged with a pressing message to it, should choose to utter themselves in the only tongue that was cosmopolitan. But already such books as had more than a provincial meaning though written in what the learned still looked on as *patois*, were beginning to be translated into the other European languages.

The invention of printing had insensibly but surely enlarged the audience which genius addresses. That there were persons in England who had learned something of French, Italian, Spanish, and of High and Low Dutch three centuries ago is shown by the dramatists of the day, but the speech of the foreigner was still generally regarded as something noxious. Later generations shared the prejudice of sturdy Abbot Samson who confirmed the manor of Thorpe " cuidam Anglico natione . . . de cujus fidelitate plenius confidebat quia bonus agricola erat et quia nesciebat loqui Gallice."[1] This was in 1182, but there is a still more amusing instance of the same prejudice so lately as 1668.

---

[1] " To a certain Englishman in whose trustworthiness he had fuller confidence because he was a good farmer and because he could not speak French."

" Erasmus hath also a notable story of a man of the same age, an Italian, that had never been in Germany, and yet he spake the German tongue most elegantly, being as one possessed of the Devil; notwithstanding was cured by a physician that administered a medicine which expelled an infinite number of *worms*, whereby *he was also freed of his knowledge of the German tongue.*" Dr. Ramesey seems in doubt whether the vermin or the language were the greater deliverance.

Even after it could no longer be maintained that no masterpiece could be written in a modern language, it was affirmed, and on very plausible grounds, that no masterpiece of style could be so written unless after sedulous study of the ancient and especially of the Grecian models. This may have been partially, but was it entirely true? Were those elements of the human mind which tease it with the longing for perfection in literary workmanship peculiar to the Greeks?

Before the new birth of letters Dante (though the general scheme of his great poem be rather mechanical than organic) had given proof of a style, which where it is best is so parsimonious in the number of its words, so goldenly sufficient in the value of them, that we must go back to Tacitus for a comparison, and perhaps not even to him for a parallel. But Dante was a great genius, and language courtesies to its natural kings.

I will take a humbler instance, the " chant-fable " of Aucassin and Nicolete rippling into song and subsiding from it unconsciously as a brook. Leaving out the episode of the King of Torelore, evidently thrust in for the groundlings, what is there like it for that unpremeditated charm which is beyond the reach of literary artifice and perhaps does not survive the early maidenhood of language? If this be not style then there is something better than style. And is there

anything so like the best epigrams of Meleager in grace of
natural feeling, in the fine tact which says all and leaves it
said unblurred by afterthought, as some little snatches of
song by nameless French minstrels of five centuries ago?

It is instructive that only fifty years after du Bellay wrote
the passage I have quoted, Bishop Hall was indirectly prais-
ing Sidney for having learned in France and brought back
with him to England that very specialty of culture which we
are told can only be got in ancient Greece, or at second hand
in ancient Rome. Speaking of some nameless rhymer, he
says of him that

> " He knows the grace of that new elegance
> Which sweet Philisides fetched late from France."

And did not Spenser (whose earliest essay in verse seems
to have been translated from du Bellay) form himself on
French and Italian models? Did not Chaucer and Gower,
the shapers of our tongue, draw from the same sources? Does
not Higgins tell us in the " Mirrour for Magistrates " that
Buckhurst, Phaer, Tuberville, Golding, and Gascoygne imitated Marot? Did not Montaigne prompt Bacon to his
Essays and Browne (unconsciously and indirectly it may be)
to his " Religio Medici?" Did not Skelton borrow his so-
called Skeltonian measure from France? Is not the verse of
" Paradise Lost " moulded on that of the " Divina Commedia?" Did not Dryden's prose and Pope's verse profit
by Parisian example?

Nay, in our own time is it not whispered that more than
one of our masters of style in English, and they, too, among
the chief apostles of classic culture, owe more of this mastery
to Paris than to Athens or Rome? I am not going to renew
the Battle of the Books, nor would I be understood as questioning the rightful place so long held by ancient and especi-

ally by Greek literature as an element of culture and that the most fruitful. But I hold this evening a brief for the modern languages and am bound to put their case in as fair a light as I conscientiously can. Your kindness has put me in a position where I am forced to reconsider my opinions and to discover, if I can, how far prejudice and tradition have had a hand in forming them.

I will not say with the Emperor Charles V, that a man is as many men as he knows languages, and still less with Lord Burleigh that such polyglottism is but " to have one meat served in divers dishes."

But I think that to know the literature of another language, whether dead or living matters not, gives us the prime benefits of foreign travel. It relieves us from what Richard Lassels aptly calls, a " Moral Excommunication;" it greatly widens the mind's range of view, and therefore of comparison, thus strengthening the judicial faculty; and it teaches us to consider the relations of things to each other and to some general scheme rather than to ourselves; above all it enlarges æsthetic charity.

It has seemed to me also that a foreign language, quite as much as a dead one, has the advantage of putting whatever is written in it at just such a distance as is needed for a proper mental perspective. No doubt this strangeness, this novelty, adds much to the pleasure we feel in reading the literature of other languages than our own. It plays the part of poet for us by putting familiar things in an unaccustomed way so deftly that we feel as if we had gained another sense and had ourselves a share in the sorcery that is practised on us. The words of our mother tongue have been worn smooth by so often rubbing against our lips or minds, while the alien word has all the subtle emphasis and beauty of some

new minted coin of ancient Syracuse. In our critical esti-
mates we should be on our guard against this charm.

In reading such books as chiefly deserve to be read in any
foreign language it is wise to translate consciously and in
words as we read. There is no such help to a fuller mastery
of our vernacular. It compels us to such a choosing and
testing, to so nice a discrimination of sound, propriety, position, and shade of meaning, that we now first learn the secret
of the words we have been using or misusing all our lives and
are gradually made aware that to set forth even the plainest
matter as it should be set forth is not only a very difficult
thing calling for thought and practice, but an affair of conscience as well.

Translating teaches us as nothing else can, not only that
there is a best way, but that it is the only way. Those who
have tried it know too well how easy it is to grasp the verbal
meaning of a sentence or of a verse. That is the bird in
the hand. The real meaning, the soul of it, that which makes
it literature and not jargon, that is the bird in the bush which
tantalizes and stimulates with the vanishing glimpses we
catch of it as it flits from one to another lurking place:

"Et fugit ad salices et se cupit ante videri." After all, I
am driven back to my Virgil again, you see, for the happiest
expression of what I was trying to say. It was these shy
allurements and provocations of Omar Khayyam's Persian
which led Fitzgerald to many a peerless phrase and made an
original poet of him in the very act of translating.

I cite this instance merely by way of hint that as a spur
to the mind, as an open-sesame to the treasures of our native
vocabulary, the study of a living language (for literary, not
linguistic ends) may serve as well as that of any which we
rather inaptly call dead.

We are told that perfection of form can be learned only of the Greeks, and it is certainly true that many among them attained to, or developed out of some hereditary germ of aptitude, a sense of proportion and of the helpful relation of parts to the whole organism which other races mostly grope after in vain. Spenser, in the enthusiasm of his new Platonism tells us that " Soul is form, and doth the body make," and no doubt this is true of the highest artistic genius. Form without soul, the most obsequious observance of the unities, the most perfect *a priori* adjustment of parts, is a lifeless thing like those machines of perpetual motion, admirable in every way but one—that they will not go.

I believe that I understand and value form as much as I should, but I also believe that some of those who have insisted most strongly on its supreme worth as the shaping soul of a work of art have imprisoned the word soul in a single one of its many meanings and the soul itself in a single one of its many functions. For the soul is not only that which gives form, but that which gives life, the mysterious and pervasive essence always in itself beautiful, not always so in the shapes which it informs, but even then full of infinite suggestion.

In literature it is what we call genius, an insoluble ingredient which kindles, lights, inspires, and transmits impulsion to other minds, wakens energies in them hitherto latent and makes them startlingly aware that they too may be parts of the controlling purpose of the world.

A book may be great in other ways than as a lesson in form, and it may be for other qualities that it is most precious to us. Is it nothing, then, to have conversed with genius? Goethe's " Iphigenie " is far more perfect in form than his " Faust," which is indeed but a succession of scenes strung together on a thread of moral or dramatic purpose, yet it is "Faust" that we read and hold dear alike for its meaning and for the delight it gives us.

And if we talk of classics, what, then, is a classic if it be not a book that forever delights, inspires, and surprises?—in which, and in ourselves, by its help, we make new discoveries every day. What book has so warmly embosomed itself in the mind and memory of men as the "Iliad?" And yet surely not by its perfection in form so much as by the stately simplicity of its style, by its pathetic truth to nature, for so loose and discursive is its plan as to have supplied plausible argument for a diversity of authorship. What work of classic antiquity has given the *bransle,* as he would have called it, to more fruitful thinking than the Essays of Montaigne, the most planless of men who ever looked before and after, a chaos indeed, but a chaos swarming with germs of evolution?

There have been men of genius, like Emerson, richly seminative for other minds; like Browning, full of wholesome ferment for other minds, though wholly destitute of any proper sense of form. Yet perhaps those portions of their writings where their genius has precipitated itself in perfect, if detached and unrelated crystals flashing back the light of our common day tinged with the diviner hue of their own nature, are and will continue to be a more precious and fecund possession of mankind than many works more praiseworthy as wholes, but in which the vitality is less abounding, or seems so because more evenly distributed and therefore less capable of giving that electric shock which thrills through every fibre of the soul.

But Samuel Daniel, an Elizabethan poet less valued now than many an inferior man, has said something to my pur-

pose far better than I could have said it. Nor is he a suspicious witness, for he is himself a master of style. He had
studied the art of writing, and his diction has accordingly
been less obscured by time than that of most of his contemporaries. He knew his classics, too, and his dullest work is
the tragedy of " Cleopatra " shaped on a classic model, pre-
sumably Seneca, certainly not the best. But he had modern
instincts, and a conviction that the later generations of men
had also their rights, among others that of speaking their
minds in such forms as were most congenial to them. In
answer to some one who had denounced the use of rhyme as
barbarous, he wrote his " Defence of Rhyme," a monument
of noble and yet impassioned prose.

In this he says, " Suffer the world to enjoy that which it
knows and what it likes, seeing whatsoever form of words
doth move delight, and sway the affections of men, in what
Scythian sort soever it be disposed and uttered, that is
true number, measure, eloquence, and the perfection of
speech."

I think that Daniel's instinct guided him to a half-truth,
which he as usual believed to include the other half also.
For I have observed that truth is the only object of man's
ardent pursuit of which every one is convinced that he and
he alone has got the whole.

I am not sure that form, which is the artistic sense of
decorum controlling the co-ordination of parts and ensuring
their harmonious subservience to a common end, can be
learned at all, whether of the Greeks or elsewhere. I am
not sure that even style (a lower form of the same faculty
or quality, whichever it be), which has to do with the perfection of the parts themselves, and whose triumph it is to
produce the greatest effect with the last possible expenditure

of material,—I am not sure that even this can be taught in any school.

If Sterne had been asked where he got that style which, when he lets it alone, is as perfect as any that I know; if Goldsmith had been asked where he got his, so equable, so easy without being unduly familiar, might they not have answered with the maiden in the ballad,

> "I gat it in my mither's wame,
> Where ye'll get never the like"?

But even though the susceptibility of art must be inborn, yet skill in the practical application of it to use may be increased,—best by practice, and very far next best by example. Assuming, however, that either form or style is to be had without the intervention of our good fairy, we can get them, or at least a wholesome misgiving that they exist and are of serious import, from the French, as Sir Philip Sidney and so many others have done, as not a few are doing now. It is for other and greater virtues that I would frequent the Greeks.

Browning, in the preface to his translation of the "Agamemnon," says bluntly, as is his wont, "learning Greek teaches Greek and nothing else." One is sometimes tempted to think that it teaches some other language far harder than Greek when one tries to read his translation.

Matthew Arnold, on the other hand, was never weary of insisting that the *grand style* could be best learned of the Greeks, if not of them only. I think it may be taught, or, at least, fruitfully suggested, in other ways. Thirty odd years ago I brought home with me from Nuremberg photographs of Peter Fischer's statues of the twelve apostles. These I used to show to my pupils and ask for a guess at their size.

The invariable answer was "larger than life." They were really about eighteen inches high, and this grandiose effect was wrought by simplicity of treatment, dignity of pose, a large unfretted sweep of drapery. This object-lesson I found more telling than much argument and exhortation. I am glad that Arnold should have been so insistent, he said so many admirable things in maintaining his thesis. But I question the validity of single verses, or even of three or four, as examples of style, whether grand or other, and I think he would have made an opponent very uncomfortable who should have ventured to discuss Homer with as little knowledge of Greek as he himself apparently had of Old French when he commented on the "Chanson de Roland."

He cites a passage from the poem and gives in a note an English version of it which is translated, not from the original, but from the French rendering by Génin who was himself on no very intimate terms with the archaisms of his mother tongue. With what he says of the poem I have little fault to find. It is said with his usual urbane discretion and marked by his usual steadiness of insight.

But I must protest when he quotes four lines, apt as they are for his purpose, as an adequate sample, and then compares them with a most musically pathetic passage from Homer. Who is there that could escape undiminished from such a comparison? Nor do I think that he appreciated as he should one quality of the poem which is essentially Homeric, I mean its invigorating energy, the exhilaration of manhood and courage that exhales from it, the same that Sidney felt in " Chevy Chase."

I believe we should judge a book rather by its total effect than by the adequacy of special parts, and is not this effect moral as well as æsthetic? If we speak of style, surely that is like good breeding, not fortuitous, but characteristic, the key which gives the pitch of the whole tune. If I should set some of the epithets with which Achilles lays Agamemnon about the ears in the first book of the "Iliad" in contrast with the dispute between Roland and Oliver about blowing the olifaunt, I am not sure that Homer would win the prize of higher breeding.

The "Chanson de Roland" is to me a very interesting and inspiring poem, certainly not to be named with the "Iliad" for purely literary charm, but equipped with the same moral qualities that have made that poem dearer to mankind than any other. When I am "moved more than with a trumpet," I care not greatly whether it be blown by Greek or Norman breath.

And this brings me back to the application of what I quoted just now from Daniel. There seems to be a tendency of late to value literature and even poetry, for their usefulness as courses of moral philosophy or metaphysics, or as exercises to put and keep the mental muscles in training. Perhaps the highest praise of a book is that it sets us thinking, but surely the next highest praise is that it ransoms us from thought. Milton tells us that he thought Spenser "a better teacher than Scotus or Aquinas," but did he prize him less that he lectured in a garden of Alcina?

To give pleasure merely is one, and not the lowest, function of whatever deserves to be called literature. Culture, which means the opening and refining of the faculties, is an excellent thing, perhaps the best, but there are other things to be had of the muses which are also good in their kind. Refined pleasure is refining pleasure too, and teaches something is her way though she be no proper schooldame. In my weaker moments I revert with a sigh, half deprecation, half relief, to the old notion of literature as holiday, as

" The world's sweet inn from care and wearisome turmoil."

Shall I make the ignominious confession that I relish Skelton's Philip Sparowe, pet of Skelton's Maystres Jane, or parts of it, inferior though it be in form, almost as much as that more fortunate pet of Lesbia? There is a wonderful joy in it to chase away what Skelton calls odius ennui, though it may not thrill our intellectual sensibility like its Latin prototype.

And in this mood the modern languages add largely to our resources. It may be wrong to be happy unless in the grand style, but it is perilously agreeable. And shall we say that the literature of the last three centuries is incompetent to put a healthy strain upon the more strenuous faculties of the mind? That it does not appeal to and satisfy the mind's loftier desires? That Dante, Machiavelli, Montaigne, Bacon, Shakespeare, Cervantes, Pascal, Calderon, Lessing, and he of Weimar in whom Carlyle and so many others have found their university, that none of these set our thinking gear in motion to as good purpose as any ancient of them all? Is it less instructive to study the growth of modern ideas than of ancient? Is the awakening of the modern world to consciousness and its first tentative, then fuller, then rapturous expression of it,

" Like the new-abashed nightingale
That slinteth first when he beginneth sing."

" Till the fledged notes at length forsake their nests,
Fluttering in wanton shoals."

less interesting or less instructive to us because it finds a readier way to our sympathy through a postern which we cannot help leaving sometimes on the latch, than through the ceremonious portal of classical prescription? Goethe went to the root of the matter when he said, "people are always talking of the study of the ancients; yet what does this mean but apply yourself to the actual world and seek to express it, since this is what the ancients also did when they were alive?"

That "when they were *alive*" has an unconscious sarcasm in it. I am not ashamed to confess that the first stammerings of our English speech have a pathetic charm for me which I miss in the wiser and ampler utterances of a tongue, not only foreign to me as modern languages are foreign, but thickened in its more delicate articulations by the palsying touch of time. And from the native wood notes of many modern lands, from what it was once the fashion to call the rude beginnings of their literature, my fancy carries away, I find, something as precious as Greek or Latin could have made it. Where shall I find the piteous and irreparable poverty of the parvenu so poignantly typified as in the " Lai de L'oiselet?" Where the secret password of all poetry with so haunting a memory as in Count Arnaldos,

> " Yo no digo esta cancion
> Sino a quien conmigo va?" [1]

It is always wise to eliminate the personal equation from our judgments of literature as of other things that nearly concern us. But what is so subtle, so elusive, so inapprehensible as this *folle du logis?* Are we to be suspicious of a book's good character in proportion as it appeals more vividly to our own private consciousness and experience? How are we to know to how many it may be making the same appeal? Is there no resource, then, but to go back humbly to the old

---

[1] " I repeat this song only to whoever goes with me."

quod semper, quod ubique, quod ab omnibus,[1] and to accept nothing as orthodox literature on which the elder centuries have not laid their consecrating hands?

The truth is, perhaps, that in reading ancient literature many elements of false judgment, partly involved in the personal equation, are inoperative, or seem to be so, which, when we read a more nearly neighboring literature, it is well nigh impossible to neutralize. Did not a part of Matthew Arnold's preference for the verses of Homer, with the thunder-roll of which he sent poor old Thoroldus about his business, spring from a secret persuasion of their more noble harmony, their more ear-bewitching canorousness? And yet he no doubt recited these verses in a fashion which would have disqualified them as barbarously for the ear of an ancient Greek as if they had been borrowed of Thoroldus himself. Do we not see here the personal fallacy's eartip? I fancy if we could call up the old *jongleur* and bid him sing to us, accompanied by his *vielle*, we should find in his verses a plaintive and not unimpressive melody such as so strangely moves one in the untutored song of the Tuscan peasant heard afar across the sunsteeped fields with its prolonged fondling of the assonants. There is no question about what is supreme in literature. The difference between what is best and what is next best is immense; it is felt instinctively; it is a difference not of degree but of kind.

And yet may we not without lese-majesty say of books what Ferdinand says of women,

> " for several virtues
> Have I liked several women; never any
> With so full soul but some defect in her
> Did quarrel with the noblest grace she owed
> And put it to the foil " ?

---

[1] The eternal, the ubiquitous, the universal.

In growing old one grows less fanatically punctual in the practice of those austerities of taste which make too constant demands on our self-denial. The ages have made up their minds about the ancients. While they are doing it about the moderns (and they are sometimes a little long about it, having the whole of time before them), may we not allow ourselves to take an honest pleasure in literature far from the highest, if you will, in point of form, not so far in point of substance, if it comply more kindly with our mood or quicken it with oppugnancy according to our need?

There are books in all modern languages which fulfil these conditions as perfectly as any, however sacred by their antiquity, can do. Were the men of the middle ages so altogether wrong in preferring Ovid because his sentiment was more in touch with their own, so that he seemed more neighborly? Or the earlier dramatists in overestimating Seneca for the same reason?

Whether it be from natural predisposition or from some occult influence of the time, there are men who find in the literature of modern Europe a stimulus and a satisfaction which Athens and Rome deny them. If these books do not give so keen an intellectual delight as the more consummate art and more musical voice of Athens enabled her to give, yet they establish and maintain, I am more than half willing to believe, more intimate and confiding relations with us.

They open new views, they liberalize us as only an acquaintance with the infinite diversity of men's minds and judgments can do, they stimulate to thought or teaze the fancy with suggestion, and in short do fairly well whatever a good book is expected to do, what ancient literature did at the Revival of Learning with an effect like that which the reading of Chapman's Homer had upon Keats. And we must not forget that the best result of this study of the ancients was the begetting of the moderns, though Dante somehow contrived to get born with no help from the Greek Hera and little more from the Roman Lucina.

As implements of education the modern books have some advantages of their own. I am told and I believe that there is a considerable number of not uningenuous youths, who, whether from natural inaptitude or want of hereditary predisposition, are honestly bored by Greek and Latin, and who yet would take a wholesome and vivifying interest in what was nearer to their habitual modes of thought and association. I would not take this for granted, I would give the horse a chance at the ancient springs before I came to the conclusion that he would not drink. No doubt, the greater difficulty of the ancient languages is believed by many to be a prime recommendation of them as challenging the more strenuous qualities of the mind.

I think there are grounds for this belief, and was accordingly pleased to learn the other day that my eldest grandson was taking kindly to his Homer. I had rather he should choose Greek than any modern tongue, and I say this as a hint that I am making allowance for the personal equation. The wise gods have put difficulty between man and everything that is worth having. But where the mind is of softer fibre and less eager of emprise, may it not be prudent to open and make easy every avenue that leads to literature, even though it may not directly lead to those summits that tax the mind and muscle only to reward the climber at last with the repose of a more ethereal air?

May we not conclude that modern literature and the modern languages as the way to it should have a more important place assigned to them in our courses of instruction, assigned to them moreover as equals in dignity, except so far as age may justly add to it, and no longer to be made to feel themselves inferior by being put below the salt?

That must depend on the way they are taught, and this on the competence and conscience of those who teach them. Already a very great advance has been made. The modern languages have nothing more of which to complain. There are nearly as many professors and assistants employed in teaching them at Harvard now as there were students of them when I was in college.

Students did I say? I meant boys who consented to spend an hour with the professor three times a week for the express purpose of evading study. Some of us learned so much that we could say " How do you do?" in several languages, and we learned little more. The real impediment was that we were kept forever in the elementary stage, that we had and could look forward to no literature that would have given significance to the languages and made them beneficent. It is very different now, and with the number of teachers the number of students has more than proportionally increased. And the reason is not far to seek. The study has been made more serious, more thorough, and therefore more inspiring.

And it is getting to be understood that as a training of the faculties, the comparative philology, at least, of the modern languages may be made as serviceable as that of the ancient. The classical superstition of the English race made them especially behindhand in this direction, and it was long our shame that we must go to the Germans to be taught the rudiments of our mother tongue.

This is no longer true. Anglo-Saxon, Gothic, Old High, and Middle High German and Icelandic are all taught not only here, but in all our chief centres of learning. When I first became interested in Old French I made a surprising discovery. If the books which I took from the college library had been bound with gilt or yellow edges, those edges stuck together, as when so ornamented they are wont to do till the leaves have been turned. No one had ever opened those books before.

> " I was the first that ever burst
> Into that silent sea."

Old French is now one of regular courses of instruction, and not only is the language taught but its literature as well.

Remembering what I remember, it seems to me a wonderful thing that I should have lived to see a poem in Old French edited by a young American scholar (present here this evening) and printed in the journal of this Society, a journal in every way creditable to the scholarship of the country. Nor as an illustration of the same advance in another language, should we forget Dr. Fay's admirable concordance of the " Divina Commedia."

But a more gratifying illustration than any is the existence and fruitful activity of this Association itself, and this select concourse before me which brings scholars together from all parts of the land, to stimulate them by personal commerce with men of kindred pursuits and to unite so many scattered energies in a single force controlled by a common and invigorated purpose.

We have every reason to congratulate ourselves on the progress the modern languages have made as well in academic as in popular consideration. They are not taught (as they could not formerly be taught) in a way that demands toil and thought of the student, as Greek and Latin, and they only, used to be taught; and they also open the way to higher intellectual joys, to pastures new and not the worse for being so, as Greek and Latin, and they only, used to do.

Surely manysidedness is the very essence of culture, and it matters less what a man learns than how he learns it. The day will come, nay, it is dawning already, when it will be understood that the masterpieces of whatever language are not to be classed by an arbitrary standard, but stand on the same level in virtue of being masterpieces; that thought, imagination, and fancy may make even a *patois* acceptable to scholars; that the poets of all climes and of all ages " sing to one clear harp in divers tones," and that the masters of prose and the masters of verse in all tongues teach the same lesson and exact the same fee.

I began by saying that I had no wish to renew the Battle of the Books. I cannot bring myself to look upon the literatures of the ancient and modern worlds as antagonists, but rather as friendly rivals in the effort to tear as many as may be from the barbarizing ploutolatry which seems to be so rapidly supplanting the worship of what alone is lovely and enduring. No, they are not antagonists, but by their points of disparity, of likeness, or contrast, they can be best understood, perhaps understood only through each other. The scholar must have them both, but may not he who has not leisure to be a scholar, find profit even in the lesser of the two if that only be attainable? Have I admitted that one is the lesser? *"O matre pulchra filia pulchrior "*[1] is perhaps what I should say here.

If I did not rejoice in the wonderful advance made in the comparative philology of the modern languages, I should not have the face to be standing here. But neither should I if I shrank from saying what I believed to be the truth, whether

---

[1] " More beautiful daughter of a beautiful mother."

here or elsewhere. I think that the purely linguistic side in the teaching of them seems in the way to get more than its fitting share. I insist only that in our college courses this should be a separate study, and that, good as it is in itself, it should, in the scheme of general instruction, be restrained to its own function as the guide to something better.

And that something better is literature. The blossoms of language have certainly as much value as its roots, for if the roots secrete food and thereby transmit life to the plant, yet the joyous consummation of that life is in the blossoms, which alone bear the seeds that distribute and renew it in other growths. Exercise is good for the muscles of mind and to keep it well in hand for work, but the true end of culture is to give it play, a thing quite as needful.

What I would urge therefore is that no invidious distinction should be made between the old learning and the new, but that students, due regard being had to their temperaments and faculties, should be encouraged to take the course in modern languages as being quite as good in point of mental discipline as any other if pursued with the same thoroughness and to the same end. And that end is literature, for there language first attains to a full consciousness of its powers and to the delighted exercise of them.

Literature has escaped that doom of Shinar which made our Association possible, and still everywhere speaks in the universal tongue of civilized man. And it is only through this record of man's joys and sorrows, of his aspirations and failures, of his thought, his speculation and his dreams, that we can become complete men, and learn both what he is and what he may be, for it is the unconscious autobiography of mankind. And has no page been added to it since the last ancient classic author laid down his pen?

WHIPPLE

EDWIN PERCY WHIPPLE, a keen and judicious American essayist and lecturer, was born at Gloucester, March 8, 1819, and was educated at the English High School of Salem. For several years he was employed in a broker's office in Boston, and in 1837 became superintendent of the reading-room of the Merchants' Exchange. This position he retained until 1860, when he determined to devote himself wholly to literature. He had begun at the age of fourteen to write for the newspapers and an article contributed to the "Boston Miscellany" on Macaulay, in 1843, attracted wide attention and secured his fame. This same year he entered the lecture field with a series of biographical and critical addresses which were published in book form in 1849 under the title "Literature and Life." He devoted himself wholly to literary work after 1860 and was for a time review editor of the "Boston Globe." His judgments on his contemporaries were regarded as unusually just and discriminating. He did not confine himself to literary topics, but treated also of finance and politics. He was a personal friend of the leading writers of his day. He was engaged on a life of Governor Andrew when he died, June 16, 1886. Among his best-known books are, "Character and Characteristic Men" (1866); "The Literature of the Age of Elizabeth" (1869); "Success and Its Conditions" (1871). After his death his selections from his writings were published under the titles, "Recollections of Eminent Men," "American Literature and Other Papers," and "Outlooks on Society, Literature, and Politics."

PATRIOTIC ORATION

DELIVERED IN BOSTON, JULY 4, 1850

THE day, gentlemen, we have here met to commemorate in the spirit of a somewhat soberer joy than rings in the noisy jubilee of the streets is not a day dedicated to liberty in the abstract but a day especially consecrated to American liberty and American independence. The true character of that liberty is to be sought in the events of our colonial history, in the manners and laws of our colonial forefathers, and above all, in the stern, brief epitome of our whole colonial life contained in that memorable Declaration,

(8022)

the maxims of whose sturdy wisdom still sound in our ears and linger in our hearts, as we have heard them read in this hall to day; a Declaration peculiar among all others of its kind, not merely for the fearless free spirit which beats and burns beneath every decisive sentence, but from its combination of clearness in the statement of particular grievances, with audacity in the announcement of general principles; a Declaration, indeed, abounding in sentiments of liberty so sinewy and bold, and ideas of liberty so exact and practical, that it bears on every immortal feature the signs of representing a people to whom liberty had been long familiar as a living law, as an organized institution, as a homely household fact. The peculiarities which distinguish the whole substance and tone of this solemn instrument are peculiarities of the American Revolution itself, giving dignity to its events and import to its principles, as they gave success to its arms.

Liberty, considered as an element of human nature, would naturally, if unchecked, follow an ideal law of development, appearing first as a dim but potent sentiment; then as an intelligent sentiment or idea; then as an organized idea, or body of institutions, recognizing mutual rights and enforcing mutual duties. But in its historical development we find that the unselfish nature of liberty is strangely intermixed with its selfish perversion; that in struggling with outward oppression it develops inward hatreds; that the sentiment is apt to fester into a malignant passion, the idea to dwindle into a barren opinion, and this passionate opinion to issue in anarchy, which is despotism disorganized, but as selfish, wolfish, and ravenous under its thousand wills as under its one. These hostile elements which make up the complex historical fact of liberty,—one positive, the other nega-

tive,—one organizing, the other destructive,—are always at
work in human affairs with beneficent or baleful energy;
but as society advances the baser elements give way by degrees to the nobler, and liberty ever tends to realize itself
in law. The most genial operation of its creative spirit is
when it appears as a still, mysterious, plastic influence,
silently and surely modifying the whole constitution of a
despotic society, stealing noiselessly into manners, insinuating itself into the administration of laws, grafting new shoots
upon the decaying trunks of old institutions, and insensibly
building up in a people's mind a character strong enough to
maintain rights which are also customs. If its most beneficent influence be seen in its gradual organization of liberties, of sentiments rooted in facts, its most barren effect for
good is when it scatters abstract opinions of freedom, true to
nothing existing in a people's practical life, and scorning all
alliance with manners or compromise with fact. This is a
fertile source of disorder, of revolts which end in massacres,
of ages of reason which end in reigns of terror; and perhaps
the failure of most of the European movements comes from
their being either mad uprisings against the pressure of intolerable miseries, or fruitless strivings to establish abstract
principles. Such principles, however excellent as proposi-
tions, can only influence a small minority of a nation, for a
nation rises only in defence of rights which have been violated, not for rights which it has never exercised; and abstract " liberty, equality, and fraternity," pushed by amiable
sentimentalists like Lamartine, and Satanic sentimentalists
like Ledru Rollin, have found their fit result in the armed
bureauocracy, now encamped in Paris under the ironical
nickname of " French Republic."

Now it was the peculiar felicity of our position that free

constitutions were planted here at the original settlement of the country, institutions which De Tocqueville considers founded on principles far in advance of the wisest political science of Europe at that day: and accordingly our Revolution began in the defence of rights which were customs, of ideas which were facts, of liberties which were laws; and these rights, ideas, and liberties, embodying as they did the common life and experience of the people, were truly considered a palpable property, an inalienable inheritance of freedom, which the Stamp Act and the other measures of colonial taxation threatened with confiscation. Parliament therefore appeared in America as a spoiler, making war upon the people it assumed to govern, and it thus stimulated and combined the opposition of all classes, for a wrong cannot but be universally perceived when it is universally felt. By thus starting up in defence of the freedom they really possessed, the colonies vastly increased it. In struggling against innovation they " innovated " themselves into independence; in battling against novelties they wrought out into actual form the startling novelty of constitutional American liberty. It was because they had exercised rights that they were such proficients in principles; it was because they had known liberty as an institution that they understood it as a science.

Thus it was not the preception of abstract opinions, but the inspiration of positive institutions which gave our forefathers the heart to brave and the ability successfully to defy the colossal power of England. But it must be admitted that in its obnoxious colonial policy England had parted with her wisdom, and in parting with her wisdom had weakened her power; falling, as Burke says, under the operation of that immutable law " which decrees vexation to

violence and poverty to rapine." The England arrayed
against us was not the England, which a few years before,
its energies wielded by the lofty and impassioned genius of
the elder Pitt, had smitten the power and humbled the pride
of two great European monarchies, and spread its fleets and
armies, animated by one vehement soul, over three quarters
of the globe. The administrations of the English government, from 1760 to the close of our Revolutionary war, were
more or less directed by the intriguing incapacity of the
King. George III is said to have possessed many private
virtues,—and very private for a long time he kept them
from his subjects, but as a monarch he was without magna-
nimity in his sentiments or enlargement in his ideas; pre-
judiced, uncultivated, bigoted, and preverse; and his boasted
morality and piety, when exercised in the sphere of government, partook of the narrowness of his mind and the obstinacy of his will; his conscience being used to transmute
his hatreds into duties and his religious sentiment to sanctify
his vindictive passions; and, as it was his ambition to rule an
empire by the petty politics of a court, he preferred to have
his folly flattered by parasites than his ignorance enlightened
by statesmen. Such a disposition in the king of a free
country was incompatible with efficiency in the conduct of
affairs, as it split parties into factions and made established
principles yield to mean personal expedients. Bute, the
King's first minister, after a short administration unexampled
for corruption and feebleness, gave away before a storm of
popular contempt and hatred. To him succeeded George
Grenville, the originator of the Stamp Act and the blunder-
ing promotor of American independence. Grenville was a
hard, sullen, dogmatic, penurious man of affairs, with a complete mastery of the details of parliamentary business, and

threading with ease all the labyrinths of English law, but limited in his conceptions, fixed in his opinions, without any of that sagacity which reads results in their principles; and chiefly distinguished for a kind of sour honesty, not infrequently found in men of harsh tempers and technical intellects. It was soon discovered that though imperious enough to be a tyrant he was not servile enough to be a tool; that the same domineering temper which enabled him to push arbitrary measures in Parliament, made him put insolent questions in the palace; and the King, in despair of a servant who could not tax America and persecute Wilkes without at the same time insulting his master, dismissed him for the Marquis of Rockingham, the leader of the great Whig connection, and a sturdy friend of the Americans both before the Revolution and during its progress. Under him the Stamp Act was repealed, but his administration soon proved too liberal to satisfy the fawning politicians who governed the understanding of the King; and the experiment was tried of a composite ministry, put together by Chatham, consisting of members selected from different factions, but without any principle of cohesion to unite them; and the anarchy, inherent in the arrangement, became portentously apparent when Chatham, driven by the gout into a state of nervous imbecility, left it to work out its mission of misrule, and its eccentric control was seized by the chancellor of the exchequer, the gay, false, dissipated, veering, presumptuous, and unscrupulous Charles Townsend. This man was so brilliant and fascinating as an orator, that Walpole said of one of his speeches, that it was like hearing Garrick act extempore scenes from Congreve. But he was without any guiding moral or political principles; and, boundlessly admired by the House of Commons and boundlessly craving its admiration, he seemed to act ever from the impulses of vanity and speak ever from the inspiration of champagne. Grenville, smarting under his recent defeat, but still doggedly bent on having a revenue raised in America, missed no opportunity of goading this versatile political roué with his sullen and bitter sarcasms. "You are cowards," said he on one occasion, turning to the treasury bench; "you are afraid of the Americans; you dare not tax America." Townsend, stung by this taunt, started passionately up from his seat, exclaiming, "Fear! cowards! dare not tax America! I do dare tax America!" and this boyish bravado ushered in the celebrated bill which was to cost England thirteen colonies, add a hundred millions of pounds to her debt, and affix an ineffaceable stain on her public character. Townsend, by the grace of a putrid fever, was saved from witnessing the consequences of his vainglorious presumption; and the direction of his policy eventually fell into the hands of Lord North, a good-natured, second-rate, jobbing statesman, equally destitute of lofty virtues and splendid vices, under whose administration the American war was commenced and consummated. Of all the ministers of George III. North was the most esteemed by his sovereign, for he had the tact to follow plans, which originated in the King's unreasoning brain and wilful disposition, and yet to veil their weak injustice in a drapery of arguments furnished from his own more enlarged mind and easier temper. Chatham and Camden thundered against him in the Lords; Burke and Fox, Cassandras of ominous and eloquent prophecy, raved and shouted statesmanship to him in the Commons, and screamed out the maxims of wisdom in ecstasies of invective; but he, good-naturedly tolerant to political adversaries, blandly indifferent to popular execration, and sleeping quietly through whole hours of philippics hot with threats of impeachment, pursued his course of court-ordained folly with the serene composure of an Ulysses or Somers. The war, as conducted by his ministry, was badly managed, but he had one wise thought which happily failed to become a fact. The command in America, on the breaking out of serious disturbances, was offered to Lord Clive; but, fortunately for us, Clive, at about that time, concluded to commit suicide, and our rustic soldiery were thus saved from meeting in the field a general, who in vigor of will and fertility of resource, was unequalled by any European commander who had appeared since the death of Marlborough. It may here be added that Lord North's plans of conciliation were the amiabilities of tyranny and benignities of extortion. They bring to mind the little French fable, wherein a farmer convokes the tenants of his barnyard, and with sweet solemnity says,—" Dear animals, I have assembled you here to advise me what sauce I shall cook you with." " But," exclaims an insurrectionary chicken, " we don't want to be eat at all !"—to which the urbane chairman replies,—" My child, you wander from the point!"

Such was the government whose policy and whose arms were directed against our rights and liberties during the Revolutionary war. As soon as the struggle commenced it was obvious that England could hold dominion over no portion of the country except what her armies occupied or wasted for the time; and that the issue of the contest turned on the question as to which would give out first, the obstinacy of the King or the fortitude of the Americans. It was plain that George III would never yield except under compulsion from the other forces of the English constitution; that as long as a corrupt House of Commons would vote supplies he would prosecute the war at whatever expense of blood and treasure to England, at whatever infliction of misery upon America. Conquest was hopeless; and Lord North before the war was half concluded was in favor of abandoning it; but all considerations of policy and humanity were lost upon the small mind and conscientiously malignant temper of the King. The peculiarity of our struggle consisted in its being with an unwise ruler, who could not understand that war waged after the objects for which it was declared have utterly failed becomes mere rapine and murder; and our energy and endurance were put to this terrible test of bearing up against the King's armies until the English nation humbling its irritated pride should be roused in our behalf and break down the King's stubborn purpose. We all know, and may we never forget, that this resistance to tyrannical innovation was no fiery outbreak of popular passion, spending itself in two or three battles and then subsiding into gloomy apathy, but a fixed and reasonable resolve rooted in character and proof against corrupt and sophistical plans of conciliation, against defeats and massacres, against universal bankruptcy and commercial ruin,—a resolve, which the sight of burning villages and cities turned into British camps only maddened into fiercer persistence, and which the slow consuming fever of an eight years' war with its soul-sickening calamities and vicissitudes could not weaken into submission. The history, so sad and so glorious, which chronicles the stern struggle in which our rights and liberties passed through the awful baptism of fire and blood, is eloquent with the deeds of many patriots, warriors, and statesmen; but these all fall into relations to one prominent and commanding figure, towering up above the whole group in unapproachable majesty, whose exalted character, warm and bright with every public and private virtue, and vital with the essential spirit of wisdom, has burst all sectional and national bounds and made the name of Washington the property of all mankind.

This illustrious man, at once the world's admiration and enigma, we are taught by a fine instinct to venerate and by a wrong opinion to misjudge. The might of his character has taken strong hold upon the feelings of great masses of men, but in translating this universal sentiment into an intelligent form, the intellectual element of this wonderful nature is as much depressed as the moral element is exalted, and consequently we are apt to misunderstand both. Mediocrity has a bad trick of idealizing itself in eulogizing him, and drags him down to its own low level while assuming to lift him to the skies. How many times have we been told that he was not a man of genius, but a person of "excellent common sense," of "admirable judgment," of "rare virtues;" and by a constant repetition of this odious cant we have nearly succeeded in divorcing comprehension from his sense, insight from his judgment, force from his virtues, and life from the man. Accordingly, in the panegyric of cold spirits, Washington disappears in a cloud of commonplaces; in the rhodomontade of boiling patriots he expires in the agonies of rant. Now the sooner this bundle of mediocre talents and moral qualities which its contrivers have the audacity to call George Washington is hissed out of existence the better it will be for the cause of talent and the cause of morals; contempt of that is the beginning of wisdom. He had no genius it seems. O no! genius we must suppose is the peculiar and shining attribute of some orator whose tongue can spout patriotic speeches, or some versifier whose muse can " Hail Columbia," but not of the man who supported states on his arm and carried America in his brain. The madcap Charles Townsend, the motion of whose pyrotechnic mind was like the whiz of a hundred rockets, is a man of genius; but George Washington raised up above the level of even eminent statesmen and with a nature moving with the still and orderly celerity of a planet round its sun,—he dwindles in comparison into a kind of angelic dunce! What is genius? Is it worth anything? Is splendid folly the measure of its inspiration? Is wisdom its base and summit,— that which it recedes from or tends toward? And by what definition do you award the name to the creator of an epic and deny it to the creator of a country? On what principle is it to be lavished on him who sculptures in perishing marble the image of possible excellence and withheld from him who built up in himself a transcendent character, indestructible as the obligations of duty and beautiful as her rewards?

Indeed, if by the genius of action you mean will enlightened by intelligence and intelligence energized by will; if force and insight be its characteristics and influence its test; and especially if great effects suppose a cause proportionably great, that is, a vital, causative mind, then is Washington most assuredly a man of genius and one whom no other American has equalled in the power of working morally and mentally on other minds. His genius it is true was of a peculiar kind, the genius of character, of thought, and the objects of thought solidified and concentrated into active faculty. He belongs to that rare class of men,—rare as Homers and Miltons, rare as Platos and Newtons,—who have impressed their characters upon nations without pampering national vices. Such men have natures broad enough to include all the facts of a people's practical life and deep enough to discern the spiritual laws which underlie, animate and govern those facts. Washington in short had that greatness of character which is the highest expression and last result of greatness of mind, for there is no method of building up character except through mind. Indeed, character like his is not built up, stone upon stone, precept upon precept, but grows up through an actual contact of thought with things,—the assimilative mind transmuting the impalpable but potent spirit of public sentiment, and the life of visible facts, and the power of spiritual laws, into individual life and power so that their mighty energies put on personality as it were and act through one centralizing human will. This process may not if you please make the great philosopher or the great poet but it does make the great man,—the man in whom thought and judgment seem identical with volition, the man whose vital expression is not in words but deeds, the man whose sublime ideas issue necessarily in sublime acts not in sublime art. It was because Washington's character was thus composed of the inmost substance and power of facts and principles that men instinctively felt the perfect reality of his comprehensive manhood. This reality enforced universal respect, married strength to repose, and threw into his face that commanding majesty which made men of the speculative audacity of Jefferson and the lucid genius of Hamilton recognize with unwonted meekness his awful superiority.

But you may say how does this account for Washington's virtues? Was his disinterestedness will? Was his patriotism intelligence? Was his morality genius? These questions I should answer with an emphatic yes, for there are few falser fallacies than that which represents moral conduct as flowing from moral opinions detached from moral character. Why, there is hardly a tyrant, sycophant, demagogue, or liberticide mentioned in history, who had not enough moral opinions to suffice for a new Eden; and Shakespeare, the sure-seeing poet of human nature, delights to put the most edifying maxims of ethics into the mouths of his greatest villains, of Angelo, of Richard III, of the uncle-father of Hamlet. Without doubt Cæsar and Napoleon could have discoursed more fluently than Washington on patriotism, as there are a thousand French republicans of the last hour's coinage who could prattle more eloquently than he on freedom. But Washington's morality was built up in warring with outward temptations and inward passions, and every grace of his conscience was a trophy of toil and struggle. He had no moral opinions which hard experience and sturdy discipline had not vitalized into moral sentiments and organized into moral powers; and these powers, fixed and seated in the inmost heart of his character, were mighty and far-sighted forces which made his intelligence moral and his morality intelligent, and which no sorcery of the selfish passions could overcome or deceive. In the sublime metaphysics of the New Testament his eye was single, and this made his whole body full of light. It is just here that so many other eminent men of action, who have been tried by strong temptations, have miserably failed. Blinded by pride or whirled on by wrath they have ceased to discern and regard the inexorable moral laws, obedience to which is the condition of all permanent success; and in the labyrinths of fraud and unrealities in which crime entangles ambition, the thousand-eyed genius of wilful error is smitten with folly and madness. No human intellect however vast its compass and delicate its tact can safely thread those terrible mazes. "Every heaven-stormer," says a quaint German, "finds his hell as sure as every mountain its valley." Let us not doubt the genius of Washington because it was identical with wisdom, and because its energies worked with and not against the spiritual order its " single eye " was gifted to divine. We commonly say that he acted in accordance with moral laws, but we must recollect that moral laws are intellectual facts, and are known through intellectual processes. We commonly say that he was so conscientious as ever to follow the path of right and obey the voice of duty. But what is right but an abstract term for rights? What is duty but an abstract term for duties? Rights and duties move not in parallel but converging lines; and how in the terror, discord, and madness of a civil war, with rights and duties in confused conflict, can a man seize on the exact point where clashing rights harmonize and where opposing duties are reconciled and act vigorously on the conception without having a conscience so informed with intelligence that his nature gravitates to the truth as by the very instinct and essence of reason?

The virtues of Washington therefore appear moral or mental according as we view them with the eye of conscience or reason. In him loftiness did not exclude breadth, but resulted from it; justice did not exclude wisdom, but grew out of it; and, as the wisest as well as justest man in America, he was pre-eminently distinguished among his contemporaries for moderation,—a word under which weak politicians conceal their want of courage, and knavish politicians their want of principle, but which in him was vital and comprehensive energy, tempering audacity with prudence, self-reliance with modesty, austere principles with merciful charities, inflexible purpose with serene courtesy, and issuing in that persistent and unconquerable fortitude in which he excelled all mankind. In scrutinizing the events of his life to discover the processes by which his character grew gradually up to its amazing height, we are arrested at the beginning by the character of his mother, a woman temperate like him in the use of words, from her clear perception and vigorous grasp of things. There is a familiar anecdote recorded of her, which enables us to understand the simple sincerity and genuine heroism she early instilled into his strong and aspiring mind. At a time when his glory rang through Europe; when excitable enthusiasts were crossing the Atlantic for the single purpose of seeing him; when bad poets all over the world were sacking the dictionaries for hyperboles of panegyric; when the pedants of republicanism were calling him the American Cincinnatus and the American Fabius—as if our Washington were honored in playing the adjective to any Roman however illustrious!—she, in her quiet dignity, simply said to the voluble friends who were striving to flatter her mother's pride into an expression of exulting praise, "that he had been a good son, and she believed he had done his duty as a man." Under the care of a mother who flooded common words with such a wealth of meaning, the boy was not likely to mistake mediocrity for excellence, but would naturally domesticate in his heart lofty principles of conduct, and act from them as a matter of course, without expecting or obtaining praise. The consequence was that in early life, and in his first occupation as surveyor, and through the stirring events of the French war, he built up character day by day in a systematic endurance of hardship; in a constant sacrific of inclinations to duty; in taming hot passions into the service of reason; in assiduously learning from other minds; in wringing knowledge, which could not be taught him, from the reluctant grasp of a flinty experience; in completely mastering every subject on which he fastened his intellect, so that whatever he knew he knew perfectly and forever, transmuting it into mind, and sending it forth in acts.

Intellectual and moral principles, which other men lazily contemplate and talk about, he had learned through a process
which gave them the toughness of muscle and bone. A man
thus sound at the core and on the surface of his nature; so
full at once of integrity and sagacity; speaking ever from
the level of his character, and always ready to substantiate
opinions with deeds; a man without any morbid egotism, or
pretension, or extravagance; simple, modest, dignified, incorruptible; never giving advice which events did not endorse
as wise, never lacking fortitude to bear calamities which resulted from his advice being overruled: such a man could not
but exact that recognition of commanding genius which inspires universal confidence. Accordingly, when the contest
between the colonies and the mother country was assuming
its inevitable form of civil war, he was found to be our
natural leader in virtue of being the ablest man among a
crowd of able men. When he appeared among the eloquent
orators, the ingenious thinkers, the vehement patriots of the
Revolution, his modesty and temperate professions could not
conceal his superiority; he at once, by the very nature of
great character, was felt to be their leader; towered up, indeed, over all their heads as naturally, as the fountain sparkling yonder in this July sun, which, in its long, dark, downward journey forgets not the altitude of its parent lake, and
no sooner finds an outlet in our lower lands than it mounts
by an impatient instinct, surely up to the level of its far-off
inland source.

After the first flush and fever of the Revolutionary excitement was over, and the haggard fact of civil war was visible
in all its horrors, it soon appeared how vitally important was
such a character to the success of such a cause. We have
already seen that the issue of the contest depended, not on

the decision of this or that battle, not on the occupation of
this or that city, but on the power of the colonists to wear
out the patience, exhaust the resources, and tame the pride of
Great Britain. The King, when Lord North threatened in
1778 to resign unless the war were discontinued, expressed his
determination to lose his crown rather than acknowledge the
independence of the rebels; he was as much opposed to that
acknowledgment in 1783 as 1778; and it was only by a pressure from without, and when the expenditures for the war
had reached a hundred million of pounds, that a reluctant consent was forced from that small, spiteful mind. Now there
was undoubtedly a vast majority of the American people
unalterably resolved on independence, but they were spread
through thirteen colonies, were not without mutual jealousies, and were represented in a Congress whose delegated
powers were insufficient to prosecute war with vigor. The
problem was, how to combine the strength, allay the suspi-
cions, and sustain the patriotism of the people during a contest peculiarly calculated to distract and weaken their energies. Washington solved this problem by the true geometry
of indomitable personal character. He was the soul of the
Revolution, felt at its center, and felt through all its parts, as
an uniting, organizing, animating power. Comprehensive as
America itself, through him, and through him alone, could
the strength of America act. He was security in defeat,
cheer in despondency, light in darkness, hope in despair, the
one man in whom all could have confidence, the one man
whose sun-like integrity and capacity shot rays of light and
heat through everything they shone upon. He would not
stoop to thwart the machinations of envy; he would not stoop
to contradict the fictions and forgeries of calumny; and he
did not need to do it. Before the effortless might of his

character they stole away and withered and died; and through no instrumentality of his did their abject authors become immortal as the maligners of Washington.

To do justice to Washington's military career we must consider that he had to fuse the hardest individual materials into a mass of national force, which was to do battle not only with disciplined armies, but with frost, famine, and disease. Missing the rapid succession of brilliant engagements between forces almost equal, and the dramatic storm and swift consummation of events which European campaigns have made familiar, there are those who see in him only a slow, sure, and patient commander, without readiness of combination or energy of movement. But the truth is the quick eye of his prudent audacity seized occasions to deliver blows with the prompt felicity of Marlborough or Wellington. He evinced no lack of the highest energy and skill when he turned back the tide of defeat at Monmouth, or in the combinations which preceded the siege of Yorktown, or in the rapid and masterly movements by which, at a period when he was considered utterly ruined, he swooped suddenly down upon Trenton, broke up all the enemy's posts on the Delaware, and snatched Philadelphia from a superior and victorious foe. Again, some eulogists have caricatured him as a passionless, imperturbable, " proper " man; but at the battle of Monmouth General Lee was privileged to discover that from those firm, calm lips could leap words hotter and more smiting than the hot June sun that smote down upon their heads. Indeed, Washington's incessant and various activity answered to the strange complexity of his position, as the heart and brain of a Revolution, which demanded not merely generalship, but the highest qualities of the statesman, the diplomatist, and the patriot. As we view him in his long seven years' struggle with the perilous difficulties of his situation, his activity constantly entangled in a mesh of conflicting considerations; with his eye fixed on Congress, on the States, and on the people, as well as on the enemy; compelled to compose sectional quarrels, to inspire faltering patriotism, and to triumph over all the forces of stupidity and selfishness; compelled to watch, and wait, and warn, and forbear, and endure, as well as to act; compelled, amid vexations and calamities which would sting the dullest sensibilities into madness, to transmute the fire of the fiercest passion into an element of fortitude; and, especially, as we view him coming out of that terrible and obscure scene of trial and temptation, without any bitterness in his virtue, or hatred in his patriotism, but full of the loftiest wisdom and serenest power; as we view all this in the order of its history, that placid face grows gradually sublime and in its immortal repose looks rebuke to our presumptuous eulogium of the genius which breathes through it!

We all know that toward the end of the wearying struggle, and when his matchless moderation and invincible fortitude were about to be crowned with the hallowing glory which liberty piously reserves for her triumphant saints and martyrs, that a committee of his officers proposed to make him king; and we sometimes do him the cruel injustice to say that his virtue overcame the temptation. He was not knave enough, or fool enough, to be tempted by such criminal baubles. What was his view of the proposal? He who had never sought popularity but whom popularity had sought; he who had entered public life not for the pleasure of exercising power but for the satisfaction of performing duty; he to be insulted and outraged by such an estimate of his services and such a conception of his character,—why, it could provoke in him nothing but an instantaneous burst of indignation and abhorrence!—and in his reply you will find that these emotions strain the language of reproof beyond the stern courtesy of military decorum.

The war ended, and our independence acknowledged, the time came when American liberty, threatened by anarchy, was to be reorganized in the constitution of the United States. As president of the convention which framed the constitution, Washington powerfully contributed to its acceptance by the States. The people were uncertain as to the equity of its compromise of opposing interests and adjustment of clashing claims. By this eloquent and learned man they were advised to adopt it; by that eloquent and learned man they were advised to reject it; but there, at the end of the instrument itself, and first among many eminent and honored names, was the bold and honest signature of George Washington, a signature which always carried with it the integrity and the influence of his character; and that was an argument stronger even than any furnished by Hamilton, Madison, and Jay. The constitution was accepted; and Washington, whose fame, to use Allston's familiar metaphor, was ever the shadow cast by his excellence, was of course unanimously elected President. This is no place to set forth the glories of his civil career. It is sufficient to say that placed amid circumstances where ignorance, vanity, or rashness would have worked ruinous mischief and disunion, he consolidated the government. One little record in his diary, just before he entered upon his office, is a key to the spirit of his administration. His journey from Mount Vernon to the seat of government was a triumphal procession. At New York the air was alive with that tumult of popular applause which has poisoned the integrity by intoxicating the pride of so many eminent generals and statesmen. What was the feeling of Washington? Did he have a misan-

thrope's cynical contempt for the people's honest tribute of
gratitude? Did he have a demagogue's fierce elation in being
the object of the people's boundless admiration? No. His
sensations, he tells us, were as painful as they were pleasing.
His lofty and tranquil mind thought of the possible reverse of
the scene after all his exertions to do good. The streaming
flags, the loud acclamations, the thunder of the cannon, and
the shrill music piercing through all other sounds,—these sent
his mind sadly forward to the solitude of his closet, where,
with the tender and beautiful austerity of his character, he
was perhaps to sacrifice the people's favor for the people's
safety, and to employ every granted power of a constitution
he so perfectly understood in preserving peace, in restraining
faction, and in giving energy to all those constitutional restraints on popular passions, by which the wisdom of to-morrow rules the recklessness of to-day.

In reviewing a life thus passed in enduring hardship and
confronting peril, fretted by constant cares, and worn by incessant drudgery, we are at first saddened by the thought that
such heroic virtue should have been purchased by the sacrifice of happiness. But we wrong Washington in bringing his
enjoyments to the test of our low standards. He has everything for us to venerate, nothing for our commiseration.
He tasted of that joy which springs from a sense of great
responsibilities willingly incurred and great duties magnanimously performed. To him was given the deep bliss of
seeing the austere countenance of inexorable duty melt into
approving smiles, and to him was realized the poet's rapturous
vision of her celestial compensations:

> "Stern Lawgiver! yet thou dost wear
>   The Godhead's most benignant grace,
> Nor know we anything so fair
>   As is the smile upon thy face."

It has been truly said that " men of intemperate minds cannot be free; their passions forge their fetters;" but no clank of any chain, whether of avarice or ambition, gave the least harshness to the movement of Washington's ample mind. In him America has produced at least one man whose free soul was fit to be liberty's chosen home. As was his individual freedom so should be our national freedom. We have seen all along that American liberty in its sentiment and idea is no opinionated, will-strong, untamable passion, bursting all bounds of moral restraint and hungering after anarchy and license, but a creative and beneficent energy, organizing itself in laws, professions, trades, arts, institutions. From its extreme practical character however it is liable to contract a taint which has long vitiated English freedom. To the Anglo-Saxon mind liberty is not apt to be the enthusiast's mountain nymph, with cheeks wet with morning dew and clear eyes that mirror the heavens, but rather is she an old dowager lady, fatly invested in commerce and manufactures, and peevishly fearful that enthusiasm will reduce her establishment and panics cut off her dividends. Now the moment property becomes timid, agrarianism becomes bold; and the industry which liberty has created, liberty must animate, or it will be plundered by the impudent and rapacious idleness its slavish fears incite. Our political institutions again are but the body of which liberty is the soul; their preservation depends on their being continually inspired by the light and heat of the sentiment and idea whence they sprung; and when we timorously suspend, according to the latest political fashion, the truest and dearest maxims of our freedom at the call of expediency or the threat of passion, when we convert politics into a mere game of interests, unhallowed by a single great and unselfish principle,—we may be sure that our worst passions are busy

" forging our fetters," that we are proposing all those intricate problems which red republicanism so swiftly solves, and giving manifest destiny pertinent hints to shout new anthems of atheism over victorious rapine. The liberty which our fathers planted and for which they sturdily contended and under which they grandly conquered, is a rational and temperate but brave and unyielding freedom, the august mother of institutions, the hardy nurse of enterprise, the sworn ally of justice and order; a liberty that lifts her awful and rebuking face equally upon the cowards who would sell and the braggarts who would pervert her precious gifts of rights and obligations; and this liberty we are solemnly bound at all hazards to protect, at any sacrifice to preserve, and by all just means to extend, against the unbridled excesses of that ugly and brazen hag, originally scorned and detested by those who unwisely gave her infancy a home, but which now, in her enormous growth and favored deformity, reels with bloodshot eyes and dishevelled tresses and words of unshamed slavishness, into halls where liberty should sit throned!

PLAYFAIR

SIR LYON PLAYFAIR, an eminent English chemist and educator, was born May 21, 1819, at Meerut, India, where his father was chief-inspector of Bengal. He was educated at the universities of St. Andrews, Edinburgh, London, and Giessen in Germany. His interest was attracted from medicine to chemistry, and after he had worked at the laboratories of Baron Liebig and of Graham, master of the mint, in 1843 he became professor of chemistry in the Royal Institution in Manchester. In 1844 he was appointed by Sir Robert Peel, member of the royal commission on public health, which did so much for modern sanitation. In successive years he was a famine commissioner to Ireland and a member of many other committees of public utility. He helped reorganize the civil service after a method which was called the Playfair scheme. Besides serving as professor in the government schools of mines and inspector-general of the government schools of science, he was professor of chemistry in the University of Edinburgh from 1858 till 1868, when he was elected member of Parliament, and sat continuously until 1892, when he was raised to the peerage. Among his other honors have been those of postmaster-general (1873-4), vice-president of the council (1886), lord-in-waiting to the queen, and a member of the Legion of Honor and many other British and foreign orders. He published many works on social topics, chemistry, and political economy. He died May 29, 1898.

THE EVOLUTION OF UNIVERSITY EXTENSION

DELIVERED IN 1894

RECENTLY the London University Commission, of which I was a member, has made its report, and during its sitting we received much evidence in favor of the University Extension scheme, as well as some evidence hostile to it. I think the opposition arose from a misunderstanding of its origin and purposes, and upon these I should like to address you. The extension of university knowledge and educational methods to the people who are unable to attend the university courses during the day, is one of the processes of evolution of popular education which has been trying to organize itself for about a century.

Universities in former times used to be more largely attended than now. Bologna University was said to be attended by 20,000 students, and Paris and Oxford by 30,000. These numbers are open to doubt, though, as there were few grammar schools, and as students entered at ten and eleven years of age, the universities were no doubt more frequented than they are now, and by a poorer class of students, who often begged their way to the university from monastery to monastery. Chaucer alludes to this when he says:

> " Busily gan for the souls to pray
> Of them that gave him wherewith to scolay."

Education in the sense we are now considering it, as attainable by the people at large in their hours of leisure after their day's work, is the product of the present century. Let us consider the conditions under which the demands for it arose.

Up to the last quarter of the eighteenth century the learned class and the working class were separated by a high impassable wall, because each spoke in a language that the other could not understand. For about two thousand years the learned class spoke, thought, and talked in Latin, and for about two centuries Greek had been raised as a second wall of separation between the learned and the people. No doubt the people were creating knowledge of another kind by enlarging their conception of things while the learned were dealing with literature and philosophy through words.

I do not allude to the early days when Rome and Greece spoke their own vernacular, and when their writers and philosophers largely recruited themselves from the people. The learned class were then the sons of citizens, and were in possession of the accumulated experiences of the people. I refer to a much later period after the dark ages when the light gradually illuminating the darkness was the borrowed light of Rome and Greece. It was then that the learned linked themselves to the past and separated themselves from the present. Then it was that they adopted the ancient languages as the expression of their thoughts and teaching, while the people went on their way without caring for the pedants whose very language was incomprehensible to them.

Among the people the industries were growing by experience and modern science was being evolved as an outcome of their enlarged conceptions. Working men then made journeys to enlarge these experiences, and the memory of the old habit still survives in the industries under such familiar names as " journeyman carpenter," " journeyman blacksmith," and so on; for the tyro was a mere apprentice until he graduated to his full position as a working man by an education not got at school but obtained in journeys, which enlarged his experiences and knowledge. When I was a student in Germany in 1838, I recollect constantly meeting parties of these journeymen on the way from one town to another. An old German saying, freely translated, explains how technical education was attained in this way:

> " Who shall pupil be? Every one.
> Who shall craftsman be? Who good work has done.
> Who shall master be? He whose thought has won."

By the end of the fifteenth century most of our present industries were fairly established in this way. During that century the printing press was introduced, and knowledge was ultimately widely spread as well as conserved. In the sixteenth century newspapers were published in the vernacular, and the people got a powerful means of recording their mental conceptions, which were chiefly those of a developing science. In England, however, newspapers did not fully establish themselves till the period of the civil war, and then they were poor in quality. They scarcely came into the life of the nation till the reign of Queen Anne, during Marlborough's victories. The learned class still adhered to their Latin and Greek, and kept themselves outside of these great movements. Latin was, in fact, the universal language for learning, being a sort of glorified Volapük. Sometimes a treatise was written in the vernacular, as when Bacon wrote in English "The Advancement of Learning," though he asked his friend Dr. Playfair to translate it into Latin, because, he says, "The privateness of the language, wherein it is written, limits my readers," and its translation into Latin "would give a second verse of that work." So also when Bacon sends his "De Augmentis Scientiarum" to the Prince of Wales, he says, it is in Latin, "as a book which will live and be a citizen of the world, as English books are not." The vernacular was, however, being introduced into our schools, though it was not generally used until the close of the eighteenth century. Learned papers and discourses were now published in English, although they were at first duplicated into Latin. A general use of the vernacular made a common road on which both the learned classes and the working classes could again travel as they had done in the grand old days of Greece and Rome, when Plato and Aristotle and Cicero and Horace spoke, and wrote, and thought in the common languages of the people.

Now again the desire for popular education, of which university extension is one of the signs. Let us see how that form of popular education became involved in this movement, among the people, who were shut off from the possibility of attending colleges of learning. Workingmen know that one of their two hands must always be employed in earning their daily bread, but they have another hand with which they could work for their own improvement and for that of the community if they only had the opportunity and knew how to employ it.

Before the age of printing books were necessarily costly, so the ancient method of obtaining knowledge was to attend public lectures or discourses, and they became the chief mode of higher education. It was so in the classical times when people flocked to the market-place in Athens to hear Socrates, and to the groves of Academus to hear Plato, or joined the Peripatetics in the walks of the Lyceum to listen to the scientific teaching of Aristotle. So it continued in every country where learning was cared for at all, and poor students went, begging on the way, to listen to lectures by Abélard in France, Chrysoloras in Italy, or Erasmus in Oxford and then at Cambridge. When printing presses multiplied books knowledge could be acquired by those who read, and was no longer confined to the few who could discourse. Public libraries for the people are, however, only inventions of our own day, and at the beginning of this century did not exist.

The people readily co-operated with Birkbeck and others in founding institutes of their own where they could read and hear lectures. One of the earliest of these exists in the city under the well-known name of the " Birkbeck Institute," which has now a new lease of active life as a systematic school of science and commerce. The people in the early part of the century were only groping in the dark for the kind of higher education which they desired. The mechanics' institutes supplemented small and defective libraries by single and unconnected lectures.

In fact, the associated members of these institutes scarcely knew what they wanted. Some joined the institutes for amusement, some for instruction. Both were proper objects of desire, but were difficult to amalgamate, so a strange mixture was made, often not very wisely, by the inexperienced managers of the new mechanics' institutes. One of the most prosperous of them asked me to give a single lecture on chemistry, in the year 1846, and sent me its program for the preceding year. It was as follows: " Wit and Humor, with Comic Songs—Women Treated in Novel Manner—Legerdemain and Spirit-Rapping—The Devil (with illustrations)—The Heavenly Bodies and the Stellar System —Palestine and the Holy Land—Speeches by Eminent Friends of Education, interspersed with Music, to be followed by a Ball. Price to the whole 2s. 6d. Refreshments in an Anteroom."

Compare your program of sound work with this motley assemblage of professors, ventriloquists, conjurers, and musicians, and you will see how much the scheme of university extension has molded the demand for knowledge among the people and turned it into channels which will refresh and irrigate the various districts through which it passes. The mechanics' institutions where they still exist have altered themselves into systematic schools, either scientific, technical, or artistic, but they have still left outside the people who have not been trained to use schools.

The universities associated to supply this want. In the universities there are always a number of zealous graduates who desire to extend to others the knowledge possessed by themselves. They are animated by the spirit of the famous Loup de Ferrières, who, a thousand years ago, wrote to Charles the Bold: " I desire to teach what I have learned and am daily learning."

This spirit led to the scheme of university extension.

Gradually, not yet completely, but surely, the people who demand your courses of lectures appreciate and follow them because they are systematic and in proper sequence; and because the lecturer also becomes the tutor to each student who really desires to understand and profit by the subject taught. In ordinary popular lectures the lecturer treats his audience as a mass, throwing his information broadcast over it, ignorant as to where it may fall, and careless as to whether the seed falls on fertile soil or on stony places where it can take no root.

When the lecturer acts also as a tutor he looks upon his audience as individuals, he drills his seed into productive soil, taking care that the ground is prepared to receive it, and that each seed gets its proper proportion of food-giving manure. The minds of the teacher and the taught get into an intellectual grapple and as the former should be the stronger man, he is enabled to drag the mind of the student from the dark holes in which it may lurk into the broad light of day.

In a college or technical school a tutorial system ought always to be combined with the lectures. Under your system of peripatetic lectures it is more difficult of application, but you do much by the weekly exercises and final examination as well as by making the courses consequential in series. The examiners for the certificates, who are not the lecturers, testify by their university experience to the good results which are attained.

To understand the object of the promoters of university extension it is important neither to exaggerate these results nor to depreciate the value of the system. The main purpose is not to educate the masses, but to permeate them with the desire for intellectual improvement, and to show them methods by which they can attain this desire. Every man who acquires a taste for learning and is imbued with the desire to acquire more of it becomes more valuable as a citizen, because he is more intelligent and perceptive. As Shakespeare says:

> " Learning is but an adjunct to ourself. . .
> It adds a precious seeing to the eye."

It is this addition of " a precious seeing to the eye " which produces progress in science. Of the five gateways of knowledge, the " eye gate " is not opened indifferently to all. The range of vision of the bat and of the eagle is very different. The most familiar objects to man, like air and water, are nothing more to the untutored intellect of man than the primrose was to Peter Bell:

> " A primrose by a river's brim
> A yellow primrose was to him,
> And it was nothing more."

Before the mind of man learns to question Nature, he is apt to look for the explanations of phenomena to the intellectual conceptions of his own untutored mind. When he knows how to put an experimental question to Nature he is on the high road to knowledge, *"Prudens quæstio dimidium scientiæ est "*—" A wise question is half of knowledge."

Thales, who flourished in the seventh century before Christ, was among the first philosophers to speculate upon the constitution of the universe. He thought everything was made out of water. The sun dipped in the evening below the western wave, and rose out of the ocean in the east mightily refreshed by its huge drink—so the sun was made out of water. Water, as the river Nile, overflowed the land of Egypt and crops grew in luxuriance—so plants were made out of water. The ocean, when it was stormy, was engaged in the manufacture of earth, and the proof is that after a storm new sand and pebbles are heaped on the shore. The real nature of water was only discovered at the end of the last century.

How little our ancestors knew about air, and how little we yet know about it in the nineteenth century! Yet, if mere observation could suffice to know a thing, air should be better understood than anything in the world. When the first man drew his first breath he began his familiarity with air. In each phase of his life man meets it at every turn. It fans him with gentle breezes and it buffets him with storms. It is never absent from every act of his existence, and the last act of his life is his inability to respire it. The first philosopher who studied air in a scientific way was Anaximenes. He lived 548 years before Christ, and men have been studying air ever since, and have laboriously brought up our knowledge to our present position. Aristotle brought his shrewd powers of observation upon air, and established that it was a material and not a spirit. A wonderful Saracen, called Alhazen, found that it had weight, and showed that it was heavier at the bottom of a mountain than at its top. Galileo again took up the study of air in 1630, and made important discoveries which led Torricelli and others to the discovery of the barometer.

It is scarcely more than a century since mankind gave up air as an element, and it is only during my lifetime that we have been taught the true chemical nature of air, and that its relation to the great phenomena of vegetable and animal life have been explained. When I was first a student of chemistry, air consisted of nitrogen and oxygen with watery vapor. During my life carbonic acid, ammonia, nitric acid, ozone, and the wide range of bacteria and like organisms have been discovered. We now know that all the foulness of the living and the products of the dead pass into the air, and are changed into the food of plants, so that the great abounding atmosphere becomes the grave of organic death and the candle of organic life. Plants and animals mutually feed on each other and the death and dissolution of one generation is needful for the growth of a succeeding one.

You see how slowly intellectual conceptions of the most common object gather round it. When we give a lecture to an ignorant audience on such subjects as air and water, we treat them from the platform of our own times—the nineteenth century. But our audience is not yet on that plane. In my old professorial days, in lecturing to classes of working men, I sometimes put myself on the platform on which Anaximenes stood 548 years before Christ, and argued as he did for the theory of the nature of air, and then mounted the ladders, taking my hearers with me, from platform to platform of discovery, till I reached that of the present day. This historical mode of illustration gave the working men a better notion of the methods of scientific discovery, and taught them more completely that science consists of conceptions obtained by a slow but steady questioning of Nature. In ancient times there was little science, because philosophers put the questions to their own minds and not to Nature. The rapid progress of science in recent times is due to our questioning Nature by means of experiment. This is the true foundation of science, as well expressed by Wordsworth:

> . . . " to the solid ground
> Of Nature trusts the mind which builds for aye."

This need of experimental inquiry does not apply to mathematics, which was a product of the opening of Greek civilization, and the achievements of the Greek geometers, Euclid, Archimedes, and Apollonius are still admirable at the present day.

If the untutored senses be sufficient to appreciate and understand what you see with your own eyes and hear with your own ears, it would not have required many thousand years for mankind to acquire our present imperfect knowledge about air and water. In explaining to our students the knowledge of to-day I think it would often be useful to show how it has been attained and how our crude faculties have become tutored faculties by close thinking, observation, and experiment upon the most familiar objects about us. Theories of the past have fallen as the leaves of trees fall, but while they existed they drew nutriment to the parent stem of knowledge. The theory of to-day is the error of to-morrow. Error in science is nothing but a shadow cast by the strong light of truth. Theories, as they arise, are an absolute necessity for the progress of science, because they collect in a common focus all the light which is shed upon a subject at a particular period. The descriptions of and arguments for the old theories I found very useful as ladders let down from the nineteenth century platform, which enabled my uneducated audience to mount to it by graduated steps, until they came to the same level of the science which I was trying to expound to them.

The world is still young and science is never old. It is sheer vanity for any generation to suppose that their state of knowledge represents the final triumph of truth. I think it is always useful in educating in modern science to show how much we owe to our ancestors by their laborious efforts to build it up. We have inherited so much from the past. Roger Bacon, writing so long ago as 1267, said: " The ancients have committed all the more errors just because they are ancients, for in matters of learning the youngest are in reality the oldest; modern generations ought to surpass their predecessors because they inherit their labors."

This thought, three centuries later, Francis Bacon put into his famous apothegm—*Antiquitas Seculi, Juventus Mundi*—antiquity in age is the youth of the world.

It is no small object in view that your purpose is to permeate the mass of people with the desire for knowledge. It is chiefly among them that great discoverers in science and great inventors in industry arise. I would refer you, as an illustration, to the past discoverers who have adoned the lecture table of the Royal Institution in Albermarle street. With scarcely an exception they have sprung directly from the people. The original founder was Benjamin Thompson, afterwards Count Rumford, a provisional schoolmaster from New England; and the institution has had as successive professors Sir Humphrey Davy, the son of a woodcarver; Young, illustrious in politics, the son, I think, of a yeoman; Faraday, a newsboy; and Tyndall, who was of humble origin.

All of these men sprang from the people. Among inventors this origin from the people is still more marked. Watt was an instrument-maker; Wheatstone, who invented our telegraphs, was a maker of musical instruments; and Bell, who added the telephone, was a teacher of deaf-mutes; Stephenson, the inventor of locomotives, an engine-tender at a colliery; Arkwright, who revolutionized the cotton industry, was a barber. These instances might be multiplied indefinitely both from modern and ancient history.

The great humanizing movements of the world have sprung from the people. The Founder of our religion did not disdain to be called the son of Joseph the carpenter, and he took his disciples from among the working men around him. Paul the tentmaker and Peter the fisherman found time to earn their daily bread and diffuse the religion of Christ. The growth of philosophy in Greece depended upon men who were using one hand to win their daily bread and the other to mold humanity. Socrates was a sculptor; Plato and Zeno were actively engaged in commerce; Aristotle was the son of a physician. They founded schools of thought, but they themselves were the products of Athens and Corinth when they were active seats of industrial activity.

I hope I have made myself intelligible when I argue that the University Extension movement is doing work of its own kind most valuable, not as an education of the people but as a means of permeating the people with a desire to be educated, and by giving them methods and subjects which they can use in continuing their education. Your opponents still object to the need of doing this, because they quote cases, such as I have mentioned, like Faraday, Watt, and Stephenson, where men of the people even in the absence of schools, educated themselves without aid from others and became great discoverers; so they say it is much more easy now to do likewise, when technical schools are covering the country.

I have spent a large portion of my life in helping to found these technical schools and therefore I fully appreciate their importance, but they do not even touch the ground covered by your movement. Such schools look to the education of a man for his daily work and only give what the Germans call Brodstudien, while the University Extension movement professes to give mental culture or what the Germans might call Verständnisstudien. No doubt one of your triumphs will be that the University Extension scheme will tend largely to feed schools of science and technical schools with students incited

to learn through your permeating influence in creating a taste
for knowledge.　This is as it should be.

During my life I have enjoyed the friendship of many men
who have risen by their own great talents, such as Dalton,
Faraday, Stephenson, Wheatstone, and Livingstone.　I knew
the great African discoverer when he rested his book on a
spinning-jenny, snatching sentence after sentence as he
passed it at work; and I attended the evening classes with him
in Glasgow and saw him pay the pennies he had saved during
the day as a cotton-spinner.

As I am recalling old memories I may say that three companions studied together in those days.　One was James
Young, a carpenter; Livingstone, a cotton-spinner; and myself, the son of a physician.　Young the carpenter established
a new industry and became very rich.　His purse was always
open to Livingstone for his African explorations; and, although he would never acknowledge it, my election committees never lacked funds from some mysterious donor, who I
always believed was my old friend, for the contributions
ceased at his death.

Were my old friends now alive, I would call them all as
witnesses as to how much trouble and suffering would have
been saved to them had they been able when young to enjoy
the advantage which you now offer to the youth of this century by giving them the materials and methods of education.
It is quite true that men of genius will cut out steps for themselves in the toilsome ascent of knowledge.　The mistake of
the argument is obvious.

All the dwellers in a plain do not surmount the mountain
which frowns upon them at the end of the valley.　A few daring spirits may reach the summit unaided and pass into the
world beyond, but the great mass of men remain in the low-

lands where they were born. We can induce many of these to make excursions which will brighten their existence, by making roads and showing them how to use the roads. Perchance in doing so we may come upon a genius and put him on his way, and wish him Godspeed! The case should not be argued by contrasting a heaven-born talent with ordinary ability. All systems of education try to draw out the mental abilities of the scholar, but they do not profess to give the gifts of God or to create special abilities in man. Such great men as I have mentioned are discoverers of new truths in science, and the bulk of mankind must be content to live on a lower plane, but their life is made the happier, more graceful, and dignified by helping them to acquire some of that knowledge which shows them how the world has advanced and how society has been improved by the advances made in science, literature, and philosophy.

In our own time science has been the great civilizing agency. Within my own memory I have seen the origin of five inventions which have had more profound effect than revolutions in altering the conditions of kingdoms and nations throughout the world. I allude to steam-locomotion, telegraphy, telephony, photography, electric lighting, and electric locomotion. The discoverers in science are the artisans of civilization, their laboratories and the workshops, and their instruments of precision and experiment are the tools with which they perform their world-labor. By the system which you pursue the people are made to take an intelligent interest in these modes of civilization. The most intelligent nation will in future be the greatest nation, and your work is to do your part in permeating the people with this general intelligence which is so necessary for their prosperity in the competition of the world.

KINGSLEY

CHARLES KINGSLEY, a famous English clergyman, author, and philanthropist, the son of an American clergyman, was born at Holne, Devonshire, June 12, 1819. He was educated at King's College, London, and Magdalen College, Cambridge, and relinquishing his early fancy for the study of law took orders in the Church of England in 1842. In the same year he became curate of Eversley, a small country parish in Hampshire, and in 1844 was appointed its rector, continuing to hold that office for the rest of his life. From the outset of his clerical career he interested himself warmly in the needs of the working classes and for that reason was often styled "the Chartist parson." With F. D. Maurice he aimed to give a Christian bias to the socialism of the day, and "Christian Socialism" as a movement may be said to date from their organization of it. One of Kingsley's sermons, "The Message of the Church to the Laboring Man," preached in a London church in 1851 caused so much discussion that the Bishop of London forbade him to preach in that diocese. Thereupon the workingmen held a large out-door meeting to support Kingsley, and presently the bishop withdrew the prohibition. In 1850 appeared Kingsley's novel "Alton Locke, Tailor and Poet," which was widely popular, especially in the United States, and its success determined him to continue writing. In 1859 he received the appointment of chaplain-in-ordinary to the Queen, and from 1860 to 1869 was professor of modern history at Cambridge University. In 1869 he was appointed a canon of Chester and in 1873 canon of Westminster. Kingsley travelled in the United States in 1874, delivering a number of lectures, but his health had already began to fail and a few months after his return he died at Eversley January 28, 1875. He was one of the most earnest men of his time and made a deep impression upon his generation. Intense enthusiasm characterizes his sermons, addresses, and novels, and much of his work bears the impress of a singularly poetic spirit. His verse, which except for a few lyrics is less known than his prose, shows him to have been a genuine poet though not a great one. His writings include "The Saints Tragedy" (1848); "Alton Locke" (1850); "Hypatia" an historical romance (1853); "Westward Ho," a romance of Elizabethan times (1855); "The Water Babies" (1863); and many other works, theological, fictitious, and political.

SERMON: THE TRANSFIGURATION

"Jesus taketh Peter, and James, and John, and leadeth them up into a high mountain apart, and was transfigured before them."—Mark ix, 2.

THE second lesson for this morning service brings us to one of the most wonderful passages in our blessed Saviour's whole stay on earth, namely, his transfiguration. The story as told by the different evangelists is this,—That our Lord took Peter, and John, and James his brother, and led them up into a high mountain apart, which mountain may be seen to this very day. It is a high peaked hill, standing apart from all the hills around it, with a small smooth space of ground upon the top, very fit, from its height and its loneliness, for a transaction like the transfiguration, which our Lord wished no one but these three to behold.

There the apostles fell asleep; while our blessed Lord, who had deeper thoughts in his heart than they had, knelt down and prayed to his Father and our Father, which is in heaven. And as he prayed the form of his countenance was changed, and his raiment became shining white as the light; and there appeared Moses and Elijah talking with him. They talked of matters which the angels desire to look into, of the greatest matters that ever happened in this earth since it was made; of the redemption of the world, and of the death which Christ was to undergo at Jerusalem.

And as they were talking the apostles awoke, and found into what glorious company they had fallen while they slept. What they felt no mortal man can tell—that moment was worth to them all the years they had lived before. When they had gone up with Jesus into the mount he was but the poor carpenter's son, wonderful enough to them, no doubt, with his wise, searching words, and his gentle, loving looks that drew to him all men who had hearts left in them, and wonderful enough, too, from all the mighty miracles which they had seen him do; but still he was merely a man like themselves, poor, and young, and homeless, who felt the heat and the cold and the rough roads as much as they did. They could feel that he spake as never man spake; they could see that God's Spirit and power was on him as it had never been on any man in their time.

God had even enlightened their reason by his Spirit, to
know that he was the Christ, the Son of the living God. But
still it does seem they did not fully understand who and what
he was; they could not understand how the Son of God
should come in the form of a despised and humble man; they
did not understand that his glory was to be a spiritual glory.

They expected his kingdom to be a kingdom of this world;
they expected his glory to consist in palaces, and armies, and
riches, and jewels, and all the magnificence with which Solo-
mon and the old Jewish kings were adorned; they thought
that he was to conquer back again from the Roman emperor
all the inestimable treasures of which the Romans had robbed
the Jews, and that he was to make the Jewish nation like the
Roman, the conquerors and masters of all the nations of the
earth. So that it was a puzzling thing to their minds why
he should be King of the Jews at the very time that he was
but a poor tradesman's son, living on charity. It was to
show them that his kingdom was the kingdom of heaven
that he was transfigured before them.

They saw his glory—the glory as of the only begotten of
the Father, full of grace and truth. The form of his countenance was changed; all the majesty, and courage, and wisdom, and love, and resignation, and pity, that lay in his noble
heart, shone out through his face, while he spoke of his death
which he should accomplish at Jerusalem—the Holy Ghost
that was upon him, the Spirit of wisdom, and love, and beauty
—the Spirit which produces everything that is lovely in
heaven and earth, in soul and body, blazed out through his
eyes, and all his glorious countenance, and made him look
like what he was—a God.

My friends, what a sight! Would it not be worth while
to journey thousands of miles, to go through all difficulties,

dangers, that man ever heard of, for one sight of that glorious face, that we might fall down upon our knees before it, and, if it were but for a moment, give way to the delight of finding something that we could utterly love and utterly adore? I say the delight of finding something to worship; for if there is a noble, if there is a holy, if there is a spiritual feeling in man, it is the feeling which bows him down before those who are greater, and wiser, and holier than himself. I say that feeling of respect for what is noble is a heavenly feeling.

The man who has lost it—the man who feels no respect for those who are above him in age, above him in knowledge, above him in wisdom, above him in goodness,—that man shall in no wise enter into the kingdom of heaven. It is only the man who is like a little child, and feels the delight of having some one to look up to, who will ever feel delight in looking up to Jesus Christ, who is the Lord of lords and King of kings. It was the want of respect, it was the dislike of feeling any one superior to himself, which made the devil rebel against God and fall from heaven. It will be the feeling of complete respect, the feeling of kneeling at the feet of one who is immeasurably superior to ourselves in everything that will make up the greatest happiness of heaven. This is a hard saying, and no man can understand it save he to whom it is given by the Spirit of God.

That the apostles had this feeling of immeasurable respect for Christ there is no doubt, else they would never have been apostles. But they felt more than this. There were other wonders in that glorious vision besides the countenance of our Lord. His raiment, too, was changed, and became all brilliant, white as the light itself. Was not that a lesson to them? Was it not if our Lord had said to them, " I am a king, and have put on glorious apparel; but whence does the glory of my raiment come? I have no need of fine linen, and purple, and embroidery, the work of men's hands; I have no need to send my subjects to mines and caves to dig gold and jewels to adorn my crown: the earth is mine and the fulness thereof. All this glorious earth with its trees and its flowers, its sunbeams and its storms, is mine. I made it; I can do what I will with it.

"All the mysterious laws by which the light and the heat flow out forever from God's throne, to lighten the sun, and the moon, and the stars of heaven—they are mine. I am the light of the world—the light of men's bodies as well as of their souls; and here is my proof of it. Look at me. I am he that ' decketh himself with light as it were with a garment, who layeth the beams of his chambers in the waters, and walketh upon the wings of the wind.' "

This was the message which Christ's glory brought the apostles—a message which they could never forget. The spiritual glory of his countenance had shown them that he was a spiritual king, that his strength lay in the spirit of power, and wisdom, and beauty, and love, which God had given him without measure; and it showed them, too, that there was such a thing as a spiritual body, such a body as each of us some day shall have if we be found in Christ at the resurrection of the just—a body which shall not hide a man's spirit when it becomes subject to the wear and tear of life, and disease, and decay; but a spiritual body—a body which shall be filled with our spirits, which shall be perfectly obedient to our spirits—a body through which the glory of our spirits shall shine out, as the glory of Christ's spirit shone out through his body at the transfiguration. Brethren, we know not yet what we shall be, but this we do know, that when he shall appear, " we shall be like him, for we shall see him as he is."

Thus our Lord taught them by his appearance that there is such a thing as a spiritual body, while, by the glory of his raiment in addition to his other miracles, he taught them that he had power over the laws of nature, and could, in his own good time, " change the bodies of their humiliation, that they might be made like unto his glorious body, according to the mighty working by which he is able to subdue all things to himself."

But there was yet another lesson which the apostles learned from the transfiguration of our Lord. They beheld Moses and Elijah talking with him:—Moses the great lawgiver of their nation, Elijah the chief of all the Jewish prophets. We must consider this a little to find out the whole depth of its meaning. You remember how Christ had spoken of himself as having come, not to destroy the Law and the Prophets, but to fulfil them. You remember, too, how he had always said that he was the person of whom the Law and the Prophets had spoken.

Here was an actual sign and witness that his words were true—here was Moses, the giver of the Law, and Elijah, the chief of the Prophets, talking with him, bearing witness to him in their own persons, and showing, too, that it was his death and his perfect sacrifice that they had been shadowing forth in the sacrifices of the law and in the dark speeches of prophecy. For they talked with him of his death, which he was to accomplish at Jerusalem.

What more perfect testimony could the apostles have had to show them that Jesus of Nazareth, their Master, was he of whom the Law and the Prophets spoke; that he was indeed the Christ for whom Moses and Elijah, and all the saints of

'old, had looked; and that he was come, not to destroy the
Law and the Prophets, but to fulfil them? We can hardly
understand the awe and the delight with which the disciples
must have beheld those blessed three—Moses, and Elias, and
Jesus Christ, their Lord, talking together before their very
eyes. For of all men in the world, Moses and Elias were to
them the greatest. All true-hearted Israelites, who knew the
history of their nation, and understood the promises of God,
must have felt that Moses and Elias were the two greatest
heroes and saviours of their nation, whom God had ever yet
raised up.

And the joy and the honor of thus seeing them face to
face, the very men whom they had loved and reverenced in
their thoughts, whom they had heard and read of from their
childhood, as the greatest ornaments and glories of their
nation—the joy and the honor, I say, of that unexpected
sight, added to the wonderful majesty which was suddenly
revealed to their transfigured Lord, seemed to have been too
much for them—they knew not what to say.

Such company seemed to them for the moment heaven
enough; and St. Peter, first finding words, exclaimed, " Lord,
it is good for us to be here. If thou wilt, let us build three
tabernacles, one for thee, and one for Moses, and one for
Elias."

Not, I fancy, that they intended to worship Moses and
Elias, but that they felt that Moses and Elias, as well as
Christ, had each a divine message, which must be listened to;
and therefore they wished that each of them might have his
own tabernacle, and dwell among men, and each teach his
own particular doctrine and wisdom in his own school. It
may seem strange that they should put Moses and Elias so on
an equality with Christ, but the truth was, that as yet they

understood Moses and Elias better than they did Christ. They had heard and read of Moses and Elijah all their lives—they were acquainted with all their actions and words—they knew thoroughly what great and noble men the Spirit of God had made them, but they did not understand Christ in like manner.

They did not yet feel that God had given him the Spirit without measure—they did not understand that he was not only to be a lawgiver and a prophet, but a sacrifice for sin, the conqueror of death and hell, who was to lead captivity captive, and receive inestimable gifts for men. Much less did they think that Moses and Elijah were but his servants—that all their spirit and their power had been given by him.

But this also they were taught a moment afterwards; for a bright cloud overshadowed them, hiding from them the glory of God the Father, whom no man hath seen or can see, who dwells in the light which no man can approach unto; and out of that cloud a voice, saying, " This is my beloved Son; hear ye him; " and then, hiding their faces in fear and wonder, they fell to the ground; and when they looked up, the vision and the voice had alike passed away, and they saw no man but Christ alone. Was not that enough for them? Must not the meaning of the vision have been plain to them? They surely understood from it that Moses and Elijah were, as they had ever believed them to be, great and good, true messengers of the living God; but that their message and their work was done—that Christ, whom they had looked for was come—that all the types of the law were realized, and all the prophecies fulfilled, and that henceforward Christ, and Christ alone, was to be their prophet and their lawgiver.

Was not this plainly the meaning of the Divine voice? For when they wished to build three tabernacles, and to honor Moses and Elijah, the Law and the Prophets, as separate from Christ, that moment the heavenly voice warned them: " This—this is my beloved Son—hear ye him and him only, henceforward."

And Moses and Elijah, their work being done, forthwith vanished away, leaving Christ alone to fulfil the Law and the Prophets, and all other wisdom and righteousness that ever was or shall be. This is another lesson which Christ's transfiguration was meant to teach them and us, that Christ alone is to be henceforward our guide; that no philosophies or doctrines of any sort which are not founded on a true faith in Jesus Christ, and his life and death, are worth listening to; that God has manifested forth his beloved Son, and that him, and him only, we are to hear.

I do not mean to say that Christ came into the world to put down human learning. I do not mean that we are to despise human learning, as so many are apt to do now-a-days; for Christ came into the world not to destroy human learning, but to fulfil it—to sanctify it—to make human learning true, and strong, and useful, by giving it a sure foundation to stand upon, which is the belief and knowledge of his blessed self.

Just as Christ came not to destroy the Law and the Prophets, but to fulfil them,—to give them a spirit and a depth in men's eyes which they never had before—just so he came to fulfil all true philosophies, all the deep thoughts which men had ever thought about this wonderful world and their own souls, by giving them a spirit and a depth which they never had before. Therefore let no man tempt you to despise learning, for it is holy to the Lord.

There is one more lesson which we may learn from our Lord's transfiguration: when St. Peter said, " Lord! it is good for us to be here," he spoke a truth. It was food for him to be there; nevertheless, Christ did not listen to his prayer. He and his two companions were not allowed to stay in that glorious company. And why? Because they had a work to do. They had glad tidings of great joy to proclaim to every creature, and it was, after all, but a selfish prayer, to wish to be allowed to stay in ease and glory on the mount while the whole world was struggling in sin and wickedness below them; for there is no meaning in a man's calling himself a Christian, or saying that he loves God, unless he is ready to hate what God hates, and to fight against that which Christ fought against, that is, sin.

No one has any right to call himself a servant of God, who is not trying to do away with some of the evil in the world around him. And, therefore, Christ was merciful when, instead of listening to St. Peter's prayer, he led the apostles down again from the mount, and sent them forth, as he did afterward, to preach the Gospel of the Kingdom to all nations. For Christ put a higher honor on St. Peter by that than if he had let him stay on the mount all his life, to behold his glory, and worship and adore. And he made St. Peter more like himself by doing so. For what was Christ's life? Not one of deep speculations, quiet thoughts, and bright visions, such as St. Peter wished to lead, but a life of fighting against evil; earnest, awful prayers and struggles within, continual labor of body and mind without, insult and danger, and confusion, and violent exertion, and bitter sorrow.

This was Christ's life—this is the life of almost every good man I ever heard of; this was St. Peter's, and St. James' and St. John's life afterwards. This was Christ's cup, which they were to drink of as well as he; this was the baptism of fire with which they were to be baptized as well as he; this was to be their fight of faith; this was the tribulation through which they, like all other great saints, were to enter into the kingdom of heaven; for it is certain that the harder a man fights against evil, the harder evil will fight against him in return; but it is certain, too, that the harder a man fights against evil, the more he is like his Saviour Christ, and the more glorious will be his reward in heaven.

It is certain, too, that what was good for St. Peter is good for us. It is good for a man to have holy and quiet thoughts, and at moments to see into the very deepest meaning of God's word and God's earth, and to have, as it were, heaven opened before his eyes; and it is good for a man sometimes actually to feel his heart overpowered with the glorious majesty of God, and to feel it gushing out with love to his blessed Saviour, but it is not good for him to stop there, any more than it was for the apostles; they had to leave that glorious vision and come down from the mount, and do Christ's work; and so have we; for, believe me, one word of warning spoken to keep a little child out of sin, one crust of bread given to a beggar-man, because he is your brother, for whom Christ died, one angry word checked, when it is on your lips, for the sake of him who was meek and lowly in heart; in short, any, the smallest, endeavor of this kind to lessen the quantity of evil which is in yourselves, and in those around you, is worth all the speculations, and raptures, and visions, and frames, and feelings in the world; for those are the good fruits of faith, whereby alone the tree shall be known, whether it be good or evil.

HOLLAND

JOSIAH GILBERT HOLLAND, an American moralist and editor, was born in Belchertown, Massachusetts July 24, 1819. The son of a poor farmer, who was also an inventor, his early educational advantages were meagre. He fitted himself for the Northampton High School, but studied so assiduously that his health was affected. After serving successively as a teacher of penmanship, an operator in a daguerreotype saloon, a copyist, and a district school master, he began the study of medicine, and, in 1844, graduated from the Berkshire Medical College. The practice of medicine was distasteful to him and he again took up the profession of teaching. He was for fifteen months superintendent of schools at Vicksburg, Mississippi, where he did an important work in elevating educational standards. At the age of thirty he returned to the North, met Mr. Samuel Bowles and joined him on the " Springfield Republican," of which he became a part owner. His "History of Western Massachusetts" and his "Timothy Titcomb Letters " were first published in the columns of the " Republican." In November, 1888, he published " Bitter Sweet," a narrative poem, which was even more successful than the " Titcomb Letters." In 1865 he issued his " Life of Abraham Lincoln," of which more than 100,000 copies were sold. The following year appeared " Katrina," a narrative poem, which had an equal sale. He had already sold his share in the " Republican " at a large increase over what he had paid for it. While traveling in Europe in 1868 he broached the idea of a new illustrated magazine. This took shape in 1870, when he began the publication of " Scribner's Monthly," afterwards the " Century Magazine." In 1872 he was elected a member of the New York board of education, of which he was afterwards president. He also served as chairman of the board of trustees of the College of the City of New York. He died in New York October 12, 1881. As a lecturer, Dr. Holland was extremely popular, having a fine presence and a musical and well-trained voice. Among his other publications were " The Bath Path " (1855); " Gold Foil Hammered from Popular Proverbs " (1859); " Arthur Bonnicastle " (1873); " Nicholas Minturn " (1876).

EULOGY OF ABRAHAM LINCOLN

DELIVERED IN SPRINGFIELD, MASSACHUSETTS, APRIL 19, 1865

WE have assembled to honor the memory of the first citizen of the republic. We have come together to say and to hear something which shall express our love for him, our respect for his character, our high estima-

tion of his services and our grief at his untimely removal from
the exalted office to which the voice of a nation had called
him. Yet the deepest of our thoughts and emotions are always dumb. The ocean's floor has no voice, but on it and
under it lie the ocean's treasures. The waves that roll and
roar above tell no story but their own. Only the surface of
the soul, like the surface of the sea, is vocal. Deep down
within every one of our hearts there are thoughts we cannot
speak, emotions that find no language, groanings that cannot
be uttered. The surprise, the shock, the pity, the sense of
outrage and of loss, the indignation, the grief, which bring us
here—which have transformed a nation jubilant with hope
and triumph into a nation of mourners—will find no full
expression here. It is all a vain show—these tolling bells,
these insignia of sorrow, these dirges, this suspension of business, these gatherings of the people, these faltering words.
The drowning man throws up his arms and utters a cry to
show that he lives, and is conscious of the element which
whelms him; and this is all that we can do.

Therefore, without trying to tell how much we loved him,
how much we honored him, and how deeply and tenderly we
mourn his loss, let us briefly trace the reasons why his death
has made so deep an impression upon us. It is not five years
since the nation knew but little of Abraham Lincoln. We had
heard of him as a man much honored by the members of a
single party—not then dominant—in his own State. We had
seen something of his work. We knew that he was held to
be a man of notable and peculiar power and of pure character
and life. Indeed, it is doubtful whether the nation knew
enough of him to justify the selection made by the convention
which presented him to the country as a candidate for its
highest office. To this office, however, he was triumphantly

elected, and since that time his life has run like a thread of gold through the history of the most remarkable period of the nation's existence.

From the first moment of his introduction to national notice he assumed nothing but duty, pretended to nothing but integrity, boasted of nothing but the deeds of those who served him. On his journey to Washington he freely and unaffectedly confessed to those who insisted on hearing him speak that he did not understand their interests, but hoped to make himself acquainted with them. We had never witnessed such frankness, and it must be confessed that we were somewhat shocked by it. So simple and artless a nature in so high a place was so unusual, so unprecedented, indeed, that it seemed unadapted to it—incongruous with it. In the society which surrounded him at the national capital, embracing in its materials some of the most polished persons of our own and other lands, he remained the same unaffected, simple-hearted man. He was not polished and did not pretend to be. He aped no foreign airs, assumed no new manners, never presumed anything upon his position, was accessible to all and preserved throughout his official career the transparent, almost boyish simplicity that characterized his entrance upon it.

I do not think that it ever occurred to Mr. Lincoln that he was a ruler. More emphatically than any of his predecessors did he regard himself as the servant of the people—the instrument selected by the people for the execution of their will. He regarded himself as a public servant no less when he issued that immortal paper, the proclamation of emancipation, then when he sat at City Point, sending telegraphic despatches to the country, announcing the progress of General Grant's army. In all places, in all circumstances, he was still the same unpretending, faithful, loyal public servant.

Unattractive in person, awkward in deportment, unrestrained in conversation, a story-lover and a story-teller, much of the society around him held him in ill-disguised contempt. It was not to be expected that fashion and courtly usage and conventional dignities and proprieties would find themselves at home with him; but even these at last made room for him, for nature's nobleman, with nature's manners, springing directly from a kind and gentle heart. Indeed, it took us all a long time to learn to love this homely simplicity, this artlessness, this direct outspeaking of his simple nature. But we did learn to love them at last, and to feel that anything else would be out of character with him. We learned that he did everything in his own way and we learned to love the way. It was Abraham Lincoln's way, and Abraham Lincoln was our friend. We had taken him into our hearts, and we would think of criticizing his words and ways no more than those of our bosom companions. Nay, we had learned to love him for these eccentricities, because they proved to us that he was not controlled by convention and precedent, but was a law unto himself.

Another reason why we loved him was that he first loved us. I do not believe a ruler ever lived who loved his people more sincerely than he. Nay, I do not believe the ruler ever lived who loved his enemies so well as he. All the insults heaped upon him by the foes of the government and the haters of his principles, purposes, and person, never seemed to generate in him a feeling of revenge or stir him to thoughts and deeds of bitterness. Throughout the terrible war over which he presided with such calmness and such power he never lost sight of the golden day, far in the indefinite future, when

peace and the restoration of fraternal harmony should come
as the result and reward of all his labors. His heart embraced in its catholic sympathies the misguided men who
were plotting his destruction, and I have no doubt that he
could and did offer the prayer: " Father, forgive them, for
they know not what they do!"   We felt—we knew—that he
suffered a thousand deaths in the destruction of the brave
lives he had summoned to the country's defence, that he sympathized with every mourner in this mourning land, that he
called us to no sacrifice which he would not gladly have
made himself, that his heart was with the humble and the
oppressed, and that he had no higher wish than to see his
people peaceful, prosperous, and happy.   He was one of us—
one with us.   Circumscribed in his affectionate regard by no
creed, or party, or caste, or color, he received everybody,
talked with everybody, respected everybody, loved everybody, and loved to serve everybody.

We loved and honored him, too, for his honesty and integrity.   He seemed incapable of deceit and insusceptible of corruption.   With almost unlimited power in his hands, possessing the highest confidence of the nation and the enthusiastic devotion of the most remarkable army the world ever
saw, with a wealth of treasure and patronage at his disposal
without precedent, and surrounded by temptations such as few
men have the power to resist, he lived and died a man with
clean hands and a name unsullied even by suspicion.   Nothing but treasonable malignity accuses him of anything more
culpable than errors of judgment and mistakes of policy.
Never, even to save himself from blame, did he seek to disguise or conceal the truth.   Never to serve himself did he
sacrifice the interests of his country.   Faithful among the
faithless, true among the false, unselfish among the grasping,

he walked in his integrity. When he spoke we believed him. Unskilled in the arts of diplomacy, unpractised in the ingenuities of indirection and intrigue, unlearned in the formalities and processes of official intercourse, he took the plain, honest truth in his hands and used it as an honest man. He was guilty of no trick, no double-meaning, no double-dealing, On all occasions, in all places, he was " Honest Abraham Lincoln," with no foolish pride that forbade the acknowledgment and correction of mistakes, and no jealousy that denied to his advisers and helpers their meed of praise. The power which this patent honesty of character and life exercised upon this nation has been one of the most remarkable features of the history of the time. The complete, earnest, immovable faith with which we have trusted his motives has been without a precedent. Men have believed in Abraham Lincoln who believed in nothing higher. Men have believed in him who had lost faith in all around him; and when he died, after demonstrating the value of his personal honesty in the administration of the greatest earthly affairs, he had become the nation's idol.

Again, we loved and honored Mr. Lincoln because he was a Christian. I can never think of that toil-worn man, rising long before his household and spending an hour with his Maker and his Bible, without tears. In that silent hour of communion he has drawn from the fountain which has fed all these qualities that have so won upon our faith and love. Ah! what tears, what prayers, what aspirations, what lamentations, what struggles, have been witnessed by the four walls of that quiet room! Aye, what food have the angels brought him there! There day after day while we have been sleeping has he knelt and prayed for us—prayed for the country, prayed for victory, prayed for wisdom and guidance, prayed for strength for his great mission, prayed for the accomplishment of his great purposes. There has he found consolation in trial, comfort in defeat and disaster, patience in reverses, courage for labor, wisdom in perplexity, and peace in the consciousness of God's approval. The man who was so humble and so brotherly among men was bowed with filial humility before God. It was while standing among those who had laid down their lives for us that he gave his heart to the One who had laid down his life for him. A praying president? A praying statesman? A praying politician? A praying commander-in-chief of armies and navies? Our foremost man, our highest man, our august ruler, our noblest dignitary, kneeling a simple-hearted child before his heavenly Father? Oh! when shall we see the like of this again? Why should we not mourn the loss of such a man as this? Why should we not love him as we have loved no other chief magistrate? He was a consecrated man—consecrated to his country and his God.

Of Mr. Lincoln's intellect I have said nothing, because there was nothing in his intellect that eminently distinguished him. An acute and strong common sense, sharply individualized by native organization and the peculiar training to which circumstances had subjected it, was his prominent characteristic. He had a perfect comprehension of the leading principles of constitutional government, a thorough belief in the right of every innocent man to freedom, a homely, straightforward mode of reasoning, considerable aptness without elegance of expression, marked readiness of illustration, and quick intuitions that gave him the element of shrewdness. How many men there are in power and out of power of whom much more than this might with truthfulness be said! No, Mr. Lincoln was not a remarkable man intellectually, or if remarkable not eminently so.   Strong without greatness, acute without brilliancy, penetrating but not profound, he was in intellect an average American in the walk of life in which the nation found him.   He was loved for the qualities of heart and character which I have attributed to him, and not for those powers and that culture which distinguish the majority of our eminent men.

In the light of these facts, let us look for a moment at what this simple-hearted, loving, honest, Christian man has done.   Without an extraordinary intellect, without the training of the schools, without a wide and generous culture, without experience, without the love of two thirds of the nation, without an army or a navy at the beginning, he has presided over and guided to a successful issue the most gigantic national struggle that the history of the world records.   He has called to his aid the best men of the time, without a jealous thought that they might overshadow him; he has managed to control their jealousies of each other and compelled them to work harmoniously; he has sifted out from weak and infected material men worthy to command our armies and lead them to victory; he has harmonized conflicting claims, interests, and policies, and in four years has absolutely annihilated the military power of a rebellion thirty years in preparation, and having in its armies the whole military population of a third of the republic, and at its back the entire resources of the men in arms and the producing power of four million slaves. Before he died he saw the rebellion in the last throes of dissolution and knew that his great work was accomplished. Could any one of the great men who surrounded him have done this work as well?   If you were doomed to go through it again would you choose for your leader any one of these before Mr. Lincoln?   We had a chance to do this but we did not do it. Mr. Lincoln's election to his second term of office, though occurring at a time when doubt and distrust brooded over the nation, was carried by overwhelming majorities. Heart and head were in the market, but we wisely chose the heart.

The destruction of the military power of the rebellion was Mr. Lincoln's special work. This he did so thoroughly that no chief magistrate will be called upon for centuries to repeat the process. He found the nation weak and tottering to destruction. He left it strong—feared and respected by the nations of the world. He found it full of personal enemies; he leaves it with such multitudes of friends that no one except at personal peril dares to insult his memory. Through this long night of peril and of sorrow, of faithlessness and fear, he has led us into a certain peace—the peace for which we have labored and prayed and bled for these long, long years.

Another work for which Mr. Lincoln will be remembered throughout all the coming generations is the practical emancipation of four million African slaves. His proclamation of emancipation was issued at the right time, and has produced, is producing, will produce, the results he sought to accomplish by it. It weakened the military power of the rebellion and has destroyed all motive to future rebellion. Besides this it accomplished that which was quite as grateful to his benevolent, freedom-loving heart, the abolition of a gigantic wrong—the emancipation of all the bondmen in the land. If he had done no more than this he would have secured for himself the fairest fame it has ever been the fortune of a good man to win. To be regarded and remembered through all coming time as the liberator of a race; to have one's name embalmed in the memory of an enfranchised people and associated with every blessing they enjoy and every good they may achieve, is a better fame than the proudest conquerors can boast. We who are white know little of the emotions which thrill the black man's heart to-day. There are no such mourners here as those simple souls among the freedmen who regarded Mr. Lincoln as the noblest personage next to Jesus Christ that ever lived. Their love is deeper than ours; their power of expression less. The tears that stream down those dark faces are charged with a pathos beyond the power of words.

Yet I know not why we may not join hands with them in perfect sympathy, for, under Providence, he has saved us from as many woes as he has them. He has enfranchised the white man as well as the black man. He freed the black man from the bondage of slavery, and he freed the white man from responsibility for it. He has removed from our national politics a power that constantly debauched them. He has destroyed an institution that was a standing disgrace to our nation, a living menace to our form of government, a loud-mouthed witness to our national hypocrisy, a dishonor to Christian civilization.

The destruction of the rebellion and the destruction of slavery are the two great achievements on which the fame of Mr. Lincoln will rest in history; but no man will write the history of these achievements justly who shall not reveal the nature of the power by which they were wrought out. The history which shall fail to show the superiority of the wisdom of an honest, humble, Christian heart over commanding and cultured intellect, will be a graceless libel on Mr. Lincoln's fame. I do not know where in the history of mankind I can find so marked an instance of the power of genuine character and the wisdom of a truthful, earnest

heart, as I see in the immeasurably great results of Mr.
Lincoln's administration. I should be false to you, false to
the occasion, false to the memory of him we mourn, and
false to the God he worshipped and obeyed, if I should fail
to adjure you to remember that all our national triumphs of
law and humanity over rebellion and barbarism have been
won through the wisdom and the power of a simple, honest,
Christian heart. Here is the grand lesson we are to learn
from the life of Mr. Lincoln. You, Christian men who
have voted, and voted, and voted again, for impure men, for
selfish men, for drunkards, for unprincipled men, for un-
christian men, because they were men of talent, or genius,
or accomplishments, or capacity for government, and because you thought that a good head was more important
than a good heart, have learned a lesson from the life and
achievements of Mr. Lincoln which you cannot forget without sin against God and crime against your country. We
have begun to be a Christian nation. We have recognized
the controlling power of Providence in our affairs. We
have witnessed in the highest seat the power of Christian
wisdom and the might of a humble, praying man. Let us
see that we remain a Christian nation—that our votes are
given to no man who cannot bring to his work the power
which has made the name of Abraham Lincoln one of the
brightest which illustrates the annals of the nation.

It was the presentiment and prophecy of Mr. Lincoln
that his own life and that of the rebellion would end together,
but little did he imagine—little did we imagine—that the
end of each would be violent. But both parties in the closing scene were in the direct exhibition of their characteristic
qualities. Mr. Lincoln went to the theatre not to please himself, but to gratify others. He went with weariness into the

crowd, that the promise under which that crowd had assembled might be fulfilled. The assassin who approached his back, and inflicted upon him his fatal wound, was in the direct exhibition of the spirit of the rebellion. Men who can perjure themselves, and betray a government confided by a trusting and unsuspecting people to their hands, and hunt and hang every man who does not sympathize with their treason, and starve our helpless prisoners by thousands, and massacre troops after they have surrendered, and can glory in these deeds, are not too good for the commission of any dastardly crime which the imagination can conceive. I can understand their shock at the enormous crime. " It will put the war back to Sumter," says one. " It is worse than the surrender of Lee's army," says another. Ah! There's the point. It severs the rebellion from the respect and sympathy of the world. The deed is so utterly atrocious—it exhibits a spirit so fiendish and desperate—that none can defend it, and all turn from it with horror and disgust.

Oh, friends! Oh, countrymen! I dare not speak the thoughts of vengeance that burn within me when I recall this shameless deed. I dare not breathe those imprecations that rise to my lips when I think of this wanton extinction of a great and beneficent life. I can hardly pray for justice, fully measured out to the mad murderer of his truest friend, for, somehow, I feel the presence of that kindly spirit, the magnetism of those kindly eyes, appealing to me to forbear. I have come into such communion with his personality that I cannot escape the power of his charity and his Christian forbearance; and the curse, rising like a bubble from the turbid waters within me, breaks into nothingness in the rarer atmosphere which he throws around me. If he could speak to me from that other shore, he would say, what all his actions and all his words said of others not less guilty than his assassin: "My murderer was mad and mistaken, as well as malignant. He thought he was doing a great and glorious deed, on behalf of a great and glorious cause. My death was necessary to the perfection of my mission, and was only one sacrifice among hundreds of thousands of others made for the same end."

Ah, that other shore! The commander-in-chief is with his army now. More are they that are with him in victory and peace than they whose names are still upon our muster-rolls. The largest body of the soldiers of the republic pitch their white tents, and unfold their golden banners, and sing their songs of triumph around him. Not his the hosts of worn and wearied bodies; not with him the riddled colors and war-stained uniforms; upon his ears breaks nevermore the dissonance of booming cannon, and clashing saber, and dying groan; but youth and life troop around him with a love purer than ours, and a joy which more than balances our grief.

Our President is dead. He has served us faithfully and well. He has kept the faith; he has finished his course. Henceforth there is laid up for him a crown of glory, which the Lord, the righteous Judge, shall give him in that day. And he who gave him to us, and who so abundantly blessed his labors, and helped him to accomplish so much for his country and his race, will not permit the country which he saved to perish. I believe in the over-ruling providence of God, and that, in permitting the life of our chief magistrate to be extinguished, he only closed one volume of the history of his dealings with this nation, to open another whose pages shall be illustrated with fresh developments of his love and sweeter signs of his mercy. What Mr. Lincoln achieved he achieved for us; but he left as choice a legacy in his Christian example, in his incorruptible integrity, and in his unaffected simplicity, if we will appropriate it, as in his public deeds. So we take this excellent life and its results, and, thanking God for them, cease all complaining and press forward under new leaders to new achievements, and the completion of the great work which he who has gone left as a sacred trust upon our hands.

BROOKS

PRESTON SMITH BROOKS, congressman and lawyer, was born in Edgefield District, South Carolina, August 4, 1819. He graduated at the South Carolina College in 1839, studied law, and was admitted to the bar in 1843. In 1844 he was elected to the State Legislature. He served as captain of the Palmetto regiment of South Carolina during most of the Mexican war, and in 1853 was elected to Congress as a States-rights Democrat, and was twice re-elected. On May 22, 1856, he made a violent and personal assault upon Charles Sumner in the United States Senate chamber, which caused great excitement and indignation throughout the country. The attack was caused by words uttered in a debate by Senator Sumner against Senator Butler, who was a relative of Mr. Brooks. In consequence of his brutal act a committee of the House reported in favor of Mr. Brooks's expulsion, but the vote was lost, as in the final action on the report the vote stood 121 to 95, while a majority of two thirds was required. After this Brooks, having had words with Anson Burlingame in a debate, challenged him to a duel, but at the appointed time and place Brooks failed to appear. Subsequently he resigned his seat in the House, but was unanimously re-elected by his constituents. He died in Washington, D. C., January 27, 1857.

SPEECH ON THE SUMNER ASSAULT

DELIVERED IN THE HOUSE OF REPRESENTATIVES, JULY 14, 1856

MR. SPEAKER,—Some time since a senator from Massachusetts allowed himself, in an elaborately prepared speech, to offer a gross insult to my State, and to a venerable friend, who is my State representative, and who was absent at the time.

Not content with that, he published to the world and circulated extensively this uncalled-for libel on my State and my blood. Whatever insults my State insults me. Her history and character have commanded my pious veneration; and in her defence I hope I shall always be prepared, humbly and modestly, to perform the duty of a son. I should have forfeited my own self-respect, and perhaps the good opinion

(8085)

of my countrymen, if I had failed to resent such an injury by calling the offender in question to a personal account. It was a personal affair, and in taking redress into my own hands I meant no disrespect to the Senate of the United States or to this House.

Nor, sir, did I design insult or disrespect to the State of Massachusetts. I was aware of the personal responsibilities I incurred and was willing to meet them. I knew, too, that I was amenable to the laws of the country, which afford the same protection to all, whether they be members of Congress or private citizens. I did not, and do not now believe, that I could be properly punished, not only in a court of law, but here also, at the pleasure and discretion of the House. I did not then, and do not now, believe that the spirit of American freemen would tolerate slander in high places and permit a member of Congress to publish and circulate a libel on another, and then call upon either House to protect him against the personal responsibilities which he had thus incurred.

But if I had committed a breach of privilege, it was the privilege of the Senate, and not of this House, which was violated. I was answerable there and not here. They had no right, as it seems to me, to prosecute me in these halls, nor have you the right in law or under the constitution, as I respectfully submit, to take jurisdiction over offences committed against them. The constitution does not justify them in making such a request, nor this House in granting it.

If, unhappily, the day should ever come when sectional or party feeling should run so high as to control all other considerations of public duty or justice, how easy it will be to use such precedents for the excuse of arbitrary power, in either house, to expel members of the minority who may have rendered themselves obnoxious to the prevailing spirit in the House to which they belong.

Matters may go smoothly enough when one House asks the other to punish a member who is offensive to a majority of its own body; but how will it be when, upon a pretence of insulted dignity, demands are made of this House to expel a member who happens to run counter to its party predilections, or other demands which it may not be so agreeable to grant?

It could never have been designed by the constitution of the United States to expose the two Houses to such temptations to collision, or to extend so far the discretionary power which was given to either House to punish its own members for the violation of its rules and orders. Discretion has been said to be the law of the tyrant, and when exercised under the color of the law and under the influence of party dictation it may and will become a terrible and insufferable despotism.

This House, however, it would seem, from the unmistakable tendency of its proceedings, takes a different view from that which I deliberately entertain in common with many others.

So far as public interests or constitutional rights are involved, I have now exhausted my means of defence. I may, then, be allowed to take a more personal view of the question at issue. The further prosecution of this subject, in the shape it has now assumed, may not only involve my friends, but the House itself, in agitations which might be unhappy in their consequences to the country.

If these consequences could be confined to myself individually, I think I am prepared and ready to meet them, here or elsewhere; and when I use this language I mean what I say.

But others must not suffer for me. I have felt more on account of my two friends who have been implicated than for myself, for they have proven that "there is a friend that sticketh closer than a brother." I will not constrain gentlemen to assume a responsibility on my account which possibly they would not run on their own.

Sir, I cannot, on my own account, assume the responsibility, in the face of the American people, of commencing a line of conduct which in my heart of hearts I believe would result in subverting the foundations of this government and in drenching this hall in blood. No act of mine, on my personal account, shall inaugurate revolution; but when you, Mr. Speaker, return to your own home and hear the people of the great North—and they are a great people—speak of me as a bad man, you will do me the justice to say that a blow struck by me at this time would be followed by revolution—and this I know.

If I desired to kill the senator, why did not I do it? You all admit that I had him in my power. Let me tell the member from New Jersey that it was expressly to avoid taking life that I used an ordinary cane, presented to me by a friend in Baltimore nearly three months before its application to the "bare head" of the Massachusetts senator. I went to work very deliberately, as I am charged—and this is admitted—and speculated somewhat as to whether I should employ a horsewhip or a cowhide; but knowing that the senator was my superior in strength, it occurred to me that he might wrest it from my hand, and then—for I never attempt anything I do not perform—I might have been compelled to do that which I would have regretted the balance of my natural life.

The question has been asked in certain newspapers why I did not invite the senator to personal combat in the mode usually adopted. Well, sir, as I desire the whole truth to be known about the matter, I will for once notice a newspaper article on the floor of the House and answer here.

My answer is that the senator would not accept a message; and, having formed the unalterable determination to punish him, I believed that the offence of " sending a hostile message," superadded to the indictment for assault and battery, would subject me to legal penalties more severe than would be imposed for a simple assault and battery. That is my answer.

Now, Mr. Speaker, I have nearly finished what I intended to say. If my opponents, who have pursued me with unparalleled bitterness, are satisfied with the present condition of this affair, I am. I return my thanks to my friends, and especially to those who are from non-slave-owning States, who have magnanimously sustained me and felt that it was a higher honor to themselves to be just in their judgment of a gentleman than to be a member of Congress for life. In taking my leave I feel that it is proper that I should say that I believe that some of the votes that have been cast against me have been extorted by an outside pressure at home, and that their votes do not express the feelings or opinions of the members who gave them.

To such of these as have given their votes and made their speeches on the constitutional principles involved, and without indulging in personal vilification, I owe my respect. But, sir, they have written me down upon the history of the country as worthy of expulsion, and in no unkindness I must tell them that for all future time my self-respect requires that I shall pass them as strangers.

And now, Mr. Speaker, I announce to you and to this House that I am no longer a member of the Thirty-fourth Congress.

CRISPI

FRANCESCO CRISPI was born at Bibera, in Sicily, October 4, 1819. He served under Garibaldi as Major at Calatafimi, in 1860, and was elected to the first Italian Parliament from Palermo a year later. He became President of the Chamber of Deputies in 1876, and Minister of the Interior in 1877, but only retained the latter office for one year. In 1878 he became Prime Minister of Italy, a post he held until 1891. He resumed office in 1893, and retained the post until 1896. In politics Crispi has always been a pronounced Liberal, and has rendered his country signal services. When the Garibaldi monument was unveiled in 1895, Crispi was fitly chosen as the orator of the occasion. However, he was never in thorough sympathy with either Mazzini or Garibaldi, and it is thought by some that to his differences with Mazzini were largely due the perpetuation of the monarchy in Italy.

AT THE UNVEILING OF GARIBALDI'S STATUE

DELIVERED AT ROME, SEPTEMBER 20, 1895

THE twentieth of September, 1870, could not be better commemorated than by the inauguration in Rome of a monument to Garibaldi, the faithful and devoted friend of Victor Emmanuel, who in 1860 accepted the plébiscite in favor of the liberation of Rome. The citizens of Rome could not be the helots of unity, the slaves of cosmopolitan patriotism. Their servitude meant the restriction of the national sovereignty, which was Italy's due in mere virtue of her existence.

The day and the place remind us of the struggle against tyranny, so laborious, yet so fruitful of liberty. The years which elapsed between July 4, 1849, and September 20,

1870, were the last years of trial for the civil power. The Church, having shown that she was powerless to live by her own resources, had to rely upon foreign bayonets, of which she in her turn became completely the slave. It was here that on April 30, after a bloody battle, Garibaldi repulsed the invader who, without provocation, had undertaken the barbarous mission of restoring tyranny. When hostilities were resumed, the defenders, although with right on their side, had to yield to force and await patiently the day of resurrection, the twentieth of September, 1870. . . .

The enemies of Italian unity have endeavored to prove that the present celebration is an insult to the head of the Catholic Church. Their object is to excite conscientious scruples against our country. But the common-sense of the people is proof against such tricks, because we all know that Christianity is a divine institution, which is not dependent upon earthly weapons for its existence. The religion of Christ preached by Paul and Chrysostom was able to sub-due the world without the aid of temporal arms, and we cannot conceive that the Vatican should persist in wishing for temporal sovereignty to exercise its spiritual mission. The Gospel, as we all believe, is truth. If it has been dis-seminated by Apostolic teachings, such teachings are suffi-cient for its existence.

It is not really for the protection and prestige of religion that our adversaries demand the restoration of the temporal power of the Holy See, but for worldly reasons, from lust of power, and from earthly covetousness. They do not con-sider that temporal sovereignty cannot be saintly and above sin, that it cannot aspire to celestial perfection in this world. Material weapons and legal violence, justified by reasons of state, should not belong to the Vicar of Christ on earth, who is to preach peace, to pray, and to pardon. Religion is not and it cannot be an affair of state. Its mission is to console believers with the hope of everlasting life, and to uphold the spirit of faith.

The Catholic Church has never enjoyed in any country so much freedom and respect as in Italy. We alone of all nations have renounced every claim to jurisdiction in ecclesiastical matters. It is a maxim of modern law that the state should have no influence in spiritual things which cannot be interfered with by the civil power without having recourse to violence. The spiritual autonomy which we protect and guarantee should be the stronghold of the Supreme Pontiff. In that stronghold he could not be assailed. Worldly matters elude his grasp, and it would be a virtue in him not to think of them. Souls are his kingdom, and he governs them so absolutely as to elicit the envy of other rulers of men. Protestant sovereigns and even princes who do not believe in Christ bow before him and reverently accept his judgments.

The Italians, by promulgating the law of May, 1871, have solved a problem which seemed incapable of solution. In this country, where freedom of thought and of conscience is acknowledged, unlimited liberty has been granted to the head of the Church with reference to his sacred office and his irresponsibility and inviolability. In regard to his acts, the Pope is subject only to God, and no human potentate can reach him. He exercises a sovereign authority over all those who believe in him, and they are many millions, while he is surrounded by all the honors and privileges of royalty without the drawbacks of civil power, without the hatred, the resentment, and the penalties inseparable from such power. No earthly prince is in a similar position or on

the same level. His position is unique. He has no territory to govern. Indeed, any extent of territory would be
inadequate for his position, and yet all the world is subject
to his spiritual empire. Were he a temporal prince his authority would be diminished, because it would be equal to
that of other rulers, and he would cease to be preëminent.
He would be exposed to continual struggles, as he has
struggled for centuries to the detriment of the faith and
of his spiritual authority. We have made him an independent sovereign, and as such he is superior to all other
princes. In this lies his power. He exercises his office by
virtue of his authority; he corresponds with all the world;
he prays; he protects, without needing protection, because
the Italian kingdom is his shield. Consequently, no earthly
weapon can reach him, and the outrages inflicted upon Bon-
iface VIII. cannot be repeated.

Catholics should be grateful to Italy for the services
which we have rendered to the Roman Pontiff. Before
September 20, 1870, he was obliged to bow before the
princes of the earth, and concordats were concessions of
divine rights made to the prejudice of the Church. It
was only when relieved of his temporal dominion that
Pius IX. could cope with Bismarck and make that man of
iron feel the power of spiritual arms. All this is our handi-
work, the work of our Parliament and our king, and we are
proud of the achievement. I will say more; it was the will
of God, because the Almighty willed that Italy should
gather her provinces together and become an equal of other
nations.

We regret to say that those who oppose this evident will
of the Creator call themselves his ministers on earth, but
they will not prevail, because Italy is strong and self-reliant

and will crush any effort at revolution. These men will not
prevail, and perhaps they may grow wiser. They are aware
that so long as they keep within lawful bounds and do not
infringe the law, they are inviolable. But they ought to
remember that if they rebel, if they revile their country and
attack our national institutions, they will lose all the benefits which they have secured by our law of guarantees,
which was granted to religion and for religion, and not
for the personal advantage of any man. They know, or
ought to know, that by inciting others to break the law
they would help Anarchism, which denies both God and
King, and they would not escape punishment.

ADDRESS TO THE ITALIAN ELECTORS

DELIVERED MAY 23, 1895

FELLOW CITIZENS, DEAREST FRIENDS,—I speak
to Italy from Rome, and this is for me, an old Italian,
the greatest comfort. Who has seen the past under-
stands me and therefore knows my mind in regard to those
to whom I owe highest honor. But the duties which
press upon us all in face of the problem which the dying
century cannot leave unsolved, and which weigh inexorably
upon us, make me tremble. Therefore I beg of you the
greatest indulgence. I will be brief and clear, as is my wont.

I held the direction of affairs from August, 1887, to February, 1891. I had it again at the end of December in 1893,
not by my will, but constrained by duty. I have never desired or sought power, conscious of its grave responsibility,

familiar with the pains which flow from it. And here let me record facts now belonging to history.

About the end of 1893 the constitution of any government whatever appeared impossible and was nearly so.

At home, rebellion already broken out in some provinces, latent in others, the national consolidarity severed; men's minds perturbed not only by evident ills, but also by the fear and almost the presentiment of greater.

Material disturbance like unto the moral—credit debased, trade hampered, revenues insufficient for the government's needs, and because of the general disorganization the fountains of public and private resources drying up.

Abroad, surprise at all this was attested by diffidence and distrust, and by its reflex action even increased the domestic difficulties. In one word, the government of the last three years had done more harm to Italy than a rout in battle. In that sad moment Italy turned her thoughts to me hopefully.

Was it well, was it ill? I can answer less than any other. Certainly the will of the crown seemed to be, and was ever, one with the will of the country, when his Majesty the King, advice being taken and it appearing that my name was proposed on all sides, including even those who are to-day my bitter enemies, wished to entrust again to me the reins of state. To refuse would have been cowardly. I obeyed.

On December 20, 1893, I spoke thus to Parliament for my colleagues and myself: " We charge upon none the actual state of things; it is the consequence of a series of events which we can record, but should not judge. We will but say that great are the difficulties to be conquered; and that to uplift credit, put in order the finances, strengthen the authority of law, and to bring the country to a true knowledge of itself, we need the support of the chamber without distinction of party.   To this end we ask of you a sacred truce. When Italy's future is assured, each shall resume his place. To combat now, to set ourselves one against the other—let me affirm it with patriotic breath, would be a crime.   When peril advances we should all unite in the common defence.

But we spoke to a chamber which could not act.   It had been disorganized because the electors had not been called to vote upon a programme based on principles.   The manner of the elections, the seductions practised, the freedom of the ballot taken from many by violence or corruption, the lavish, lawless, promises impressed on the new representation the stamp of an original sin.   The chamber showed itself convinced of this, like us, when it consented to the revision of the electoral lists, explicitly declaring its own corrupt origin.

At all events the contagion of good appeared at first to be possible and effective.   Whether it were the sinking of public and private fortunes, the shame of recent ill success and proved incapacity, and the fear of arousing by partisan instability the popular wrath—a productive period of restorative work even with that chamber seemed possible.   The effect was soon felt.

The sight of Italy showing herself capable of re-creating her government, with sincere and practical seriousness, surrounded by the sympathy of the country, gave new life to foreign confidence.   At home rebellion was turned, credit uplifted, the finances on the way to restoration, through a programme dependent upon the truth, replaced a false consideration for the taxpayer with the evident utility of a final effort.   This effort, partially, but with some reluctance agreed to by the chamber, was accepted by the nation with that good sense which is the real basis of Italian character.

The path was regained, the career resumed. The moment for evil to reassert itself had therefore come.

The violent, certain of the unpopularity to which they would have condemned themselves, had been silent while there was danger of disruption, the unworthy who had been hurled from power, the incapable who had had to put away ambition and should have renounced it, now all took up the cry, and when we were almost at the goal, the invidious and jealous coalition of the disaffected sought to turn Parliament from its path and to again cast the country over a precipice of miseries.

Thus the national tribune became a seat for defamation; parliamentary immunity, an immunity of offence, and personal encounters replaced the contest for principles.

Calumny is no new weapon in politics; in democratic countries it has succeeded to the mediæval poison and dagger, and recourse to it is had all the more readily, when the pebble of some unsuccessful David, or the bullet of some fanatical assassin have failed. Never was it so clamorous, violent, and insinuating, keen and comprehensive as now, tricked out artfully and ably ordered.

It counted upon the disguise which such warfare would arouse in a man who, reaching the decline of a long and wearisome career, must aspire before all else for peace.

If I had yielded and bent before this new system for provoking ministerial crises by defamation, accepting the convenient theory that a minister (however much culumniated), ought to defend himself and resign his powers meanwhile, thus giving to the meanest of insulters a right to change the government of the country—the country would have quickly seen with more disgust than wonder, vituperation freshly changed into hosannas.

But before to-day I learned to suffer in the fulfilment of duty, and I resisted. I resisted because I could prove that more than ever there was political nihilism outside the government, and because war was being made far less upon the man than upon the régime he represented.

I never compromise and they all know it. I resisted and my suffering was dear to me, because to suffer for a just cause is the greatest of honors. Ours was just and most noble; and since the means of which a Parliament ordinarily disposes were insufficient to unveil the plot, the ministry concordantly proposed to the crown the prorogation of the session. This was without hesitation, but not without regret.

Still we all took comfort that in the prorogation we all submitted ourselves to the primary judgment of the country, and this judgment was as explicit as just.

This régime, which is wont to be called the decree-law, is a serious matter; it is declared to be in contradiction to the statute by those who have been first to recur to it, not alone needlessly, but fruitlessly, for the finances of the State and national economy. Our use of it apart from our purity of intention was legitimized by success.

To be sure the very insuccess of the most fierce and predatory opposition made these opponents still more fanatical. Insomuch that losing entirely the sense of patriotism and humanity more than one among them augured—to the advantage of barbarisms—defeat to those arms which we had been obliged to take up in Africa, to defend ourselves from treason and to guard civilization.

But victory smiled upon us. Our soldiery, valorous, patient, and ready for fatigue, battle, and sacrifice, the stuff for heroes to-day as for martyrs yesterday, strengthened by wise organization, guided by that wise boldness which is one national tradition in war, renewed the bright days of that glory which seemed to have set forever.

Blessed be that victory! The Italian heavens, clouded by the fogs of defamation, shone again, and the atmosphere, heavy with speculation and scandal, cleared away. A thrill of renewing vigor ran through the national fibre, and a wave of sympathetic respect flowed in from all the world.

We can to-day vaunt of peace with honor, since if bloody conquests have spoken of our valor, our diplomacy has found pleasure and success in demonstrating the union of our interests and our ideals. From Morocco to the extreme Orient, from one America to the other, my colleague of the foreign department has proven that equity is with Italy, and equity means advantage. So that there has never been as now such cordial relationships between our own and other governments—never greater respect for our country in its international rights. Thus was crushed the other story of provocative politics; proved futile the attempt to gain belief in a plan of crazy adventure in Africa, while we were measuring only too closely our successes by our immediate financial possibilities, watched over with the glance of a miser by my friend and colleague of the treasury, and by other eminent associates not less severe than he; accused men of acting as slave-traders in the face of our country—but all this in vain, the opposition at last shifted over to an effort to excite compassion as victims—or authors, as might be—of a social conflict.

But we do not hide from ourselves certainly either the gravity or the urgency of the forms which the social problem assumes among us. Is it possible to distinguish socialists from anarchists?

Certain it is that in other countries—although one cannot tell clearly where socialism ends and anarchy begins—there is serious study and sincere conviction, together with an assumption of great interest in the masses which can make respectable that principle of socialism which is indeed a negation of individual freedom, while anarchy is only perpetual war.

But among us on the other hand there are only the caprices of theorists changing their programme daily, banners waving in the wind of popularity; shameful sentimentality shifting from one object to its extreme opposite; and the ambition of politicians turning indifferently to any party if only they may succeed; even good faith undeniable to many is seldom strengthened by authority. Indeed this propaganda of socialism has brought no benefit to the real sufferings of our people, sufferings which I shall be the last to deny. So socialists and anarchists have accomplished nothing but to distract the government from effective provisions, to render repressive laws inevitable as the exceptional but necessary result of their behavior. We might have responded with violence which the peril and the injury to society would have justified, to the crimes committed with weapons, dynamite, and fire, to robbery, to evil provocation wrought with wicked words upon ignorant and senseless crowds. But we have limited ourselves in most instances to that measure of preservation found in the supervision of a prescribed residence and restriction of that personal liberty which had been abused.

Further, what was the disposition of the government toward those on whom less merited punishment has fallen, is proved by the clement measures proposed by us to the king's compassion, and by the many who have been liberated in these recent months, no less than the care given to studying that part of the social problem dependent upon legislative provisions, as attested by projects which may be opportunely modified, but show undeniable inspiration.

Yet we have seen these projects combatted by the very people who on the other hand allied themselves with the authors and encouragers of disorder—a monstrous amalgamation of contradictions. Aristocracy, socialism, radicalism, and anarchy were to be seen marching in affectionate embrace, one party approving whatever legitimate demands another made, and together all aiming at a general destruction. Thus the disorder is double—material and moral.

One would say that history teaches nothing to those who should most treasure its lessons, still they aspire by governing the country to become historical themselves. This is no republic, and we have not then to fear that the excesses of any sort of radical will lead us to Cæsarism; the modifying power here is fortunately permanent and loyal, and our institutions rest upon the heart as well as the good sense of the people.

Still it is edifying—this strange marriage which unites in the name of liberty, those who are for opposite reasons the negation of it—those who invoked the scaffold in its defence, and they would attain it by distinction.

Liberty does not lack in Italy, but a wise use of it rather. It is less in our habits than in our legislation, where I think it an honor to have taken a large part. This the public knows so well that every renewed effort to bind together those who would make liberty the pretext for vain agitation, falls under popular indifference.

The statesman's duty is to oppose public opinion whenever he sees it deviate from the ends toward which it should tend for the good of the fatherland, and guilty are they who yield and flatter, in the craze for mere popularity, when they should protest and resist. We needed no proof of it, for the conviction was deep and general that a new chamber was indispensable—new in origin, elementally in part, in discipline, in programme and a firm will to adhere thereto. Therefore it is that we have summoned the electors, and that we stand before you that you may judge us according to our desires and our accomplishments.

Our intentions are not to be counted with those which pave the infernal streets. All have seen and know how they have been prevented from becoming facts and by whom. Facts they will yet become if you continue your favor in this same effort.

In spite of most adverse circumstances and of the attempt of the hostile coalition to arrest government action, this has moved on surely, and this ministry, presenting itself for judgment to the nation, has to credit results so incontestable that our adversaries, knowing them undeniable, have had to seek elsewhere arms with which to fight us.

More and better we feel we can do when we may labor no longer alone, but with the concurrence of Parliament We desire above all to make the Italian people forget the dark and shameful things which have perturbed in this late period of its national life—and this with a civil as well as material reparation.

The union into a political statehood lived in Italian thought before it came to pass. Such thought was the Italian's ideal patrimony and fortune; and foreigners themselves, though dominating it, respected it, such light beamed from it and hallowed the cause of our redemption. To-day memories are not life but death; hence the supreme need of a national education, serving above all as a stimulus to good. Instead there is moral inertia in many, and, worse yet, such a scorn of what is patriotic, spiritually active, and fruitful, that the best can sometimes accomplish little.

I tried to put Italians on their guard against this scepticism of thought and action when I pointed out the existence of a new monster, bearing upon its banner "Neither God nor Chief," and summoned to combat it a gathering of honest men of whatever faith, inscribing instead upon our banner, "With God and the King for Fatherland." Some made believe to be afraid, crying out against me as a reactionist, pretending that I sought to initiate an anti-liberal movement and renounce the conquests of civilization.

Puerile accusation! The modern state lives not without liberty in all classes of its society, in every manifestation of its practical vitality. But as liberty means not license, and as the liberty of each finds natural limits in the liberty of all, there is no offence to liberty in reacting against nihilism of every kind—of conscience no less than of government.

Government should imply providence, and to be provident a government must be free in its actions. But on account of much that happened during the last period of the closed legislative session the need has become most evident that some points scarcely indicated in the constitution should be elucidated and confirmed by a duly sanctioned ministerial responsibility.

But to prevent the repetition of past melancholy phenomena you must assume your share of the burden, Italian electors, renouncing nihilism above all things, at the polls.

If you wish the public life to develop itself as you would have it, you must begin by participating in it, by a judicious use of your own votes. Choose, then, between us and our friends and our adversaries! Who and what we are you have seen to know! What our adversaries are and what they could give you needs not to be said. Conspirators disguised as moralists, knowing that the country was with it, they have substituted calumny for criticism, some careless, others even desirous that perils should gather about our institutions in their overthrow of the existing government.

Why thus destroy? Because a coalition of anarchists, monarchists, " plebiscite " radicals, federal republicans, socialists, and pseudo-conservatives could have no other aspiration. Before such discordant elements could combine in real unity they must begin by converting one another, which their own contradictory programmes recognize as impossible. If it conquered it could not form a government even of the worst, and assuredly not good. But it will not conquer!

The dilemma before the electors to-day is simple but solemn—the choice between the national monarchy and social, moral, and political anarchy. To fight such anarchy is the duty now imposed on every good citizen.

In the king, symbol and strong safeguard of national unity, the king surrounded by democratic institutions, is our trust. Let not fail that trust. Neither by doubt nor by the withholding of votes. To refrain from the ballot is desertion in the hour of battle; to doubt, the first step toward defeat.

So I make my appeal to all Italians, and I believe that my voice will be heard, because all good men have herein one common interest. Parties must be reformed upon honest and logical bases, so that there may be an interchange of ideas between men and their government. And the renunciation of power will be welcome to me when I can retire without baseness, without fear for the security of our institutions.

Let us unite our hearts then, elevating them in the sentiment of a supreme duty, alert and calm as in the best of days, assured that the work of social pacification and the reorganization of the state are no less important than the struggles for independent unity and their national, final development.

Close up, then, around the king, and with our glance bent on the Cross of Savoy, resplendent upon the nation's banner, let us, too, cry " *In hoc signo vinces!* "

[Special translation by Mary E. Adams.]

RAYMOND

H ENRY JARVIS RAYMOND, a noted American journalist and orator, was born in Lima, New York, January 24, 1820, and educated at the University, of Vermont. He studied law for a year or two in New York city after his graduation, and then taking up the profession of journalism was an assistant editor of the "New York Tribune," 1841-43, and editor of the "New York Courier and Enquirer," 1843-50. He entered the State legislature as a Whig member in 1849 and was re-elected in the following year. On September 18, 1851, he issued the first number of the "New York Times," the editor of which he remained for the rest of his life. Raymond was a delegate to the Baltimore Whig convention of 1852, making there a strong speech explaining northern sentiment on the questions then at issue, and in the organization of the Republican party in 1856 took a prominent part. He declined a nomination for the governorship of New York in 1857, and in 1860 favored Seward as a presidential candidate. During the civil war Raymond was again a member of the State legislature, and in 1864 he entered Congress, making there in December, 1865, a notable speech in which he maintained that the southern States had never been out of the Union. He was a supporter of the reconstruction policy of President Johnson and wrote an "Address and Declaration of Principles," which the loyalists' convention at Philadelphia put forth in 1866. He declined a renomination to Congress and also the Austrian mission tendered him by President Johnson. He died in New York city June 18, 1869. Raymond was an orator of considerable power, but is best known as a journalist, who exerted a most beneficial influence in raising the level of newspaper controversy. His published writings comprise "Political Lessons of the Revolution" (1854); "Letters to Mr. Yancy" (1860); "History of the Administration of President Lincoln" (1864), revised in 1865 as "Life and Public Services of Abraham Lincoln."

SPEECH ON RECONSTRUCTION

DELIVERED IN THE HOUSE OF REPRESENTATIVES, DEC. 21, 1865.

M R. CHAIRMAN,—I should be glad, if it meet the sense of those members who are present, to make some remarks upon the general question before the House; but I do not wish to trespass at all upon their disposition in regard to this matter. I do not know, however, that there will be a better opportunity to say what little I have to say than is now offered; and if the House shall indicate no other wish, I will proceed to say it.

I need not say that I have been gratified to hear many things which have fallen from the lips of the gentleman from Ohio [Mr. Finck], who has just taken his seat. I have no party feeling, nor any other feeling, which would prevent me from rejoicing in the indications apparent on that side of the House of a purpose to concur with the loyal people of the country, and with the loyal administration of the government, and with the loyal majorities in both Houses of Congress, in restoring peace and order to our common country. I cannot, perhaps, help wishing, sir, that these indications of an interest in the preservation of our government had come somewhat sooner. I cannot help feeling that such expressions cannot now be of as much service to the country as they might once have been.

If we could have had from that side of the House such indications of an interest in the preservation of the Union, such heartfelt sympathy with the efforts of the government for the preservation of that Union, such hearty denunciation of those who were seeking its destruction, while the war was raging, I am sure we might have been spared some years of war, some millions of money, and rivers of blood and tears.

But, sir, I am not disposed to fight over again battles now happily ended. I feel, and I am rejoiced to find that members on the other side of the House feel, that the great problem now before us is to restore the Union to its old integrity, purified from everything that interfered with the full development of the spirit of liberty which it was made to enshrine.

I trust that we shall have a general concurrence of the members of this House and of this Congress in such measures as may be deemed most fit and proper for the accomplishment of that result. I am glad to assume and to believe that there is not a member of this House, nor a man in this country, who does not wish, from the bottom of his heart, to see the day speedily come when we shall have this nation— the great American Republic—again united, more harmonious in its action than it ever has been, and forever one and indivisible. We in this Congress are to devise the means to restore its union and its harmony, to perfect its institutions, and to make it in all its parts and in all its action, through all time to come, too strong, too wise, and too free ever to invite or ever to permit the hand of rebellion again to be raised against it.

Now, sir, in devising those ways and means to accomplish that great result, the first thing we have to do is to know the point from which we start, to understand the nature of the material with which we have to work—the condition of the territory and the States with which we are concerned. I had supposed at the outset of this session that it was the purpose of this House to proceed to that work without discussion, and to commit it almost exclusively, if not entirely, to the joint committee raised by the two Houses for the consideration of that subject.

But, sir, I must say that I was glad when I perceived the distinguished gentleman from Pennsylvania [Mr. Stevens], himself the chairman on the part of this House of that great committee on reconstruction, lead off in a discussion of this general subject, and thus invite all the rest of us who choose to follow him in the debate. In the remarks which he made in this body a few days since, he laid down, with the clearness and the force which characterize everything he says and does, his point of departure in commencing this great work.

I had hoped that the ground he would lay down would be such that we could all of us stand upon it and co-operate with him in our common object. I feel constrained to say, sir— and do it without the slightest disposition to create or to exaggerate differences—that there were features in his exposition of the condition of the country with which I cannot concur. I cannot for myself start from precisely the point which he assumes.

In his remarks on that occasion he assumed that the States lately in rebellion were and are out of the Union. Throughout his speech—I will not trouble you with reading passages from it—I find him speaking of those States as " outside of the Union," as " dead States," as having forfeited all their rights and terminated their State existence. I find expressions still more definite and distinct; I find him stating that they " are and for four years have been out of the Union for all legal purposes;" as having been for four years a " separate power," and " a separate nation."

His position therefore is that these States, having been in rebellion, are now out of the Union and are simply within the jurisdiction of the constitution of the United States as so much territory to be dealt with precisely as the will of the conqueror, to use his own language, may dictate. Now, sir, if that position is correct it prescribes for us one line of policy to be pursued very different from the one that will be proper if it is not correct.

His belief is that what we have to do is to create new States out of this territory at the proper time—many years distant—retaining them meantime in a territorial condition and subjecting them to precisely such a state of discipline and tutelage as Congress or the government of the United States may see fit to prescribe. If I believed in the premises which

he assumes, possibly, though I do not think probably, I
might agree with the conclusion he has reached.

But, sir, I cannot believe that this is our condition. I cannot believe that these States have ever been out of the Union
or that they are now out of the Union. I cannot believe
that they ever have been or are now in any sense a separate
power. If they were, sir, how and when did they become so?
They were once States of this Union—that every one con-
cedes; bound to the Union and made members of the Union
by the constitution of the United States. If they ever went
out of the Union it was at some specific time and by some
specific act.

I regret that the gentleman from Pennsylvania [Mr.
Stevens] is not now in his seat. I should have been glad
to ask him by what specific act and at what precise time any
one of those States took itself out of the American Union.
Was it by the ordinance of secession? I think we all agree
that an ordinance of secession passed by any State of this
Union is simply a nullity, because it encounters in its practical operation the constitution of the United States, which
is the supreme law of the land. It could have no legal
actual force or validity. It could not operate to effect any
actual change in the relations of the State adopting it to the
national government, still less to accomplish the removal of
that State from the sovereign jurisdiction of the constitution
of the United States.

Well, sir, did the resolutions of the States, the declarations
of their officials, the speeches of members of their legislatures, or the utterances of their press accomplish the result?
Certainly not. They could not possibly work any change
whatever in the relations of these States to the general government. All their ordinances and all their resolutions were

simply declarations of a purpose to secede. Their secession, if it ever took place, certainly could not date from the time when their intention to secede was first announced.

After declaring that intention they proceeded to carry it into effect. How? By war. By sustaining their purpose by arms against the force which the United States brought to bear against it. Did they sustain it? Were their arms victorious? If they were then their secession was an accomplished fact. If not it was nothing more than an abortive attempt—a purpose unfulfilled. This, then, is simply a question of fact and we all know what the fact is. They did not succeed. They failed to maintain their ground by force of arms—in other words, they failed to secede.

But the gentleman from Pennsylvania [Mr. Stevens] insists that they did secede, and that this fact is not in the least affected by the other fact that the constitution forbids secession. He says that the law forbids murder, but that murders are nevertheless committed. But there is no analogy between the two cases. If secession had been accomplished, if these States had gone out and overcome the armies that tried to prevent their going out, then the prohibition of the constitution could not have altered the fact.

In the case of murder the man is killed, and murder is thus committed in spite of the law. The fact of killing is essential to the committal of the crime; and the fact of going out is essential to secession. But in this case there was no such fact. I think I need not argue any further the position that the rebel States have never for one moment, by any ordinances of secession, or by any successful war, carried themselves beyond the rightful jurisdiction of the constitution of the United States.

They have interrupted for a time the practical enforcement and exercise of that jurisdiction; they rendered it impossible for a time for this government to enforce obedience to its laws; but there has never been an hour when this government, or this Congress, or this House, or the gentleman from Pennsylvania himself, ever conceded that those States were beyond the jurisdiction of the constitution and laws of the United States. . . .

Why, sir, if there be no constitution of any sort in a State, no law, nothing but chaos, then that State would no longer exist as an organization. But that has not been the case, it never is the case in great communities, for they always have constitutions and forms of government. It may not be a constitution or form of government adapted to its relation to the government of the United States; and that would be an evil to be remedied by the government of the United States.

That is what we have been trying to do for the last four years. The practical relations of the governments of those States with the government of the United States were all wrong—were hostile to that government. They denied our jurisdiction and they denied that they were States of the Union, but their denial did not change the fact; and there was never any time when their organizations as States were destroyed. A dead State is a solecism, a contradiction in terms, an impossibility.

These are, I confess, rather metaphysical distinctions, but I did not raise them. Those who assert that a State is destroyed whenever its constitution is changed, or whenever its practical relations with this government are changed, must be held responsible for whatever metaphysical niceties may be necessarily involved in the discussion. I do not know, sir, that I have made my views on this point clear to the gentleman from Pennsylvania [Mr. Kelley], who has questioned me upon it, and I am still more doubtful whether, even if they are intelligible, he will concur with me as to their justice. But I regard these States as just as truly within the jurisdiction of the constitution, and therefore just as really and truly States of the American Union now, as they were before the war.

Their practical relations to the constitution of the United States have been disturbed, and we have been endeavoring through four years of war to restore them and make them what they were before the war. The victory in the field has given us the means of doing this; we can now re-establish the practical relations of those States to the government. Our actual jurisdiction over them, which they vainly attempted to throw off, is already restored. The conquest we have achieved is a conquest over the rebellion, not a conquest over the States whose authority the rebellion had for a time subverted.

For these reasons I think the views submitted by the gentleman from Pennsylvania [Mr. Stevens] upon this point are unsound. Let me next cite some of the consequences which it seems to me must follow the acceptance of his position. If, as he asserts, we have been waging war with an independent power, with a separate nation, I cannot see how we can talk of treason in connection with our recent conflict, or demand the execution of Davis or anybody else as a traitor.

Certainly if we were at war with any other foreign power we should not talk of the treason of those who were opposed to us in the field. If we were engaged in a war with France and should take as prisoner the Emperor Napoleon, certainly we would not talk of him as a traitor or as liable to execution. I think that by adopting any such assumption as that of the honorable gentleman we surrender the whole idea of treason and the punishment of traitors.

I think, moreover, that we accept virtually and practically the doctrine of State sovereignty, the right of a State to withdraw from the Union, and to break up the Union at its own will and pleasure. I do not see how upon those premises we can escape that conclusion. If the States that engaged in the late rebellion constituted themselves by their ordinances of secession or by any of the acts with which they followed those ordinances, a separate and independent power, I do not see how we can deny the principles on which they professed to act or refuse assent to their practical results. I have heard no clearer, no stronger statement of the doctrine of State sovereignty as paramount to the sovereignty of the nation than would be involved in such a concession. Whether he intended it or not the gentleman from Pennsylvania [Mr. Stevens] actually assents to the extreme doctrines of the advocates of secession.

SHERMAN

WILLIAM TECUMSEH SHERMAN, a distinguished American officer in the War of the Rebellion, was born at Lancaster, Ohio, February 8, 1820. He graduated at West Point in 1840, and after serving for a time in Florida and California and seeing no chance for promotion, he resigned in 1853 and became a banker in San Francisco. When the civil war broke out he was head of the Louisiana Military Academy. In May, 1861, he took his commis-ion as colonel, but after the battle of Bull Run was appointed brigadier-general of volunteers. In August of the same year having been sent to Kentucky he demanded 200,000 men and agreed to put an end to the war there. But he was regarded as a visionary and was relieved of his command. After the battle of Shiloh, where he had a chance to distinguish himself, he was made major-general and became Grant's right-hand man in the operations around Vicksburg. In July, 1863, having been appointed a brigadier in the regular army he drove General Johnston out of Jackson, Mississippi, and once more rendered efficient assistance to Grant at Chattanooga. In March, 1864, he was appointed to the command of the Army of the Southwest, and in April began his operations against Atlanta, which was evacuated on the first of September. He undertook and carried out successfully the famous march to the sea, reaching Savannah on the tenth of December. He was made major-general and received the thanks of Congress. In February moving north he captured Charleston and by the seventh of February reached Columbia. He aimed to cut off Lee's retreat or else to join Grant before Richmond, but Lee surrendered on the ninth of April. Sherman made terms with General Johnston. For four years he commanded the Mississippi division, and when Grant became President Sherman was appointed head of the army. In 1874 he was retired at his own request. He died in New York February 14, 1891. Sherman was distinguished for his dogged perseverance, his generosity, and his simplicity. He contributed to the literature of the war his own memoirs, which were first published in 1875, and in a revised edition in 1891.

THE ARMY AND NAVY

ADDRESS DELIVERED AT THE BANQUET OF THE NEW ENGLAND
SOCIETY, DECEMBER 22, 1875

MR. PRESIDENT AND GENTLEMEN OF THE NEW ENGLAND SOCIETY,—I confess that I never come to a New England festival in the city of New York without commingling feelings of pleasure and dread: pleasure, because I am always certain of finding here

all that can satisfy the palate, the fancy, the eye, and, better
still, the wit and good feeling that always abound; and dread,
at being compelled to face an audience such as this, every
one of whom could teach me, and before whom I should be
silent. Whenever I see the name of my friend Choate, I am
sure of an abundant supply of that exquisite wit for which
he is famous, and this, added to the many other attractions
of your New England Society, will ever draw me hither, if
time and distance permit.

Though I had hoped to sit to-night and listen to others,
I find myself allotted to the old familiar toast, " The Army
and Navy," and had a right to expect in this great seaport
some representative of the navy to relieve me at least of
that branch of the subject, but I look about me and see
none of them present. Where is Porter, or your Vice-Ad-
miral Rowan, or Paulding, or some other representative of
that most honorable body who carry our flag to the uttermost
parts of the earth, and cause it to be respected everywhere,
who should avail themselves of an occasion like this to speak
a few words for their honored comrades? The subject is a
noble one, and would inspire any speaker. We know but
little of the " Mayflower," which, two hundred and fifty-five
years ago, brought the small band of Pilgrims to the dreary
shores of Plymouth Bay, but there are hundreds of gentlemen who well remember those gallant clippers that used to
sail for California—the " Huntress," the " Maid of the
Mist," the " White Cloud," the " Mist of the Morning."
How beautiful! But all are gone. In like manner did you
use to go down to the Battery to see depart for foreign service the old frigates such as the " Constitution " and " Independence," so clean and beautiful, with their tiers of 18-
pound carronades, bull-dogs then, but mere pop-guns now,

still the same with which our gallant tars fought great battles, and the same with which Nelson fought and won at Tra-
falgar. Steam and modern improvement have changed all
these, and in their stead what do we have? Low black monsters made of iron and driven by steam; nothing visible above
water but small towers, called pepper-boxes, with their pairs
of heavy guns, with long, projecting beams with torpedoes
at the ends, like devil-fish, dangerous sea-monsters, and with
uncouth names like " Canonicus," " Sassacus," etc. But
these changes are necessary, and our navy must conform, and
we cannot but admire their courage and patriotism in so
gracefully conforming, to the necessities of service. I confess I do not want to go to sea in such sea-monsters, and, had
I to choose, would far prefer to accept death on the deck of
the old " Constitution."

Change, however, is universal—you are no more like the
old Pilgrim Fathers than are the contents of this room like
the utensils and tin cups which furnished the cabins at Plymouth. Still the lessons of Plymouth Rock remain, and other
Plymouths exist on our remote borders. I can take any of
you to-day to some of our military posts on the upper Missouri or in Arizona where the soldiers have to practise the
same economy, the same self-denial, which the Pilgrims did
in their days of trial and exposure, and I assure you that your
words of greeting will be as welcome to them in their rude
huts and dugouts as though they were your guests here to-
night. How all is changed! Houses and palaces have taken
the place of huts, and abundance replaces the scanty tin cup
of shelled corn; but with them nature is the same. The cold
pinches now as it did then; hunger is the same. Distance
and privation of the society of family and friends remain as
they were when our Pilgrim Fathers banished themselves

from all that was valued on earth for the sake of principle, and our little army to-day is fulfilling the same general object in preparing the way for others to follow, who will extract from the rock its hidden gold and silver and make the desert to blossom with the rose and the corn. The little army of which I have spoken is scattered from the frozen regions of Pembina to that other arid region of Arizona, where General Porter has said the surgeon once recommended that dropsy patients be introduced to increase the supply of water.

Our country is very large, extending from the frigid to the torrid zone; from the Atlantic to the Pacific; and our little regular army of 25,000 men is the connecting link between the present and future; but, in the language of your toast, it is essentially an army of peace, preparing the way for future States and future civil communities, and I hope the day will come when even at Fort Yuma there will be a celebration like this at Delmonico's, celebrating their past hardships and privations in abundance and luxury. I repeat that the army is now one of peace, engaged in preparing the way for the expansion of peaceful communities. But I see that your minds and thoughts revert to a period only ten years ago, when this whole nation was in arms, when all were soldiers, when, in fact, we were struggling for a national existence. I did not wish to refer to this, but somehow we naturally revert to it. Then the army was numbered by millions of men and the war was essentially a struggle between two branches of civilization. The North prevailed and naturally their phase of civilization became predominant, and the principles of Plymouth Rock became the standard for this country. By it I mean that freedom of thought and speech, the assertion of the rights of man, the individual to go where he chooses, and to exercise all the privileges of a freeman, which characterized our fathers—a freedom that conceded to all others the same rights and privileges he claimed for himself, giving to the black man absolute freedom and assuring to the Japanese, whose minister sits side my side, that his people may freely come and soon enjoy all the privileges and advantages of the native-born American. Still my belief is that the English-speaking races that first settled our Atlantic shores will prevail on this continent, that their civilization will prevail over all others; that their forms of education, refinement, fidelity to contracts, forms of business, will be the standard law and custom of the country. As to our Southern brethren I believe it is universally conceded that since the Christian era there never has been a case where the conquerors so promptly conceded to the conquered all the rights they themselves possessed, not only the rights to live in peace, to share in the business and prosperity of the whole country, but actually to share in its government, and the army was among the first to share with them their rations the moment hostilities ceased; and I believe, if they accept these terms in the spirit they were granted, that peace henceforth will prevail in all our country; but should they have anything in reserve, any boast of the " Old Confederacy," that a storm would arise in the land tenfold more furious than was the last.

I am sorry to hear so much talk in New York of hard times. I don't see the evidences of it in your streets. I see magnificent equipages and elegantly dressed people, and the signs of luxury and extravagance everywhere. If your Pilgrim Fathers had possessed one tenth of the luxuries you now enjoy, they would have considered themselves rich. And were you all to practise their economy in a short while all these complaints would cease. The fact is, too many of our people flock to the cities and want to be merchants and business men. The solution is in the west, where millions of acres remain in a state of nature. In the border States there is land enough to give occupation to another forty millions of people. Food is abundant, but of course there you cannot have the luxuries and advantages of New York city. Therefore I advise the young men, instead of staying here as clerks and porters in stores, to " go west," for there is abundant room and occupation for all who are willing to work. Excuse me. I had no intention to take up so much time or to touch on so great a variety of subjects, but have been drawn on by your interest.

In conclusion I will say that I hear that the necessities of the country will compel a further reduction of our little army. If such be the case, so be it. For one, I am willing to set the example and try once more to turn my sword into a pruning-hook and earn a living as I did before the war; but I advise all in authority to bear in mind the advice of Washington, always to preserve and maintain in this country the nucleus of an army; especially a knowledge of the art of war, so that when danger does come we may not have to do, as we did in our revolutionary days, send to Germany for another Steuben, to teach our soldiers the common drill.

DEVENS

CHARLES DEVENS, orator, jurist, and soldier, was born in Charlestown, Massachusetts, April 4, 1820. He graduated at Harvard College in 1838, studied at the Harvard Law School and began the practice of law in 1841. In 1848-49 he was a member of the State Senate, and from 1849 to 1853 held the office of United States marshal for the district of Massachusetts. In 1854 he resumed the practice of law in Worcester, but on April 19, 1861, entered the army, having accepted the office of major, commanding an independent battalion of rifles. He served in this capacity for three months, and in July was appointed colonel of the Fifteenth Massachusetts Volunteers. With this regiment he served until 1862, when he was made brigadier-general. Gen. Devens was in the battles of Fair Oaks, Antietam, Fredericksburg, and Chancellorsville, and was several times wounded. After the evacuation of Richmond Devens's troops were the first to occupy it, and he was afterwards brevetted major-general for his gallant conduct at the capture of the city. Gen. Devens remained in the service a year after the termination of hostilities, and then, at his own request, was mustered out in June, 1866. He immediately resumed the practice of his profession in Worcester, and in April, 1867, was appointed a justice of the superior court of Massachusetts. In 1873 he was made a justice of the supreme judicial court of the State, and in 1877 became attorney-general in the cabinet of President Hayes. On his return to Massachusetts he was reappointed a justice of the supreme judicial court, which office he continued to hold until his death, which occurred in Boston January 7, 1891. Gen. Devens was an eloquent and forcible orator, an accomplished jurist, and a gallant soldier. Among his most famous addresses were those delivered at the centennial celebration of the battle of Bunker Hill and the dedication of the soldiers' monuments in Boston and Worcester.

SONS OF HARVARD

SPEECH AT COMMEMORATION EXERCISES HELD AT CAMBRIDGE, JULY 21, 1865

THE sons of Harvard who have served their country on field and flood, in deep thankfulness to Almighty God, who has covered their heads in the day of battle and permitted them to stand again in these ancient halls and under these leafy groves, sacred to so many memories of youth and learning, and in yet deeper thankfulness for the

(8121)

crowning mercy which has been vouchsafed in the complete triumph of our arms over rebellion, return home to-day. Educated only in the arts of peace, unlearned in all that pertained especially to the science of war, the emergency of the hour threw upon them the necessity of grasping the sword.

Claiming only that they have striven to do their duty, they come only to ask their share in the common joy and happiness which our victory has diffused and meet this imposing reception. When they remember in whose presence they stand; that of all the great crowd of the sons of Harvard who are here to-day there is not one who has not contributed his utmost to the glorious consummation; that those who have been blessed with opulence have expended with the largest and most lavish hand in supplying the government with the sinews of war and sustaining everywhere the distressed upon whom the woes of war fell; that those less large in means although not in heart have not failed to pour out most tenderly of time and care, of affection and love, in the thousand channels that have been opened; that the statesmen and legislators whose wise counsels and determined spirit have brought us thus far in safety and honor are here,—would that their task were as completely done as ours!—yet sure I am that in their hands "the pen will not lose by writing what the sword has won by fighting;" that the poets whose fiery lyrics roused us as when

"Tyrtæus called aloud to arms,"

and who have animated the living and celebrated the dead in the noblest strains are here; that our orators whose burning words have so cheered the gloom of the long controversy are here, although with all we lament that one voice so often heard through the long night of gloom was not permitted to greet with us the morning.   Surrounded by memories such as his, surrounded by men such as these, we may well feel at receiving this noble testimonial of your regard that it is rather you who are generous in bestowing than we who are rich in deserving.   Nor do we forget the guests who honor us by their presence to-day, chief among whom we recognize his Excellency the Governor of Massachusetts, who although he wears the civilian's coat bears as stout a heart as beats under any soldier's jacket, and who has sent his men by the thousands and tens of thousands to fight in this great battle; and the late commanding general of the Army of the Potomac under whom so many of us have fought.   If the wide and comprehensive plans of our great lieutenant-general have marked him as the Ulysses of a holier and mightier epic than Homer ever dreamed, in the presence of the great captain who fairly turned the tide of the rebellion on the hills above Gettysburg, we shall not have to look far for its Achilles.

Yet, sir, speaking always of others as you have called on me to speak for them it seems to me that the record of the sons of the university who have served in the war is not unworthy of her.   In any capacity where service was honorable or useful they have rendered it.   In the departments of science they have been conspicuous, and the skill of the engineer upon whom we so often depended was not seldom derived from the schools of this university.   In surgery they have by learning and judgment alleviated the woes of thousands.   And in the ministration of that religion in whose name this university was founded they have not been less devoted; not only have cheering words gone forth from their pulpits, but they have sought the hospitals where the wounded were dying, or like Fuller at Fredericksburg, have laid down their lives on the field where armed hosts were contending.

All these were applying the principles of their former education to new sets of circumstances; but, as you well remember, by far the larger portion of our number were of the combatants of the army, and the facility they displayed in adopting the profession of arms affords an admirable addition to the argument by which it has been heretofore maintained that the general education of our colleges was best for all who could obtain it, as affording a basis upon which any superstructure of usefulness might be raised. Readily mastering the tactics and detail of the profession, proving themselves able to grapple with its highest problems, their courage and gallantry were proverbial.

It would be a great mistake to suppose that all that was added to our army by such men as these was merely what it gained in physical force and manly prowess. Our neighbors on the other side of the water, whose attachment to monarchy is so strong that it sometimes makes them unjust to republics, have sometimes attacked the character and discipline of our army. Nothing could be more unjust. The federal army was noble, self-sacrificing, devoted always, and to the discipline of that army no men contributed more than the members of this university and men such as they. They bore always with them the loftiest principle in the contest and the highest honor in all their personal relations. Disorder in camp, pillage and plunder, found in them stern and unrelenting foes. They fought in a cause too sacred, they wore a robe too white, to be willing to stain or sully it with such corruption.

Mr. President, I should ill do the duty you have called on me to perform if I forgot that this ceremonial is not only a reception of those who return, but a commemoration of those who have laid down their lives for the service of the country.

He who should properly have spoken for us, the oldest of our graduates, although not of our members who have fought in this war,—Webster of the class of 1833, sealed his faith with his life on the bloody field of the second Manassas, dying for the constitution of which his great father was the noblest expounder. For those of us who return to-day, whatever our perils and dangers may have been, we cannot feel that we have done enough to merit what you so generously bestow; but for those with whom the work of this life is finished and yet who live forever inseparably linked with the great names of the founders of the Republic, and not them alone, but the heroes and martyrs of liberty everywhere, we know that no honor can be too much. The voices which rang out so loud and clear upon the charging cheer that heralded the final assault in the hour of victory, that in the hour of disaster were so calm and resolute as they sternly struggled to stay the slow retreat are not silent yet. To us and those who will come after us, they will speak of comfort and home relinquished, of toil nobly borne, of danger manfully encountered, of life generously surrendered, and this not for pelf or ambition, but in the spirit of the noblest self-devotion and the most exalted patriotism. Proud as we who are here to-day have a right to be that we are the sons of this university, and not deemed unworthy of her when these are remembered, we may well say, " Sparta had many a worthier son than we."

ORATION AT THE DEDICATION OF THE SOLDIERS' AND SAILORS' MONUMENT ON BOSTON COMMON

DELIVERED IN BOSTON, SEPTEMBER 17, 1877

M R. MAYOR, FELLOW CITIZENS, AND COM-RADES,—On the anniversary of a day thrice memorable as that of the first settlement of this town in 1630; as that of the adoption of the constitution of the United States in 1789; as that of a great battle fought for the Union on the soil of Maryland in 1862 (the victorious commander in which is to-day among our most honored and illustrious guests), we have assembled to dedicate this monument to the memory of the brave who fell in that great conflict which, commencing for the unity of the government, broadened and deepened into one for the equal rights of all men.

Before we part, some words should be spoken seeking to express, however inadequately, our gratitude to those to whom it is devoted. Yet our ceremonial will be but vain and empty if its outward acts are not the expressions of feelings deeper than either acts or words. Its true dedication is to be found in the emotions which have been kindled by the occasion itself, and to which every heart has yielded.

Here in this city, the capital of Massachusetts, a State from which more than sixty gallant regiments were sent to the field under the inspiration of her illustrious governor, who now himself sleeps with those whom he sent forth to battle, we seek to surrender by this solemn act, from the age that is passing to the ages that are coming, for eternal memory and honor, the just fame of those who have died for the Union.

This is no monument to the glories of war. While great changes for good have been wrought, and great steps taken toward liberty and civilization, by the convulsive energies exhibited in wars, these are but exceptions to the great rule that, of all the causes which have degraded nations, opposed human progress, and oppressed industry, war has been one of the worst. If this were its object it were better far that the stones which compose it had slumbered in their native quarries. No pomp and circumstance, no waving of banners, no dancing of plumes, can lend to war true dignity. This is to be found alone in a great and noble cause.

Nor is this a monument to valor only. There is something honorable in the true solider who, resolutely hazarding life, stands for the flag he follows; but there is that which is higher and nobler here. Among the finest monuments of Europe is that which is found in the beautiful valley of Lucerne to the memory of the Swiss Guard who fell around Louis XVI when the furious mob had stormed his palace. Placed in a niche of the limestone cliff, of which it forms a part, a lion pierced with a spear still holds in his death-grip the shield on which are carved the arms of the Bourbon. Few works of art are more majestic or more fully show the hand of the master. It is courage only that it honors, and you wonder at the power which has so enobled and dignified it when the great idea of patriotism was wanting. The Swiss whom it commemorates simply did bravely the work which they had contracted to do when the subjects of the king, whose bread they had eaten and whose wine they had drank, deserted him.

The men whom we commemorate were brave as these, yet their place in history is not with them. It is with the soldiers of liberty who have fallen a willing sacrifice for country with

patriotic devotion.   It is with the Swiss who at Sempach or
Morgarten, in defence of their own freedom, broke the power
of the House of Austria, and not with the mercenaries whom
they have sent to fight the battles of Europe.

The sentiment of this monument is patriotism.   The men
whom it honors were soldiers, courageous to the death; but
it is their cause which sets them apart, for just honor and
commendation, among the millions who have laid down their
lives upon the battle-field.   Patriotism such as theirs is the
highest of civic virtues, the noblest form of heroism.   Those
who perilled their lives in obedience to its promptings could
gain no more than those who remained at home in inglorious
ease; and yet they laid aside their hopes of comfort to die
for us.

That the government they had lived under might be preserved, that the just and equal rights of all men might be
maintained, they encountered disease, danger, and death in
all the horrid forms in which they present themselves to
every one who takes his place in the ranks of an army, with
the solemn belief that in no other way could they discharge
the obligation imposed upon them by their birthright as citizens of a free country.   Whatever might be its difficulties
and dangers, their path was so clearly indicated that they
deemed they could not err in following it.   When they
fought and fell they could not know but that their efforts
would be in vain, and the great Flag, the symbol of our
united sovereignty, be rent asunder; but they were ready
to risk all and to dare all in the effort to deserve success.

They were animated by no fierce fire of ambition; no desire to exalt themselves; no expectation of attaining those
rewards which are gained by great chieftains.   They had
no such hopes.   They knew well that all the honor they

could obtain was that general meed of praise awarded to all who serve faithfully, but which would not separate them from others who had been brave and true. No doubt, as the blood of youth was high in their veins they looked forward, in some instances, to the stern joy of the conflict; but beyond and above its tempest, fire, and smoke they beheld and strove for the great objects of the contest.

To-day they have seemed to come again as when they moved out in serried lines with the flag which they went to defend waving above their heads. Again we have seemed to see them, their faces lighted with patriotic enthusiasm, and we have recalled the varied scenes of their stern and manly service which was to end in a soldier's death for the country to which they had devoted themselves; in each and every fortune patient and determined, staining their cause with no weakness or cowardice, dishonoring it by no baseness or cruelty.

When we reflect how little our system of education is calculated to adapt men to the restraints of military service, how inconsistent its largeness and freedom is with that stern control which necessarily marks a system intended to give a single mind the power which is embodied in thousands of men, we may well wonder at the ready submission which was always given to its exactions.

To some the possession of marked military qualities, adapting them to control others, gave prominence; to some mere accidents of time or circumstance may have given high commands; while others, not less worthy, filled only their places and did their duty in the ranks. But those who led must often have felt that their highest desire should be to be worthy of the devotion of those who followed. The distinctions necessary to discipline have long since passed away.

Side by side, on fields bought by their blood, " no useless coffins around their breasts," but wrapped in the blanket which is the soldier's martial shroud, awaiting the coming of the Eternal Day, they rest together.

What matter is it while men have given of their utmost in intellect, strength, and courage, and of their blood to the last drop, whether they fell with the stars of the general, the eagles of the colonel, on their shoulders, or in the simple jacket of the private? Wherever " on fame's eternal camping-ground their silent tents are spread," in the tangled wildwood, in the stately cemetery, or in nameless graves, not even marked by the word " unknown," the earth that bears them dead bears not alive more true or noble men. To-day we remember them all, without regard to rank or race, seeking to honor those whom we cannot by name identify.

If we do not commend patriotism such as these men exhibited, to whom are we to turn in the hour of danger which may come to those who are to succeed us, as it did to ourselves? Lessons such as they have given are not to be idly neglected when the time is gone when their services have ceased to be of immediate value. We shall not need to go to Marathon and Platea for examples, whose brethren have shed their blood on fields as fiercely contested as those; and it would be idle to go anywhere for examples unless, in rendering homage to the valor and patriotism displayed by our brethren, we seek to reconsecrate ourselves to the same virtues.

Every instinct of justice calls upon us for the appropriate meed of praise, every suggestion of wisdom counsels that we omit no opportunity to instil into others the admiration with which their deeds are regarded. The fables of romance, which, in some form, each nation of Europe has, that in great emergencies their illustrious chiefs will return again to rescue them, are not altogether myths. To each people that loves bravery and patriotism come again in their hour of trial the old heroic souls, although the form and garb they wear is of their present age and time.

The time for natural tears has passed. To every heart the years have brought their new store of joys and sorrows since these men made their great sacrifice for country. The structure that we have reared stands to honor, and not to mourn, the dead. So shall it stand when we in our turn are gone, to teach its lesson of duty nobly done, at the expense of life itself, to those who are in turn to take upon themselves the duties of life.

Those whose names it honors were known and loved by us, and are not to be recalled but with that manly sorrow born of respect and love. There are those also to whom they were even nearer and dearer than to us, who knew them as comrades, whose homes are forever darkened by the absence of the light of affection which their presence shed around them. But the age comes swiftly on which is to know them only by their deeds. We commend them to the grave and impartial tribunal of history as patriotic and devoted citizens; we invoke the considerate judgment of the world upon the justice of their cause; we renew and reiterate the assertion that there was a solemn duty laid upon them by their time, their place, their country, and that such duty they met and performed. To them, as to the Spartans who fell around their king in stern defence of the liberties of Greece, changing but the name of the battle-field, apply the words which Simonides uttered:

> " Of those who at Thermopylæ were slain,
>   Glorious the doom and beautiful th ot.
>   Their tomb an altar, men from tears re rain,
>   Honor and praise, but mourn them not."

Although this monument may often be passed as a thing of custom, although the lesson which it teaches may seem to be forgotten, yet in the hour of trial, if it is to come to others as it came to us, it will be freshly remembered. As in the Roman story which tells of Hannibal, the mightiest enemy Rome ever knew, it is related that his father, Hamilcar, himself a chieftain and a warrior, whose renown has been eclipsed by that of his greater son, brought him when a child of nine years old into the Temple of the Gods, that he might lift his little hands to swear eternal hostility to the tyranny of Rome: so shall those who succeed us come here to swear hostility, not to one grasping power only, but to every tyranny that would enslave the body or enchain the mind of man, and eternal devotion to the great principles of civil and religious liberty.

Nor is this monument, while it asserts our belief in the fidelity of these men, in any sense unkind or ungenerous toward those with whom they were engaged in deadly strife. It bears no words of boasting or unseemly exultation, and the assertion of the justice of their cause, though firmly made, is yet not made in any harsh or controversial spirit. We recognize fully that those with whom they warred were our countrymen; we know their valor and determination; we know that no foot of ground was yielded to us until to hold it became impossible, and that they resisted until men and means utterly and hopelessly failed.

Whatever we may think of their cause, that as a people they believed in it cannot fairly be questioned. Men do not sacrifice life and property without stint or measure except in the faith that they are right. Upon individuals we may charge unreasonable temper, intolerance, passion, and the promptings of a selfish and ill-regulated ambition; but the whole body of a people do not act from motives thus personal, and have a right to have their bravery and sincerity admitted, even if more cannot be conceded.

The great conflict was fought out and the victory won which has established forever, if the force of arms can establish anything, that the Republic is one and indivisible, and amid the roar of battle and the clash of arms the institution of slavery, which divided us as a nation, which made of the States two classes diverse and discordant, has passed away. Perhaps, if we had fully known all that it was to cost, both at the North and South, we should have hesitated more than we did before engaging in a strife so deadly and terrible.

Yet, as we consider all the woes which must have followed the dismemberment of the Union, as we contemplate the vast gain for peace, freedom, and equality by the emancipation of the subject race from slavery and the dominant race itself from the corrupting influence of this thraldom, who shall say that we have any right to deplore the past except with mitigated grief? We are yet too near the events through which we were swept upon the bloody currents of the war to appreciate their full extent and magnitude, or all the consequences which are to flow from them.

We know already that we enter upon a higher plane of national life, when it is established that there are no exceptions to the great rules of liberty among men, and that each is entitled to the just rewards of his labor and the position to which his talents, ability, and virtue entitle him. As we stand here in memory of our gallant dead we urge upon all who have contended with them to unite with us in the effort to make of our new and regenerated government, purified by the fires of our civil conflict, a Republic more noble and more august than its founders had dared to hope.

Among all patriotic men there is everywhere an earnest desire that there shall be full peace and reconciliation between the sections of the Union. Whatever may have been former divisions there is nothing in the events of the past, there is nothing in the present condition of things, which should forbid this. We can stand, firmly and securely stand, upon that which has been definitely settled by the war.

Ours was not a mere conflict of dynasties or of families, like the English Wars of the Roses, in which the great houses of York and Lancaster disputed the English crown. It was a great elemental conflict, in which two opposite systems of civilization were front to front and face to face. It was necessary that one or the other should conquer and that it should be settled whether the continent should be all free or all slave. Yet the history of civil wars demonstrates that the widest and saddest differences of religion, the most radical differences as to the form of government, have not prevented firm union when the cause of dissension was obliterated.

Now that it is determined that Union is to exist, it must be rendered one of mutual respect and regard as well as of mutual interest. Unless this is the case there is no cohesive pressure of either internal or external force strong enough to maintain it. There must have been a party victorious and a party vanquished; but there is no true victory anywhere unless the conclusion is for the interest of each and all. It is not the least of the just claims that the American revolution has upon the friends of liberty everywhere, that, while it terminated in the dismemberment of the British empire, it left the English a more free people than they would have been but for its occurrence. It settled for them more firmly the great safeguards of English liberty in the right of the habeas corpus, the trial by jury, and the great doctrine that representation must accompany taxation. We speak of it as the victory of Adams and Jefferson, but it was not less that of Chatham and Burke.

I should deem the war for the Union a failure, I should think the victory won by these men who have died in its defence barren, if it shall not prove in every larger sense won for the South as well as the North; if it shall not be shown that it is better for her that the contest against its rightful authority failed.

It is not to be expected that opinion will be changed by edicts, even when those edicts are maintained by force. The changes of opinion must be gradual and must be the effect of that time which enables feeling to subside and the judgment to act. Already there are brave and reflecting men who fought against us who do not hesitate to acknowledge that the end was well for them as for us, and who look forward hopefully to better results than could have been expected from a Confederacy which, if it had been founded, would have been at the mercy of each individual State.

Nor is there any one bold enough to say, now that the system of slavery is destroyed, he would raise a hand or lift a finger to replace it. That the cause for which they have suffered so much will still be dear to those who have fought for it, or with whom it is associated by tender and affectionate recollections of those whom they have loved, who have fallen in its defence, is to be expected. To such sentiments and feelings it is a matter of indifference whether there is defeat or success. They would exist, indeed, even if the reason and judgment should concede the cause to have been unwise. Certainly we ourselves, had the war for the Union failed, would not the less have believed it just and necessary, nor the less have honored the memory of those engaged in it. When results are accepted cordially we can ask no more until the softening influences of time have done their work.

On the fields which were ploughed by the fierce artillery the wheat has been dancing fresh and fair in the breezes of the summer that is gone; and as the material evidences of the conflict pass away, so let each feeling of bitterness disappear, as together, both North and South, we strive to render the Republic one whose firm yet genial sway shall protect with just and equal laws each citizen who yields obedience to her power.

Asking for ourselves no rights that we do not freely concede to others, demanding no restraints upon others that we do not readily submit to ourselves, yielding a generous obedience to the constitution in all its parts, both new and old, let us endeavor to lift ourselves to that higher level of patriotism which despises any narrow sectionalism and rejoices in a nationality broad enough to embrace every section of the Union and each one of its people, whether high or humble, rich or poor, black or white.

There is no division to-day among the States of the Union such as existed when the constitution was formed. In each and all the great principles of liberty and equal rights are the same, to be alike respected as the only basis upon which the government can stand. Whatever may have been the sorrows or the losses of the war, there is no sorrow that cannot find its recompense in the added grandeur and dignity of the whole country.

Comrades, it is the last time that we, who have marched under the flag and been the soldiers of the Union in its mortal struggle, shall gather in such numbers as meet to-day. We are an army to whom can come no recruits. The steady, resistless artillery of time hurls its deadly missiles upon us, and each hour we are fewer and weaker. But, as we stand together thus, as we remember how nobly and bravely life's work was done by these men whom we have sought to commemorate, let us believe that the tie which binds us to them in a great and holy cause is not wholly dissolved. Their worldly task is done, their solemn oath, which we took side by side with them, is performed. For us life brings each day its new duties and new responsibilities.

In the classic mythology, which was the religion of the ancient world, it was fabled that the heroes were demi-gods. Raised above the race of man, and yet not so far but their example might be imitated, they served to animate those who yet struggled with their mortal surroundings. So should these, our heroes, while the dust of life's conflict is yet on us, inspire us to loftier purposes and nobler lives. And, as we leave them to their glorious repose and their pure and noble fame, let us go forth exalted by these hours of communion with them.

Above them, as we depart, we utter the ancient form of words, and yet in no formal way, which conclude the proclamations of the State whose children they were: "God save the Commonwealth of Massachusetts!" And to this we add, with not less of fervor or solemnity, the prayer which was in their hearts and upon their lips as they died: "God save the Union of the American States!"

VALLANDIGHAM

C LEMENT LAIRD VALLANDIGHAM, a once prominent American politician, was born at New Lisbon, Ohio, July 29, 1820, and educated at Jefferson College in Pennsylvania. He studied law and was admitted to the bar in 1842, and after practising his profession for a short time in Columbus, Ohio, removed to Dayton in the same State. He sat in the State legislature, 1845-46, and edited the "Dayton Empire," 1847-49. During this period he became well known not only as an able lawyer and an eloquent speaker, but as an extreme pro-slavery advocate. After several unsuccessful congressional contests he entered Congress at length in 1858, and served there until 1863. In Congress he made several singularly audacious attacks upon the administration for its conduct of the Civil War, on December 5, 1862, offering a series of resolutions directed against the war, and in the following January delivering an impassioned speech condemning it. After the expiration of his congressional term, Vallandigham delivered many bitter and violent speeches in Ohio against the administration, and in May, 1863, was arrested by General Burnside for having declared the war to be "cruel and unnecessary," tried by court-martial and sentenced to close imprisonment. His sentence was however changed by President Lincoln to banishment within the Confederate lines. The arrest and sentence provoked extended controversy in the press and in public gatherings, the Democrats as a body denouncing the action of the military commission, and the Republicans justifying it in some cases and in others regretting it. Not meeting with a cordial reception in the South, Vallandigham escaped to Canada, and while in exile was nominated for governor of Ohio, but was defeated by a large majority. The next year he returned to Ohio unmolested and resumed his profession. During the conduct of a murder trial at Lebanon, Ohio, on June 17, 1871, Vallandigham attempted to illustrate his theory of the shooting; in doing this the pistol was accidentally discharged, killing him instantly.

SPEECH ON THE WAR AND ITS CONDUCT

DELIVERED IN THE HOUSE OF REPRESENTATIVES, JANUARY 14, 1863

S IR,—I am one of that number who have opposed abolitionism, or the political development of the anti-slavery sentiment of the North and West, from the beginning. In school, at college, at the bar, in public assemblies, in the legislature, in Congress, boy and man, in time of peace and in time of war, at all times and at every sacrifice, I have fought against it. It cost me ten years' exclusion from office and honor at that period of life when honors are sweetest. No matter; I learned early to do right and to wait.

Sir, it is but the development of the spirit of intermeddling, whose children are strife and murder. Cain troubled himself about the sacrifices of Abel and slew his brother. Most of the wars, contentions, litigations, and bloodshed, from the beginning of time have been its fruits. The spirit of non-intervention is the very spirit of peace and concord.

I do not believe that if slavery had never existed here we would have had no sectional controversies. This very civil war might have happened fifty, perhaps a hundred, years later. Other and stronger causes of discontent and of dis-union, it may be, have existed between other states and sections, and are now being developed every day into maturity. The spirit of intervention assumed the form of abolitionism because slavery was odious in name and by association to the Northern mind, and because it was that which most obviously marks the different civilizations of the two sections.

The South herself, in her early and later efforts to rid her-self of it, had exposed the weak and offensive parts of slavery to the world. Abolition intermeddling taught her at last to search for and defend the assumed social, economic, and political merit and values of the institution. But there never was an hour from the beginning when it did not seem to me as clear as the sun at broad noon that the agitation in any form, in the North and West, of the slavery question must sooner or later end in disunion and civil war.

This was the opinion and prediction for years of Whig and Democratic statesmen alike; and, after the unfortunate dissolution of the Whig party in 1854, and the organization of the present Republican party upon the exclusive anti-slavery and sectional basis, the event was inevitable, because in the then existing temper of the public mind, and after the education through the press and the pulpit, the lecture and the political canvass, for twenty years, of a generation taught to hate slavery and the South, the success of that party, possessed as it was of every engine of political, business, social, and religious influence, was certain.

It was only a question of time, and short time. Such was its strength, indeed, that I do not believe that the union of the Democratic party in 1860 on any candidate, even though he had been supported also by the entire so-called conservative or anti-Lincoln vote of the country, would have availed to defeat it; and, if it had, the success of the Abolition party would only have been postponed four years longer. The disease had fastened too strongly upon the system to be healed until it had run its course.

The doctrine of "the irrepressible conflict" had been taught too long and accepted too widely and earnestly to die out until it should culminate in secession and disunion, and, if coercion were resorted to, then in civil war. I believed from the first that it was the purpose of some of the apostles of that doctrine to force a collision between the North and the South, either to bring about a separation or to find a vain but bloody pretext for abolishing slavery in the States. In any event I knew, or thought I knew, that the end was certain collision and death to the Union.

Believing thus, I have for years past denounced those who taught that doctrine with all the vehemence, the bitterness, if you choose—I thought it a righteous, a patriotic bitterness—of an earnest and impassioned nature. Thinking thus, I forewarned all who believed the doctrine, or followed the party which taught it, with a sincerity and a depth of conviction as profound as ever penetrated the heart of man.

And when, for eight years past, over and over again, I have proclaimed to the people that the success of a sectional anti-slavery party would be the beginning of disunion and civil war in America, I believed it. I did.

I had read history and studied human nature and meditated for years upon the character of our institutions and form of government, and of the people south as well as north; and I could not doubt the event.

But the people did not believe me, nor those older and wiser and greater than I. They rejected the prophecy and stoned the prophets. The candidate of the Republican party was chosen president. Secession began. Civil war was imminent. It was no petty insurrection, no temporary combination to obstruct the execution of the laws in certain States, but a revolution, systematic, deliberate, determined, and with the consent of a majority of the people of each State which seceded.

Causeless it may have been, wicked it may have been, but there it was—not to be railed at, still less to be laughed at, but to be dealt with by statesmen as a fact. No display of vigor or force alone, however sudden or great, could have arrested it even at the outset. It was disunion at last. The wolf had come, but civil war had not yet followed. In my deliberate and solemn judgment there was but one wise and masterly mode of dealing with it. Non-coercion would avert civil war and compromise crush out both abolitionism and secession. The parent and the child would thus both perish.

But a resort to force would at once precipitate war, hasten secession, extend disunion, and while it lasted utterly cut off

all hope of compromise. I believed that war, if long enough
continued, would be final, eternal disunion. I said it; I
meant it; and accordingly to the utmost of my ability and
influence I exerted myself in behalf of the policy of non-
coercion. It was adopted by Mr. Buchanan's administration
with the almost unanimous consent of the Democratic and
Constitutional Union parties in and out of Congress; and in
February, with the consent of a majority of the Republican
party in the Senate and the House.

But that party most disastrously for the country refused
all compromise. How, indeed, could they accept any? That
which the South demanded, and the Democratic and conservative parties of the North and West were willing to grant, and
which alone could avail to keep the peace and save the Union
implied a surrender of the sole vital element of the party,
and its platform, of the very principle, in fact, upon which
it had just won the contest for the presidency, not, indeed, by
a majority of the popular vote—the majority was nearly a
million against it,—but under the forms of the constitution.

Sir, the crime, the " high crime," of the Republican party,
was not so much its refusal to compromise, as its original
organization upon a basis and doctrine wholly inconsistent
with the stability of the constitution and the peace of the
Union.

The president-elect was inaugurated; and now, if only the
policy of non-coercion could be maintained, and war thus
averted, time would do its work in the North and the South,
and final peaceable adjustment and reunion be secured.
Some time in March it was announced that the president had
resolved to continue the policy of his predecessor, and even
go a step farther, and evacuate Sumter and the other federal forts and arsenals in the seceded States. His own party,

acquiesced; the whole country rejoiced. The policy of non-coercion had triumphed, and for once, sir, in my life, I found myself in an immense majority.

No man then pretended that a union founded in consent could be cemented by force. Nay, more, the President and the secretary of state went farther. Said Mr. Seward, in an officio-diplomatic letter to Mr. Adams: "For these reasons, he (the President) would not be disposed to reject a cardinal dogma of theirs (the secessionists), namely, that the federal government could not reduce the seceding States to obedience by conquest, although he were disposed to question that proposition. But in fact the President willingly accepts it as true. Only an imperial or despotic government could subjugate thoroughly disaffected and insurrectionary members of the State."

Pardon me, sir, but I beg to know whether this conviction of the President and his secretary is not the philosophy of the persistent and most vigorous efforts made by this administration, and first of all through this same secretary, the moment war broke out, and ever since till the late elections, to convert the United States into an imperial or despotic government?

But Mr. Seward adds, and I agree with him: "This federal republican system of ours is, of all forms of government, the very one which is most unfitted for such a labor."

This, sir, was on the 10th of April, and yet that very day the fleet was under sail for Charleston. The policy of peace had been abandoned. Collision followed; the militia were ordered out; civil war began.

Now, sir, on the 14th of April, I believed that coercion would bring on war, and war disunion. More than that, I believed what you all believe in your hearts to-day, that the

South could never be conquered—never. And not that only but I was satisfied—and you of the Abolition party have now proved it to the world—that the secret but real purpose of the war was to abolish slavery in the States. In any event, I did not doubt that, whatever might be the momentary impulses of those in power, and whatever pledges they might make, in the midst of the fury, for the constitution, the Union, and the flag, yet the natural and inexorable logic of revolutions would sooner or later drive them into that policy and with it to its final but inevitable result, the change of our present democratical form of government into an imperial despotism. These were my convictions on the 14th of April.

Had I changed them on the 15th, when I read the President's proclamation, and become convinced that I had been wrong all my life, and that all history was a fable, and all human nature false in its development from the beginning of time, I would have changed my public conduct also. But my convictions did not change. I thought that if war was disunion on the 14th of April it was equally disunion on the 15th and at all times.

Believing this I could not as an honest man, a union man, and a patriot lend an active support to the war; and I did not. I had rather my right arm were plucked from its socket and cast into eternal burnings than with my convictions to have thus defiled my soul with the guilt of moral perjury. Sir, I was not taught in that school which proclaims that " all is fair in politics." I loathe, abhor, and detest the execrable maxim. I stamp upon it. No State can endure a single generation whose public men practise it. Whoever teaches it is a corrupter of youth. What we most want in these times, and at all times, is honest and independent public men.

That man who is dishonest in politics is not honest at heart in anything; and sometimes moral cowardice is dishonesty. Do right; and trust to God, and truth, and the people. Perish office, perish honors, perish life itself; but do the thing that is right, and do it like a man.

Certainly, sir, I could not doubt what he must suffer who dare defy the opinions and the passions, not to say the madness, of twenty millions of people. Had I not read history? Did I not know human nature? But I appealed to time; and right nobly hath the avenger answered me. I did not support the war; and to-day I bless God that not the smell of so much as one drop of its blood is upon my garments. Sir, I censure no brave man who rushed patriotically into this war; neither will I quarrel with any one here or elsewhere who gave to it an honest support. Had their convictions been mine, I too would doubtless have done as they did. With my convictions I could not.

But I was a representative. War existed—by whose act no matter—not by mine. The President, the Senate, the House, and the country all said that there should be war— war for the Union; a union of consent and good will. Our Southern brethren were to be whipped back into love and fellowship at the point of the bayonet. O, monstrous delusion! I can comprehend a war to compel a people to accept a master; to change a form of government; to give up territory; to abolish a domestic institution—in short, a war of conquest and subjugation; but a war for union! Was the Union thus made? Was it ever thus preserved?

Sir, history will record that after nearly six thousand years of folly and wickedness in every form and administration of government—theocratic, democratic, monarchic, oligarchic, despotic, and mixed—it was reserved to American statesmanship in the nineteenth century of the Christian era to try the grand experiment on a scale the most costly and gigantic in its proportions, of creating love by force and developing fraternal affection by war! And history will record, too, on the same page the utter, disastrous, and most bloody failure of the experiment.

But to return: the country was at war; and I belonged to that school of politics which teaches that when we are at war the government—I do not mean the executive alone, but the government—is entitled to demand and have, without resistance, such number of men and such amount of money and supplies generally as may be necessary for the war, until an appeal can be had to the people. Before that tribunal alone, in the first instance, must the question of the continuance of the war be tried. This was Mr. Calhoun's opinion, and he laid it down very broadly and strongly in a speech on the loan bill in 1841. Speaking of supplies, he said: " I hold that there is a distinction in this respect between a state of peace and war. In the latter the right of withholding supplies ought ever to be held subordinate to the energetic and successful prosecution of the war. I go further, and regard the withholding of supplies, with a view of forcing the country into a dishonorable peace, as not only to be what it has been called, moral treason, but very little short of actual treason itself."

Upon this principle, sir, he acted afterward in the Mexican war. Speaking of that war in 1847 he said: "Every senator knows that I was opposed to the war; but none but myself knows the depth of that opposition. With my conception of its character and consequences it was impossible for me to vote for it." And again, in 1848: " But after war was declared by authority of the government I acquiesced in what I could not prevent, and which it was impossible for me to arrest; and I then felt it to be my duty to limit my efforts to give such direction to the war as would as far as possible prevent the evils and dangers with which it threatened the country and its institutions."

Sir, I adopt all this as my own position and my defence, though perhaps in a civil war I might fairly go farther in opposition. I could not, with my convictions, vote men and money for this war, and I would not as a representative vote against them. I meant, that without opposition, the President might take all the men and all the money he should demand, and then to hold him to a strict accountability before the people for the results. Not believing the soldiers responsible for the war or its purposes or its consequences, I have never withheld my vote where their separate interests were concerned. But I have denounced from the beginning the usurpations and the infractions, one and all, of law and constitution, by the President and those under him; their repeated and persistent arbitrary arrests, the suspension of habeas corpus, the violation of freedom of the mails, of the private house, of the press, and of speech, and all the other multiplied wrongs and outrages upon public liberty and private right which have made this country one of the worst despotisms on earth for the past twenty months, and I will continue to rebuke and denounce them to the end; and the people, thank God, have at last heard and heeded and rebuked them too. To the record and to time I appeal again for my justification.

And now, sir, I recur to the state of the Union to-day. What is it? Sir, twenty months have elapsed, but the rebellion is not crushed out; its military power has not been broken; the insurgents have not dispersed. The Union is not restored; nor the constitution maintained; nor the laws enforced. Twenty, sixty, ninety, three hundred, six hundred days have passed; a thousand millions been expended; and three hundred thousand lives lost or bodies mangled; and to-day the Confederate flag is still near the Potomac and the Ohio, and the Confederate government stronger, many times, than at the beginning. Not a State has been restored, not any part of any State has voluntarily returned to the Union. And has anything been wanting that Congress, or the States, or the people in their most generous enthusiasm, their most impassionate patriotism, could bestow?

Was it power? And did not the party of the executive control the entire federal government, every State government, every county, every city, town, and village in the North and West?

Was it patronage? All belonged to it. Was it influence? What more? Did not the school, the college, the church, the press, the secret orders, the municipality, the corporation, railroads, telegraphs, express companies, the voluntary association, all, all yield it to the utmost?

Was it unanimity? Never was an administration so supported in England or America. Five men and half a score of newspapers made up the opposition.

Was it enthusiasm? The enthusiasm was fanatical. There has been nothing like it since the Crusades.

Was it confidence? Sir, the faith of the people exceeded that of the patriarch. They gave up constitution, law, right, liberty, all at your demand for arbitrary power that the rebellion might, as you promised, be crushed out in three months and the Union restored.

Was credit needed? You took control of a country,

young, vigorous, and inexhaustible in wealth and resources, and of a government almost free from public debt, and whose good faith had never been tarnished. Your great national loan bubble failed miserably as it deserved to fail; but the bankers and merchants of Philadelphia, New York, and Boston lent you more than their entire banking capital. And when that failed, too, you forced credit by declaring your paper promises to pay a legal tender for all debts.

Was money wanted? You had all the revenues of the United States, diminished indeed, but still in gold. The whole wealth of the country, to the last dollar lay at your feet. Private individuals, municipal corporations, the State governments, all in their frenzy, gave you money or means with reckless prodigality. The great eastern cities lent you $150,000,000. Congress voted, first, $250,000,000 and next $500,000,000 more in loans; and then, first $50,000,000, next $10,000,000, then $90,000,000, and in July last, $150,000,000 in treasury notes; and the secretary has issued also a paper " postage currency," in sums as low as five cents, limited in amount only by his discretion.

Nay, more : already since the 4th of July, 1861, this House has appropriated $2,017,864,000, almost every dollar without debate and without a recorded vote. A thousand millions have been expended since the 15th of April, 1861; and a public debt or liability of $1,500,000,000 already incurred. And to support all this stupendous outlay and indebtedness, a system of taxation, direct and indirect, has been inaugurated, the most onerous and unjust ever imposed upon any but a conquered people.

Money and credit, then, you have had in prodigal profusion. And were men wanted? More than 1,000,000 rushed to arms; 75,000 first (and the country stood aghast at the multitude), then 83,000 more were demanded; and 310,000 responded to the call. The President next asked for 400,000, and Congress in their generous confidence, gave him 500,000; and, not to be outdone, he took 637,000. Half of these melted away in their first campaign; and the President demanded 300,000 more for the war, and then drafted yet another 300,000 for nine months. The fabled hosts of Xerxes have been out-numbered.

And yet victory, strangely, follows the standard of the foe. From Great Bethel to Vicksburg, the battle has not been to the strong. Yet every disaster except the last has been followed by a call for more troops, and every time so far they have been promptly furnished. From the beginning the war has been conducted like a political campaign, and it has been the folly of the party in power that they have assumed that numbers alone would win the field in a contest not with ballots but with musket and sword.

But numbers, you have had almost without number—the largest, best appointed, best armed, fed, and clad host of brave men, well organized and well disciplined, ever marshalled. A navy, too, not the most formidable perhaps, but the most numerous and gallant, and the costliest in the world, and against a foe almost without a navy at all. Thus with 20,000,000 people, and every element of strength and force at command—power, patronage, influence, unanimity, enthusiasm, confidence, credit, money, men, and army and a navy the largest and the noblest ever set in the field, or afloat upon the sea; with the support, almost servile, of every State, county, and municipality in the North and West, with a Congress swift to do the bidding of the executive; without opposition anywhere at home and with an arbitrary power which neither the Czar of Russia nor the Emperor of Austria dare exercise; yet after nearly two years of more vigorous prosecution of war than ever recorded in history; after more skirmishes, combats and battles than Alexander, Cæsar, or the first Napoleon ever fought in any five years of their military career, you have utterly, signally, disastrously—I will not say ignominiously—failed to subdue 10,000,000 "rebels," whom you had taught the people of the North and West not only to hate, but to despise.

Rebels, did I say? Yes, your fathers were rebels, or your grandfathers. He who now before me on canvas looks down so sadly upon us, the false, degenerate, and imbecile guardians of the great Republic which he founded, was a rebel. And yet we, cradled ourselves in rebellion and who have fostered and fraternized with every insurrection in the nineteenth century everywhere throughout the globe, would now, forsooth, make the word " rebel " a reproach.

Rebels certainly they are; but all the persistent and stupendous efforts of the most gigantic warfare of modern times have through your incompetency and folly availed nothing to crush them out, cut off though they have been, by your blockade from all the world, and dependent only upon their own courage and resources. And yet they were to be utterly conquered and subdued in six weeks or three months.

Sir, my judgment was made up and expressed from the first. I learned it from Chatham: " My lords, you cannot conquer America." And you have not conquered the South. You never will. It is not in the nature of things possible; much less under your auspices. But money you have expended without limit, and blood poured out like water. Defeat, debt, taxation, sepulchres, these are your trophies. In vain, the people gave you treasure, and the soldier yielded

up his life. "Fight, tax, emancipate, let these," said the
gentleman from Maine [Mr. Pike] at the last session, " be
the trinity of our salvation."

Sir, they have become the trinity of your deep damna-
tion. The war for the Union is, in your hands, a most
bloody and costly failure. The President confessed it on the
22d of September, solemnly, officially, and under the broad
seal of the United States. And he has now repeated the
confession. The priests and rabbis of abolition taught him
that God would not prosper such a cause. War for the
Union was abandoned; war for the negro openly begun,
and with stronger battalions than before. With what
success? Let the dead at Fredericksburg and Vicksburg
answer.

And now, sir, can this war continue? Whence the money
to carry it on? Where the men? Can you borrow? From
whom? Can you tax more? Will the people bear it? Wait
till you have collected what is already levied. How many
millions more of " legal tender "—to-day, forty-seven per
cent. below the par of gold—can you float? Will men enlist
now at any price? Ah, sir, it is easier to die at home. I beg
pardon; but I trust I am not " discouraging enlistments." If
I am, then first arrest Lincoln, Stanton, Halleck, and some of
your other generals, and I will retract; yes, I will recant.
But can you draft again? Ask New England—New York.
Ask Massachusetts. Where are the nine hundred thousand?
Ask not Ohio—the Northwest. She thought you in earnest,
and gave you all, all—more than you demanded.

> " The wife whose babe first smiled that day,
>   The fair, fond bride of yester eve,
> And aged sire and matron gray,
> Saw the loved warriors haste away,
>   And deemed it sin to grieve."

Sir, in blood she has atoned for her credulity; and now there is mourning in every house, and distress and sadness in every heart. Shall she give you any more?

But ought this war to continue? I answer, no—not a day, not an hour. What then? Shall we separate? Again I answer, no, no, no! What then? And now, sir, I come to the grandest and most solemn problem of statesmanship from the beginning of time; and to the God of heaven, illuminer of hearts and minds, I would humbly appeal for some measure, at least, of light and wisdom and strength to explore and reveal the dark but possible future of this land.

DAWSON

JOHN WILLIAM DAWSON, an eminent Canadian scientist and educator, was born in October, 1820, at Pictou, Nova Scotia, where his father, the younger son of a Scotch farmer, had settled to engage in business in 1811. He went first to a private school, then to the grammar school and college at Pictou. At the age of fifteen he helped his father in his printing establishment and gained some knowledge of that art. He was especially interested in natural history, mineralogy, geology, and chemistry, and in 1840 he went to Edinburgh to complete his training in those sciences. He returned to Nova Scotia in 1847, and in 1855 was appointed principal of McGill University, which he succeeded in raising to a high degree of efficiency. He took an active part in the establishment of the Royal Society of Canada. In 1884 he was active in promoting the meeting of the British Association at Montreal and was knighted in recognition of his distinguished services in the cause of science and education. In 1886 he presided over the meeting of the Association in Birmingham. Failing health obliged him to resign his principalship in May, 1893, and he died November 19, 1899. Among his works may be mentioned " Archaia " (1858); " Story of the Earth and Man " (1872); " Dawn of Life " (1875); " Origin of the World " (1877); " Fossil Men " (1878); " Change of Life in Geological Time " (1880); " Egypt and Syria " (1885); " The Meeting-Place of Geology and History " (1894), and " Fifty Years of Work in Canada " (1901).

ON THE HIGHER EDUCATION OF WOMEN

FROM LECTURE DELIVERED OCTOBER, 1871, BEFORE THE LADIES' EDUCATIONAL ASSOCIATION

THE ancient Stoics, who derived much of their philosophy from Egypt and the East, believed in a series of great cosmical periods, at the end of each of which the world and all things therein were burned by fire, but only to reappear in the succeeding age on so precisely the same plan that one of these philosophers is reported to have held that in each succeeding cycle there would be a new Xantippe to scold a new Socrates. I have sometimes thought that this illustration expressed not merely their idea of cosmical revolutions, but also the irrepressible and ever recurring conflict of the rights and education of women. Notwithstanding all that may be said to the contrary, I believe that Xantippe was as good a wife as Socrates, or any of his contemporary Greeks deserved. She no doubt kept his house in order, prepared his dinners, and attended to his collars and buttons (if he used such things) and probably had a general love and respect for him. But she was quite incapable of seeing any sense or reason in his philosophy, and must have regarded it as a vexatious waste of time, and possibly as a chronic source of impecuniosity in family affairs.

The educated Greek of her day had small respect for woman, and had no idea of any other mission for her than that of being a domestic drudge. No one had ever taught Xantippe philosophy, hence she despised it, and being a woman of character and energy she made herself felt as a thorn in the flesh of her husband and his associates. In this way Xantippe derived from her husband's wisdom only a provocation of her own bad temper, and he lost all the benefits of the loving sympathy of a kindred soul; and thus the best and purest of heathen philosophers found no help-meet for him.

So Xantippe becomes a specimen of the typical uneducated woman in her relation to the higher departments of learning and human progress. In ordinary circumstances she may be a useful household worker. If emancipated from this she may spread her butterfly wings in thoughtless frivolity, but she treats the higher interests and efforts of humanity with stolid unconcern, or insipid levity, or interferes in them with a capricious and clamorous tyranny. In what she does and in what she leaves undone she is equally a drag on the progress of what is good and noble, and the ally and promoter of what is empty, useless, and wasteful. If the Stoics anticipated a perpetual succession of such women they might well be hopeless of the destinies of mankind.

But the Stoics wanted that higher light as to the position and destiny of woman which the Gospel has given to us; and it is a relief to turn from their notions to the testimony of the Word of God. The Bible has some solution for each of the difficult problems of human nature, and it has its own theory on the subject of woman's relations to man.

In the old record in Genesis, Adam, the earth-born, finds no helpmeet for him among the creatures, sprung, like himself, from the ground, but he is given that equal helper in the woman made from himself. In this new relation he assumes a new name. He is no longer Adam, the earthy, but Ish, lord of creation, and his wife is Isha,—he the king and she the queen of the world. Thus in Eden there was a perfect unity and equality of man and woman, as both Moses and our Saviour in commenting on this passage indicate,— though Milton, usually so correct as an interpreter of Genesis, seems partially to overlook this. But a day came when Isha in the exercise of her independent judgment was tempted to sin, and tempted her husband in turn.

Then comes a new dispensation of labor and sorrow and subjection, the fruit, not of God's original arrangement, but of man's fall. Simple as a nursery tale, profounder than any philosophy, this is the Bible theory of the subjection of woman, and of that long succession of wrongs, and sufferings, and self-abnegation which have fallen to her lot as the partner of man in the struggle for existence in a sin-cursed world.

But even here there is a gleam of light. The seed of the woman is to bruise the head of the serpent, and Isha receives a new name, Eve, the mother of life. For in her, in every generation, from that of Eve to that of Mary of Bethlehem, resided the glorious possibility of bringing forth the Deliverer from the evils of the fall. This great prophetic destiny formed the banner of woman's rights, borne aloft over all the generations of the faithful, and rescuing woman from the degradation of heathenism, in which while mythical goddesses were worshipped the real interests of living women were trampled under foot.

The dream of the prophets was at length realized, and in Christianity, for the first time since the gates of Eden closed on fallen man, woman obtained some restoration of her rights. Even here some subjection remains because of present imperfection, but it is lost in the grand status of children of God, shared alike by man and woman; for according to St. Paul, with reference to this divine adoption, there is "neither male nor female."

Our Lord himself has given to the same truth a still higher place, when in answer to the quibble of the Sadducees he uttered the remarkable words, "They who shall be accounted worthy to obtain that world, neither marry nor are given in marriage, for they are equal to the angels."

If both men and women had a higher appreciation of the dignity of their position as children of God; if they would more fully realize that world which was so shadowy to philosophic Sadducee and ritualistic Pharisee, though so real to the mind of Christ, we should have very little disputation about the relative rights here of men or women, and would be more ready to promote every effort, however humble, which may tend to elevate and dignify both. Nor need we fear that we shall ever, by any efforts we can make, approach too near to that likeness to the angels which embraces all that is excellent in intellectual and moral strength, and in exemption from physical evil.

But what bearing has all this on our present object?
Much in many ways, but mainly in this, that while it re-
moves the question of the higher training of women altogether from the sphere of the silly and flippant nonsense so
often indulged in on the subject, it shows the heaven-born
equality of man and woman as alike in the image and likeness of God; the evil origin of the subjection and degradation inflicted on the weaker sex, and the restored position
of woman as a child of God under the Gospel, and as an
aspirant for an equal standing, not with man only, but with
those heavenly hosts which excel in strength.

In this light of the Book of Books, let us proceed to consider some points bearing on our present duty in reference
to this great subject.

Only a certain limited proportion of men or women can
go on to a higher education, and those who are thus selected
are either those who by wealth and social position are enabled to claim this privilege, or those who intend to enter
into professions which are believed to demand a larger
amount of learning. The question of the higher education
of women in any country depends very much on the relative
numbers of these classes among men and women, and on the
views which may be generally held as to the importance of
education for ordinary life, as contrasted with professional
life.

Now, in this country the number of young men who receive a higher education merely to fit them for occupying
a high social position is very small. The greater number of
young men who pass through our colleges do so under the
compulsion of a necessity to fit themselves for certain professions. On the other hand, with the exception of those
young women who receive an education for the profession

of teaching, the great majority of those who obtain what is regarded as higher culture do so merely as a means of general improvement, and to fit themselves better to take their proper place in society.

Certain curious and important consequences flow from this. An education obtained for practical professional purposes is likely to partake of this character in its nature, and to run in the direction rather of hard utility than of ornament; that which is obtained as a means of rendering its possessor agreeable is likely to be æsthetical in its character, rather than practical or useful.

An education pursued as a means of bread-winning is likely to be sought by the active and ambitious of very various social grades; but that which is thought merely to fit for a certain social position is likely to be sought almost exclusively by those who move in that position. An education intended for recognized practical uses is likely to find public support, and to bear a fair market price; that which is supposed to have a merely conventional value as a branch of refined culture is likely to be at a fancy price. Hence it happens that the young men who receive a higher education, and by means of this attain to positions of responsibility and eminence, are largely drawn from the humbler strata of society, while the young women of those social levels rarely aspire to similar advantages.

On the other hand, while numbers of young men of wealthy families are sent into business with a merely commercial education at a very early age, their sisters are occupied with the pursuit of accomplishments of which their more practical brothers never dream. When to all this is added the frequency and rapidity of changes in social standing in a country like this, it is easy to see that an educational chaos

must result, most amusing to any one who can philosophically
contemplate it as an outsider, but most bewildering to those
who have any practical concern with it, especially, I should
suppose, to careful and thoughtful mothers whose minds are
occupied with the connections which their daughters may
form and the positions which they may fill in society.

The educational problem which these considerations
present admits, I believe, of but two general solutions. If
we could involve women in the same necessity for independent exertion and professional work as men, I have no
doubt that in the struggle for existence they would secure
to themselves an equal, perhaps a greater, share of the more
solid kinds of higher education. Some strong-minded women
and chivalrous men in our day favor this solution, which has,
it must be confessed, some show of reason in older countries,
where from unhealthy social conditions great numbers of unmarried women have to contend for their own subsistence.

But it is opposed by all the healthier instincts of our humanity, and in countries like this, where very few women
remain unmarried, it would be simply impracticable. A better solution would be to separate, in the case of both sexes,
professional from general education and to secure a large
amount of the latter of a solid and practical character for
both sexes, both for its own sake and because of its beneficial
results in the promotion of our well-being, considered as individuals, as well as in our family, social, and professional
relations.

This solution also has its difficulties, and it cannot, I fear,
ever be fully worked out until either a higher intellectual
and moral tone is reached in society, or until nations visit
with proper penalties the failure on the part of those who
have the means to give to their children the highest attain-

able education, and with this also to provide the funds for educating all those who in the lower schools prove themselves to be possessed of promising abilities. It may be long before such laws can be instituted even in the more advanced communities.

In the meantime, in aid of that higher appreciation of the benefits of education that may supply a better, if necessarily less effectual stimulus, I desire to direct your attention to a few considerations which show that young women,— viewed not as future lawyers, physicians, politicians, or even teachers, but as future wives and mothers,—should enjoy a high and liberal culture, and which may help us to understand the nature and means of such culture.

The first thought that arises on this branch of the subject is that woman was intended as the helpmate of man. And here I may first speak of that kind and loving ministry of woman which renders life sweet and mitigates its pains and sorrows, and which is to be found not solely among the educated and refined, but among the simplest and least cultured,—a true instinct of goodness, needing direction, but native to the heart of woman, in all climes and in all states of civilization.

Yet it is sad to think how much of this holy instinct is lost and wasted through want of knowledge and thought. How often do labor and self-sacrifice become worse than useless because not guided by intelligence; how often an influence that would be omnipotent for good becomes vitiated and debased into a power that enervates and enfeebles the better resolutions of men, and involves them and their purposes in its own inanity and frivolity.

No influence is so powerful for good over young men as that of educated female society. Nothing is so strong to uphold the energies, or to guide the decisions of the greatest and most useful men as the sympathy and advice of one who can look at affairs from without (from the quiet sanctuary of home), and can bring to bear on them the quick tact and ready resources of a cultivated woman's mind. In this, the loftier sphere of domestic duty, in her companionship and true copartnership with man, woman requires high culture quite as much as if she had, alone and unshielded, to fight the battle of life.

It may be said that, after all, the intelligence of the average woman is quite equal to that of the average man, and that highly educated women would not be appreciated by the half-educated men who perform most of the work of the world. Granting this, it by no means follows that the necessity for the education of women is diminished. Every Xantippe cannot have a Socrates, but every wise and learned woman can find scope for her energies and abilities. If need be she may make something even of a very common-place man. She can greatly improve even a fool, and can vastly enhance the happiness and usefulness of a good man should she be so fortunate as to find one.

But it is in the maternal relation that the importance of the education of woman appears most clearly. It requires no very extensive study of biography to learn that it is of less consequence to a man what sort of father he may have had than what sort of mother. It is, indeed, a popular impression that the children of clever fathers are likely to exhibit the opposite quality. This I do not believe, except in so far as it results from the fact that men in public positions, or immersed in business are apt to neglect the oversight of their children.

But it is a noteworthy fact that eminent qualities in men

may often be traced to similar qualities in their mothers. Knowledge, it is true, is not hereditary, but high mental qualities are so, and experience and observation seem to prove that the transmission is chiefly through the mother's side. But leaving this physiological view, let us look at the purely educational. Imagine an educated mother training and molding the powers of her children, giving to them in the years of infancy those gentle yet permanent tendencies which are of more account in the formation of character than any subsequent educational influences, selecting for them the best instructors, encouraging and aiding them in their difficulties, rejoicing with them in their successes, able to take an intelligent interest in their progress in literature and science.

How ennobling such an influence, how fruitful of good results, how certain to secure the warm and lasting gratitude of those who have received its benefits when they look back in future life on the paths of wisdom along which they have been led! What a contrast to this is the position of an untaught mother finding her few superficial accomplishments of no use in the work of life, unable wisely to guide the rapidly developing life of her children, bringing them up to repeat her own failures and errors, or perhaps to despise her as ignorant of what they must learn!

Truly, the art and profession of a mother is the noblest and most far-reaching of all, and she who would worthily discharge its duties must be content with no mean preparation. It is worth while also to say here that these duties and responsibilities in the future are not to be measured altogether by those of the past.

Several features of the present movement afford, I think, especial reasons for congratulation. One is, that this is an association of ladies for educational purposes, originating with ladies, carried on by them, and supported by their contributions. Another is that the movement is self-supporting and not sustained by any extraneous aid. It will I hope attract to itself endowments which may give it a stronger and higher character, but its present position of independence is the best guarantee for this as well as for all other kinds of success. Again, this association embraces nearly all that is elevated in social and educational standing in our city, and has thus the broadest and highest basis that can be attained among us for any effort whatever.

We are not alone nor are we indeed in the van of this great work. I need not speak of the United States, where the magnificent Vassar College (with which the name of one of our excellent and learned women was connected so usefully), Cornell University, the University of Michigan, and others, have marked strongly the popular sentiment as to the education of women.

In Canada itself, Toronto, and even Quebec and Kingston, have preceded us, though I think in the magnitude of our success we may hope to excel them all.

In the mother country the Edinburgh Association—which has afforded us the model for our own—the North of England Educational Council, the Bedford College in London, the Cheltenham College, the Hitchin College, Cambridge (since developed into Girton College), also Newnham College, the Lady Margaret Somerville Halls at Oxford, the Alexandra College in Dublin, are all indications of the intensity and direction of the current.

On the continent of Europe, Sweden has a state college for women; the Victoria Lyceum at Berlin has the patronage of the Princess Royal; the University of Paris has established classes for ladies; and even St. Petersburg has its university for women.

All these movements have originated not only in our time, but within a few years, and they are evidently the dawn of a new educational era, which, in my judgment, will see as great an advance in the education of our race as that which was inaugurated by the revival of learning and the establishment of universities for men in a previous age. It implies not only the higher education of women, but the elevation, extension, and refinement of the higher education of men. Colleges for women will, as new institutions, be free from many evil traditions which cling about the old seats of learning.

They will start with all the advantages of our modern civilization. They will be animated by the greater refinement, tact, and taste of woman. They will impress many of these features upon our older colleges, with which, I have no doubt, they will become connected under the same university organizations. They will also greatly increase the demand for a higher education among young men.

An Edinburgh professor is reported to have said to some students who asked ignorant questions, "Ask your sisters at home, they can tell you,"—a retort which I imagine few young men would lightly endure.

So soon as young men find that they must attain to higher education before they can take a creditable place in the society of ladies we shall find them respecting science and literature almost as much as money and attaching to the services of the college professor as much importance as to those of their tailor.

ON THE PROGRESS OF SCIENCE IN CANADA

AN ADDRESS DELIVERED BEFORE THE ROYAL SOCIETY OF CANADA
IN MAY 1882

WE meet to-day to inaugurate a new era in the progress of Canadian literature and science, by the foundation of a body akin to those great national societies which in Great Britain and elsewhere have borne so important a part in the advancement of science and letters.

The idea of such a society for this country may not be altogether new, but if broached at all, it has been abandoned, from the inability of its advocates to gather together from our widely distributed provinces the elements necessary to its success. Now it presents itself under different and happier conditions.

In the mother country the reign of Queen Victoria, our gracious sovereign, has been specially marked by the patronage of every effort for the growth of education, literature, science, and art, not only on her part but on that of the lamented Prince Consort and of other members of the royal family. It is fitting that here too the representative of royalty should exert the same influence, and our present Governor-General [The Marquis of Lorne] has undoubtedly both a personal and an hereditary right to be the patron of progress and culture in literature and science. Since the political consolidation of the Canadian Dominion, improved means of intercourse have been welding together our formerly scattered Provinces and have caused much more intimate relations than formerly to subsist between men of letters and science.

We are sometimes told that the enterprise in which we are engaged is premature, that like some tender plant too early exposed to the frosts of our Canadian spring it will be nipped and perish.

But we must remember that in a country situated as this is, nearly everything is in some sense premature. It is with us a time of breaking up of ground and of sowing and planting, not a time of reaping or gathering fruit, and unless this generation of Canadians is content, like those that have preceded it, to sow what others must reap in its full maturity, there will be little hope for our country.

In Canada at present, whether in science, in literature, in art, or in education, we look around in vain for anything that is fully ripe. We see only the rudiments and beginnings of things, but if these are healthy and growing we should regard them with hope and should cherish and nurture them as the germs of greater things in the future. Yet there is a charm in this very immaturity, and it brings with it great opportunities.

We have the freedom and freshness of a youthful nationality. We can trace out new paths which must be followed by our successors; we have a right to plant wherever we please the trees under shade of which they will sit. The independence which we thus enjoy, and the freedom to originate which we can claim, are in themselves privileges, but privileges that carry with them great responsibilities.

Allow me to present to you a few thoughts bearing on this aspect of our position, and in doing so, to confine myself chiefly to the side of science, since my friend Dr. Chauveau, who is to follow me, is so much better able to lay such before you from a literary point of view.

Young though our country is we are already the heirs of

the labors of many eminent workers in science who have passed away or have been removed from this country.

In geology, the names of Bigsby, Bayfield, Baddeley, Logan, Lyell, Billings, Hector, and Isbister will occur to all who have studied the geological structure of Canada, and there are younger men like McOuat and Hartley—too early snatched away—who have left behind them valuable records of their labors.

In botany and zoology we can point to Michaux, Pursh, Hooker, Shepherd, Bourgeau, Douglas, Menzies, Richardson, Lord, and Brunet.

These are but a few of the more eminent laborers in the natural history of this country, without mentioning the many living workers who still remain. Were it the object of this society merely to collect and reproduce, and bring up to date, what these older men have done, it would have no small task before it. But to this we have to add the voluminous reports of the geological survey, and the numerous papers and other publications of the men who are still with us.

In natural science we thus have a large mass of accumulated capital on which to base our future operations, along with an unlimited scope for further efforts and researches.

The older men among us know how much has been done within the lifetime of the present generation. When as a young man I began to look around for means of scientific education there was no regular course of natural science in any of our colleges, though chemistry and physics were already taught in some of them. There were no collections in geology or natural history, except the private cabinets of a few zealous workers.

The Geological Survey of Canada had not then been thought of. There were no special schools of practical science, no scientific libraries, no scientific publications, and scarcely any printed information accessible. In these circumstances, when I proposed to devote myself to geological pursuits I had to go abroad for training not equal to that which can now be obtained in many of our Canadian colleges. Nor at that time were there public employments in this country to which a young geologist or naturalist could aspire. It is true this was more than forty years ago, but in looking back it would seem but as yesterday were not these years marked by the work that has been done, the mass of material accumulated, and the scientific institutions established within this time. Those who began their scientific work under such circumstances may be excused for taking somewhat hopeful views as to the future.

Perhaps at present the danger is that we may be content to remain in the position we have reached without attempting anything further; and, however inconsistent this may be, it is easy to combine the fear that any movement in advance may be rash or premature with the self-satisfied belief that we have already advanced so far that little remains to be attained.

We must bear in mind, however, that we have still much to do to place ourselves on a level with many other countries. With the exception of the somewhat meagre grants to the Geological Survey and to the Meteorological Service, the government of Canada gives nothing in aid of scientific research. What is done for scientific education by local societies must under our system be done by the separate Provinces, and is necessarily unequal and imperfect. Few large endowments have been given for scientific purposes. We have had no national societies or associations comparable with those of other countries.

Yet we are looking forward to a great future. Wealth and population are moving rapidly onward, and the question is whether culture of the higher grade shall keep pace with the headlong rush of material progress. Various elements may enter into the answer to this question, but undoubtedly the formation of such a society as this is one of these, and of the utmost importance; and even though at the present time the project may fail of success, or be only partially effective (of which, however, I have no apprehension), it must be renewed till finally enabled to firmly establish itself.

Another consideration bearing on this question is the vastness of the territory which we possess, and for the scientific development of which we have assumed the responsibility. Canada comprises one half of the great North American continent, reaching for three thousand miles from east to west and extending from south to north from the latitudes of 45 degrees and 49 degrees to the Polar Sea. In this area we have representatives of all the geological formations—from the Laurentian and Huronian, to which Canada has the honor of giving names, to the Post-pliocene and modern. Of some of these formations we have more magnificent developments than has any other country.

In zoology our land area extends from the land of the musk-ox in the north to that of the rattlesnake in the south, and we have perhaps the greatest area possessed by any country for the study of fresh-water animals. Our marine zoology includes that of the North Atlantic, the North Pacific, and of the Arctic Ocean. In botany we have the floras of the Atlantic and Pacific slopes, of the western plains, and of the Arctic zone. In physical, astronomical, and meteorological investigations we have the advantage of vast area and of varied climate and conditions. These circumstances in themselves imply responsibilities in connection with the progress of science, not here only but throughout the world.

Much is no doubt being done to cultivate these vast fields of research, and I would not for a moment underrate the efforts being made and the arduous labors, perils, and privations to which the pioneers in these fields are even now subjected; but what is being done is relatively insignificant.

Many letters from abroad reach me every year asking for information, or reference, as to Canadian workers in specialties which no one here is studying; and I know that most of our active naturalists are continually driven by such demands to take up lines of investigation in addition to those already more than sufficient to occupy their time and energy. Were it not for the aid indirectly given us by the magnificent and costly surveys and commissions of the United States, which freely invade Canadian territory whenever they find any profitable ground that we are not occupying, we would be still more helpless in these respects. Is there not in these circumstances reason for combination of effort and for the best possible arrangements for the distribution of our small force over the vast area which it has to maintain?

I have dwelt sufficiently long on topics which indicate that the time has fully come for the institution of the Royal Society of Canada. Let us turn for a moment to the consideration of the ends which it may seek to attain and the means for their attainment.

I would place here first the establishment of a bond of union between the scattered workers now widely separated in different parts of the Dominion. Our men of science are so few and our country so extensive that it is difficult to find in any one place, or within reasonable distance of each other, half a dozen active workers in science. There is thus great lack of sympathy and stimulus and of the discussion and interchange of ideas, which tend so much to correct as well as to encourage. The lonely worker finds his energies flag and is drawn away by the pressure of more popular pursuits. Even if this society can meet but once a year, something may be done to remedy the evils of isolation.

Again, means are lacking for the adequate publication of results. True, we have the reports of the Geological Survey, and transactions are published by some of the local societies, but the resources at the disposal of these bodies are altogether inadequate, and for anything extensive or costly we have to seek means of publication abroad.

This can be secured only under special circumstances; and while in this way the published results of Canadian science become so widely scattered as to be accessible with difficulty, much that would be of scientific value fails altogether of adequate publication, especially in the matter of illustration.

Thus, the Canadian naturalist is often obliged to be content with the publication of his work in an inferior style and poorly illustrated, so that it has an aspect of inferiority to work really no better, which in the United States or in the mother country has the benefit of sumptuous publication and illustration. On this account he has often the added mortification of finding his work overlooked or neglected; and not infrequently, whilst he is looking in vain for means of publication the credit of that which he has attained by long and diligent labor is taken away from him by its previous issue elsewhere.

In this way, also, it very often happens that collectors who have amassed important material of great scientific value are induced to place it in the hands of specialists in other countries, who have at their command means of publication not possessed by equally competent men here. The injury which Canadian science and the reputation of Canada sustain in this way is well known to many who are present and who have been personal sufferers.

Should this society have sufficient means placed at its disposal to publish transactions,—I shall not say equal to those of the Royal Society of London, or the Smithsonian Institute at Washington, but to those of such bodies as the Philadelphia Academy, or the Boston Society of Natural History,—an incalculable stimulus would be given to science in Canada by promoting research, by securing to this country the credit of the work done in it, by collecting the information now widely scattered, and by enabling scientific men abroad to learn what is being done here. It is not intended that such means of publication should be limited to the work or papers of members of the society.

In this respect it will constitute a judicial body to decide as to what may deserve publication. Its transactions should be open to good papers from any source, and should thus enable the younger and less known men of science to add to their own reputation and to that of the country, and so to prepare the way for their admission to membership of this society.

Few expenditures of public money are more profitable to the State than those which promote scientific publication. The actual researches made imply much individual labor and expense, no part of which falls on the public funds, and by the comparatively small cost of publication the country gets the benefit of the results obtained, its mental and industrial progress is stimulated, and it acquires reputation abroad.

This is now so well understood that in most countries public aid is given to research as well as to publication. Here we may be content, in the first instance, with the latter alone, but if the society is at first sustained by the government, it may be hoped that, as in older countries, private benefactions and bequests will flow into it, so that eventually it may be able, not merely to afford means of publication, but to extend substantial aid to young and struggling men of science who are following out under difficulties important investigations.

In return for aid given to this society the government may also have the benefit of its advice, as a body of experts, in any case of need. The most insignificant natural agencies sometimes attain to national importance. A locust, a midge or a parasitic fungus may suddenly reduce to naught the calculations of a finance minister.

The great natural resources of the land and of the sea are alike under the control of laws known to science. We are occasionally called on to take our part in the observation of astronomical or atmospheric phenomena of world-wide interest. In such cases it is the practice of all civilized governments to have recourse to scientific advice, and in a society like this our government can command a body of men free from the distracting influence of private and local interests, and able to warn against the schemes of charlatans and pretenders.

Another object which we should have in view is that of concentrating the benefits of the several local societies scattered through the Dominion. Some of these are of long standing and have done much original work.

The Literary and Historical Society of Quebec is, I believe, the oldest of these bodies, and its transactions include not merely literature and history, but much that is of great value in natural science, while it has been more successful than any of our other societies in the accumulation of a library.

The Natural History Society of Montreal, of which I have had the honor to be a member for twenty-seven years, is now in its fifty-third year. It has published seventeen volumes of proceedings, including probably a larger mass of original information respecting the natural history of Canada than is to be found in any other publication. It has accumulated a valuable museum and has done much to popularize science. It has twice induced the American Association for the Advancement of Science to hold its meeting in Canada, and was the first body to propose the establishment of a Geological Survey.

The Canadian Institute of Toronto, occupying the field of literature as well as of science, although a younger, has been a more vigorous society, and its transactions are equally voluminous and valuable. The Natural History Society of St. John, New Brunswick, though it has not published so much, has carried out some very important researches in local geology which are known and valued throughout the world.

The Nova Scotian Institute of Natural Science is a flourishing body and publishes valuable transactions. The Institût Canadien of Quebec, and the Ottawa Natural History Society are also very useful institutions. The new Natural History Society of Manitoba has entered on a vigorous and hopeful career.

There are also in the Dominion some societies of great value, cultivating more restricted fields than those above referred to, and of a character rather special than local. As examples of these I may mention the Entomological Society of Canada, the Historic Society, and the Numismatic Society of Montreal.

Did I suppose that this society would interfere with the prosperity of such local bodies, I should be slow to favor its establishment. I believe, however, that the contrary effect will be produced. They are sustained by the subscriptions and donations of local members and of the Provincial legislatures, while this society must depend on the Dominion Parliament, from which they draw no aid. They will find abundant scope for their more frequent meetings in the contributions of local laborers, while this will collect and compare these and publish such portions as may be of wider interest. This society will also, it is hoped, furnish means of publication for memoirs too bulky and expensive to appear in local transactions.

There should, however, be a closer association than this. It is probable that nearly all of the local societies are already represented among our members by gentlemen who can inform us as to their work and wishes. We should therefore be prepared at once to offer terms of friendly union. For this purpose it would be well to give to each of them an associate membership for its president, and for one or two of its officers nominated by itself and approved by our council. Such representatives would be required to report to us for our transactions the authors and subjects of all their original papers, and would be empowered to transmit to us for publication such papers as might seem deserving of this and make suggestions as to any subjects of research which might be developed by local investigation. The details of such association may, I think, readily be arranged on terms mutually advantageous and conducive to the attainment of the objects we all have in view.

It would be a mistake to suppose that this society should include all our literary and scientific men, or even all those of some local standing. It must consist of selected and representative men who have themselves done original work of at least Canadian celebrity. Beyond this it would have no resting-place short of that of a great popular assemblage, whose members would be characterized rather by mere receptivity than by productiveness. In this sense it must be exclusive in its membership; but inclusive, in that it offers its benefits to all.

It is somewhat surprising at first sight, and indicative of the crude state of public opinion on such matters that we sometimes find it stated that a society so small in its membership will prove too select and exclusive for such a country as this; or find the suggestion thrown out that the society should become a professional one by including the more eminent members of the learned professions.

If we compare ourselves with other countries, I rather think the wonder is that so many names should have been proposed for membership of this society. Not to mention the strict limitations in this respect, placed on such societies in the mother country and on the continent of Europe, we have a more recent example in the National Academy of Sciences in the United States. That country is probably as democratic in its social and public institutions as Canada, and its scientific workers are certainly in the proportion of forty to one of ours. Yet the original members of the Academy were limited to fifty, and though subsequently the maximum was raised to one hundred, this number has not as yet been attained. Yet public opinion in the United States would not have tolerated a much wider selection, which would have descended to a lower grade of eminence, and so would have lowered the scientific prestige of the country.

Science and literature are at once among the most

democratic and the most select of the institutions of society. They throw themselves freely into the struggle of the world, recognize its social grades, submit to the criticism of all, and stand or fall by the vote of the majority, but they absolutely refuse to recognize, as entitled to places of importance, any but those who have earned their titles for themselves. Thus it happens that the great scientific and literary societies must consist of few members, even in the oldest and most populous countries, while on the other hand their benefits are for all, and they diffuse knowledge through the medium of larger and more popular bodies whose membership implies capacity for receiving information though not for doing original work. The younger men of science and literature must be content to earn their admission into the higher ranks, but have, in the fact that such higher rank is accessible to them, an encouragement to persevere, and in the meantime may have all their worthy productions treated in precisely the same manner as are those of their seniors.

Finally we, who have been honored with the invitation to be the original members of this society, have a great responsibility and a high duty laid upon us. We owe it to the large and liberal scheme, conceived by his Excellency the Governor-General, to carry out this plan in the most perfect manner possible, not with regard to personal, party, or class views, but to the great interests of Canada and its reputation before the world. We should approve ourselves first, unselfish and zealous literary and scientific men, and next, Canadians, in that widest sense of the word, in which we shall desire at any personal sacrifice to promote the best interests of our country, and this, in connection with a pure and elevated literature and a true, profound, and practical science.

We aspire to a great name. The title of "Royal

Society," which, with the consent of her gracious Majesty the Queen, we hope to assume, is one dignified in the mother country by a long line of distinguished men, who have been fellows of its Royal Society. The name may provoke comparisons not favorable to us, and though we may hope to shelter ourselves from criticism by pleading the relatively new and crude condition of science and literature in this country, we must endeavor with God's blessing on earnest and united effort to produce by our cultivation of the almost boundless resources of the country which has fallen to us as our inheritance, works which shall entitle us without fear of criticism to take to ourselves worthily and justly this proud name of "The Royal Society of Canada."

BURLINGAME

A NSON BURLINGAME, a distinguished American diplomatist, was born in New Berlin, New York, November 14, 1820. After obtaining an education at the University of Michigan he studied law at Harvard University, beginning the practice of his profession in Boston in 1846. He engaged actively in politics and soon became the popular orator of the new Free-Soil party; during the campaign of 1848 acquiring a very wide reputation as an able public speaker. He entered the State senate in 1852, and represented Massachusetts in Congress, 1854-60. He vehemently denounced the assault made upon Senator Sumner by Preston Brooks in 1856, and was challenged therefor by Brooks. Burlingame accepted the challenge, appointing a locality in Canada as the place of meeting, but Brooks declined to travel through the North in order to reach it. Burlingame was one of the founders of the Republican party and one of its favorite orators. He was appointed minister to Austria in 1861, but that country declined to receive him on account of his speeches in behalf of Hungarian independence, and of his motion in Congress that Austria's opponent, Sardinia, should be recognized as a first-class power. He was then sent as minister to China, and in 1867 was appointed by the Chinese regent special envoy from China to the United States. Accepting the office he returned to the United States at the head of the Chinese mission the next year, and in July, 1868, negotiated what is known as "The Burlingame Treaty." This treaty constitutes in effect China's earliest official recognition of the principles of international law. He then visited England, France, Denmark, Sweden, Holland, and Prussia in behalf of the Chinese government, negotiating important treaties in all of these countries but France. He was about to enter upon a similar mission in Russia when his death took place at St. Petersburg, Russia, February 22, 1870. Many of his speeches were issued singly, but no complete collection has been made.

MASSACHUSETTS AND SUMNER

DELIVERED IN THE HOUSE OF REPRESENTATIVES, JUNE 21, 1856

M R. CHAIRMAN,—the House will bear witness that I have not pressed myself upon its deliberations. I never before asked its indulgence. I have assailed no man; nor have I sought to bring reproach upon any man's State. But, while such has been my course, as well as the course of my colleagues from Massachusetts, upon this floor,

(8180)

certain members have seen fit to assail the State which we represent, not only with words, but with blows.

In remembrance of these things, and seizing the first opportunity which has presented itself for a long time, I stand here to-day to say a word for old Massachusetts—not that she needs it; no, sir; for in all that constitutes true greatness—in all that gives abiding strength—in great qualities of head and heart—in moral power—in material prosperity—in intellectual resources and physical ability—by the general judgment of mankind, according to her population, she is the first State.

There does not live the man anywhere who knows anything to whom praise of Massachusetts would not be needless. She is as far beyond that as she is beyond censure. Members here may sneer at her; they may praise her past at the expense of her present; but I say with a full conviction of its truth that Massachusetts, in her present performances, is even greater than in her past recollections. And when I have said this, what more can I say?

Sir, although I am here as her youngest and humblest member, yet, as her representative, I feel that I am the peer of any man upon this floor. Occupying that high standpoint with modesty, but with firmness, I cast down her glove to the whole band of her assailants.

She has been assailed in the House and out of the House, at the other end of the Capitol, and at the other end of the avenue. There have been brought against her general charges and specific charges. I am sorry to find at the head of the list of her assailants the President of the United States, who not only assails Massachusetts, but the whole North. He defends one section of the Union at the expense of the other. He declares that one section has ever been mindful of its constitutional obligations and that the other has not. He declares that if one section of our country were a foreign country the other would have just cause of war against it.

And to sustain these remarkable declarations he goes into an elaborate perversion of history, such as that Virginia ceded her lands against the interests of the South for the benefit of the North; when the truth is, she ceded her lands, as New York and other States did, for the benefit of the whole country. She gave her lands to freedom, because she thought freedom was better than slavery; because it was the policy of the times, and events have vindicated that policy.

It is a perversion of history when he says that the territory of the country has been acquired more for the benefit of the North than for the South; he says that substantially. Sir, out of the territory thus acquired five slave States, with a pledge for four more, and two free States have come into the Union; and one of these as we all know fought its way through a compromise degrading to the North.

The North does not object to the acquisition of territory when it is desired, but she desires that it shall be free. If such a complexion had been given to it, how different would have been the fortunes of the Republic to-day! This may be ascertained by comparing the progress of Ohio with that of any slave State in the Mississippi Valley. It will appear more clearly by comparing the free with the slave regions. I have not time to do more than to present a general picture.

Freedom and slavery started together in the great race on this continent. In the very year the Pilgrim Fathers landed on Plymouth Rock, slaves landed in Virginia. Freedom has gone on, trampling down barbarism and planting States—building the symbols of its faith by every lake and every river, until now the sons of the Pilgrims stand by the shores of the Pacific. Slavery has also made its way toward the setting sun. It has reached the Rio Grande on the south; and the groans of its victims and the clank of its chains may be heard as it slowly ascends the western tributaries of the Mississippi River.

Freedom has left the land bespangled with free schools and filled the whole heavens with the shining towers of religion and civilization. Slavery has left desolation, ignorance, and death in its path. When we look at these things; when we see what the country would have been had freedom been given to the Territories; when we think what it would have been but for this blight in the bosom of the country; that the whole South—that fair land God has blessed so much—would have been covered with cities, and villages, and railroads, and that in the country, in the place of twenty-five millions of people thirty-five millions would have hailed the rising morn exulting in republican liberty; when we think of these things how must every honest man—how must every man with brains in his head or heart in his bosom—regret that the policy of old Virginia in her better days did not become the animating policy of this expanding Republic!

It is a perversion of history, I say, when the President intimates that the adoption of the constitution abrogated the ordinance of 1787. It was recognized by the first Congress which assembled under the constitution; and it has been sanctioned by nearly every President from Washington down.

It is a perversion of history when the President intimates that the Missouri Compromise was made against the interests of the South and for the benefit of the North. The truth— the unmistakable truth—is that it was forced by the South on

the North. It received the almost united vote of the South.
It was claimed as a victory of the South.

The men who voted for it were sustained in the South;
and those who voted for it in the North passed into oblivion;
and though some of them are physically alive to-day they
are as politically dead as are the President and his immediate
advisers.

Not only has the President perverted history but he has
turned sectionalist. He has become the champion of sectionalism. He makes the extraordinary declaration that if
a State is refused admission into the Union because her constitution embraced slavery as an institution then one section
of the country would of necessity be compelled to dissolve its
connection with the people of the other section!

What does he mean? Does he mean to say that there are
traitors in the South? Does he mean to say if they were
voted down that then they ought not to submit? If he does,
and if they mean to back him in the declaration, then I say
the quicker we try the strength of this great government the
better. Not only has he said that, but members have said on
this floor again and again that if the Fugitive Slave Law,
which has nothing sacred about it—which I deem unconstitutional—which South Carolina deems unconstitutional—if
that law be repealed that this Union will then cease to exist.

I say that it is not for the President and members on this
floor to determine the life of this Union; this Union rests
in the hearts of the American people and cannot be
eradicated thence. Whenever any person shall lift his hand
to smite down this Union the people will subjugate him to
liberty and the constitution. I do not wish to dwell on the
President and what he has said. Notwithstanding all this
perversion of history—notwithstanding his violated pledges

—and notwithstanding his warlike exploits at Greytown and Lawrence—his servility has been repaid with scorn.

I am glad of it. The South was right. When a man is false to the convictions of his own heart and to freedom he cannot be trusted with the delicate interests of slavery. I cannot express the delight I feel in the poetic justice that has been done; but at the same time I am not unmindful of the deep ingratitude that first lured him to ruin and then deserted and left him alone to die.

If I were not too much of a native American I would quote and apply to him the old Latin words " *De mortuis nil nisi bonum* "—" Speak nothing but good of the dead." I can almost forgive him, considering his condition, the blistering words he let fall upon us the other night when he went through the ordeal of ratifying the nomination of James Buchanan. He said that we had received nothing at the hands of the government save its protection and its political blessings. We have not certainly received any offices; and as for its protection and political blessings let the silence above the graves of those who sleep in their bloody shrouds in Kansas answer.

There have been general and specific charges made against old Massachusetts. The general charge when expressed in polite language is that she has not been faithful to her constitutional obligations. I deny it. I call for proof, I ask when? where? how? I say, on the contrary, that from the time when this government came from the brains of her statesmen and the unconquerable arms of her warriors she has been loyal to it.

In peace she has added to it renown; and in war her sons have crowded the way to death as to a festival. She has quenched the fires of rebellion on her own soil without federal aid, and when the banners of nullification flew in the southern sky, speaking through the lips of Webster, in Faneuil Hall, she stood by Jackson and the Union. No man speaking in her name—no man wearing her ermine, or clothed with her authority—ever did anything or said anything, or decided anything, not in accordance with her constitutional obligations. Yet, sir, the hand of the federal government has been laid heavily upon her.

That malignant spirit which has usurped this government through the negligence of the people, too long has pursued her with rancor and bitterness. Before its invidious legislation she has seen her commerce perish and ruin, like a devastating fire, sweep through her fields of industry, but amid all these things Massachusetts has always lifted up her voice with unmurmuring devotion to the Union.

She has heard the federal drum in her streets. She has protected the person of that most odious man—odious both at the North and the South—the slave-hunter. She has protected him when her soil throbbed with indignation from the sea to the New York line. Sir, the temples of justice there have been clothed in chains. The federal courts in other States have been closed against her, and her citizens have been imprisoned, and she has had no redress.

Yet, notwithstanding all these things, Massachusetts has always been faithful and loyal to the constitution. You may ask why, if she has been so wronged, so insulted, has she been so true and faithful to the Union? Sir, because she knew, in her clear head, that these outrages came not from the generous hearts of the American people. She knew that when justice should finally assume the reins of government all would be well. She knew that when the government ceased to foster the interests of slavery alone her interests would be regarded and the whole country be blessed. It was this high constitutional hope that has always swayed the head and heart of Massachusetts and which has made her look out of the gloom of the present and anticipate a glorious future. So much in relation to the general charge against Massachusetts.

There are specific charges upon which I shall dwell for a moment. One is that she has organized an "Emigrant Aid Society." Did you not tell Massachusetts that the people of Kansas were to be left perfectly free to mold her institutions as they thought best? She knew and she told you that your doctrine of squatter sovereignty was a delusion and a snare. She opposed it as long as she could here; and when she could do it no longer she accepted the battle upon your pledge of fair play. She determined to make Kansas a free State.

In this high motive the Emigrant Aid Society had its origin. Its objects are two-fold—freedom for Kansas and pecuniary reward. And it is so organized that pecuniary benefit cannot flow to stockholders, except through the prosperity of those whom it aids. The idea of the society is this: to take capital and place it in advance of civilization; to take the elements of civilization, the saw-mill, the church, the schoolhouse, and plant them in the wilderness, as an inducement to the emigrant. It is a peaceful society. It has never armed one man; it has never paid one man's passage to Kansas. It never asked—though I think it should have asked—the political sentiments of any man whom it has assisted to emigrate to Kansas. It has invested $100,000, and it has conducted from Massachusetts to Kansas from twelve to fifteen hundred of the flower of her people.

Such is the Emigrant Aid Society, such is its origin, and

such its action. It is this society, so just and legal in its origin and its action, that has been made the pretext for the most bitter assaults upon Massachusetts. Sir, it is Christianity organized. How have these legal and these proper measures been met by those who propose to make Kansas a slave State? The people of Massachusetts would not complain if the people who differ from them should go there to seek a peaceful solution of the conflicting questions. But how have they been met? By fraud and violence, by sackings, and burnings, and murders.

Laws have been forced upon them, such as you have heard read to-day by the gentleman from Indiana [Mr. Colfax], so atrocious that no man has risen here to defend one single one of them. Men have been placed over them whom they never elected, and this day, as has been stated by the gentleman from Indiana, civil war rages from one end of Kansas to the other. Men have been compelled to leave their peaceful pursuits, and starvation and death stare them in the face, and yet the government stands idle—no, not idle; it gives its mighty arm to the side of the men who are trampling down law and order there.

The United States troops have not been permitted to protect the free State men. When they have desired to do so they have been withdrawn. I cannot enter into a detail of all the facts. It is a fact that war rages there to-day. Men kill each other at sight. All these things are known and nobody can deny them. All the western winds are burdened with the news of them, and they are substantiated equally by both sides.

Has the government no power to make peace in Kansas and to protect citizens there under the organic law of the Territory? I ask, in the name of old Massachusetts, if our honest citizens who went to Kansas to build up homes for themselves and to secure the blessings of civilization, are not entitled to protection? She throws the responsibility upon this administration, and holds it accountable; and so will the people at the polls next November.

Another charge is that Massachusetts has passed a personal liberty bill. Well, sir, I say that Massachusetts for her local legislation is not responsible to this House or to any member of it. I say, sir, if her laws were as bad as those atrocious laws of Kansas, you can do nothing with her. I say, if her statute books instead of being filled with generous legislation—legislation which ought to be interesting to her assailants, because it is in favor of the idiotic and the blind—were filled, like those of the State of Alabama, with laws covering the State with whipping-posts, keeping half of her people in absolute slavery, and nearly all of the other half in subjection to twenty-nine thousand slaveholders; if the slaveholders themselves were not permitted to trade with or teach their slaves as they choose; if ignorance were increasing faster than the population, I say, even then, you could not do anything here with the local laws of Massachusetts. I say, the presumption is, that the law, having been passed by a sovereign State, is constitutional.

If it is not constitutional, then, sir, when the proper tribunal shall have decided that question, what is there, I ask, in the history of Massachusetts which will lead us to believe that she will not abide by that result? I say there is nothing in the history of the State of Mississippi, or of South Carolina, early or recent, which makes Massachusetts desirous of emulating their example. I, sir, agree with the South Carolina authority I have quoted here in regard to the legislation of Massachusetts.

Sir, my time is passing away and I must hasten on. The State of Massachusetts is the guardian of the rights of her citizens and of the inhabitants within her border line. If her citizens go beyond the line into distant lands or upon the ocean then they look to the federal arm for protection. But old Massachusetts is the State which is to secure to her citizens the inestimable blessing of trial by jury and the writ of habeas corpus.

All these things must come from her and not from the federal government. I believe, with her great statesmen and with her people, that the Fugitive Slave Law is unconstitutional. Mr. Webster, as an original question, thought it was not constitutional; Mr. Rantoul, a brilliant statesman of Massachusetts, said the same thing; they both thought that the clause of the constitution was addressed to the States. Mr. Webster bowed to the decision of the supreme court in the Prigg case; Mr. Rantoul did not.

Massachusetts believes it to be unconstitutional; but whether it be constitutional or not she means so long as the federal government undertakes to execute that law, that the federal government shall do it with its own instruments, vile or otherwise. She says that no one clothed with her authority shall do anything to help in it so long as the federal government undertakes to do it. But, sir, I pass from this.

I did intend to reply *seriatim* to all the attacks which have been made upon the State, but I have not half time enough. The gentleman from Mississippi [Mr. Bennett] after enumerating a great many things he desired Massachusetts to do, said, amongst other things, that she must tear out of her statute book this personal liberty law. When she had done that and a variety of other things too numerous to mention, then he said " the South would forgive Massa-

chusetts." The South forgive Massachusetts! Sir, forgiveness is an attribute of divinity. The South has it not. Sir,
forgiveness is a higher quality than justice, even. The
South—I mean the slave power—cannot comprehend it.

Sir, Massachusetts has already forgiven the South too
many debts and too many insults. If we should do all the
things the gentleman from Mississippi desired us to do, then
the gentleman from Alabama [Mr. Shorter] comes in and
insists that Massachusetts shall do a great variety of other
things before the South probably will forgive her.

Among other things, he desired that Massachusetts should
blot out the fact that General Hull, who surrendered De-
troit, had his home in Massachusetts. Why, no, sir; she
does not desire even to do that, for then she would have to
blot out the fact that his gallant son had his home there—
that gallant son who fell fighting for his country in the same
war at Lundy's Lane—that great battle, where Colonel Mil-
ler, a Massachusetts man by adoption, when asked if he
could storm certain heights, replied, in a modest Massachusetts manner, " I will try, sir." He stormed the heights.

The gentleman desires, also, that we should blot out the
history of the connection of Massachusetts with the last war.
Oh, no! She cannot do that. She cannot so dim the lustre of
the American arms. She cannot so wrong the Republic.
Where, then, would be your great sea-fights? Where, then,
would be the glory of " Old Ironsides," whose scuppers ran
red with Massachusetts blood? Where, then, would be the
history of the daring of those brave fishermen, who swarmed
from all her bays and all her ports, sweeping the enemy's
commerce from the most distant seas?

Ah, sir! she cannot afford to blot out that history. You,
sir, cannot afford to let her do it—no, not even the South.

She sustained herself in the last war; she paid her own expenses and has not yet been paid entirely from the treasury of the nation. The enemy hovered on her coast with his ships, as numerous almost as the stars. He looked on that warlike land and the memory of the olden time came back upon him. He remembered how, more than forty years before, he had trodden on that soil; he remembered how vauntingly he invaded it and how speedily he left it. He turned his glasses toward it and beheld its people rushing from the mountains to the sea to defend it; and he dared not attack it. Its capital stood in the salt sea spray, yet he could not take it. He sailed south, where there was another capital, not far from where we now stand, forty miles from the sea. A few staggering, worn-out sailors and soldiers came here. They took it. How it was defended let the heroes of Bladensburg answer!

Sir, the gentleman from South Carolina [Mr. Keitt] made a speech; and if I may be allowed to coin a word, I will say it had more cantankerosity in it than any speech I ever heard on this floor.

It was certainly very eloquent in some portions—very eloquent indeed, for the gentleman has indisputably an eloquent utterance and an eloquent temperament. I do not wish to criticise it much, but it opens in the most extraordinary manner with a " weird torchlight," and then he introduces a dead man, and then he galvanizes him, and puts him in that chair, and then he makes him " point his cold finger " around this hall.

Why, it almost frightens me to allude to it. And then he turns it into a theatre, and then he changes or transmogrifies the gentleman from Indiana [Mr. Colfax], who has just spoken, into a snake and makes him " wriggle up to the foot-

lights;" and then he gives the snake hands, and then " mailed
hands," and with one of them he throws off Cuba, and with
the other clutches all the Canadas.   Then he has men with
" glozing mouths," and they are " singing psalms through
their noses," and are moving down upon the South " like an
army with banners."   Frightful, is it not?   He talks about
rotting on dead seas.   He calls our party at one time a
" toad," and then he calls it a " lizard;" " and more, which
e'en to mention would be unlawful."   Sir, his rhetoric seems
to have the St. Vitus's dance.   He mingles metaphors in
such a manner as would delight the most extravagant
Milesian.

But I pass from his logic and his rhetoric, and also over
some historical mistakes, much of the same nature as those
made by the President, which I have already pointed out,
and come to some of his sentences, in which terrific questions
and answers explode.   He answers hotly and tauntingly that
the South wants none of our vagabond philanthropy.   Sir,
when the yellow pestilence fluttered its wings over the southern States and when Massachusetts poured out her treasures
to a greater extent in proportion to her population than any
other State, was that vagabond philanthropy?   I ask the
people of Virginia and Louisiana.

But, sir, the gentleman was most tender and most plaintive when he described the starving operatives.   Why, sir,
the eloquence was most overwhelming upon some of my colleagues.   I thought I saw the iron face of our speaker soften
a little when he listened to the unexpected sympathy of the
gentleman with the hardships of his early life.   Sir, he was
an operative from boyhood to manhood—and a good one,
too.

Ah, sir, he did not appreciate, as he tasted the sweet bread of honest toil, his sad condition; he did not think, as he stood in the music of the machinery which came from his cunning hand, how much better it would have been for him had he been born a slave and put under the gentleman from South Carolina—a kind master, as I have no doubt he is—where he would have been well fed and clothed, and would have known none of the trials which doubtless met him on every hand. How happy he would have been if, instead of being a Massachusetts operative, he had been a slave in South Carolina, fattening, singing, and dancing upon the banks of some southern river.

Sir, if the gentleman will go to my district and look upon those operatives and mechanics; if he will look upon some of those beautiful models which come from their brains and hands, and which from time to time leap upon the waters of the Atlantic, out-flying all other clippers, bringing home wealth and victory with all the winds of heaven, he might have reason to change his views. Let him go there, and, even after all he said, he may speak to those men and convince them if he can of their starving condition. I will guaranty his personal safety. I believe the people of Massachusetts would pour forth their heart's blood to protect even him in the right of freedom of speech; and that is saying a great deal after all that has happened.

Let him go to the great county of Worcester—that beehive of operatives and Abolitionists, as it has been called—and he will find the annual product of that county greater, in proportion to the population, than that of any other equal population in the world, as will be found by reference to a recent speech of ex-Governor Boutwell, of our State. The next county, I believe, in respect to the amount of products in proportion to population, is away up in Vermont.

Sir, let him go and look at these men—these Abolitionists, who, we are told, meddle with everybody's business but their own. They certainly take time enough to attend to their own business to accomplish these results which I have named.

The gentleman broke out in an exceedingly explosive question, something like this: I do not know if my memory can do justice to the language of the gentleman, but it was something like this: "Did not the South, equally with the North, bare her forehead to the god of battles?" I answer plainly, No, sir, she did not; she did not.

Sir, Massachusetts furnished more men in the Revolution than the whole South put together, and more by ten-fold than South Carolina. I am not including, of course, the militia—the conjectured militia furnished by that State. There is no proof that they were ever engaged in any battle. I mean the regulars; and I say that Massachusetts furnished more than ten times as many men as South Carolina. I say on the authority of a standard historian, once a member of this House (Mr. Sabine, in his history of the loyalists), that more New England men now lie buried in the soil of South Carolina than there were of South Carolinians who left their State to fight the battles of the country.

I say, when General Lincoln was defending Charleston he was compelled to give up its defence because the people of that city would not fight. When General Greene, that Rhode Island blacksmith, took command of the Southern army South Carolina had not a federal soldier in the field; and the people of that State would not furnish supplies to his army; while the British army in the State were furnished with supplies almost exclusively from the people of South Carolina. While the American army could not be recruited, the ranks of the British army were rapidly filled from that State.

The British post of Ninety-Six was garrisoned almost exclusively from South Carolina. Rawdon's reserve corps was made up almost entirely by South Carolinians. Of the eight hundred prisoners who were taken at the battle of King's Mountain—of which we have heard so much—seven hundred of them were Southern Tories. The Maryland men gained the laurels of the Cowpens. Kentuckians, Virginians, and North Carolinians gained the battle of King's Mountain. Few South Carolinians fought in the battles of Eutaw, Guilford, etc. They were chiefly fought by men out of South Carolina; and they would have won greater fame and brighter laurels if they had not been opposed chiefly by the citizens of the soil. Well might the British commander boast that he had reduced South Carolina into allegiance.

But, sir, I will not proceed further with this history, out of regard for the fame of our common country; out of regard for the patriots—the Sumters, the Marions, the Rutledges, the Pinckneys, the Haynes—truer patriots, if possible, than those of any other State.

Out of regard for these men I will not quote from a letter of the patriot Governor Mathews to General Greene, in which he complains of the selfishness and utter imbecility of a great portion of the people of South Carolina.

But, Mr. Chairman, all these assaults upon the State of Massachusetts sink into insignificance compared with the one I am about to mention. On the 19th of May it was announced that Mr. Sumner would address the Senate upon the Kansas question. The floor of the Senate, the galleries, and avenues leading thereto, were thronged with an expectant audience; and many of us left our places in this House to hear the Massachusetts orator.   To say that we were delighted with the speech we heard would but faintly express the deep emotions of our hearts awakened by it.   I need not speak of the classic purity of its language, nor of the nobility of its sentiments.   It was heard by many; it has been read by millions.   There has been no such speech made in the Senate since the days when those Titans of American eloquence—the Websters and the Haynes—contended with each other for mastery.

It was severe, because it was launched against tyranny.   It was severe as Chatham was severe when he defended the feeble colonies against the giant oppression of the mother country.   It was made in the face of a hostile Senate.   It continued through the greater portion of two days; and yet during that time the speaker was not once called to order. This fact is conclusive as to the personal and parliamentary decorum of the speech.   He had provocation enough.   His State had been called hypocritical.   He himself had been called " a puppy," " a fool," " a fanatic," and " a dishonest man."   Yet he was parliamentary from the beginning to the end of his speech.   No man knew better than he did the proprieties of the place, for he had always observed them. No man knew better than he did parliamentary law, because he had made it the study of his life.   No man saw more clearly than he did the flaming sword of the constitution, turning every way, guarding all the avenues of the Senate. But he was not thinking of these things; he was not thinking then of the privileges of the Senate nor of the guarantees of the constitution; he was there to denounce tyranny and crime, and he did it.   He was there to speak for the rights of an empire, and he did it bravely and grandly.

So much for the occasion of the speech.   A word, and I

shall be pardoned, about the speaker himself. He is my friend; for many and many a year I have looked to him for guidance and light, and I never looked in vain. He never had a personal enemy in his life; his character is as pure as the snow that falls on his native hills; his heart overflows with kindness for every being having the upright form of man; he is a ripe scholar, a chivalric gentleman, and a warm-hearted, true friend. He sat at the feet of Channing, and drank in the sentiments of that noble soul. He bathed in the learning and undying love of the great jurist, Story; and the hand of Jackson, with its honors and its offices, sought him early in life, but he shrank from them with in-stinctive modesty. Sir, he is the pride of Massachusetts. His mother Commonwealth found him adorning the highest walks of literature and law, and she bade him go and grace somewhat the rough character of political life. The people of Massachusetts—the old, and the young, and the middle-aged—now pay their full homage to the beauty of his public and private character. Such is Charles Sumner.

On the 22d day of May, when the Senate and the House had clothed themselves in mourning for a brother fallen in the battle of life in the distant State of Missouri, the senator from Massachusetts sat in the silence of the Senate Chamber, en-gaged in the employments appertaining to his office when a member from this House, who had taken an oath to sustain the constitution, stole into the Senate, that place which had hitherto been held sacred against violence, and smote him as Cain smote his brother.

One blow was enough; but it did not not satiate the wrath of that spirit which had pursued him through two days. Again and again, quicker and faster fell the leaden blows, until he was torn away from his victim, when the senator from Massachusetts fell in the arms of his friends, and his blood ran down on the Senate floor. Sir, the act was brief and my comments on it shall be brief also. I denounce it in the name of the constitution it violated. I denounce it in the name of the sovereignty of Massachusetts, which was stricken down by the blow. I denounce it in the name of civilization, which it outraged. I denounce it in the name of humanity. I denounce it in the name of that fair play which bullies and prize-fighters respect. What! strike a man when he is pinioned—when he cannot respond to a blow! Call you that chivalry? In what code of honor did you get your authority for that? I do not believe that member has a friend so dear who must not in his heart of hearts condemn the act. Even the member himself, if he has left a spark of that chivalry and gallantry attributed to him, must loathe and scorn the act. God knows, I do not wish to speak unkindly or in a spirit of revenge; but I owe it to my manhood and the noble State I in part represent, to express my deep abhorrence of the act. But much as I reprobate the act, much more do I reprobate the conduct of those who were by and saw the outrage perpetrated. Sir, especially do I notice the conduct of that senator recently from the free platform of Massachusetts, with the odor of her hospitality on him, who stood there, not only silent and quiet while it was going on, but when it was over approved the act. And worse: when he had time to cool, when he had slept on it, he went into the Senate Chamber of the United States and shocked the sensibilities of the world by approving it. Another senator did not take part because he feared his motives might be questioned, exhibiting as extraordinary a delicacy as that individual who refused to rescue a drowning mortal because he had not been introduced to him. Another was

not on good terms; and yet if rumor be true, that senator
has declared that himself and family are more indebted to
Mr. Sumner than to any other man; yet when he saw him
borne bleeding by, he turned and went on the other side.
Oh, magnanimous Slidell! Oh, prudent Douglas! Oh, audacious Toombs!

Sir, there are questions arising out of this which far trans-
cend those of a mere personal nature. Of those personal
considerations I shall speak when the question comes properly before us, if I am permitted to do so. The higher question involves the very existence of the government itself. If,
sir, freedom of speech is not to remain to us, what is all this
government worth? If we from Massachusetts, or any other
State—senators, or members of the House—are to be called
to account by some " gallant nephew " of some " gallant
uncle," when we utter something which does not suit their
sensitive natures, we desire to know it. If the conflict is to
be transferred from this peaceful, intellectual field to one
where it is said, " honors are easy and responsibilities equal,"
then we desire to know it. Massachusetts, if her sons and
representatives are to have the rod held over them, if these
things are to continue, the time may come—though she utters
no threats—when she may be called upon to withdraw them
to her own bosom, where she can furnish to them that protection which is not vouchsafed to them under the flag of
their common country. But while she permits us to remain,
we shall do our duty—our whole duty. We shall speak
whatever we choose to speak, when we will, where we will,
and how we will, regardless of all consequences.

Sir, the sons of Massachusetts are educated at the knees
of their mothers in the doctrines of peace and good will, and
God knows, they desire to cultivate those feelings—feelings

of social kindness and public kindness. The House will bear witness that we have not violated or trespassed upon any of them; but, sir, if we are pushed too long or too far, there are men from the old Commonwealth of Massachusetts who will not shrink from a defence of freedom of speech, and the honored State they represent, on any field where they may be assailed.

COLERIDGE

SIR JOHN DUKE, LORD COLERIDGE, an English chief justice and orator, the son of Sir John Taylor Coleridge, an English jurist, was born at Ottery Saint Mary, Devonshire, December 3, 1820. He was educated at Eton, and Balliol College, Oxford, and after gaining a fellowship at Exeter College studied law and was called to the bar at the Middle Temple in 1847. He became recorder of Portsmouth in 1855, queen's counsel in 1861, and from 1865 to 1873 sat in the House of Commons as member for Exeter. Although Coleridge early became famous as a " silver-tongued " speaker his practice for a long period was of limited extent, but after the lapse of years his services came more frequently into demand and he was retained as counsel in a number of celebrated cases. In 1868 he was appointed solicitor-general, in 1871 attorney-general, and in 1873 he became chief justice of the court of common pleas, and was created Baron Coleridge. On the death of Six Alexander Cockburn, Coleridge succeeded him as lord chief justice of England. In 1833 Chief Justice Coleridge made a tour in the United States, where he was received with much enthusiasm and made a number of eloquent speeches and addresses. His death took place in London, June 1, 1894. Coleridge was a very finished speaker, his forensic efforts wanting neither the graces of style nor able reasoning combined with impressiveness of statement. His tastes were strongly literary, and although he wrote no book he contributed frequently to periodicals and journals. He was a brilliant conversationalist, and his friendships, both literary and professional, were extensive. In politics he was a Liberal, giving warm support to his life-long friend, Gladstone, both in and out of office.

ON THE VALUE OF CLEAR VIEWS AS TO THE LAWS REGULATING THE ENJOYMENT OF PROPERTY

FROM ADDRESS TO THE GLASGOW JURIDICAL SOCIETY IN THE QUEEN'S ROOMS, MAY 25, 1887

IT seems an elementary proposition that a free people can deal as it thinks fit with its common stock, and can prescribe to its citizens rules for its enjoyment, alienation, and transmission. Yet in practice this seems to be anything but admitted. There are estates in these islands of more than a million acres. These islands are not very large. It is plainly conceivable that estates might grow to fifteen million acres or to more. Further, it is quite reasonably possible that the growth of a vast emporium of commerce might be checked, or even a whole trade lost to the country by the simple will of one, or it may be more than one, great landowner.

Sweden is a country, speaking comparatively, small and poor; but I have read in a book of authority that in Sweden at the time of the Reformation three fifths of the land were in mortmain and what was actually the fact in Sweden might come to be the fact in Great Britain. These things might be for the general advantage, and if they could be shown to be so, by all means they should be maintained. But if not, does any man possessing anything which he is pleased to call his mind deny that a state of law under which such mischiefs could exist, under which a country itself would exist, not for its people but for a mere handful of them, ought to be instantly and absolutely set aside?

Certainly there are men who, if they do not assert, imply the negative. A very large coal owner some years ago interfered with a high hand in one of the coal strikes. He sent for the workmen. He declined to argue but he said, stamping with his foot upon the ground, "All the coal within so many square miles is mine, and if you do not instantly come to terms not a hundredweight of it shall be brought to the surface, and it shall all remain unworked."

This utterance of his was much criticised at the time. By some it was held up as a subject for panegyric and a model for imitation; the manly utterance of one who would stand no nonsense, determined to assert his rights of property and to tolerate no interference with them. By others it was denounced as insolent and brutal, and it was suggested that if a few more men said such things, and a few men acted on them, it would very probably result in the coal owners having not much right of property left to interfere with. To me it seemed then, and seems now, an instance of that density of perception and inability to see distinctions between things inherently distinct of which I have said so much.

I should myself deny that the mineral treasures under the soil of a country belong to a handful of surface proprietors in the sense in which this gentleman appeared to think they did. That fifty or a hundred gentlemen, or a thousand, would have a right, by agreeing to shut the coal mines, to stop the manufactures of Great Britain and to paralyze her commerce seems to me, I must frankly say, unspeakably absurd.

It is not even the old idea about such things. Coal-mining is comparatively recent; but the custom of bounding as to tin in Cornwall, the customs of the High Peak in Derbyshire as to lead, the legal rule everywhere as to gold and silver, are enough to show that in these matters the general advantage was in former days openly and avowedly regarded, and that when rights of private property interfered with it they were summarily set at naught. To extend to coal and copper the old law applicable to tin and lead may be wise or foolish, but is surely no more an assault on property itself than was the old law which prescribed that, in certain places, and under certain circumstances, the owner of the surface should not prevent the winning of mineral treasure by others entirely unconnected with him or with the surface land. It is not to the point to say that these laws were found to be inconvenient, and have in some places and to some extent been abrogated.

It may be so. Inconvenience, that is, that they were not in practice found to be for the general advantage, is a very good reason for abrogating them. That they existed and had to be modified on grounds of expediency is a proof of the point for which I am contending, namely, that these old laws show that the distinction I think so important was early and largely recognized; and that while property itself was acknowledged, the laws of its enjoyment were regulated according to what was thought to be the general advantage.

I am told, but I do not know of my own knowledge, that the laws in Prussia against the landowner and in favor of the discoverer and winner of mineral treasures are still more stringent than those of Cornwall or Derbyshire, yet, I suppose, that no one will contend that in Prussia the laws of property are disregarded, or that the principle of property is unsafe.

Take again, for a moment, the case of perpetuities, to which I have more than once alluded, as exemplified in gifts *inter vivos*, or in what, by a common but strange abuse of language, are called " munificent bequests," after a man has had all the enjoyment possible to him, to religious or charitable objects. Persons either not capable of attributing definite meaning to their language, or at least not accustomed to do so, talk of any interference with such dispositions as immoral, and brand it as sacrilege.

The wisest clergyman who ever lived, as Mr. Arnold calls Bishop Butler, pointed out nearly 150 years ago that all property is and must be regulated by the laws of the community; that we may with a good conscience retain any property whatever, whether coming from the Church or no, to which the laws of the State give title; that no man can give what he did not receive; and that, as no man can himself have a perpetuity, so he cannot give it to any one else. No answer has ever been attempted to Bishop Butler; none seems pos-

sible; yet men go on, like the Priest and Levite, pass it by
on the other side and repeat the parrot cry of immorality
and sacrilege without ever taking the trouble to clear their
minds, perhaps being congenitally unable to do so, or to ascertain whether there is any argument which will " hold " upon
which to justify the charge. These are they who

> " might move
> The wise man to that scorn which wisdom holds
> Unlawful ever,"

and from whom I part with this one word. There may be
abundant and very good reasons for maintaining the inviolability of all gifts or bequests in perpetuity, there may be
abundant and very good reasons for maintaining the contrary, but to call names does not advance an argument; abuse
is not reasoning, and moderate and reasonable men are apt
to distrust the soundness of a cause which needs such arts
and employs such weapons.

Furthermore, it is often said that you may no doubt alter
the laws of property on a proper case being shown for the
alteration. Sensible men see that what Bishop Butler calls
" plain absurdities " follow from any other doctrine. It
would indeed be difficult, in the face of railway bills, gas bills,
water bills, tramway bills, dock bills, harbor bills (the catalogue is endless) passed by the hundred every year through
both Houses of Parliament, to deny that private property
may be rightly interfered with for the public good, even
when the public is represented chiefly, if not entirely, by a
small band of speculators.

But then it is said you have no right to do it, except on
proper compensation. I ask respectfully, however, what is
the exact meaning of these words, especially " right " and
" proper " ? Is the absolute right,—right, I say, not power,

for that no man questions,—is the absolute right of the State intended to be denied to deal with the common stock with or without compensation; and by proper compensation is it meant that the compensation is to be proper in the opinion of the person compensated, or the person compensating or of whom?

Or is it intended to say only that any change in the tenure of property or of the laws of property made by law should be made with as little suffering to individuals as may be, and with as much consideration as possible for the present holders and present expectants of property, whether real or personal. If the latter proposition is intended no man in his senses will differ from it.   Men to whose personal loss the law is altered are, as matter of common fairness, to be considered in every way, and nothing should be done to their detriment which it is possible to avoid.   Every one will agree in this.

But if the right is questioned, and if the sufficiency of the compensation is to be determined by the person compensated, let this be considered.   A foreign army lands, or a foreign fleet threatens our coasts.   The general in command of the district, in the name of the Sovereign, that is, of the State, orders the destruction of a house which, if left standing, might be an important military position for the invading army; or it may be, as a military precaution, a large tract of cultivated country, gardens, orchards, or the like, has to be laid entirely waste.   Have the owners a claim, a legal right, to compensation?

It has been decided for centuries, in accordance with good sense, most certainly not.   *Salus populi suprema lex.*[1]   Take another case which has actually happened.   Parliament supplies the funds for a great public and national harbor,

---

[1] The safety of the people is the paramount law.

created by a huge breakwater, which the officers of the Sovereign construct. The effect of this great national work is to turn the tide of the sea full on to the lands of a beach-bounded proprietor some miles off, who could only save his land from utter destruction by the erection of a long and massive sea wall. Has he a claim, a legal right, to compensation? Again I answer most certainly not. *Salus populi suprema lex.*

Many other cases might be put to which the answer would be the same but these are enough for my purpose. And now as to the sufficiency of the compensation. The property is taken and often in the opinion of him who loses it no compensation is sufficient. Suppose the possessor of an ancient and beautiful house, endeared to him by a thousand tender and noble memories, is told that he must part with it for the public good. The public good comes to him, perhaps, represented by an engineer, a contractor, an attorney, a parliamentary agent, and a parliamentary counsel. He is very likely well off in point of money and does not at all want the compensation; but he is a man of feeling, or, if you will, of imagination, and he does want his house. He does not believe in the public caring two straws for the railway between Eatanswill and Mudborough. He thinks it hard that the engineer and the rest of them should pull down his old hall, and root up his beautiful pleasure-grounds.

But he is told that the public good requires it, that a jury will give him compensation, and that he has no cause for complaint; and told sometimes by the very people who, when it is proposed to apply the same process for the same reasons to other rights or laws of property, are frantic in their assertion of the sacredness of these laws, and vehemently maintain that to touch one of them is to assail the existence of property and dissolve society. Once more let us see things as they are, recognize distinctions, admit consequences, clear our minds, and if we must differ, as probably we must, let us differ without calling names or imputing motives.

These are individual instances; but all history, and in a high degree the history of these islands is full of examples in which the principle has been unhesitatingly applied to whole classes in the name of the public good. To corporations it has been constantly extended, artificial persons so far as the corporation itself goes, we know, yet made up of individuals who have had to submit to deprivation of property and consequent loss of position without a shadow of compensation.

Monasteries, colleges, convents, corporation boroughs, and other corporations have all at different times of our history and under different circumstances been thought either partly or entirely inconsistent with the general welfare; and accordingly their property has been taken from them, sometimes wholly, sometimes in part, sometimes by compulsory sale, sometimes by simple removal. Great proprietors in many cases now stand in the place of these corporations without any injury to the principle of property, though as a consequence of great changes in the laws regulating its enjoyment. And if in times to come, by the same means and for the same reasons other classes of the nation were to stand in the place of these great proprietors, it would not more follow then than it has followed now that the principle of property would be assailed, though the laws by which it is enjoyed might change.

All laws of property must stand upon the foot of general advantage; a country belongs to the inhabitants; in what proportions and by what rules its inhabitants are to own it must be settled by the law; and the moment a fragment of the people set up rights inherent in themselves and not founded on the public good, " plain absurdities " follow.

This at least seems to have been the view which consciously or unconsciously governed the English lawyers who invented, so greatly to the general advantage, the laws of copyhold. When the tenants had created the farms and built the homesteads on land which they held at the will of the lord, and out of which by the theory of the law they could be turned at his pleasure, though they had made one and built the other; and in respect of which, by the same theory, the lord might have made them pay a heavy rent for what was the fruit of their own hands; the English lawyers intervened with the healing doctrine of the custom of the manor by which fixity of tenure was secured to the tenant and the lord's exactions were curbed within fixed and reasonable limits. Compulsory enfranchisement has followed of late years; but the mitigating effect of manorial custom in harsher times can hardly be overrated; and the absence of such an influence in the sister island, where there are no manors, has sharpened and intensified those hostile feelings between the lord and the tenant which are apt to grow up even in the most favorable circumstances and under the best system of land laws in the world.

HELMHOLTZ

HERMANN LUDWIG FERDINAND VON HELMHOLTZ was born at Potsdam in 1821, and after receiving a university education took a medical degree. At the age of twenty-two he was appointed military physician in his native town, and continued the practice of his profession for some time. Six years later, however, he was invited to occupy the chair of Professor of Physiology at Königsberg, and henceforth he devoted himself to scientific research. He held, successively, professorships at Bonn and Heidelberg, but spent the latter part of his life in Berlin. He is well known as the inventor of the ophthalmoscope, as the writer of "The Theory of the Conservation of Force," "The Doctrine of Tone-Generation," and other epoch-making works, and as the author of discoveries in acoustics and optics, which have challenged the attention of the scientific world. He died in 1894.

THE MYSTERY OF CREATION

ADDRESS DELIVERED AT HEIDELBERG IN 1871

ALL life and all motion on our earth is, with few exceptions, kept up by a single force, that of the sun's rays, which bring to us light and heat. They warm the air of the hot zones; this becomes lighter and ascends, while the colder air flows toward the poles. Thus is formed the great circulation of the passage winds. Local differences of temperature over land and sea, plains and mountains, disturb the uniformity of this great motion, and produce for us the capricious change of winds. Warm aqueous vapors ascend with the warm air, become condensed into clouds, and fall in the cooler zones, and upon the snowy tops of the mountains, as rain and as snow. The water collects

(8211)

in brooks, in rivers, moistens the plains, and makes life possible; crumbles the stones, carries their fragments along, and thus works at the geological transformation of the earth's surface. It is only under the influence of the sun's rays that the variegated covering of plants of the earth grows; and while they grow, they accumulate in their structure organic matter, which partly serves the whole animal kingdom as food, and serves man more particularly as fuel. Coals and lignites, the sources of power of our steam engines, are remains of primitive plants, the ancient production of the sun's rays.

Need we wonder if, to our forefathers of the Aryan race in India and Persia, the sun appeared as the fittest symbol of the Deity? They were right in regarding it as the giver of all life—as the ultimate source of almost all that has happened on earth.

But whence does the sun acquire this force? It radiates forth a more intense light than can be attained with any terrestrial means. It yields as much heat as if fifteen hundred pounds of coal were burned every hour upon each square foot of its surface. Of the heat which thus issues from it, the small fraction which enters our atmosphere furnishes a great mechanical force. Every steam engine teaches us that heat can produce such force. The sun, in fact, drives on earth a kind of steam engine whose performances are far greater than those of artificially constructed machines. The circulation of water in the atmosphere raises, as has been said, the water evaporated from the warm tropical seas to the mountain heights; it is, as it were, a water-raising engine of the most magnificent kind, with whose power no artificial machine can be even distantly compared. I have previously explained the mechanical equivalent of heat. Calculated by that standard, the work which the sun produces by its radiation is equal to the constant exertion of seven thousand horse power for each square foot of the sun's surface.

For a long time experience had impressed on our mechanicians that a working force cannot be produced from nothing; that it can only be taken from the stores which nature possesses, which are strictly limited, and which cannot be increased at pleasure—whether it be taken from the rushing water or from the wind; whether from the layers of coal, or from men and from animals, which cannot work without the consumption of food. Modern physics has attempted to prove the universality of this experience to show that it applies to the great whole of all natural processes, and is independent of the special interests of man. These have been generalized and comprehended in the all-ruling natural law of the conservation of force. No natural process, and no series of natural processes, can be found, however manifold may be the changes which take place among them, by which a motive force can be continuously produced without a corresponding consumption. Just as the human race finds on earth but a limited supply of motive forces, capable of producing work, which it can utilize but not increase, so also must this be the case in the great whole of nature. The universe has its definite store of force, which works in it under ever-varying forms; is indestructible, not to be increased, everlasting and unchangeable like matter itself. It seems as if Goethe has an idea of this when he makes the earth-spirit speak of himself as the representative of natural force:

"In the currents of life, in the tempests of motion,
In the fervor of art, in the fire, in the storm,
            Hither and thither,
            Over and under
            Wend I and wander.
            Birth and the grave,
            Limitless ocean,
            Where the restless wave
            Undulates ever
            Under and over,
            Their seething strife
            Heaving and weaving
            The changes of life.
    At the whirling loom of time unawed,
    I work the living mantle of God."

Let us return to the special question which concerns us here: Whence does the sun derive this enormous store of force which it sends out?

On earth the processes of combustion are the most abundant source of heat. Does the sun's heat originate in a process of this kind? To this question we can reply with a complete and decided negative, for we now know that the sun contains the terrestrial elements with which we are acquainted. Let us select from among them the two, which, for the smallest mass, produce the greatest amount of heat when they combine; let us assume that the sun consists of hydrogen and oxygen, mixed in the proportion in which they would unite to form water. The mass of the sun is known, and also the quantity of heat produced by the union of known weights of oxygen and hydrogen. Calculation shows that under the above supposition the heat resulting from their combustion would be sufficient to keep up the radiation of heat from the sun for three thousand and twenty-one years. That, it is true, is a long time, but even profane history teaches that the sun has lighted and warmed us for three thousand years, and geology puts it beyond doubt that this period must be extended to millions of years.

Known chemical forces are thus so completely inadequate, even on the most favorable assumption, to explain the production of heat which takes place in the sun, that we must quite drop this hypothesis.

We must seek for forces of far greater magnitude, and these we can only find in cosmical attraction. We have already seen that the comparatively small masses of shooting stars and meteorites can produce extraordinarily large amounts of heat when their cosmical velocities are arrested by our atmosphere. Now, the force which has produced these great velocities is gravitation. We know of this force as one acting on the surface of our planet when it appears as terrestrial gravity. We know that a weight raised from the earth can drive our clocks, and that in like manner the gravity of the water rushing down from the mountains works our mills.

If a weight fall from a height and strike the ground, its mass loses, indeed, the visible motion which it had as a whole—in fact, however, this motion is not lost; it is transferred to the smallest elementary particles of the mass, and this invisible vibration of the molecules is the motion of heat. Visible motion is transformed by impact into the motion of heat.

That which holds in this respect for gravity holds also for gravitation. A heavy mass, of whatever kind, which is suspended in space separated from another heavy mass, represents a force capable of work. For both masses attract each other, and, if unrestrained by centrifugal force, they move toward each other under the influence of this attraction; this takes place with ever-increasing velocity; and if this velocity is finally destroyed, whether this be suddenly by collision, or gradually by the friction of movable parts, it develops the corresponding quantity of the motion of heat, the amount of which can be calculated from the equivalence, previously established, between heat and mechanical work.

Now we may assume with great probability that very many more meteors fall upon the sun than upon the earth, and with greater velocity, too, and therefore give more heat. Yet the hypothesis that the entire amount of the sun's heat which is continually lost by radiation is made up by the fall of meteors, a hypothesis which was propounded by Mayer, and has been favorably adopted by several other physicists, is open, according to Sir W. Thomson's investigations, to objection; for, assuming it to hold, the mass of the sun should increase so rapidly that the consequences would have shown themselves in the accelerated motion of the planets. The entire loss of heat from the sun cannot, at all events, be produced in this way; at the most a portion, which, however, may not be inconsiderable.

If, now, there is no present manifestation of force sufficient to cover the expenditure of the sun's heat, the sun must originally have had a store of heat which it gradually gives out. But whence this store? We know that the cosmical forces alone could have produced it. And here the hypothesis, previously discussed as to the origin of the sun, comes to our aid. If the mass of the sun had been once diffused in cosmical space, and had then been condensed —that is, had fallen together under the influence of celestial gravity—if, then, the resultant motion had been de-

stroyed by friction and impact with the production of
heat, the new world produced by such condensation must
have acquired a store of heat, not only of considerable, but
even of colossal magnitude.

Calculation shows that, assuming the thermal capacity
of the sun to be the same as that of water, the temperature might be raised to twenty-eight million of degrees, if
this quantity of heat could ever have been present in the
sun at one time. This cannot be assumed, for such an
increase of temperature would offer the greatest hindrance
to condensation. It is probable rather that a great part of
this heat which was produced by condensation began to
radiate into space before this condensation was complete.
But the heat which the sun could have previously developed by its condensation would have been sufficient to
cover its present expenditure for not less than twenty-
two million years of the past.

And the sun is by no means so dense as it may become. Spectrum analysis demonstrates the presence of
large masses of iron and of other known constituents
of the rocks. The pressure which endeavors to con-
dense the interior is about eight hundred times as great
as that in the centre of the earth; and yet the density of
the sun, owing probably to its enormous temperature, is
less than a quarter of the mean density of the earth.

We may, therefore, assume with great probability that
the sun will still continue in its condensation, even if it
only attained the density of the earth—though it will
probably become far denser in the interior, owing to
the enormous pressure—this would develop fresh quanti-
ties of heat, which would be sufficient to maintain for an
additional seventeen million years the same intensity of

sunshine as that which is now the source of all terrestrial life.

. . . .

The term of seventeen million years which I have given may, perhaps, become considerably prolonged by the gradual abatement of radiation by the new accretion of falling meteors, and by still greater condensation than that which I have assumed in that calculation. But we know of no natural process which could spare our sun the fate which has manifestly fallen upon other suns. This is a thought which we only reluctantly admit; it seems to us an insult to the beneficent Creative Power which we otherwise find at work in organisms, and especially in living ones. But we must reconcile ourselves to the thought that, however we may consider ourselves to be the centre and final object of creation, we are but as dust on the earth; which again is but a speck of dust in the immensity of space; and the previous duration of our race, even if we follow it far beyond our written history, into the era of the lake dwellings or of the mammoth, is but an instant compared with the primeval times of our planet, when living beings existed upon it, whose strange and unearthly remains still gaze at us from their ancient tombs; and far more does the duration of our race sink into insignificance compared with the enormous periods during which worlds have been in process of formation, and will still continue to form when our sun is extinguished, and our earth is either solidified in cold, or is united with the ignited central body of our system.

But who knows whether the first living inhabitants of the warm sea on the young world, whom we ought, perhaps, to honor as our ancestors, would not have regarded our present cooler condition with as much horror as we look on a world without a sun? Considering the wonderful adaptability to the conditions of life which all organisms possess, who knows to what degree of perfection our posterity will have been developed in seventeen million years, and whether our fossilized bones will not, perhaps, seem to them as monstrous as those of the Ichthyosaurus now do; and whether they, adjusted for a more sensitive state of equilibrium, will not consider the extremes of temperature within which we now exist to be just as violent and destructive as those of the older geological times appear to us? Yea, even if sun and earth should solidify and become motionless, who could say what new worlds would not be ready to develop life? Meteoric stones sometimes contain hydrocarbons; the light of the heads of comets exhibits a spectrum which is most like that of the electrical light in gases containing hydrogen and carbon. But carbon is the element, which is characteristic of organic compounds, from which living bodies are built up. Who knows whether these bodies, which everywhere swarm through space, do not scatter germs of life wherever there is a new world, which has become capable of giving a dwelling-place to organic bodies? And this life we might, perhaps, consider as allied to ours in its primitive germ, however different might be the form which it would assume in adapting itself to its new dwelling-place.

However this may be, that which most arouses our moral feelings at the thought of a future, though possibly very remote, cessation of all living creation on the earth is more particularly the question whether all this life is not an aimless sport, which will ultimately fall a prey to destruction by brute force. Under the light of Darwin's great thought, we begin to see that, not only pleasure and joy, but also pain, struggle, and death, are the powerful means by which Nature has built up her finer and more perfect forms of life. And we men know more particularly that in our intelligence, our civic order, and our morality we are living on the inheritance which our forefathers have gained for us, and that which we acquire in the same way will, in like manner, ennoble the life of our posterity. Thus the individual who works for the ideal objects of humanity, even if in a modest position, and in a limited sphere of activity, may bear without fear the thought that the thread of his own consciousness will one day break. But even men of such free and large order of minds as Lessing and David Strauss could not reconcile themselves to the thought of a final destruction of the living race, and with it of all the fruits of all past generations.

As yet we know of no fact, which can be established by scientific observation, which would show that the finer and complex forms of vital motion could exist otherwise than in the dense material of organic life: that it can propagate itself as the sound-movement of a string can leave its originally narrow and fixed home and diffuse itself in the air, keeping all the time its pitch, and the most delicate shade of its color-tint; and that, when it meets another string attuned to it, starts this again or excites a flame ready to sing to the same tone. The flame even, which of all processes in inanimate nature is the closest type of life, may become extinct, but the heat which it produces continues to exist—indestructible, im-perishable, as an invisible motion, now agitating the molecules of ponderable matter, and then radiating into boundless space as the vibration of an ether. Even there it retains the characteristic peculiarities of its origin, and it reveals its history to the inquirer who questions it by the spectroscope. United afresh, these rays may ignite a new flame, and thus, as it were, acquire a new bodily existence.

Just as the flame remains the same in appearance, and continues to exist with the same form and structure, although it draws every minute fresh combustible vapor, and fresh oxygen from the air, into the vortex of its ascending current; and just as the wave goes on in unaltered form, and is yet being reconstructed every moment from fresh particles of water, so also in the living being it is not the definite mass of substance which now constitutes the body to which the continuance of the individual is attached. For the material of the body, like that of the flame, is subject to continuous and comparatively rapid change—a change the more rapid the livelier the activity of the organs in question. Some constituents are renewed from day to day, some from month to month, and others only after years. That which continues to exist as a particular individual is like the flame and the wave—only the form of motion which continually attracts fresh matter into its vortex and expels the old. The observer with a deaf ear only recognizes the vibration of sound as long as it is visible and can be felt, bound up with heavy matter. Are our senses, in reference to life, like the deaf ear in this respect?

TUPPER

SIR CHARLES TUPPER, a distinguished Canadian statesman, was born at Amherst, Nova Scotia, July 2, 1821, and educated in public and private schools. He studied medicine at Edinburgh University and returning to Nova Scotia began practice in his native town, and soon reaching the top of his profession was president of the Canadian Medical Association, 1857-70. Entering the Nova Scotia legislature in 1855, as member for the Cumberland district, he quickly became prominent there and was provincial secretary, 1855-60. While in England in 1858 on business connected with the intercolonial railway he sounded a number of prominent statesmen regarding the project for a confederation of the Provinces of British North America. He was prime minister of Nova Scotia, 1864-67, during which period he passed the free school law, and after the union of the Provinces he sat in the Dominion House of Commons until 1870, when he entered the cabinet as president of the council. He filled the position of minister of internal revenue, 1872-73, was minister of public works, 1878-79, and minister of railways and canals, 1879-84. He was knighted in 1879 by the Marquis of Lorne acting for the queen, and in 1888 was created a baronet for his services in connection with the Fisheries Treaty at Washington. He was high commissioner for Canada in London, 1883-87, and after a year as minister of finance in the Canadian cabinet was recalled to London as high commissioner in 1888. In January, 1898, he entered the Dominion cabinet as secretary of state and later in the same year was for a short time prime minister of Canada. His party being defeated in June he resigned this post and at the assembling of the Canadian Parliament in the following August became leader of the Opposition. He has received many honorary degrees from various universities and had held a number of important offices in addition to the already named.

IN FAVOR OF A PROTECTIVE POLICY

FROM SPEECH DELIVERED IN THE CANADIAN HOUSE OF COMMONS,
MARCH 14, 1879

I CONFESS that I am very much surprised at the forcible though fallacious address to which we have all listened for the last two or three hours. I did suppose, sir, that, brought face to face, as the people of this country have been under the administration of public affairs, by the honorable gentleman who has just taken his seat, with a condition of things that is calculated to arrest the attention of every patriotic man in Canada, I did suppose that that honorable gentleman would feel that it was a duty he owed to this House, that he owed to this country, not to indulge in such animadversions as he has indulged in in reference to the proposals that have just been made to the House, but to lend to the ministry of the day and to my honorable friend, the finance minister of Canada, all the aid and all the assistance that he could, in order that some measures might be adopted to retrieve that position of affairs into which that honorable gentleman has largely contributed to bring this country.

The honorable gentleman talks of incapacity, talks of recklessness, talks of ignorance. I ask the members of this House who have listened to him for the last five years whether in the whole of this country can be found a more striking monument of all those excellencies than the honorable gentleman himself? Five years ago, when I ventured some modest criticisms of the policy that he propounded to the House, he expressed his regret that no finance minister of the then late administration had a seat in the House. That regret was not confined to himself. No man felt it more than I did. No one felt it more than the gentlemen who were associated with me, and I am glad to know that that feeling became widespread throughout the country; that every year the experience that the people of Canada had of the administration, of its fiscal and financial affairs by the honorable gentleman induced a deeper, wider, and stronger feeling as to the absolute necessity of bringing back to the aid and assistance of this country the gentleman under whose financial management it had prospered before.

The honorable gentleman himself has heard the plaudits given to-night to the budget speech delivered by my honor-

able friend, coming, I was going to say, from the whole
House, so small was the number of those who did not join
in applauding the able effort of my honorable friend that it
seemed to come not from a section of this House, but from
the entire chamber. I congratulate the House, I congratulate the country, that my honorable friend [Mr. Tilley] is
back in the position he occupied in 1873—back in the position he occupied when the late government handed over to
their successors in office the conduct of the affairs of the
country, which was then in the highest condition of prosperity of any country on the face of the globe—back to the
position he occupied when the honorable gentleman, instead
of inheriting years of accumulated deficits, inherited years
of accumulated surpluses—back, I say, to a condition of
things that would compare favorably with the administration of public affairs in any country in the world. . . .

Now the honorable gentleman says he wonders the finance
minister is not appalled at the spectre which is conjured up
before us. Well, sir, I think my honorable friend, looking
round this Parliament, which I am proud to say in my judgment, surpasses in independence, character, intellect, and
talent any Parliament that ever sat within these walls, my
honorable friend must see that the great mass of the representatives of the people are not appalled, and that if there is
any spectre present it is in the honorable gentleman's
imagination.

Let him look at Canada to-day and compare it with what
it was when he assumed the financial management of this
country, and what will he find? Where wealth, prosperity,
happiness, and progress were in Canada he will find gaunt
poverty and distress pervading the country from end to end.
That is what he will find. I do not envy the honorable gen-

tleman his feelings when he casts his eye over the horizon
of his country and finds here and there spectres gaunt with
famine and distress; poverty where wealth existed before;
hunger where plenty was known.   I sympathize with the
honorable gentleman when he feels that had he addressed
himself like a statesman to meet the emergency as my honorable friend has met it, the prosperity we enjoyed when
he took office would be enjoyed now.

There are spectres, but they are not spectres of which my
honorable friend, the finance minister, need be afraid, and
if his policy is what I believe it is, and if it has the effect
in Canada it had before, he will have nothing to regret. We
are told that it is un-British.   When did it become un-
British? How did Great Britain attain the position of
prominence and distinction she occupies as a manufacturing
country? Was it by a free-trade policy? Was it by unnecessary expenditure and deficits that all the interests of
the country were allowed to become impoverished?

No. It was by protecting and fostering the industries of
the country, by developing the great resources Providence
had given to the country, that she became so great and prosperous. When she followed that policy long enough to be
enabled to bid defiance to the world she changed her policy,
believing that the example she was giving would be followed
by other countries.

Unfortunately for England that policy was not followed
by other countries, and the most thoughtful men, the most
able statesmen, the most distinguished men in commercial
circles are to-day turning their attention seriously to the
question as to whether, in adopting that policy of free trade,
England had not made a mistake, and as to whether it might
not well, at no distant day, be reconsidered.

They say it is not British. But I say it is eminently British. From what source do we find the industries of Canada paralyzed? Is it from competition with England? No. That is fair and legitimate competition—a competition in which we have the protection of 3,000 miles of sea. That which breaks down the industries of Canada is the policy of unfair, unjust, and illegitimate trade on the part of our American neighbors who have their own market for themselves and can afford to send their surplus products over here at slaughtering prices, knowing that when they have thus stamped out Canadian industries they can put up the price and recoup themselves.

What about the iron industry? Every person who knows anything about the subject is aware that Providence has given us not only magnificent mines of iron and coal, inexhaustible and of the best quality, for the manufacture of iron in close proximity to the iron deposits. The moment that interest was established, and British and Canadian capital was invested in that industry—the moment Americans found that American iron was being driven out of this market—they sent their agents here to ascertain at what price iron could be bought. They said, " We can supply you with iron equal in quality and at less cost than you can obtain it elsewhere." It is indeed well known that the agents came here and stated whatever was the price of iron in Canada they would supply it at ten per cent less.

That was not from a charitable disposition, or a desire to promote the prosperity of Canada, but from a desire to crush our industries and enrich themselves after our industries were destroyed. Under these circumstances it is not strange that the idea should force itself upon the minds of members of the government, looking to the prosperity of the country.

"It is necessary, not that we should adopt a hostile attitude against our neighbors, but that we should pay them the compliment of saying that their policy is so wise and just that we are disposed to follow it."

I believe the result of this imposition of a duty on coal will be to bring about free trade in that article between the two countries. Nova Scotia coal, which formerly was largely shipped to New York and Boston markets, was shut out by a duty of seventy-five cents per ton. Was not free trade to be expected as the natural result, when the Americans find Canada declaring if they shut Nova Scotia coal out of the market of the Eastern States we must adopt a policy of protection to our own industry as they were protecting theirs, and give Nova Scotia coal owners the Ontario market. I believe within two years from the adoption of the national policy—not a policy of hostility to the United States, but one of following the system they had adopted to foster their industries—they will give us a free market for coal in the United States.

While adopting measures to meet the government of the United States by a tariff somewhat analogous to their own, and to protect the mining, manufacturing, and agricultural interests of Canada against the unfair competition of our neighbors across the lines, my honorable friend the finance minister also proposes to insert in the bill the statement that when the Americans shall reduce their tariff on these natural products we will reduce ours to the same extent, and that when they wipe out the duties altogether, we will admit their products free. At no distant day we shall enjoy all the advantages which we possessed under the Reciprocity Treaty.

I believe, in the interests of Ontario, it is a wise policy to develop the coal industry of Nova Scotia. That Province is an important part of the Dominion, and twelve million dollars of capital invested in coal mines cannot lie dead and unremunerative without inflicting great injury on the whole country. Nova Scotia has common interests with the other Provinces and contributes to the general revenue and it is, therefore, the duty of Parliament to adopt all legitimate measures to promote and foster its industries. What would be the effect of pursuing a contrary course? In the present state of the labor market in the United States, coal can be produced at exceedingly low prices, and if the Nova Scotia coal industries are not fostered they will be crushed out, and the people so employed will go to swell the ranks of those engaged in building up that great country to the south of the line. Send your own people to populate the United States and what happens? When the coal industries of Nova Scotia are destroyed the Americans will raise the price of coal to the people of Ontario and they will have to pay it. And why is not coal a legitimate subject for taxation? Do you not tax cloth, hats, boots, and indeed everything that the poor man consumes? You are willing to tax sugar fifty per cent and impose heavy duties on tea and coffee. And where can you draw the line between fuel and the other necessaries of life?

My honorable friend the finance minister had reduced the duties on the necessaries of life by $400,000 a year. He has decreased the expenditure for the year by about $800,000, taking into account the sinking fund and interest on the additional debt that was required.

The honorable member for Centre Huron objected to the iron industry being fostered in the manner proposed. The honorable gentleman objects to coal being fostered in the same way. Does he not know that the history of the world shows that every country that possessed coal and iron has risen to greatness just in proportion as it has developed those industries? This I know, that in England and Belgium, where coal and iron abound, the progress of those countries is indicated as by a barometer, and has risen just in proportion to the output of the coal and the development of the iron mines. The coal industries of the country will not only be benefitted by protection, but the very fact that these industries are promoted,—that there is an increased demand for the coal,—will lower its costs for consumption to every person who requires to use it. If a mine has a capacity for an output of 100,000 tons of coal and there is only a demand for 30,000, it will cost the miner $1.50 a ton to put that coal at its pit's mouth, whereas if there was a larger demand he could bring it out at a better profit for $1.25. So, looking at what nature has endowed this country with these deposits of coal and iron, I believe that a wiser and more judicious policy could not be contemplated than the policy under which these great industries are to have fair play, and to have the same consideration that all other industries are entitled to.

I did not intend to prolong these observations for two reasons, first, because it is not necessary, as the honorable gentleman, as I have already said, in his somewhat rambling speech managed to knock down all the men of straw he considered he had set up, and left little for me to demolish. But there is one thing I must refer to, and that is the denunciation of my honorable friend for allowing duties to be paid in anticipation of this tariff. Does he forget that he was so anxious to get money paid in, in anticipation of the duties of 1874, that he actually put it in the governor's speech?

Does not the honorable gentleman know that for three

long years we have been saying from these benches that the
tariff would be reconstructed in this sense the moment we
came into power? Does he not know that from one end of
the country to the other we have openly put it before the
country as a question of public policy from which there was
no escape, that either this country must go to ruin, or that
there must be a radical reconstruction of the tariff? But
when there was no such expectation, when no man in this
country dreamed of a deficit except himself—and he did not
dream of it, because he had the evidence to the contrary
before his eyes—the honorable gentleman knowing that, and
having that knowledge within himself, put into the governor's speech the announcement that startled every man in
this country, and drove them with a rush to the Custom-
houses. And yet he had been denouncing my honorable
friend of being guilty of a great moral turpitude, for declaring to this country that we intended to make this change in
its fiscal affairs.

I have but one remark more to make and I sit down. I
did not believe that any party necessity, that any feeling of
jealousy of the gentleman who had gone before him or of
the gentleman who came after him in the administration of
the government, could have induced the honorable gentleman to invite the hostile action of the United States. I say
the language the honorable gentleman used—the language
that he unfairly, unpatriotically, and dishonestly used, because, sir, it is not true. I say that language was unworthy
the mouth of any Canadian statesman. I say that declarations on the floor of the Parliament of Canada, going to-
morrow morning down to New York and Washington, that
we are at the feet of the Americans—the declarations that
we are as clay in the hands of the potter, that we live by

their favor, that they have it in their power to adopt a policy that will crush us—I say that that was an unpatriotic statement, and I repeat that it is not true.

We have one half of this continent and not the worst half of it either. We have a country of divers resources of the most varied character. We have the great granary of the world, for a finer granary does not exist than the great northwest; and with this great and magnificent country and all its enormous resources, were we to assent to the view of the honorable gentleman, we should be unworthy the name of freemen, of the British origin of which we all pride ourselves—we should be unworthy of numbering among our people that great nationality descended from old France, having the same energy of character that has rendered France to-day one of the most prosperous countries—and under the protective system—that has ever been seen.

The honorable gentleman deplores the different nationalities and the different religions. Why, it is that which makes a country great. I say that this country is a greater country because there is a different race and a different language and a different religion. It has been found in all countries that nothing tends to stimulate the progress and prosperity of a country, and to develop all its institutions, whether civil or religious, more than a natural rivalry among freemen—that is to be found in such a country as this. Under these circumstances I trust never to hear from the mouth of any Canadian statesman in this House or out of it, the unpatriotic declaration that this great country of ours occupies so humiliating, so degrading a position as that which the language of the honorable gentleman indicated.

A NATIONAL MEASURE

[Extracts from the notable speech delivered by Sir Charles Tupper in the Canadian House of Commons on December 14, 1880, in presenting the resolutions providing for a grant of twenty-five million dollars and twenty-five million acres of land to the Canadian Pacific Railway Company in order to aid the company in constructing the line which now extends across Canada from the Atlantic to the Pacific Ocean.]

MR. CHAIRMAN,—It affords me very much pleasure to rise for the purpose of submitting a motion to this House in relation to the most important question that has ever engaged the attention of this Parliament—a motion which submits for the approval of this House the means by which the great national work, the Canadian Pacific Railway, shall be completed and operated hereafter in a way that has more than once obtained the approval of this House, and the sanction of the people of this country, and upon terms more favorable than any that have ever previously been offered to the House.

I shall be obliged, Mr. Chairman, to ask the indulgence of the House while at some considerable length I place before it the grounds upon which I affirm that this resolution embodies the policy of the Parliament of Canada as expressed on more than one occasion, and that these resolutions present terms for the consideration of this Parliament, for the completion of this work, more favorable than any previously submitted; and, sir, I have the less hesitation in asking the indulgence of the House, because I ask it mainly for the purpose of repeating to the House statements made by gentlemen of much greater ability than myself, and occupying positions in this House and country second to no other. But for what took place here yesterday I would have felt warranted in expressing the opinion that the resolutions, grave and important as they are, would receive the unanimous consent of this Parliament.

I would, I say, have been warranted in arriving at that conclusion—but for the very significant indications that were made from the other side of the House—because these resolutions only ask honorable gentlemen on both sides of the House to affirm a proposition to which they have again and again, as public men, committed themselves. I need not remind the House that when my right honorable friend, the leader of the government, occupied in 1871 the same position which he now occupies, the policy of constructing a great line of Canadian Pacific railway that would connect the two great oceans which form the eastern and western boundaries of the Dominion of Canada, received the approval of the House. Not only did the policy of accomplishing that great work receive the indorsation of a large majority in the Parliament of the country, but in specific terms, the means by which that work should be accomplished were embodied in a form of a resolution and submitted for the consideration of the Parliament. . . .

I say that this company embraces capitalists, both of our own and other countries, who are men of highest character; men, whose names are the best guarantees that could be offered the people of Canada, that any enterprise they may undertake will be successful. With regard to the terms of the contract, I do not hesitate to say that no greater injury could have been inflicted on the people of Canada than to have made the conditions of the agreement so onerous that instead of ensuring their successful fulfilment they would have led to failure. I say that the moment the contract is signed everything we can do for the purpose of obtaining the best terms in our power has been done, always under the impression that we owed it to Canada to make a contract that was capable of fulfilment; to give those gentlemen a fair contract and afford them a fair opportunity of grappling with this great, this gigantic enterprise, that we were so anxious to transfer from our shoulders to theirs.

And I would ask this House whether this being a contract involving the great business importance that it does, is one to sit down and cavil over, in the ordinary acceptation of the term, in relation to contracts, and to drive the most difficult bargain that could be driven, and perhaps lead to what occurred when we made the contract in 1873, with terms largely in excess of those that this contract contains? That was not a contract that was capable of fulfilment, because the parties were unable, in the then condition of the country, to raise the capital that was necessary. Now, we approach this question in that spirit, and I would ask every member of this House, if we should not be unworthy of representing the Parliament of Canada in the discharge of the public business, if we had not felt in the interests of Canada, that this arrangement should be one that would obtain the command of the capital that was required, and that would enable the parties engaged in this great work to make it thoroughly successful as I trust it will be. We have reason to know that all that a command of capital can do they have the advantage of; we have reason to know that all that skill and energy and a knowledge of precisely such work will do, has been secured, in order to make this a successful contract, and I would ask honorable gentlemen opposite what more is desirable or necessary. . . .

When I rose I expressed the pride and pleasure it gave me as a member of the government of Canada to be able in the

year 1880, to propound to Parliament a measure for its
adoption which will secure in ten years the construction of the
Pacific railway, upon terms more favorable than the most
enthusiastic friend of the railway had ventured to hope this
Parliament would have the opportunity of putting its seal of
ratification to. I have read at some length the able and
eloquent statements of honorable gentlemen opposite to show
that no men are more bound as honorable and patriotic statesmen to give this measure their hearty support than those
gentlemen themselves. I am glad to know that if ever there
were a measure presented for the consideration of this House,
worthy and likely to receive its hearty adoption, it is the
measure I have the honor of submitting for its consideration.
I have the satisfaction of knowing that throughout this intelligent country every man breathed more freely when he
learned that the great, enormous undertaking of constructing and operating the railway was to be lifted from the
shoulders of the government, and the liability the country
was going to incur was what was to be brought within, not over
the limit, which in its present financial condition it is prepared to meet; within such limits that the proceeds from the
sale of land to be granted by Parliament for the construction of the line, would wipe out all liabilities at no distant day.
But this is the slightest consideration in reference to this
question. It is a fact that under the proposals now submitted for the Parliament to consider, this country is going
to secure the construction and operation of the gigantic work
which is to give new life and vitality to every section of
this Dominion. No greater responsibility rests upon any
body of men in this Dominion than rests upon the government of Canada, placed as it is in a position to deal with the
enormous work of the development of such a country as

Providence has given us; and I say we should be traitors to ourselves and to our children if we should hesitate to secure on terms such as we have the pleasure of submitting to Parliament the construction of this work, which is going to develop all the enormous resources of the northwest, and to pour into that country a tide of population which will be a tower of strength to every part of Canada, a tide of industrious and intelligent men who will not only produce national as well as individual wealth in that section of the Dominion, but will create such a demand for the supplies which must come from the older Provinces, as will give new life and vitality to every industry in which those Provinces are engaged.

Under these circumstances we had a right to expect that support, which in justice to themselves and their position as statesmen, honorable gentlemen opposite should give us. I say, sir, that looking at this matter from a party point of view —the lowest point of view—I feel that these gentlemen, by following the course they propose, are promoting the interests of the party now in power, just as they promoted our interests when they placed themselves in antagonism to the national policy which the great mass of the people desired.

But I say I am disappointed at their course. I regret it, notwithstanding that it conduces to the interests of our own party. On past occasions I made the most earnest appeal in my power to those gentlemen to sink on one great national question partisan feelings and to enable both sides of this House and both parties of this country to unite in a great measure that did not require to be dragged down into the arena of party, and which would be promoted and largely promoted by a combination of both of the great parties in this country.

The honorable gentlemen refused to respond to that ap-

peal and therefore I will not waste time on the present occasion by pointing out to them how desirable it is now, but
I did hope when we abandoned this railway as a government
work and when it became a commercial undertaking it would
be otherwise; and one of the reasons—one of the great necessities for changing our base—one of the great necessities
to place this work on a commercial footing at the earliest
opportunity—was that we became aware from the events of
the last two sessions that while we dealt with it as a government railway it was to be dragged down from its high position to the arena of partisan politics.

In order to obstruct the government, in order to prevent
our carrying out the policy as we were carrying it out, these
gentlemen were driven to assume the unpatriotic attitude of
decrying the credit and capabilities of our country and
damaging the prospects of this great work.

I am glad that we have triumphed over such opposition
and that despite the obstruction we have surmounted the
great difficulty—that despite all the obstruction they could
throw in our way, the time has come when enlightened
capitalists best acquainted with the resources of Canada are
prepared to throw themselves into the constrution of this
great railway. I say, that I was in hope, now that we have
abandoned it as a government work and it is placed on a commercial foundation, that those gentlemen could, without loss
of party prestige, unite with us on this great question and
on giving this syndicate, who are charged with this important
and onerous undertaking, that fair, handsome, and generous
support that men engaged in a great national work in any
country are entitled to receive at the hands, not only of the
government of the country, but of every patriotic member
of the Parliament.

Sir, I say I have been disappointed, but I hope upon future reflection at no distant day when the results of this measure which we are now submitting for the approval of Parliament and which I trust and confidently expect will obtain the sanction of this House, will be such as to compel these gentlemen openly and candidly to admit that in taking the course which we have followed we have done what is calculated to promote the best interests of the country and that it has been attended with a success exceeding our most sanguine expectations.

I can only say in conclusion after some five-and-twenty years of public life I shall feel it the greatest source of pleasure that the quarter of a century has afforded me, as I am satisfied that my right honorable friend beside me will feel that it crowns the success of his public life, that while premier of this country his government was able to carry through Parliament a measure of such inestimable value to the progress of Canada; so I can feel if I have no other bequest to leave my children after me the proudest legacy I would desire to leave was the record that I was able to take an active part in the promotion of this great measure, by which I believe Canada will receive an impetus that will make it a great and powerful country at no distant date.

BRECKINRIDGE

JOHN CABELL BRECKENRIDGE or BRECKINRIDGE, an American politician and soldier, was born near Lexington, Kentucky, January 21, 1821. He was educated at Centre College, in his own State, and after studying law at Transylvania University established himself in practice at Lexington. During the Mexican War he held a major's commission and at its close he entered the lower house of the State legislature. He was sent to Congress in 1851 as Democratic representative, and after serving several times was elected to the vice-presidency in 1856. In 1860 he was the presidential candidate of the Anti-Douglas Democrats, receiving seventy-two electoral votes. In the same year he was elected to the United States Senate, and after advocating there the cause of the South for a short time during Lincoln's administration, he resigned his seat and joined the Confederacy in the autumn of 1861, soon receiving an appointment as major-general. From January, 1865, until the fall of the Confederacy, Breckinridge was Confederate secretary of war. After the surrender of Lee in April, 1865, Breckinridge went to Europe, but returned in 1868 and spent the remainder of his life in his native State, dying at Lexington, May 17, 1875.

ADDRESS PRECEDING THE REMOVAL OF THE SENATE

ON the 6th of December, 1819, the Senate assembled for the first time in this Chamber, which has been the theatre of their deliberations for more than thirty-nine years.

And now the strifes and uncertainties of the past are finished. We see around us on every side the proofs of stability and improvement. The Capitol is worthy of the Republic. Noble public buildings meet the view on every hand. Treasures of science and the arts begin to accumulate. As this flourishing city enlarges it testifies to the wisdom and forecast that dictated the plan of it. Future generations will not be disturbed with questions concerning the centre of population, or of territory, since the steamboat, the railroad, and the telegraph have made communication almost instantaneous. The spot is sacred by a thousand memories, which are so many pledges that the city of Washington, founded by him and bearing his revered name, with its beautiful site, bounded by picturesque eminences, and the broad Potomac, and lying within view of his home and his tomb, shall remain forever the political capital of the United States.

It would be interesting to note the gradual changes which have occurred in the practical working of the government since the adoption of the constitution; and it may be appropriate to this occasion to remark one of the most striking of them.

At the origin of the government the Senate seemed to be regarded chiefly as an executive council. The President often visited the chamber and conferred personally with this body; most of its business was transacted with closed doors, and it took comparatively little part in the legislative debates. The rising and vigorous intellects of the country sought the arena of the House of Representatives as the appropriate theatre for the display of their powers. Mr. Madison observed, on some occasion, that being a young man and desiring to increase his reputation, he could not afford to enter the Senate; and it will be remembered that so late as 1812 the great debates which preceded the war and aroused the country to the assertion of its rights took place in the other branch of Congress. To such an extent was the idea of seclusion carried that when this chamber was completed no seats were prepared for the accommodation of the public; and it was not until many years afterward that the semicircular gallery was erected which admits the people to be witnesses of your proceedings. But now, the Senate, besides its peculiar relations to the executive department of the government, assumes its full share of duty as a co-equal branch of the legislature; indeed from the limited number of its members and for other obvious reasons the most important questions, especially of foreign policy, are apt to pass first under discussion in this body,—and to be a member of it is justly regarded as one of the highest honors which can be conferred on an American statesman.

It is scarcely necessary to point out the causes of this change, or to say that it is a concession both to the importance and to the individuality of the States, and to the free and open character of the government.

In connection with this easy but thorough transition, it is worthy of remark that it has been effected without a charge from any quarter that the Senate has transcended its constitutional sphere—a tribute at once to the moderation of the Senate, and another proof to thoughtful men of the comprehensive wisdom with which the framers of the constitution secured essential principles without inconveniently embarrassing the action of the government.

The progress of this popular movement in one aspect of it, has been steady and marked. As the origin of the government, no arrangements in the Senate were made for spectators; in this chamber about one third of the space is allotted to the public; and in the new apartment the galleries cover two thirds of its area. In all free countries the admission of the people to witness legislative proceedings is an essential element of public confidence; and it is not to be anticipated that this wholesome principle will ever be abused by the substitution of partial and interested demonstrations for the expression of a matured and enlightened public opinion. Yet it should never be forgotten that not France, but the turbulent spectators within the hall, awed and controlled the French assembly. With this lesson and its consequences before us, the time will never come when the deliberations of the Senate shall be swayed by the blandishments or the thunders of the galleries.

It is impossible to disconnect from an occasion like this a crowd of reflections on our past history and of speculations on the future. The most meagre account of the Senate involves a summary of the progress of our country. From year to year you have seen your representation enlarge; again and again you have proudly welcomed a new sister into the confederacy; and the occurrences of this day are a material and impressive proof of the growth and prosperity of the United States. Three periods in the history of the Senate mark in striking contrast three epochs in the history of the Union.

On the 3d of March, 1789, when the government was organized under the constitution, the Senate was composed of the representatives of eleven States containing three millions of people.

On the 6th of December, 1819, when the Senate met for the first time in this room it was composed of the representatives of twenty-one States containing nine millions of people.

To-day it is composed of the representatives of thirty-two States containing more than twenty-eight millions of people, prosperous, happy, and still devoted to constitutional liberty. Let these great facts speak for themselves to all the world.

The career of the United States cannot be measured by that of any other people of whom history gives account; and the mind is almost appalled at the contemplation of the prodigious force which has marked their progress. Sixty-nine years ago thirteen States, containing three millions of in-

JOHN C. BRECKINRIDGE

habitants, burdened with debt, and exhausted by the long war of independence, established for their common good a free constitution on principles new to mankind, and began their experiment with the good wishes of a few doubting friends and the derision of the world. Look at the result to-day; twenty-eight millions of people, in every way happier than an equal number in any other part of the globe! the centre of population and political power descending the western slopes of the Alleghany Mountains, and the original thirteen States forming but the eastern margin on the map of our vast possessions.

See besides, Christianity, civilization, and the arts given to a continent; the despised colonies grown into a power of the first class, representing and protecting ideas that involve the progress of the human race; a commerce greater than that of any other nation; free interchange between States; every variety of climate, soil, and production, to make a people powerful and happy—in a word, behold present greatness, and in the future an empire to which the ancient mistress of the world in the height of her glory could not be compared. Such is our country; aye, and more—far more than my mind could conceive or my tongue could utter. Is there an American who regrets the past? Is there one who will deride his country's laws, pervert her constitution, or alienate her people? If there be such a man, let his memory descend to prosperity laden with the execrations of all mankind.

So happy is the political and social condition of the United States, and so accustomed are we to the secure enjoyment of a freedom elsewhere unknown, that we are apt to under-value the treasures we possess, and to lose in some degree the sense of obligation to our forefathers. But when the

strifes of faction shake the government and even threaten it
we may pause with advantage long enough to remember that
we are reaping the reward of other men's labors.　This
liberty we inherit; this admirable constitution, which has survived peace and war, prosperity and adversity, this double
scheme of government, State and Federal, so peculiar and so
little understood by other powers, yet which protects the
earnings of industry and makes the largest personal freedom
compatible with public order; these great results were not
achieved without wisdom and toil and blood—the touching
and heroic record is before the world.　But to all this we
were born, and, like heirs upon whom has been cast a great
inheritance, have only the high duty to preserve, to extend,
and to adorn it.　The grand productions of the era in which
the foundations of this government were laid, reveal the
deep sense its founders had of their obligations to the whole
family of man.　Let us never forget that the responsibilities
imposed on this generation are by so much the greater than
those which rested on our revolutionary ancestors, as the
population, extent, and power of our country surpass the
dawning promise of its origin.

It would be a pleasing task to pursue many trains of
thought, not wholly foreign to this occasion, but the temptation to enter the wide field must be rigorously curbed; yet I
may be pardoned, perhaps, for one or two additional reflections.

The Senate is assembled for the last time in this chamber.
Henceforth it will be converted to other uses; yet it must
remain forever connected with great events, and sacred to
the memories of the departed orators and statesmen who here
engaged in high debates and shaped the policy of their
country.　Hereafter the American and the stranger, as they

wander through the Capitol, will turn with instinctive rever-ence to view the spot on which so many and great materials have accumulated for history. They will recall the images of the great and the good, whose renown is the common prop-erty of the Union; and, chiefly, perhaps, they will linger around the seats once occupied by the mighty three, whose names and fame, associated in life, death has not been able to sever; illustrious men, who in their generation sometimes divided, sometimes led, and sometimes resisted public opin-ion—for they were of that higher class of statesmen who seek the right and follow their convictions.

There sat Calhoun, the senator, inflexible, austere, op-pressed, but not overwhelmed by his deep sense of the im-portance of his public functions; seeking the truth, then fearlessly following it—a man whose unsparing intellect compelled all his emotions to harmonize with the deductions of his rigorous logic, and whose noble countenance habitu-ally wore the expression of one engaged in the performance of high public duties.

This was Webster's seat. He, too, was every inch a senator. Conscious of his own vast powers, he reposed with confidence on himself; and scorning the contrivances of smaller men, he stood among his peers all the greater for the simple dignity of his senatorial demeanor. Type of his northern home, he rises before the imagination, in the grand and granite outline of his form and intellect, like a great New England rock, repelling a New England wave. As a writer, his productions will be cherished by statesmen and scholars while the English tongue is spoken. As a senatorial orator, his great efforts are historically associated with this chamber, whose very air seems to vibrate beneath the strokes of his deep tones and his weighty words.

On the outer circle sat Henry Clay, with his impetuous and ardent nature untamed by age, and exhibiting in the Senate the same vehement patriotism and passionate eloquence that of yore electrified the House of Representatives and the country. His extraordinary personal endowments, his courage, all his noble qualities, invested him with an individuality and a charm of character which in any age would have made him a favorite of history. He loved his country above all earthly objects. He loved liberty in all countries. Illustrious man!—orator, patriot, philanthropist—whose light, at its meridian, was seen and felt in the remotest parts of the civilized world; and whose declining sun as it hastened down the west threw back its level beams in hues of mellowed splendor, to illuminate and to cheer the land he loved and served so well.

All the States may point with gratified pride to the services in the Senate of their patriotic sons. Crowding the memory come the names of Adams, Hayne, Wright, Mason, Otis, Macon, Pinckney, and the rest—I cannot number them—who, in the record of their acts and utterances, appeal to their successors to give the Union a destiny not unworthy of the past. What models were these, to awaken emulation or to plunge in despair! Fortunate will be the American statesman who in this age or in succeeding times shall contribute to invest the new hall to which we go with historic memories like those which cluster here.

And now, senators, we leave this memorable chamber, bearing with us unimpaired the constitution we received from our forefathers. Let us cherish it with grateful acknowledgments to the Divine Power who controls the destinies of empires and whose goodness we adore. The structures reared by men yield to the corroding tooth of time.

These marble walls must molder into ruin; but the principles of constitutional liberty, guarded by wisdom and virtue, unlike material elements, do not decay. Let us devoutly trust that another Senate, in another age, shall bear to a new and larger chamber this constitution vigorous and inviolate, and that the last generation of posterity shall witness the deliberations of the representatives of American States still united, prosperous, and free.

DA SILVA

L UIZ AUGUSTO REBELLO DA SILVA, an eminent Portuguese statesman and author, was born in Lisbon, Portugal, April 2, 1821, and died
there September 19, 1871. He was educated at the University of Coimbra
and early adopted a literary career, contributing to various literary and
political journals. In 1845 he was made a secretary of the council of state,
and after his entry into the Cortes as deputy in 1848 his talents as an orator
made him especially prominent. In 1869 and 1870 he was secretary of
marine and colonial affairs. He became a member of the Lisbon Academy
of Sciences in 1854, and in 1858 received an appointment as professor of
national and general history, and was a member of several learned societies.
Beside his many contributions to literary and political periodicals he published a number of popular works, among which are " The Youth of King
John V " (1851-53); " A History of Portugal " (1861).

EULOGY OF ABRAHAM LINCOLN

[The death of Abraham Lincoln was deeply felt throughout Europe;
crowned heads and parliaments hastened to express their horror at the
crime committed by Wilkes Booth. The Portuguese Parliament was not
behind the other foreign parliaments; and in the Chamber of Peers the
eloquent voice of Señor Rebello da Silva was raised, giving utterance to
his noble sentiments respecting the sad catastrophe. The following eulogy
was delivered in the Chamber of Peers at Lisbon, August 12, 1865.]

M R. PRESIDENT,—I desire to offer to the chamber
some observations on a subject I deem most grave
for the purpose of introducing a motion which I
intend to lay upon the table.

The chamber has been made aware by the official documents in the foreign journals that a flagrant outrage has
recently covered with mourning a great nation beyond the
Atlantic, the powerful republic of the United States. President Lincoln has been assassinated in the theatre, almost in
the arms of his wife!

The perpetration of so foul a deed has caused the deepest

grief in America and throughout all the courts of Europe. Cabinets and parliaments have evinced the most universal sorrow at an event so grievous.

It belongs to civilized communities, it becomes almost a duty with all constituted political bodies, to accompany their manifestations with the sincere expression of horror at facts and crimes so infamous.

Through a fatality or a sublime disposition or unfathomable mystery of Providence—which is the more Christian interpretation of history—it often happens, not only in the life of nations but in that of individuals, when the loftiest heights have been reached, the boldest destinies fulfilled, even the last degrees of human greatness attained, when the way is suddenly made smooth, and the horizon casts off its clouds and shadows, and smiles flooded with light, that then an unseen hand is lifted in the darkness; that a power, secret and inexorable, is armed in silence, and waving the dagger of Brutus, pointing the cannon of Wellington, or offering the poisoned cup of Asiatic herbs, hurls the conqueror, crowned with laurels, from his height at the feet of Pompey's statue, like Cæsar; at the feet of fortune, weary with following him, like Napoleon; at the feet of the Colossus of irritated Rome, like Hannibal.

The mission of great men and heroes makes them seem to us almost like demigods; for they receive for a moment from on high the omnipotence which revolutionizes societies and transfigures nations; they pass like tempests in their car of fire to see themselves dashed at last in an instant against the eternal barriers of the impossible, barriers which no one can remove, where they all find the pride of their ephemeral power reduced to nought and humbled to the dust—for immutable and great alone is God.

Death overtakes them, or ruin reaches them in their ipogee, to show to princes, to conquerors, and to people that their hour is one only and short, that their work is fragile as the work of man, so soon as the pillar of fire which guided them is extinguished and night falls upon their way; the new paths they had opened for themselves, and through which they thought to pass boldly and secure, become gulfs which open and swallow them, when, as instruments of the designs of the Most High, the days of their empire and their enterprise shall have been counted and finished.

Thus is seen a terrible example, a memorable lesson in the catastrophe of the most noted characters of history. So come to us to-day, stained with the illustrious blood of one of its most honored citizens, the recent pages of the annals of the powerful republic of the United States. Its President, when the first quadrennium was closed of a government, in which strife was his heritage, falls suddenly, struck down before his own triumph; and from his cold and powerless hands escape loosely the reins of an administration which the perseverance and energy of his will, the co-operation of his fellow citizens, and the loftiness and prestige of the great idea he symbolized and defended, have made immortal with a name proclaimed by millions of voices and votes on the fields of battle and in the assemblies of the people.

Reconducted, elevated a second time on the shields of popular favor to the supreme direction of affairs, at the moment when the heat of civil strife was appeased, when the union of that vast dilacerated body gave promise in its restoration to bind up the wounds through which for so many months flowed in torrents the generous blood of the free; almost in the arms of victory, surrounded by those who most loved him, in the bosom of his popular court, he suddenly encounters death, and the ball of an obscure fanatic closes and seals the golden book of his destinies at the moment, too, when every prosperity seemed to welcome him to length of days and festive favor.

It is not a king who disappears in the obscurity of the tomb, burying with him, like Henry IV, the future of vast plans; it is the chief of a glorious people, who leaves behind him as many successors as there are abettors of his idea, co-operators in his noble and well-aimed aspirations. The purple of a throne is not covered with mourning, the heart of a great empire is shrouded in grief. The cause of which he was the strenuous champion did not die with him; but all wept for his loss, through their horror of the deed and the occasion and through the hopes founded on his pure and benevolent motives.

Lincoln, martyr to the broad principle which he repre-sented in power and struggle, belongs now to history and posterity. Like Washington, whose idea he continued, his name will be inseparable from the memorable epochs to which he is bound and which he expresses. If the Defender of Independence freed America, Lincoln unsheathed with out hesitation the sword of the Republic, and with its point erased and tore out from the statutes of a free people, the anti-social stigma, the anti-humanitarian blasphemy, the sad, shameful, infamous codicil of old societies, the dark, repug-nant abuse of slavery, which Jesus Christ first condemned from the top of the cross, proclaiming the equality of man before God, which nineteen centuries of civilization reared in the Gospel have proscribed and rejected as the opprobrium of our times.

At the moment when he was breaking the chains of a luck-less race, when he was seeing in millions of rehabilitated slaves millions of future citizens, when the bronze voice of Grant's victorious cannon was proclaiming the emancipation of the soul, of the conscience, and of toil, when the scourge was about to fall from the hands of the scourgers, when the ancient slave pen was about to be transformed, for the captive, into a domestic altar; at the moment when the stars of the Union, sparkling and resplendent with the golden fires of liberty were waving over the subdued walls of Petersburg and Richmond . . . the sepulchre opens and the strong, the powerful enters it. In the midst of triumphs and acclamations there appeared to him a spectre, like that of Caesar in the Ides of March, saying to him, " You have lived."

Far be it from me to approve or condemn the civil strife which divides and covers with blood two brother sections of the American people. I am neither their judge nor their censor. I honor the principle of liberty, wherever cherished and maintained; but I can also honor and admire another principle, not less sacred and glorious, that of independence. May the progressive virtue of our age reunite those whom discord has divided and reconcile ideas which are in the hearts and aspirations of all generous souls!

In this struggle which in magnitude exceeds all we have seen or heard of in Europe, the vanquished of to-day are worthy of the great race from which they sprang. Lee and Grant are two giants, whom history will keep inseparable. But the hour of peace is perchance about to strike. Lincoln desired it as the crown of his labors, the glorious result of so many sacrifices. After force, let there be forbearance; after the brave fury of battles, the fraternal embrace of citizens.

These were the motives which governed him, these the last virtuous desires he entertained; and it is at this moment (perchance a rare one) when a great soul is so potent for good, when a single mind is worth whole legions as a pacificator, that the hand of an assassin is raised in treachery and cuts the threads of plans and purposes so lofty and so noble.

If the American nation were not a people tried in the experiences and strifes of government, could any one perchance calculate the fatal consequences of this sudden blow? Who knows if the conflagration of civil war would not have spread to the remotest confines of these federal States in all the pomp of its horrors? Happily, it will not be so. While public opinion and the journals condemn the deed severely and justly, and their horror is excited against the fatal crime —sentiments which are those of all civilized Europe—they give honorable heed to ideas of peace and forbearance, as though the great man who advocated these ideas had not disappeared from the arena of the world. And I use the term advisedly, "great man," for he is truly great who rises to the loftiest heights from profound obscurity, relying solely on his own merits—as did Napoleon, Washington, Lincoln. For these arose to power and greatness, not through any favor or grace of a chance-cradle, or genealogy, but through the prestige of their own deeds, through the nobility which begins and ends with themselves—the sole offspring of their own works. He is more to be envied who makes himself great and famous through his genius and deeds, than he who is born with hereditary titles.

Lincoln was of this privileged class; he belonged to this aristocracy. In infancy, his energetic soul was nourished by poverty. In youth he learned through toil the love of liberty and respect for the rights of man. Even to the age of twenty-two, educated in adversity, his hands made callous by honorable labor, he rested from the fatigues of the field, spelling out in the pages of the Bible, in the lessons of the Gospel, in the fugitive leaves of the daily journal, which the Aurora opens and the night disperses—the first rudiments of instruction which his solitary meditations ripened.

Little by little, light was infused into that spirit, the wings put forth and grew strong with which he flew. The chrysalis felt one day the ray of the sun, which called it to life, broke its involucrum, and launched forth fearlessly from the darkness of its humble cloister into the luminous spaces of its destiny. The farmer, day-laborer, shepherd, like Cincinnatus, left the ploughshare in the half-broken furrow, and legislator of his own State, and afterward of the great Republic, saw himself proclaimed in the tribunal the popular chief of many millions of people, the maintainer of the holy principle inaugurated by Wilberforce. What strife, what scenes of agitation, what a series of herculean labors and incalculable sacrifices, were not involved and represented, in the glory of their results, during these four years of war and government? Armies in the field, such as, since the remotest periods, there has been no example! Huge battles, which saw the sun rise and set twice or thrice without victory inclining to the one or the other side! Marches, in which thousands of victims, whole legions, piled with the dead, each fragment of the conquered earth! Assaults which, in audacity and slaughter, reduced to insignificance the exploits of Attila and the Huns.

What stupendous obsequies for the scourge of slavery! What a lesson, terrible and salutary from a great people, still rich and vigorous with youth, to the timid vacillations of old Europe, before a destiny contested by principles so sacred!

These were the monuments, the million marks of his

career. If the sword was in his hands the instrument, and liberty the inspiration and strength of his efforts, he was not unfaithful to them. Above the thorns in his path, through the tears and blood of so many holocausts he was able at last to see the promised land. It was not vouchsafed to him to plant therein, in expiation, the auspicious olive-tree of concord. When he was about to reunite the broken bond of the Union; when he was about to infuse anew the life-giving spirit of free institutions into the body of the country, its scattered and bloody members rejoined and recemented; when the standard of the Republic—the funeral clamors silenced and the agonies of pride and defeat consoled,— was about to be again raised, covering with its glorious folds all the children of the same common soil, purified from the indelible stain of slavery . . . the athlete reels and falls in the arena, showing that he, too, was but a mortal.

I deem this sketch sufficient. The chamber, through inclination, through a sense of duty, through its institution, not only conservative, but as the faithful guardian of traditions and principles, will not be, surely will not desire to be, backward in joining in the manifestations which the elective House has just voted, co-operating with the enlightened cabinets and parliaments of Europe. Silence in the presence of such outrages belongs only to Senates dumb and disinherited of all high sentiments and aspirations.

Voting this motion the Chamber of Peers associates itself in the grief of all civilized nations. The crime, which shortened the days of President Lincoln, martyr to the great principles in which our age most glories, is almost, is in essence, a regicide; and a monarchical country cannot refrain from detesting and condemning it.

The descendants of those who first revealed to the Europe

of the sixteenth century the new way, which, through the barriers of stormy and unknown seas, opened the gates of the kingdom of the Aurora, will not be the last to bend over the gravestone of a great magistrate, who was likewise the guide of his people through fearful tempests, and who succeeded in conducting them triumphantly to the overthrow of the last vestige of the citadel of slavery. To each epoch and each people, its task and its meed of glory; to each illustrious hero his crown of laurel, or his civic crown.

STORRS

RICHARD SALTER STORRS, an American clergyman and orator of distinction, was born in Braintree, Massachusetts, August 22, 1821, the son of a Congregationalist minister of the same name, for sixty-two years pastor in Braintree. He was educated at Amherst College, and after studying law for a short time with Rufus Choate relinquished it for the study of theology, which he pursued at Andover Theological Seminary. After a year's pastorate at Brookline, Massachusetts, he accepted a call to the newly organized Church of the Pilgrims in Brooklyn, New York, of which he was pastor for over fifty years. As a pulpit orator he was known far beyond the limits of his own denomination, and as a speaker on public occasions attained great popularity, his influence, both as clergyman and layman, having been of the most beneficent character. He died June 5, 1900. His sermons and addresses, which are noted for the classical polish of their style, were delivered without notes. His principal writings include "The Constitution of the Human Soul" (1856); "Conditions of Success in Preaching Without Notes" (1875); "Early American Spirit and the Genesis of It" (1875); "John Wycliffe and the First English Bible" (1880); "Recognition of the Supernatural in Letters and Life" (1881); "Manliness in the Scholar" (1883); "Divine Origin of Christianity Indicated by Its Historical Effects" (1884); "Prospective Advance of Christian Missions" (1885); "Bernard of Clairvaux" (1892); "Forty Years of Pastoral Life;" "Foundation Truths of American Missions" (1897).

THE RISE OF CONSTITUTIONAL LIBERTY

CENTENNIAL ORATION DELIVERED AT THE ACADEMY OF MUSIC, NEW YORK, JULY 4, 1876

MR. PRESIDENT, FELLOW CITIZENS,— The long-expected day has come, and passing peacefully the impalpable line which separates ages, the Republic completes its hundredth year. The predictions in which affectionate hope gave inspiration to political prudence are fulfilled. The fears of the timid, and the hopes of those to whom our national existence is a menace, are alike disappointed. The fable of the physical world becomes the fact of the political; and after alternate sunshine and storm, after heavings of the earth which only deepened its roots, and ineffectual blasts of lightning whose lurid threat died in the air, under a sky now raining on it benignant influence, the century-plant of American independence and popular government bursts into this magnificent blossom of a joyful celebration illuminating the land!

With what desiring though doubtful expectation those whose action we commemorate looked for the possible coming of this day, we know from the records which they have left. With what anxious solicitude the statesmen and the soldiers of the following generation anticipated the changes which might take place before this centennial year should be reached, we have heard ourselves, in their great and fervent admonitory words. How dim and drear the prospect seemed to our own hearts fifteen years since, when, on the Fourth of July, 1861, the thirty-seventh Congress met at Washington with no representative in either House from any State south of Tennessee and western Virginia, and when a determined and numerous army, under skilful commanders, approached and menaced the capital and the government — this we surely have not forgotten; nor how, in the terrible years which followed, the blood and fire, and vapor of smoke, seemed oftentimes to swim as a sea, or to rise as a wall, between our eyes and this anniversary.

"It cannot outlast the second generation from those who founded it," was the exulting conviction of the many who loved the traditions and state of monarchy, and who felt them insecure before the widening fame in the world of our prosperous Republic. "It may not reach its hundredth year," was the deep and sometimes the sharp apprehension of those who felt, as all of us felt, that their own liberty, welfare, hope, with the brightest political promise of the world, were bound up with the unity and the life of our nation. Never was solicitude more intense, never was prayer to Almighty God more fervent and constant — not in the earliest beginnings of our history, when Indian ferocity threatened that history with a swift termination; not in the days of supremest trial amid the Revolution — than in those years when the nation seemed suddenly split asunder, and forces which had been combined for its creation were clinched and rocking back and forth in bloody grapple on the question of its maintenance.

The prayer was heard. The effort and the sacrifice have come to their fruitage, and to-day the nation — still one, as at the start, though now expanded over such immense spaces, absorbing such incessant and diverse elements from other lands, developing within it opinions so conflicting, interests so various, and forms of occupation so novel and manifold — to-day the nation, emerging from the toil and the turbulent strife, with the earlier and the later clouds alike swept out of its resplendent stellar arch, pauses from its work to remember and rejoice; with exhilarated spirit to anticipate its future, with reverent heart to offer to God its great *Te Deum*.

Not here alone, in this great city, whose lines have gone out into all the earth, and whose superb progress in wealth, in culture, and in civic renown is itself the most illustrious token of the power and beneficence of that frame of government under which it has been realized; not alone in yonder — I had almost said adjoining — city, whence issued the paper that first announced our national existence, and where now rises the magnificent exposition, testifying for all progressive States to their respect and kindness toward us, the radiant clasp of diamond and opal on the girdle of the sympathies which interweave their peoples with ours; not alone in Boston, the historic town, first in resistance to

British aggression and foremost in plans for the new and popular organization, one of whose citizens wrote his name, as if cutting it with a plowshare, at the head of all on our great charter, another of whose citizens was its intrepid and powerful champion, aiding its passage through the Congress; not there alone, nor yet in other great cities of the land, but in smaller towns, in villages and hamlets, this day will be kept, a secular Sabbath, sacred alike to memory and to hope.

Not only, indeed, where men are assembled, as we are here, will it be honored. The lonely and remote will have their parts in this commemoration. Where the boatman follows the winding stream or the woodman explores the forest shades; where the miner lays down his eager drill beside rocks which guard the precious veins, or where the herdsman, along the sierras, looks forth on the seas which now reflect the rising day, which at our midnight shall be gleaming like gold in the setting sun; there also will the day be regarded as a day of memorial. The sailor on the sea will note it, and dress his ship in its brightest array of flags and bunting. Americans dwelling in foreign lands will note and keep it.

London itself will to-day be more festive because of the event which a century ago shadowed its streets, incensed its Parliament, and tore from the crown of its obstinate King the chiefest jewel. On the boulevards of Paris, in the streets of Berlin, and along the levelled bastions of Vienna, at Marseilles, and at Florence, upon the silent liquid ways of stately Venice, in the passes of the Alps, under the shadow of church and obelisk, palace and ruin, which still prolong the majesty of Rome; yet, farther east, on the Bosphorus and in Syria; in Egypt which writes on the front of its compartment in the great exhibition: " The oldest people of the world sends its morning greeting to the youngest nation; " along the heights behind Bombay, in the foreign hongs of Canton, in the "Islands of the Morning," which found the dawn of their new age in the startling sight of an American squadron entering their bays — everywhere will be those who have thought of this day, and who join with us to greet its coming.

No other such anniversary, probably, has attracted hitherto such general notice. You have seen Rome, perhaps, on one of those shining April days when the traditional anniversary of the founding of the city fills its streets with civic processions, with military display, and the most elaborate fireworks in Europe; you may have seen Holland in 1872, when the whole country bloomed with orange on the three hundredth anniversary of the capture by the sea-beggars of the City of Briel, and of the revolt against Spanish domination which thereupon flashed on different sides into sudden explosion. But these celebrations, and others like them, have been chiefly local. The world outside has taken no wide impression from them. This of ours is the first of which many lands, in different tongues, will have had report. Partly because the world is narrowed in our time, and its distant peoples are made neighbors by the fleeter machineries now in use; partly because we have drawn so many to our population from foreign lands, while the restless and acquisitive spirit of our people has made them at home on every shore; but partly, also, and essentially, because of the nature and the relations of that event which we commemorate, and of the influence exerted by it on subsequent history, the attention of men is more or less challenged, in every centre of commerce and of thought, by this anniversary.

Indeed, it is not unnatural to feel — certainly it is not irreverent to feel — that they who by wisdom, by valor, and by sacrifice, have contributed to perfect and maintain the institutions which we possess, and have added by death, as well as by life, to the lustre of our history, must also have an interest in this day; that in their timeless habitations they remember us beneath the lower circle of the heavens, are gl d in our joy, and share and lead our grateful praise. To a spirit alive with the memories of the time, and rejoicing in its presage of nobler futures, recalling the great, the beloved, the heroic, who have labored and joyfully died for its coming, it will not seem too fond an enthusiasm to feel that the air is quick with shapes we cannot see, and glows with faces whose light serene we may not catch! They who counselled in the Cabinet, they who defined and settled the law in decisions of the bench, they who pleaded with mighty eloquence in the Senate, they who poured out their souls in triumphant effusion for the liberty which they loved in forum or pulpit, they who gave their young and glorious life as an offering on the field, that government for the people and by the people might not perish from the earth — it cannot be but that they, too, have part and place in this jubilee of our history! God make our doings not unworthy of such spectators, and make our spirit sympathetic with theirs, from whom all selfish passion and pride have now forever passed away!

The interest which is felt so distinctly and widely in this anniversary reflects a light on the greatness of the action which it commemorates. It shows that we do not unduly exaggerate the significance or the importance of that; that it had really large, even world-wide, relations, and contributed an effective and a valuable force to the furtherance of the cause of freedom, education, humane institutions, and popular advancement, wherever its influence has been felt. Yet when we consider the action itself it may easily seem but slight in its nature, as it was certainly commonplace in its circumstances. There was nothing even picturesque in its surroundings, to enlist for it the pencil of the painter, or help to fix any luminous image of that which was done on the popular memory.

In this respect it is singularly contrasted with other great and kindred events in general history; with those heroic and fruitful actions in English history which had especially prepared the way for it, and with which the thoughtful student of the past will always set it in intimate relations.

When, five centuries and a half before, on the 15th of June, and the following days, in the year of our Lord 1215, the English barons met King John in the long meadow of Runnymede, and forced from him the Magna Charta — the strong foundation and steadfast bulwark of English liberty, concerning which Mr. Hallam has said in our own time that " all which has been since obtained is little more than as confirmation or commentary "— no circumstance was wanting of outward pageantry to give dignity, brilliance, impressiveness to the scene. On the one side, was the King with the bishops and gentry who adhered to him, and the Papal legate before whom he had lately rendered his homage. On the other side was the great and determined majority of the barons of England, with multitudes of knights, armed vassals and retainers. Stephen Langton, Archbishop of Canterbury, the head of the English clergy, was with them; the bishops of London, Winchester, Lincoln, Worcester, Rochester, and of other great Sees. The Earl of Pembroke, daring and wise, of vast and increasing power in the realm, was at their head. Robert Fitz Walter, whose fair daughter Matilda the profligate King had forcibly abducted, was marshal of the army — the "Army of God and the Holy Church." William Longsword, Earl of Salisbury, half-brother of the King, was with the barons. The Earls of Albemarle, Arundel, Gloucester, Hereford, Norfolk, Oxford, were in the array; the great Earl Warrenne, who claimed the same right of the sword in his barony which William the Conqueror had had in the kingdom; the Constable of Scotland, Hubert de Burgh, Seneschal of Poictou, and many other powerful nobles. Some burgesses of London were present as well; and doubtless there mingled with the throng those skilful clerks whose pens had drawn the great instrument of freedom, and whose training in language had given a remarkable precision to its exact clauses and cogent terms.

Pennons and banners streamed at large, and spear-heads gleamed above the host. The June sunshine flashed, reflected from inlaid shields and damascened armor. The terrible bows of the English yeomen hung on their shoulders. The voice of trumpets and clamoring bugles was in the air. The whole scene was vast as a battle, though bright as a tournament; splendid, but threatening, like burnished clouds, in which lightnings sleep. The King, one of the handsomest men of the time, though cruelty, perfidy and every foul passion must have left their traces on his face, was especially fond of magnificence in dress, wearing, we are told, on one Christmas occasion a rich mantle of red satin, embroidered with sapphires and pearls, a tunic of white damask, a girdle lustrous with precious stones, and a baldric from his shoulder, crossing his breast, set with diamonds and emeralds, while even his gloves — as, indeed, is still indieated on his fine effigy in Worcester Cathedral — bore similar ornaments, the one a ruby, the other a sapphire.

Whatever was superb, therefore, in that consummate age of royal and baronial state, whatever was splendid in the glittering and grand apparatus of chivalry, whatever was impressive in the almost more than princely pomp of the prelates of the Church —

> " The boast of heraldry, the pomp of power
> And all that beauty, all that wealth e'er gave "

— all this was marshalled on that historic plan in Surrey where John and the barons faced each other, where Saxon king and Saxon earl had met in council before the Norman had footing in England; and all combined to give a fit magnificence of setting to the great charter there granted and sealed.

The tower of Windsor — not of the present castle and palace, but of the earlier detached fortress which already crowned the cliff, and from which John had come to the field — looked down on the scene. On the one side low hills inclosed the meadow; on the other the Thames flowed brightly by, seeking the capital and the sea. Every feature of the scene was English, save one; but over all loomed, in a portentous and haughty stillness, in the ominous presence of the envoy from Rome, that ubiquitous power, surpassing all others, which already had once laid the kingdom under interdict, and had exiled John from Church and throne, but to which, later, he had been reconciled, and on which now he secretly relied to annul the charter which he was granting.

The brilliant panorama illuminates the page which bears its story. It rises still as a vision before one, as he looks on the venerable parchment originals, preserved to our day in the British Museum. If it be true, as Hallam has said, that from that era there was a new soul in the people of England, it must be confessed that the place, the day, and all the circumstances of that new birth, were fitting to the great and the vital event.

That age passed away, and its peculiar splendor of aspect was not thereafter to be repeated. Yet when, four hundred years later, on the 7th of June, 1628, the Petition of Right, the second great charter of the liberties of England, was presented by Parliament to Charles I, the scene and its accessories were hardly less impressive.

Into that law — called a petition, as if to mask the deadly energy of its blow upon tyranny — had been collected by the skill of its framers all the heads of the despotic prerogative which Charles had exercised, that they might all together be smitten with one tremendous destroying stroke. The King, enthroned in his chair of state, looked forth on those who waited for his word, as still he looks, with his forecasting and melancholy face, from the canvas of Vandyck. Before him were assembled the nobles of England — in peaceful array, and not in armor, but with a civil power in their hands which the older gauntlets could not have held, and with the memories of a long renown almost as visible to themselves and to the King, as were the tapestries suspended on the walls.

Crowding the bar, behind these descendants of the earlier barons, were the members of the House of Commons, with whom the law now presented to the King had had its origin, and whose boldness and tenacity had constrained the peers, after vain endeavor to modify its provisions, to accept them as they stood. They were the most powerful body of representatives of the kingdom that had yet been convened; possessing a private wealth, it was estimated, surpassing threefold that of the peers, and representing not less than they, the best life and the oldest lineage of the kingdom which they loved.

Their dexterous, dauntless, and far-sighted sagacity is yet more evident, as we look back, than their wealth or their breeding; and among them were men whose names will be familiar while England continues. Wentworth was there, soon to be the most dangerous of traitors to the cause of which he was then the champion, but who then appeared as resolute as ever to vindicate the ancient, lawful, and vital liberties of the kingdom; and Pym was there, who not long after was to warn the dark and haughty apostate that he never again would leave pursuit of him so long as his head stood on his shoulders; Hampden was there, considerate and serene, but inflexible as an oak; once imprisoned already for his resistance to an unjust taxation, and ready again to suffer and to conquer in the same supreme cause. Sir John Eliot was there, eloquent and devoted, who had tasted also the bitterness of imprisonment, and who, after years of its subsequent experience, was to die a martyr in the Tower. Coke was there, seventy-seven years of age, but full of fire as full of fame, whose vehement and unswerving hand had had chief part in framing the petition. Selden was there, the repute of whose learning was already continental. Sir Francis Seymour, Sir Robert Philips, Strode, Hobart, Denzil Holles, and Valentine — such were the Commoners; and there, not impossibly for the first time in his life, faced the King, a silent young member who had come now to his first Parliament, at the age of twenty-nine, from the borough of Huntingdon, Oliver Cromwell.

In a plain cloth suit he stood among his colleagues. But they were often splendid and even sumptuous in dress; with embroidered doublets and coats of velvet, with flowing collars of rich lace, the swords by their sides with flashing hilts, their very hats jewelled and plumed, the abundant dressed and perfumed hair falling in curls upon their shoulders. Here and there were those who still more distinctly symbolized their spirit with steel corselets, overlaid with lace and rich embroidery.

So stood they in the presence, representing to the full the wealth and genius and stately civic pomp of England, until the King had pronounced his assent, in the expressed customary form, to the law which confirmed the popular liberties; and when, on hearing his unequivocal final assent, they burst into loud, even passionate, acclamations of victorious joy, there had been from the first no scene more impressive in that venerable hall, whose history went back to Edward the Confessor.

In what sharp contrast with the rich ceremonial and the splendid accessories of these preceding kindred events, appears that modest scene at Philadelphia, from which we gratefully date to-day a hundred years of constant and prosperous national life!

In a plain room of an unpretending and recent building — the lower east room of what then was a State House, what since has been known as the " Independence Hall "— in the midst of a city of probably thirty thousand inhabitants — a city which preserved its rural aspect and the quaint simplicity of whose plan and structures had always been marked among American towns — were assembled somewhat less than fifty persons, to consider a paper prepared by a young Virginia lawyer, giving reasons for a resolve which the Assembly had adopted two days before. They were farmers, planters, lawyers, physicians, surveyors of land, with one eminent Presbyterian clergyman. A majority of them had been educated at such schools, or primitive colleges, as then existed on this continent, while a few had enjoyed the rare advantage of training abroad and foreign travel; but a considerable number, perhaps twenty in all, and among them some of the most influential, had had no other education than that which they had gained by diligent reading while at their trades or on their farms.

The figure to which our thoughts turn first is that of the author of the careful paper on the details of which the discussion turned. It has no special majesty or charm — the slight, tall frame, the sun-burned face, the gray eyes spotted with hazel, the red hair which crowns the head; but already, at the age of thirty-three, the man has impressed himself on his associates as a master of principles, and of the language in which those principles find their expression, so that his colleagues have left to him, almost wholly, the work of preparing the important Declaration. He wants readiness in debate, and so is now silent; but he listens eagerly to the vigorous argument and the forcible appeals of one of his fellows on the committee, Mr. John Adams, and now and then speaks with another of the committee, much older than himself — a stout man, with a friendly face, in a plain dress, whom the world already had heard something of as Benjamin Franklin. These three are, perhaps, most prominently before us as we recall the vanished scene, though others were there of fine presence and cultivated manners, and though all impress us as substantial and respectable representative men, however harsh the features of some, however brawny their hands with labor. But certainly nothing could be more unpretending, more destitute of pictorial charm, than that small assembly of persons for the most part quite unknown to previous fame, and half of whose names it is not probable that half of us in this assembly could now repeat.

After a discussion somewhat prolonged, as it seemed at the time, especially as it had been continued from previous days, and after some minor amendments of the paper, toward evening it was adopted, and ordered to be signed by the President and Secretary; and so the transaction was complete. Whatever there was of proclamation and bell-ringing appears to have come on subsequent days. It was a full month before the paper was signed by the members. It must have been nearly or quite the same time before the news of its adoption had reached the remoter parts of the land.

If pomp of circumstances were necessary to make an event like this great and memorable, there would have been others in our own history more worthy far of our commemoration. As matched against multitudes in general history, it would sink into instant and complete insignificance. Yet here, to-day, a hundred years from the adoption of that paper, in this city which counts its languages by scores, and beats with the tread of a million feet, in a land whose enterprise flies abroad over sea and land on the rush of engines not then imagined, in a time so full of exciting hopes that it hardly has leisure to contemplate the past, we pause from all our toil and traffic, our eager plans and impetuous debate, to commemorate the event. The whole land pauses, as I have said; and some distinct impression of it will follow the sun, wherever he climbs the steep of heaven, until in all countries it has more or less touched the thoughts of men.

Why is this? is a question, the answer to which should interpret and vindicate our assemblage. It is not simply because a century happens to have passed since the event thus remembered occurred. A hundred years are always closing from some event, and have been since Adam was in his prime. There was, of course, some special importance in the action there accomplished — in the nature of that action, since not in its circumstances — to justify such long record of it; and that importance it is ours to define. In the perspective of distance the small things disappear, while the great and eminent keep their place. As Carlyle has said, " A king in the midst of his body guards, with his trumpets, war horses, and gilt standard-bearers, will look great, though he be little; only some Roman Carus can give audience to satrap ambassadors, while seated on the ground, with a woollen cap, and supping on boiled peas like a common soldier."

What was, then, the great reality of power in what was done one hundred years since which gives it its masterful place in history, makes it Roman and regal amid all its simplicity?

Of course, as the prime element of its power it was the action of a people and not merely of persons; and such action of a people has always a momentum, a public force, a historic significance, which can pertain to no individual arguments or appeals. There are times, indeed, when it has the energy and authority in it of a secular inspiration; when the supreme soul which rules the world comes through it to utterance, and a thought surpassing man's wisest plan, a will transcending his strongest purpose, is heard in its commanding voice.

It does not seem extravagant to say that the time to which our thoughts are turned was one of these. For a century and a half the emigrants from Europe had brought hither,

not the letters alone, the arts and industries or the religious
convictions, but the hardy moral and political life which had
there been developed in ages of strenuous struggle and work.
France and Germany, Holland and Sweden, as well as England, Scotland, and Ireland, had contributed to this. The
Austrian Tyrol, the Bavarian highlands, the Bohemian plain,
Denmark, even Portugal, had had their part in this colonization. The ample domain which here received the earliest
immigrants had imparted to them of its own oneness, and
diversities of language, race and custom had fast disappeared
in the governing unity of a common aspiration, and a common purpose to work out through freedom a nobler well-
being.

The general moral life of this people, so various in origin,
so accordant in spirit, had only risen to grander force through
the toil and strife, the austere training, the long patience of
endurance, to which it here had been subjected. The expo-
sures to heat and cold and famine, to unaccustomed labors,
to alterations of climate unknown in the Old World, to
malarial forces brooding above the mellow and drainless
recent lands — these had fatally stricken many; but those
who survived were tough and robust, the more so, perhaps,
because of the perils which they had surmounted. Education was not easy, books were not many, and the daily newspaper was unknown; but political discussion had been always
going on, and men's minds had gathered unconscious force
as they strove with each other, in eager debate, on questions
concerning the common welfare. They had had much
experience in subordinate legislation on the local matters
belonging to their care, had acquired dexterity in performing public business, and had often had to resist or amend
the suggestions or dictates of royal governors. For a recent

people, dwelling apart from older and conflicting States, they had a large experience in war, the crack of the rifle being never unfamiliar along the near frontier, where disciplined skill was often combined with savage fury to sweep with sword or scar with fire their scattered settlements.

By every species, therefore, of common work, of discussion, endurance, and martial struggle, the descendants of the colonists scattered along the American coast had been allied to each other. They were more closely allied than they knew. It needed only some signal occasion, some summons to sudden heroic decision, to bring them into instant general combination; and Huguenot and Hollander, Swede, German and Protestant Portuguese, as well as Englishman, Scotchman, Irishman, would then forget that their ancestors had been different, in the supreme consciousness that they now had a common country, and, before all else, were all of them Americans.

That time had come. That consciousness had for fifteen years been quickening in the people, since the "Writs of Assistance" had been authorized by Parliament, in 1761, and Otis, resigning his honorable position under the crown, had flung himself against the alarming innovation with an eloquence as blasting as the stroke of the lightning which in the end destroyed his life. With every fresh invasion by England of their popular liberties, with every act which threatened such invasion by providing opportunity and the instruments for it — the sense of a common privilege and right of a common inheritance of the country they were fashioning out of the forest, of a common place in the history of the world, had been increased among the colonists. They were plain people, with no strong tendencies to the ideal. They wanted only a chance for free growth; but they must have that, and have it together, though the continent cracked. The diamond is formed, it has sometimes been supposed, under a swift, enormous pressure of masses meeting, and forcing the carbon into a crystal. The ultimate spirit of the American colonists was formed in like manner; the weight of a rocky continent beneath, the weight of an oppression only intolerable because undefined, pressing on it from above. But now that spirit, of inestimable price, reflecting light from every angle, and harder to be broken than anything material, was suddenly shown in acts and declarations of conventions and assemblies from the Penobscot to the St. Mary's.

Any commanding public temper, once established in a people, grows bolder, of course, more inquisitive and inventive, more sensible of its rights, more determined on its future, as it comes more frequently into exercise. This in the colonies lately had had the most significant of all its expressions, up to that point, in the resolves of popular assemblies that the time had come for a final separation from the Kingdom of Great Britain. The eminent Congress of two years before had given it powerful reinforcement. Now, at last, it entered the representative American Assembly, and claimed from that the ultimate word. It found what it sought. The Declaration was only the voice of that supreme, impersonal force, that will of communities, that universal soul of the State.

The vote of the colony, then thinly covering a part of the spaces not yet wholly occupied by this great State, was not, indeed, at once formally given for such an instrument. It was wisely delayed, under the judicious counsel of Jay, till a provincial congress could assemble, specially called and formally authorized to pronounce the deliberate resolve of the colony; and so it happened that only twelve colonies voted at first for the great Declaration, and that New York was not joined to the number till five days later. But Jay knew, and all knew, that, numerous, wealthy, eminent in character, high in position as were those here and elsewhere in the country — in Massachusetts, in Virginia, and in the Carolinas — who were by no means yet prepared to sever their connection with Great Britain, the general and governing mind of the people was fixed upon this with a decision which nothing could change, with a tenacity which nothing could break. The forces tending to that result had wrought to their development with a steadiness and strength which the stubbornest resistance had hardly delayed. The spirit which now shook light and impulse over the land was recent in its precise demand, but as old in its birth as the first Christian settlements, and it was that spirit — not of one, nor of fifty, not of all the individuals in all the conventions, but the vaster spirit which lay behind — which put itself on sudden record through the prompt and accurate pen of Jefferson.

He was himself in full sympathy with it, and only by reason of that sympathy could give it such consummate expression. Not out of books, legal researches, historical inquiry, the careful and various studies of language, came that document; but out of repeated public debate, out of manifold personal and private discussion, out of his clear, sympathetic observation of the changing feeling and thought of men, out of that exquisite personal sensibility to vague and impalpable popular impulses which was in him innately combined with artistic taste, an ideal nature and rare power of philosophical thought. The voice of the cottage, as well as the college, of the church, as well as the legislative assembly, was in the paper. It echoed the talk of the farmer in homespun, as well as the classic eloquence of Lee, or the terrible tones of Patrick Henry. It gushed at last from the pen of its writer, like the fountain from the roots of Lebanon, a brimming river when it issues from the rock; but it was because its sources had been supplied, its fulness filled by unseen springs; by the rivulets winding far up among the cedars, and percolating through hidden crevices in the stone; by melting snows, whose white sparkle seemed still on the stream; by fierce rains, with which the basins above were drenched; by even the dews, silent and wide, which had lain in stillness all night upon the hill.

The Platonic idea of the development of the State was thus realized here; first ethics, then politics. A public opinion, energetic and dominant, took its place from the start as the chief instrument of the new civilization. No dashing manœuvers of skilful commanders, no sudden burst of popular passion, was in the Declaration; but the vast mystery of a supreme and imperative public life, at once diffused and intense — behind all persons, before all plans, beneath which individual wills are exalted, at whose touch the personal mind is inspired, and under whose transcendent impulse the smallest instrument becomes of a terrific force. That made the Declaration, and that makes it now, in its modest brevity, take its place with Magna Charta and the Petition of Right, as full as they of vital force, and destined to a parallel permanence.

Because this intense common life of a determined and manifold people has not behind them other documents, in form similar to this, and in polish and cadence of balanced phrase perhaps its superiors, have no hold like that which it keeps on the memory of men. What papers have challenged

the attention of men within the century, in the stately Spanish tongue, in Mexico, New-Granada, Venezuela, Bolivia, or
in the Argentine Republic, which the people themselves
now hardly remember? How the resonant proclamations
of German, or of French Republicans, of Hungarian or
Spanish revolutionists and patriots, have vanished as sound
absorbed in the air! Eloquent, persuasive, just, as they
were, with a vigor of thought, a fervor of passion, a fine
completeness and symmetry of expression in which they
could hardly be surpassed, they have only now a literary
value. They never became great general forces. They
were weak, because they were personal; and history is too
crowded, civilization is too vast, to take much impression
from occasional documents. Only then is a paper of secular
force or long remembered when behind it is the ubiquitous
energy of the popular will, rolling through its words in vast
diapason, and charging the clauses with tones of thunder.

Because such an energy was behind it, our Declaration
had its majestic place and meaning, and they who adopted
it saw nowhere else

> " So rich advantage of a promised glory
> As smiled upon the forehead of their action."

Because of that we read it still, and look to have it as
audible as now among the dissonant voices of the world, when
other generations in long succession have come and gone!

But further, too, it must be observed that this paper,
adopted a hundred years since, was not merely the declaration of a people, as distinguished from eminent and cultured
individuals — a confession before the world of the public
State-faith, rather than a political thesis — but it was also
the declaration of a people which claimed for its own a great
inheritance of equitable laws and of practical liberty, and

which now was intent to enlarge and enrich that. It had roots in the past and a long genealogy, and so it had a vitality inherent, and an immense energy.

They who framed it went back, indeed, to first principles. There was something philosophic and ideal in their scheme, as always there is when the general mind is deeply stirred. It was not superficial. Yet they were not undertaking to establish new theories, or to build their State upon artificial plans and abstract speculations. They were simply evolving out of the past what therein had been latent; were liberating into free exhibition and unceasing activity a vital force older than the history of their colonization, and wide as the lands from which they came. They had the sweep of vast impulses behind them. The slow tendencies of centuries came to sudden consummation in their Declaration, and the force of its impact upon the affairs and the mind of the world was not to be measured by its contents alone, but by the relation in which these stood to all the vehement discussion and struggle of which it was the latest outcome. This ought to be always distinctly observed.

The tendency is strong, and has been general, among those who have introduced great changes in the government of States, to follow some plan of political, perhaps of social innovation, which enlists their judgment, excites their fancy, and to make a comely theoretical habitation for the national household, rather than to build on the old foundations, expanding the walls, lifting the height, enlarging the doorways, enlightening with new windows the halls, but still keeping the strength and renewing the age, of an old and venerated structure. You remember how in France, in 1789 and the following years, the schemes of those whom Napoleon called the "ideologists," succeeded each other, no one of them gaining a permanent supremacy, though each included important elements, till the armed Consulate of 1799 swept them all into the air, and put in place of them one masterful genius and ambitious will. You remember how in Spain, in 1812, the new constitution proclaimed by the Cortes was thought to inaugurate with beneficent provisions a wholly new era of development and progress; yet how the history of the splendid peninsula, from that day to this, has been but the record of a struggle to the death between the old and the new, the contest as desperate, it would seem, in our time as it was in the first.

It must be so always when a preceding state of society and government, which has got itself established through many generations, is suddenly superseded by a different fabric, however more evidently conformed to right reason. The principle is not so strong as the prejudice. Habit masters invention. The new and theoretic shivers its force on the obstinate coherence of the old and the established. The modern structure falls and is replaced, while the grim feudal keep, though scarred and weatherworn, the very cement seeming gone from its wall, still scowls defiance at the red right hand of the lightning itself.

It was no such rash speculative change which here was attempted. The people whose deputies framed our Declaration were largely themselves descendants of Englishmen; and those who were not had lived long enough under English institutions to be impressed with their tendency and spirit. It was, therefore, only natural that even when adopting that ultimate measure which severed them from the British crown, they should retain all that had been gained in the motherland through centuries of endurance and strife. They left nothing that was good; they abolished the bad, added the needful, and developed into a rule for the continent the splendid precedents of great former occasions. They shared still the boast of Englishmen that their constitution " has no single date from which its duration is to be reckoned," and that " the origin of the English law is as undiscoverable as that of the Nile." They went back themselves for the origin of their liberties to the most ancient muniments of English freedom. Jefferson had affirmed, in 1774, that a primitive charter of American independence lay in the fact that as the Saxons had left their native wilds in the north of Europe, and had occupied Britain — the country which they left asserting over them no further control, nor any dependence of them upon it — so the Englishmen coming hither had formed, by that act, another State over which Parliament had no rights, in which its laws were void till accepted.

But while seeking for their liberties so archaic a basis, neither he nor his colleagues were in the least careless of what subsequent times had done to complete them. There was not one element of popular right, which had been wrested from the crown and nobles in any age, which they did not keep; not an equitable rule for the transfer or the division of property, for the protection of personal rights, or for the detection and punishment of crime, which was not precious in their eyes. Even chancery jurisdiction they retained, with the distinct tribunals, derived from the ecclesiastical courts, for probate of wills, and the English technicalities were maintained in the courts almost as if they were sacred things. Especially that of equality of civil rights among all commoners, which Hallam declares the most prominent characteristic of the English constitution — the source of its permanence, its improvement, and its vigor — they perfectly retained; they only more sharply affirmatively declared it.

And even in renouncing their allegiance to the King and putting the united colonies in his place, they felt themselves acting in intimate harmony with the spirit and drift of the ancient constitution. The executive here was to be elective, not hereditary, to be limited and not permanent in the term of his functions; and no established peerage should exist. But each State retained its governor, legislature, its ancient statute and common law; and, if they had been challenged for English authority for their attitude toward the crown, they might have replied in the words of Bracton, the Lord Chief Justice five hundred years before, under the reign of Henry III, that the law makes the king: "There is no king where will and not law bears rule; " "if the king were without a bridle, that is the law, they ought to put a bridle upon him." They might have replied in the words of Fox, speaking in Parliament in daring defiance of the temper of the House, but with many supporting him, when he said that in declaring independence they [the Americans] "had done no more than the English had done against James II."

They had done no more; though they had not elected another king in place of him whom they renounced. They had taken no step so far in advance of the then existing English constitution as these which the Parliament of 1640 took in advance of the previous Parliaments which Charles had dissolved. If there was a right more rooted than another in that constitution, it was the right of the people which was taxed to have its vote in the taxing legislature. If there was anything more accordant than another with its historic temper and tenor, it was that the authority of the king was determined when his rule became tyrannous. Jefferson had but perfectly expressed the doctrine of the lovers of freedom in England for many generations when he said in his " Sum-

mary View of the Rights of America," in 1774, that "the
monarch is no more than the chief officer of the people,
appointed by the laws, and circumscribed with definite
powers, to assist in working the great machine of government,
erected for their use, and, consequently, subject to their
superintendence;" that "kings are the servants, not the
proprietors, of the people," and that a nation claims its
rights " as derived from the laws of nature, not as the gift
of their chief magistrate."

That had been the spirit, if not as yet the formulated
doctrine of Raleigh, Hampden, Russell, Sidney — of all the
great leaders of liberty in England. Milton had declared
it in a prose as majestic as any passage of the "Paradise
Lost." The commonwealth had been built on it, and the
whole revolution of 1688. And they who now framed it
into their permanent organic law, and made it supreme in
the country they were shaping, were in harmony with the
noblest inspirations of the past. They were not innovating
with a rash recklessness. They were simply accepting and
reaffirming what they had learned from luminous events
and illustrious men. So their work had a dignity, a strength
and a permanence, which can never belong to mere fresh
speculations. It interlocked with that of multitudes going
before. It derived a virtue from every field of struggle in
England ; from every scaffold hallowed by free and consecrated blood ; from every hour of great debate. It was only
the complete development into law for a separated people
of that august ancestral liberty, the germs of which had
preceded the Heptarchy, the gradual definition and establishment of which had been the glory of English history. A
thousand years brooded over the room where they asserted
hereditary rights. Its walls showed neither portraits nor

mottoes; but the Kaiser-saal at Frankfurt was not hung around with such recollections. No titles were worn by those plain men; but there had not been one knightly soldier or one patriotic and prescient statesman, standing for liberty in the splendid centuries of its English growth, who did not touch them with unseen accolade and bid them be faithful. The paper which they adopted, fresh from the pen of its young author, and written on his hired pine table, was already, in essential life, of a venerable age; and it took immense impulse, it derived an instant and vast authority from its relation to that undying past in which they, too, had grand inheritance, and from which their public life had come.

Englishmen themselves now recognize this, and often are proud of it. The distinguished representative of Great Britain at Washington may think his government, as no doubt he does, superior to ours, but his clear eye cannot fail to see that English liberty was the parent of ours, and that the new and broader continent here opened before it suggested that expansion of it which we celebrate to-day. His ancestors, like ours, helped to build the Republic; and its faithfulness to the past, amid all innovations, was one great secret of its earliest triumph, has been one source from that day to this of its enduring and prosperous strength.

The Congress, and the people behind it, asserted for themselves hereditary liberties, and hazarded everything in the purpose to complete them. But they also affirmed with emphasis and effect another right, more general than this, which made their action significant and important to other people; which made it, indeed, a signal to the nations of the right of each to assert for itself the just prerogative of forming its government, electing its rulers, ordaining its laws, as might to it seem most expedient. Hear again the immortal words: "We hold these truths to be self-evident . . . that to secure these [inalienable] rights, governments are instituted among men, deriving their just powers from the consent of the governed; that whenever any form of government becomes destructive of these ends, it is the right of the people to alter or abolish it, and to institute new government, laying its foundations in such principles, and organizing its powers in such form, as to them shall seem most likely to effect their safety and happiness."

This is what the party of Bentham called "the assumption of natural rights, claimed without the slightest evidence of their existence, and supported by vague and declamatory generalities." This is what we receive as the decisive and noble declaration, spoken with the simplicity of a perfect conviction, of a natural right as patent as the continent; a declaration which challenged at once the attention of mankind, and which now is practically assumed as a premise in international relations and public law.

Of course, it was not a new discovery. It was old as the earliest of political philosophers; as old, indeed, as the earliest communities, which, becoming established in particular locations, had there developed their own institutions, and repelled with vehemence the assaults that would change them. But in the growth of political societies, and the vast expansion of imperial states, by the conquest of those adjacent and weaker, the right, so easily recognized at the outset, so germane to the instincts, so level with the reason of every community, had widely passed out of men's thoughts; and the power of a conquering state to change the institutions and laws of a people, or impose on it new ones — the power of a parent state to shape the forms and prescribe the rules of the colonies

which went from it — had been so long and abundantly exercised that the very right of the people thus conquered or
colonial, to consult its own interests in the frame of its
government, had been almost forgotten. It might be a high
speculation of scholars or a charming dream of political
enthusiasts. But it was not a maxim for the practical
statesman; and, whatever its correctness as an ideal principle,
it was vain to expect to see it established in a world full of
kings, who claimed each for himself an authority from God,
and full of states intent on grasping and governing by their
law adjacent domains. The revolt of the Netherlands
against Spanish domination had been the one instance in
modern history in which the inherent right of a people to
suit itself in the frame of its government had been proclaimed and then maintained; and that had been a
paroxysmal revolt against tyranny so crushing and cruelties
so savage that they took it out of the line of examples. The
Dutch Republic was almost as exceptional, through the fierce
wickedness which had crowded it into being, as was Switzer-
land itself on its Alpine heights. For an ordinary state to
claim self-regulation, and found its government on a *plebis*
cite, was to contradict precedent, and to set at defiance
European tradition.

Our fathers, however, in a somewhat vague way, had
held from the start that they had right to an autonomy,
and that acts of Parliament and appointments of the crown
took proper effect upon these shores only by reason of their
assent. Their charters were held to confirm this doctrine.
This conviction, at first practical and instinctive rather than
theoretic, had grown with their growth, and had been intensified into positive affirmation and public exhibition, as the
British rule infringed more sharply on their interests and

their hopes. It had finally become the general and decisive conviction of the colonies. It had spoken already in armed resistance to the troops of the king. It had been articulated, with gathering emphasis, in many resolves of assemblies and conventions. It was now finally, most energetically, set forth to the world in the great Declaration; and in that utterance, made general not particular, and founding the rights of the people in this country on principles as wide as humanity itself, there lay an appeal to every nation — an appeal whose words took unparalleled force, were illuminated and made rubrical, in the fire and blood of the following war.

When the Emperor Ferdinand visited Innsbruck — that beautiful town of the Austrian Tyrol — in 1838, it is said that the inhabitants wrote his name in immense bonfires along the sides of the precipitous hills which shelter the town. Over a space of four or five miles extended that colossal illumination, till the heavens seemed on fire in the far-reflected, up-streaming glow. The right of a people, separated from others, to its own institutions — our fathers wrote this in lines so vivid and so large that the whole world could see them; and they followed that writing with the consenting thunders of so many cannon that even the lands across the Atlantic were shaken and filled with the long reverberation.

The doctrine had, of course, in every state its two-fold internal application, as well as its front against external powers. On the one hand, it swept with destroying force against the notion so long maintained of the right of certain families in the world, called Hapsburg, Bourbon, Stuart, or whatever, to govern the rest; and wherever it was received it made the imagined divine right of kings an obsolete and contemptible fiction. On the other hand, it smote with equal energy against the pretensions of any minority within the state, whether banded together by the ties of descent, or of neighborhood in location, or of common opinion, or supposed common interest, to govern the rest; or even to impair the established and paramount government of the rest by separating themselves organically from it.

It was never the doctrine of the fathers that the people of Kent, Cornwall, or Lincoln, might sever themselves from the rest of England, and while they had their voice and vote in the public councils might assert the right to govern the whole, under threat of withdrawal if their minor vote were not suffered to control. They were not seeking to initiate anarchy, and to make it thenceforth respectable in the world by support of their suffrages. They recognized the fact that the state exists to meet permanent needs, is the ordinance of God as well as the family; and that he has determined the bounds of men's habitation, by rivers, seas, and mountain chains, shaping countries as well as continents into physical coherence, while giving one man his birth on the north of the Pyrenees, another on the south, one on the terraced banks of the Rhine, another in English meadow or upland. They saw that a common and fixed habitation, in a country thus physically defined, especially when combined with community of descent, of permanent public interest, and of the language on which thought is interchanged — that these make a people; and such a people, as a true and abiding body-politic, they affirmed had right to shape its government, forbidding others to intermeddle.

But it must be the general mind of the people which determined the questions thus involved; not a dictating class within the state, whether known as peers or associated commoners, whether scattered widely, as one among several political parties, or grouped together in some one section, and having a special interest to encourage. The decision of the general public mind, as deliberately reached, and authentically declared, that must be the end of debate; and the right of resistance, or the right of division, after that, if such right exist, it is not to be vindicated from their Declaration. Any one who thought such government by the whole intolerable to him was always at liberty to expatriate himself, and find lsewhere such other institutions as he might prefer. But ie could not tarry, and still not submit. He was not a nonarch, without the crown, before whose contrary judgment and will the public councils must be dumb. While dwelling in the land and having the same opportunity with others to seek the amendment of what he disapproved, the will of the whole was binding upon him; and that obligation he could not vacate by refusing to accept it. If one could not, neither could ten, nor a hundred, nor a million, who still remained a minority of the whole.

To allow such a right would have been to make government transparently impossible. Not separate sections only, but counties, townships, school districts, neighborhoods, must have the same right; and each individual, with his own will for his final law, must be the complete ultimate state.

It was no such disastrous folly which the fathers of our Republic affirmed. They ruled out kings, princes, peers, from any control over the people; and they did not give to a transient minority, wherever it might appear, on whatever question, a greater privilege, because less defined, than that which they jealously withheld from these classes. Such a tyranny of irresponsible occasional minorities would have seemed to them only more intolerable than that of classes organized, permanent, and limited by law. And when it was affirmed by some, and silently feared by many others, that in our late immense civil war the States which adhered to the old constitution had forgotten or discarded the principles of the earlier Declaration, those assertions and fears were alike without reason. The people which adopted the Declaration when distributed into colonies was the people which afterward established the confederation of 1781, imperfect enough, but whose abiding renown it is that under it the war was ended. It was the same people which framed the constitution when compacted into States. " We the people of the United States, do ordain and establish the following constitution," so runs the majestic and vital instrument. It contains provisions for its own emendation. When the people will they may set it aside, and put in place of it one wholly different; and no other nation can intervene. But while it continues, it and the laws made normally under it are not subject to resistance by a portion of the people conspiring to direct or limit the rest. And, whensoever any pretension like this shall appear, if ever again it does appear, it will undoubtedly as instantly appear that even as in the past so in the future, the people, whose the government is, and whose complete and magnificent domain God has marked out for it, will subdue resistance, compel submission, forbid secession, though it cost again, as it cost before, four years of war, with treasure uncounted and inestimable life.

The right of a people upon its own territory, as equally against any classes within it or any external powers, this is the doctrine of our Declaration. We know how it here has been applied, and how settled it is upon these shores for the time to come. We know, too, something of what impression it instantly made upon the minds of other peoples, and how they sprang to greet and accept it. In the fine image of Bancroft, "the astonished nations, as they read that all men are created equal, started out of their lethargy, like those who have been exiles from childhood, when they suddenly hear the dimly remembered accents of their mother tongue."

The theory of scholars was now become the maxim of a State. The diffused ineffectual nebulous light had got itself concentrated into an orb; and the radiance of it, penetrating and hot, shone afar. You know how France responded to it; with passionate speed seeking to be rid of the terrific establishments in Church and State which had nearly crushed the life of the people, and with a beautiful, though credulous, unreason trying to lift by the grasp of the law into intelligence and political capacity the masses whose training for thirteen centuries had been despotic. No operation of natural law was any more certain than the failure of that too daring experiment. But the very failure involved progress from it — involved, undoubtedly, that ultimate success which it was vain to try to extemporize. Certainly the other European powers will not again intervene, as they did, to restore a despotism which France had abjured, and with foreign bayonets to uphold institutions which it does not desire. Italy, Spain, Germany, England — they are not republican in the form of their government, nor as yet democratic in the distribution of powers. But each of them is as full of this organic, self-demonstrating doctrine as is our own land; and England would send no troops to Canada to compel its submission if it should decide to set up for itself. Neither Italy nor Spain would maintain a monarchy a moment longer than the general mind of the country preferred it. Germany would be fused in the fire of one passion if any foreign nation whatever should assume to dictate the smallest change in one of its laws.

The doctrine of the proper prerogative of kings, derived from God, which in the last century was more common in Europe than the doctrine of the centrality of the sun in our planetary system, is now as obsolete among the intelligent as are the epicycles of Ptolemy. Every government expects to stand henceforth by assent of the governed, and by no other claim or right. It is strong by beneficence, not by tradition, and at the height of its military successes it circulates appeals and canvasses for ballots. Revolution is carefully sought to be averted by timely and tender amelioration of the laws. The most progressive and liberal states are most evidently secure, while those which stand, like olive-trees at Tivoli, with feeble arms supported on pillows and hollow trunks filled up with stone, are palpably only tempting the blast. An alliance of sovereigns, like that called the Holy, for reconstructing the map of Europe, and parcelling out the passive peoples among separate governments, would to-day be no more possible than would Charlemagne's plan for reconstructing the Empire of the West. Even Murad, Sultan of Turkey, now takes the place of Abdul, the deposed, " by the Grace of God and the will of the people; " and that accomplished and illustrious prince, whose empire under the Southern Cross rivals our own in its extent, and most nearly approaches it on this hemisphere in stability of institutions and in practical freedom, has his surest title to the throne which he honors in his wise liberality, and his faithful endeavor for the good of his people. As long as in this he continues as now a recognized leader among the monarchs — ready to take and seek suggestions from even a democratic Republic — his throne will be steadfast as the water-sheds of Brazil; and while his successors maintain his spirit no domestic insurrections will test the question whether they retain that celerity in movement with which Dom Pedro has astonished Americans.

It is no more possible to reverse this tendency toward popular sovereignty, and to substitute for it the right of families, classes, minorities, or of intervening foreign states, than it is to arrest the motion of the earth, and make it swing the other way in its annual orbit. In this, at least, our fathers' Declaration has made its impression on the history of mankind.

It was the act of a people and not of persons, except as these represented and led it. It was the act of a people not starting out on new theories of government so much as developing into forms of law and practical force a great and gradual inheritance of freedom. It was the act of a people declaring for others as for itself the right of each to its own form of government without interference from other nations, without restraint by privileged classes.

It only remains, then, to ask the question how far it has contributed to the peace, the advancement, and the permanent welfare of the people by which it was set forth — of other nations which it has affected. And to ask this question is almost to answer it. The answer is as evident as the sun in the heavens.

It cannot certainly be affirmed that we in America, any more than persons or peoples elsewhere, have reached as yet the ideal state of private liberty combined with a perfect public order, or of culture complete and a supreme character. The political world, as well as the religious, since Christ was on earth, looks forward, not backward, for its millennium. That golden age is still to come which is to shine in the perfect splendor reflected from him who is ascended; and no prophecy tells us how long before the advancing race shall reach and cross its glowing marge, or what long effort, or what tumults of battle, are still to precede.

In this country, too, there have been immense special impediments to hinder wide popular progress in things which are highest. Our people have had a continent to subdue. They have been from the start in constant migration. Westward, from the counties of the Hudson and the Mohawk, around the lakes, over the prairies, across the great river, westward still, over alkali plains, across terrible cañons, up gorges of the mountains where hardly the wild goat could find footing; westward always, till the Golden Gate opened out on the sea which has been made 10,000 miles wide, as if nothing less could stop the march — this has been the popular movement from almost the day of the great Declaration. Tomorrow's tents have been pitched in new fields, and last year's houses await new possessors.

With such constant change, such wide dislocation of the mass of the people from early and settled home associations, and with the incessant occupation of the thoughts by the great physical problems presented — not so much by any struggle for existence as by harvests for which the prairies waited, by mills for which the rivers clamored, by the coal and the gold which offered themselves to the grasp of the miner — it would not have been strange if a great and dangerous decadence had occurred in that domestic and private virtue of which home is the nursery, in that generous and reverent public spirit which is but the effluence of its combined rays. It would have been wholly too much to expect that, under such influences, the highest progress should have been realized in speculative thought, in artistic culture, or in the researches of pure science.

Accordingly, we find that in these departments not enough has been accomplished to make our progress signal in them, though here and there the eminent souls, "that are like stars and dwell apart," have illumined themes highest with their high interpretations. But history has been cultivated among us with an enthusiasm, to an extent hardly I think to have been anticipated among a people so recent and expectant; and Prescott, Motley, Irving, Ticknor, with him upon whose splendid page all American history has been amply illustrated, are known as familiarly and honored as highly in Europe as here. We have had, as well, distinguished poets, and have them now, to whom the nation has been responsive, through whom the noblest poems of the Old World have come into the English tongue, rendered in fit and perfect music, and some of whose minds, blossoming long ago in the solemn and beautiful fancies of youth, with perennial energy still ripen to new fruit as they near or cross their four score years. In medicine and law, as well as in theology, in fiction, biography, and the vivid narrative of exploration and discovery, the people whose birthday we commemorate has added something to the possession of men. Its sculptors and painters have won high places in the brilliant realm of modern art. Publicists like Wheaton, jurists like Kent, have gained a celebrity reflecting honor on the land; and if no orator so vast in knowledge, so profound and discursive in philosophical thought, so affluent in imagery, and so glorious in diction as Edmund Burke has yet appeared, we must remember that centuries were needed to produce him elsewhere, and that any of the great parliamentary debaters, aside from him, have been matched or surpassed in the hearing of those who have hung with rapt sympathetic attention on the lips of Clay or of Rufus Choate, or have felt themselves listening to the mightiest mind which ever touched theirs when they stood beneath the imperial voice in which Webster spoke.

In applied science there has been much done in the country, for which the world admits itself our grateful debtor. I need not multiply illustrations of this from locomotives, printing presses, sewing machines, revolvers, steam reapers, bank locks. One instance suffices, most signal of all. When Morse, from Washington, thirty-two years ago, sent over the wires his word to Baltimore, "What hath God wrought," he had given to all the nations of mankind an instrument the most sensitive, expansive, quickening, which the world yet possesses. He had bound the earth in electric network.

England touches India to-day, and France, Algeria, while we are in contact with all the continents upon these scarcely perceptible nerves. The great strategist like Von Moltke, with these in his hands, from the silence of his office directs campaigns, dictates marches, wins victories; the statesman in the Cabinet inspires and regulates the distant diplomacies; while the traveller in any port or mart is by the same marvel of mechanism in instant communication with all centres of commerce. It is certainly not too much to say that no other invention of the world in this century has so richly deserved the medals, crosses, and diamond decorations, the applause of Senates, the gifts of Kings, which have been showered upon its author, as did this invention, which finally taught and utilized the lightnings whose nature a signer of the great Declaration had made apparent.

But after all it is not so much in special inventions, or in eminent attainments made by individuals, that we are to find the answer to the question, "What did that day, a hundred years since, accomplish for us?" Still less is it found in the progress we have made in outward wealth and material success. This might have been made, approximately at least, if the British supremacy had here continued. The prairies would have been as productive as now, the mines of copper and silver and gold as rich and extensive, the coalbeds as vast, and the cotton-fields as fertile, if we had been born the subjects of the Georges or of Victoria. Steam would have kept its propulsive force, and sea and land have been theatres of its triumph. The river would have been as smooth a highway for the commerce which seeks it; and the leap of every mountain stream would have given as swift and constant a push to the wheels that set spindles and saws in motion. Electricity itself would have lost no property, and might have become as completely as now the fire-winged messenger of the thought of mankind.

But what we have now, and should not have had except for that paper which the Congress adopted, is the general and increasing popular advancement in knowledge, vigor, as I believe in moral culture, of which our country has been the arena, and in which lies its hope for the future. The independence of the nation has acted with sympathetic force on the personal life which the nation includes. It has made men more resolute, aspiring, confident, and more susceptible to whatever exalts. The doctrine that all by creation are equal — not in respect of physical force or of mental endowment, of means for culture or inherited privilege, but in respect of immortal faculty, of duty to each other, of right to protection, and to personal development — this has given manliness to the poor, enterprise to the weak, a kindling hope to the most obscure. It has made the individuals of whom the nation is composed more alive to the forces which educate and exalt.

There has been incessant motive, too, for the wide and

constant employment of these forces. It has been felt that, as the people is sovereign here, that people must be tuned in mind and spirit for its august and sovereign function. The establishment of common schools for a needful primary secular training has been an instinct of society, only recognized and repeated in provisions of statutes. The establishment of higher schools, classical and general, of colleges, scientific and professional seminaries, has been as well the impulse of the nation, and the furtherance of them a care of government. The immense expansion of the press in this country has been based fundamentally upon the same impulse; and has wrought with beneficent general force in the same direction. Religious instruction has gone as widely as this distribution of secular knowledge.

It used to be thought that a Church dissevered from the State must be feeble. Wanting wealth of endowments and dignity of titles — its clergy entitled to no place among the peers, its revenues assured by no legal enactments — it must remain obscure and poor, while the absence of any external limitations, of parliamentary rubrics and a legal creed, must leave it liable to endless division, and tend to its speedy disintegration into sects and schisms. It seemed as hopeless to look for strength, wealth, beneficence, for extensive educational and missionary work, to such churches as these, as to look for aggressive military organization to a company of farmers, or for the volume and thunder of Niagara to a thousand sinking and separate rills.

But the work which was given to be done in this country was so great and momentous, and has been so constant that matching itself against that work the Church, under whatever name, has realized a strength, and developed an activity, wholly fresh in the world in modern times. It has not been antagonized by that instinct of liberty which always awakens against its work, where religion is required by law. It has seized the opportunity. Its ministers and members have had their own standards, leaders, laws, and sometimes have quarrelled, fiercely enough, as to which were the better. But in the work which was set them to do, to give to the sovereign American people the knowledge of God in the Gospel of his Son, their only strife has been one of emulation — to go the farthest, to give the most, and to bless most largely the land and its future. The spiritual incentive has of course been supreme; but patriotism has added its impulse to the work. It has been felt that Christianity is the basis of republican empire, its bond of cohesion, its life-giving law; that the ancient manuscript copies of the Gospels sent by Gregory to Augustine at Canterbury, and still preserved on sixth century parchments at Oxford and Cambridge — more than Magna Charta itself these are the roots of English liberty; that Magna Charta and the Petition of Right with our completing Declaration, were possible only because these had been before them. And so in the work of keeping Christianity prevalent in the land, all Christian churches have eagerly striven. Their preachers have been heard where the pioneer's fire scarce was kindled. Their schools have been gathered in the temporary camp, not less than in the hamlet or town. They have sent their books with lavish distribution, they have scattered their Bibles like leaves of Autumn, where settlements were hardly more than prophesied. In all languages of the land they have told the old story of the law and the cross, a present redemption and a coming tribunal. The highest truths, most solemn and inspiring, have been the truths most constantly in hand. It has been felt that, in the best sense, a muscular Christianity was indispensable where

men lifted up axes upon the thick trees. The delicate speculations of the closet and the schools were too dainty for the
work; and the old confessions of councils and reformers,
whose undecaying and sovereign energy no use exhausts, have
been those always most familiar where the trapper on his
stream or the miner in his gulch has found priest or minister
on his track.

Of course not all the work has been fruitful. Not all
God's acorns come to oaks, but here and there one. Not all
the seeds of flowers germinate, but enough to make some
radiant gardens. And out of all this work and gift has come
a mental and moral training to the nation at large such as it
certainly would not have had except for this effort, the effort
for which would not have been made on a scale so immense
except for the incessant aim to fit the nation for its great
experiment of self-regulation. The Declaration of Independence has been the great charter of public education; has given
impulse and scope to this prodigious missionary work.

The result of the whole is evident enough. I am not here
as the eulogist of our people beyond what facts justify. I
admit, with regret, that American manners sometimes are
coarse, and American culture very imperfect; that the noblest
examples of a consummate training imply a leisure which
we have not had, and are perhaps most easily produced where
social advantages are more permanent than here, and the law
of heredity has a wider recognition. We all know too well
how much of even vice and shame there has been in our
national life; how corruption has entered high places in the
government, and the blister of its touch has been upon laws,
as well as on the acts of prominent officials. And we know
the reckless greed and ambition, the fierce party spirit, the
personal wrangles and jealous animosities, with which our

Congress has been often dishonored; at which the nation —
sadder still — has sometimes laughed in idiotic unreason.

But knowing all this, and with the impression of it full on
our thoughts, we may exult in the real, steady, and prophesy-
ing growth of a better spirit toward dominance in the land.
I scout the thought that we, as a people, are worse than our
fathers! John Adams, at the head of the War Department,
in 1776, wrote bitter laments of the corruption which existed
in even that infant age of the Republic, and of the spirit
of venality, rapacious and insatiable, which was then the most
alarming enemy of America. He declared himself ashamed
of the age he lived in! In Jefferson's day all Federalists
expected the universal dominion of French infidelity. In
Jackson's day all Whigs thought the country gone to ruin
already, as if Mr. Biddle had had the entire public hope
locked up in the vaults of his terminated bank. In Polk's
day the excitements of the Mexican War gave life and germi-
nation to all seeds of rascality. There has never been a time
— not here alone but in any country — when the fierce light
of incessant inquiry blazing on men in public life would not
have brought out such forces of evil as we have seen, or
when the condemnation which followed the discovery would
have been sharper. And it is among my deepest convictions
that, with all which has happened to debase and debauch it,
the nation at large was never before more mentally vigorous
or morally sound than it is to-day.

Gentlemen, the demonstration is around us. This city, if
any place on the continent, should have been the one where
a reckless wickedness should have had sure prevalence, and
reforming virtue the least chance of success. Starting in
1790 with a white population of less than 30,000 — growing
steadily for forty years, till that population has multiplied

sixfold — taking into itself from that time on such multitudes of emigrants from all parts of the earth that the dictionaries of the languages spoken in its streets would make a library — all forms of luxury coming with wealth, and all means and facilities for every vice — the primary elections being always the seed-bed out of which springs its choice of rulers, with the influence which it sends to the public councils — its citizens so absorbed in their pursuits that oftentimes, for years together, large numbers of them have left its affairs in hands the most of all unsuited to so supreme and delicate a trust — it might well have been expected that while its docks were echoing with a commerce which encompassed the globe, while its streets were thronged with the eminent and the gay from all parts of the land, while its homes had in them uncounted thousands of noble men and cultured women, while its stately squares swept out year by year across new space, while it founded great institutions of beneficence and shot new spires upward toward heaven, and turned the rocky waste to a pleasure-ground famous in the earth, its government would decay, and its recklessness of moral ideas, if not as well of political principles, would become apparent.

Men have prophesied this, from the outset till now. The fear of it began with the first great advance of the wealth, population, and fame of the city; and there have not been wanting facts in its history which served to renew if not to justify the fear.

But when the war of 1861 broke on the land, and shadowed every home within it, this city — which had voted by immense majorities against the existing administration, and which was linked by a million ties with the great communities that were rushing to assail it — flung out its banners from window and spire, from City Hall and newspaper office, and poured its wealth and life into the service of sustaining the government, with a swiftness and strength and a vehement energy that were never surpassed. When, afterward, greedy and treacherous men, capable and shrewd, deceiving the unwary, hiring the skilful, and molding the very law to their uses, had concentrated in their hands the government of the city, and had bound it in seemingly invincible chains while they plundered its treasury — it rose upon them, when advised of the facts, as Samson rose upon the Philistines; and the two new cords that were upon his hands no more suddenly became as flax that was burned than did those manacles imposed upon the city by the craft of the Ring.

Its leaders of opinion to-day are the men — like him who presides in our assembly — whom virtue exalts and character crowns. It rejoices in a chief magistrate as upright and intrepid in a virtuous cause as any of those whom he succeeds. It is part of a State whose present position, in laws, and officers, and the spirit of its people does no discredit to the noblest of its memories. And from these heights between the rivers, looking over the land, looking out on the earth to which its daily embassies go, it sees nowhere beneath the sun a city more ample in its moral securities, a city more dear to those who possess it, a city more splendid in promise and in hope.

What is true of the city is true, in effect, of all the land. Two things, at least, have been established by our national history, the impression of which the world will not lose. The one is, that institutions like ours, when sustained by a prevalent moral life throughout the nation, are naturally permanent. The other is, that they tend to peaceful relations with other states. They do this in fulfilment of an organic tendency, and not through any accident of location. The same tendency will inhere in them, whosoever established.

In this age of the world, and in all the states which Christianity quickens, the allowance of free movement to the popular mind is essential to the stability of public institutions. There may be restraint enough to guide and keep such movement from premature exhibition. But there cannot be force enough used to resist it, and to reverse its gathering current. If there is, the government is swiftly overthrown, as in France so often, or is left on one side, as Austria has been by the advancing German people; like the Castle of Heidelberg, at once palace and fortress, high-placed and superb, but only the stateliest ruin in Europe, when the rail train thunders through the tunnel beneath it, and the Neckar sings along its near channel as if tower and tournament never had been. Revolution, transformation, organic change, have thus all the time for this hundred years been proceeding in Europe; sometimes silent, but oftener amid thunders of stricken fields; sometimes pacific, but oftener with garments rolled in blood.

In England the progress has been peaceful, the popular demands being ratified by law whenever the need became apparent. It has been vast as well as peaceful in the extension of suffrage, in the ever-increasing power of the Commons, in popular education. Chatham himself would hardly know his own England if he should return to it. The throne continues, illustrated by the virtues of her who fills it, and the ancient forms still obtain in Parliament. But it could not have occurred to him or to Burke that a century after the ministry of Grenville the embarkation of the Pilgrims would be one of the prominent historical pictures on the panels of the lobby of the House of Lords, or that the name of Oliver Cromwell, and of Bradshaw, president of the high court of justice, would be cut in the stone in Westminster Abbey, over the places in which they were buried, and whence their decaying bodies were dragged to the ditch and the gibbet. England is now, as has been well said, "an aristocratic Republic, with a permanent executive." Its only perils lie in the fact of that aristocracy, which, however, is flexible enough to endure, of that permanence in the executive which would hardly outlive one vicious prince.

What changes have taken place in France I need not remind you, nor how uncertain is still its future. You know how the swift, untiring wheels of advance or reaction have rolled this way and that in Italy and in Spain; how Germany has had to be reconstructed; how Hungary has had to fight and suffer for that just place in the Austrian councils which only imperial defeat surrendered. You know how precarious the equilibrium now is in many states between popular rights and princely prerogative; what armies are maintained to fortify governments: what fear of sudden and violent change, like an avalanche tumbling at the touch of a foot, perplexes nations. The records of change make the history of Europe. The expectation of change is almost as wide as the continent itself.

Meantime, how permanent has been the Republic, which seemed at the outset to foreign spectators a mere sudden insurrection, a mere organized riot! Its organic law, adopted after exciting debate, but arousing no battle, and enforced by no army, has been interpreted and peacefully administered, with one great exception, from the beginning. It has once been assailed with passion and skill, with splendid daring and unbounded self-sacrifice, by those who sought a sectional advantage through its destruction. No monarchy of the world could have stood that assault. It seemed as if the last fatal Apocalypse had come, to drench the land with plague and flood, and wrap it in a fiery gloom. The Republic

—" pouring, like the tide into a breach,
With ample and brim fulness of its force,"

subdued the Rebellion, restored the dominion of the old constitution, amended its provisions in the contrary direction from that which had been so fiercely sought, gave it guarantees of endurance while the continent lasts, and made its ensigns more eminent than ever in the regions from which they had been expelled. The very portions of the people which then sought its overthrow are now again its applauding adherents — the great and constant reconciling force, the tranquillizing irenarch, being the freedom which it leaves in their hands.

It has kept its place, this Republic of ours, in spite of the rapid expansion of the nation over territory so wide that the scanty strip of the original state is only as a fringe on its immense mantle. It has kept its place, while vehement debates, involving the profoundest ethical principles, have stirred to its depths the whole public mind. It has kept its place, while the tribes of mankind have been pouring upon it, seeking the shelter and freedom which it gave. It saw an illustrious President murdered by the bullet of an assassin. It saw his place occupied as quietly by another as if nothing unforeseen or alarming had occurred. It saw prodigious armies assembled for its defence. It saw those armies at the end of the war marching in swift and long procession up the streets of the capital, and then dispersing into their former peaceful citizenship, as if they had had no arms in their hands. The general before whose skill and will those armies had been shot upon the forces which opposed them, and

whose word had been their military law, remained for three
years an appointed officer of the government he had saved.
Elected then to be the head of that government, and again
re-elected by the ballots of his countrymen, in a few months
more he will have retired, to be thenceforth a citizen like the
rest, eligible to office, and entitled to vote, but with no thought
of any prerogative descending to him or to his children from
his great service and military fame. The Republic, whose
triumphing armies he led, will remember his name and be
grateful for his work; but neither to him nor to any one else
will it ever give sovereignty over itself.

From the Lakes to the Gulf its will is the law, its dominion
complete. Its centripetal and centrifugal forces are balanced, almost as in the astronomy of the heavens. Decen-
tralizing authority, it puts his own part of it into the hand
of every citizen. Giving free scope to private enterprise,
allowing not only but accepting and encouraging each movement of the public reason which is its only terrestrial rule,
there is no threat, in all its sky, of division or downfall. It
cannot be successfully assailed from without, with a blow at
its life, while other nations continue sane.

It has been sometimes compared to a pyramid, broad-
based and secure, not liable to overthrow, as is obelisk or
column, by storm or age. The comparison is just, but it is
not sufficient. It should rather be compared to one of the
permanent features of nature, and not to any artificial construction — to the river, which flows like our own Hudson,
along the courses that nature opens, forever in motion, but
forever the same; to the lake, which lies on common days
level and bright in placid stillness, while it gathers its fulness from many lands, and lifts its waves in stormy strength
when winds assail it; to the mountain, which is not artisti-

cally shaped, and which only rarely, in some supreme sunburst, flushes with color, but whose roots the very earthquake cannot shake, and on whose brow the storms fall hurtless, while under its shelter the cottage nestles, and up its sides the gardens climb.

So stands the Republic:

> " Whole as the marble, founded as the rock,
> As broad and general as the casing air."

What has been the fact? Lay out of sight that late evil war which could not be averted when once it had been threatened, except by the sacrifice of the government itself and a wholly unparalleled public suicide, and how much of war with foreign powers has the century seen? There has been a frequent crackle of musketry along the frontiers, as Indian tribes which refused to be civilized have slowly and fiercely retreated toward the West. There was one war declared against Tripoli, in 1801, when the Republic took by the throat the African pirates to whom Europe paid tribute, and when the gallantry of Preble and Decatur gave early distinction to our Navy. There was a war declared against England, in 1812, when our seamen had been taken from under our flag, from the decks, indeed, of our national ships, and our commerce had been practically swept from the seas. There was a war affirmed already to exist in Mexico in 1846, entered into by surprise, never formally declared, against which the moral sentiment of the nation rose widely in revolt, but which in its result added largely to our territory, opened to us Californian treasures, and wrote the names of Buena Vista and Monterey on our short annals.

That has been our military history: and if a people, as powerful and as proud, has anywhere been more peaceable also in the last 100 years, the strictest research fails to find it.

Smarting with the injury done us by England during the crisis of our national peril, in spite of the remonstrances presented through that distinguished citizen who should have been your orator to-day; while hostile taunts had incensed our people; while burning ships had exasperated commerce, and while what looked like artful evasions had made statesmen indignant — with a half million men who hardly yet laid down their arms, with a navy never before so vast or so fitted for service — when a war with England would have had the force of passion behind it, and would, at any rate, have shown to the world that the nation respects its starry flag and means to have it secure on the seas — we referred all differences to arbitration, appointed commissioners, tried the cause at Geneva with advocates, not with armies, and got a prompt and ample verdict. If Canada now lay next to Yorkville, it would not be safer from armed incursion than it is when divided by only a custom house from all the strength of this Republic.

The fact is apparent, and the reason not less so. A monarchy, just as it is despotic, finds incitement to war — for preoccupation of the popular mind; to gratify nobles, officers, the army; for historic renown. An intelligent republic hates war, and shuns it. It counts standing armies a curse only second to an annual pestilence. It wants no glory, but from growth. It delights itself in arts of peace, seeks social enjoyment and increase of possessions, and feels instinctively that, like Israel of old, "its strength is to sit still." It cannot bear to miss the husbandman from the fields, the citizen from the town, the house-father from the home, the worshipper from the church. To change or shape other people's institutions is no part of its business. To force them to accept its forms of government would simply contradict and nullify its charter. Except, then, when it is startled into passion, by the cry of a suffering under oppression which stirs its pulses into tumult, or when it is assailed in its own rights, citizens, property, it will not go to war, nor even then if diplomacy can find a remedy for the wrong. " Millions for defence," said Cotesworth Pinckney to the French directory, when Talleyrand in their name had threatened him with war, " but not a cent for tribute." He might have added, " and not a dollar for aggressive strife."

It will never be safe to insult such a nation, or to oppress its citizens, for the reddest blood is in its veins, and some Captain Ingraham may always appear to lay his little sloop-of-war alongside the offending frigate, with shotted guns and a peremptory summons. There is a way to make powder inexplosive; but, treat it chemically how you will, the dynamite will not stand many blows of the hammer. The detonating tendency is too permanent in it. But if left to itself, such a people will be peaceful, as ours has been. It will foster peace among the nations. It will tend to dissolve great permanent armaments, as the light conquers ice, and Summer sunshine breaks the glacier which a hundred trip-hammers could only scar. The longer it continues the more widely and effectively its influence spreads, the more will its benign example hasten the day, so long foretold, so surely coming, when

" The war-drum throbs no longer, and the battle-flags are furled
In the Parliament of man, the Federation of the world."

It will not be forgotten, in the land or in the earth, until the stars have fallen from their poise, or until our vivid morning star of republican liberty, not losing its lustre, has seen its special brightness fade in the ampler effulgence of a freedom universal!

But while we rejoice in that which is past, and gladly recognize the vast organic mystery of life which was in the Declaration, the plans of Providence which slowly and silently, but with ceaseless progression, had led the way to it, the immense and enduring results of good which from it have flown, let us not forget the duty which always equals privilege, and that of peoples, as well as of persons, to whomsoever much is given shall only therefore the more be required. Let us consecrate ourselves, each one of us, here, to the further duties which wait to be fulfilled, to the work which shall consummate the great work of the fathers!

Mr. President, fellow citizens, to an extent too great for your patience, but with a rapid incompleteness that is only too evident as we match it with the theme, I have outlined before you a few of the reasons why we have the right to commemorate the day whose hundredth anniversary has brought us together, and why the paper then adopted has interest and importance not only for us, but for all the advancing sons of men. Thank God that he who framed the Declaration, and he who was its foremost champion, both lived to see the nation they had shaped growing to greatness, and to die together, in that marvellous coincidence, on its semi-centennial! The fifty years which have passed since then have only still further honored their work. Mr. Adams was mistaken in the day which he named as the one to be most fondly remembered. It was not that on which independence of the Empire of Great Britain was formally resolved. It was that on which the reasons were given which justified the act, and the principles were announced which made it of general significance to mankind. But he would have been absolutely right in saying of the fourth day what he did say of the second: it " will be the most remarkable epoch in the

history of America: to be celebrated by succeeding generations as the great anniversary festival, commemorated as the
day of deliverance, by solemn acts of devotion to Almighty
God, from one end of the continent to the other."

From barren soils come richest grapes, and on severe and
rocky slopes the trees are often of toughest fibre. The wines
of Rüdesheim and Johannisberg cannot be grown in the fatness of the gardens, and the cedars of Lebanon disdain the
levels of marsh and meadow. So a heroism is sometimes
native to penury which luxury enervates, and the great resolution which sprang up in the blast and blossomed under
inclement skies, may lose its shapely and steadfast strength
when the air is all of summer softness. In exuberant
resources is to be the coming American peril — in a swiftly-
increasing luxury of life. The old humility, hardihood,
patience, are too likely to be lost when material success again
opens, as it will, all avenues to wealth, and when its brilliant
prizes solicit, as again they will, the national spirit.

Be it ours to endeavor that that temper of the fathers which
was nobler than their work shall live in the children, and exalt
to its tone their coming career; that political intelligence,
patriotic devotion, a reverent spirit toward him who is above,
an exulting expectation of the future of the world, and a
sense of our relation to it, shall be as of old, essential
forces in our public life, that education and religion shall
keep step all the time with the nation's advance, and
be forever instantly at home wherever its flag shakes out its
folds.

In a spirit worthy of the memories of the past let us set
ourselves to accomplish the tasks which in the sphere of
national politics still await completion. We burn the sunshine of other years when we ignite the wood or coal upon

our hearths. We enter a privilege which ages have secured in our daily enjoyment of political freedom. While the kindling glow irradiates our homes, let it shed its lustre on our spirit and quicken it for its further work. Let us fight against the tendency of educated men to reserve themselves from politics, remembering that no other form of activity is so grand or effective as that which affects, first the character, and then the revelation of character in the government, of a great and free people. Let us make religious dissensions here, as a force in politics, as absurd as witchcraft. Let party names be nothing to us, in comparison with that costly and proud inheritance of liberty and of law which parties exist to conserve and enlarge, which any party will have here to maintain if it would not be buried at the next cross-roads, with a stake throught its breast. Let us seek the unity of all sections of the Republic through the prevalence in all of mutual respect, through the assurance in all of local freedom, through the mastery in all of that supreme spirit which flashed from the lips of Patrick Henry when he said, in the first Continental Congress, "I am not a Virginian, but an American." Let us take care that labor maintains its ancient place of privilege and honor, and that industry has no fetters imposed of legal restraint or of social discredit to hinder its work or to lessen its wage. Let us turn and overturn in public discussion, in political change, till we secure a civil service, honorable, intelligent, and worthy of the land, in which capable integrity, not partisan zeal, shall be the condition of each public trust; and let us resolve that whatever it may cost, of labor and of patience, of sharper economy and of general sacrifice, it shall come to pass that wherever American labor toils, wherever American enterprise plans, wherever American commerce reaches, thither again shall go as of old the country's coin — the American eagle, with the encircling stars and golden plumes!

In a word, fellow citizens, let each of us live in the blessing and the duty of our great citizenship, as those who are conscious of unreckoned indebtedness to a heroic and prescient past, the grand and solemn lineage of whose freedom runs back beyond Bunker Hill or the "Mayflower," runs back beyond muniments and memories of men, and has the majesty of far centuries upon it! Let us live as those for whom God hid a continent from the world till he could open all its scope to the freedom and faith of gathered peoples, from many lands, to be a nation to his honor and praise! Let us live as those to whom he commits the magnificent trust of blessing peoples many and far, by the truths which he has made our life, and by the history which he helps us to accomplish.

Let us not be unmindful of this ultimate and inspiring lesson of the hour. By all the memories of the past, by all the impulses of the present, by the noblest instincts of our own souls, by the touch of his sovereign spirit upon us, God make us faithful to the work and to him! that so not only this city may abide in long and bright tranquillity of peace, when our eyes have shut forever on street and spire, and populous square: that so the land, in all its future, may reflect an influence from this anniversary; and that, when another century has passed, the sun which then ascends the heavens may look on a world advanced and illumined beyond our thought, and here may behold the same great nation, born of struggle, baptized into liberty, and in its second terrific trial purchased by blood, then expanded and multiplied till all the land blooms at its touch, and still one in its life, because still pacific, Christian, free!

MAGEE

WILLIAM CONNOR MAGEE, a distinguished prelate of the English church, was the grandson of William Magee, an archbishop of Dublin, and was born at Cork, Ireland, December 17, 1821. He was educated at Trinity College, Dublin, was ordained in the Anglican church in 1844, and was for two years a curate in the parish of Saint Thomas in Dublin. In 1848 he accepted a curacy at Saint Saviour's Church in Bath, England, and was incumbent of the Octagon Proprietary Chapel in the same city, 1850-59. After a year in London as curate of Quebec Chapel he accepted the Irish living of Enniskillen, where he remained, 1860-64. His eloquence as a preacher had meanwhile attracted much attention both in England and Ireland and led to his being made dean of Cork in 1866, and dean of the Chapel Royal of Dublin, two years later. He was Donellan lecturer at Trinity College, Dublin, 1865-66, and in 1868 preached a very memorable sermon before the Church Congress in Dublin on "The Breaking of the Net," while his sermon before the British Association at Norwich the same year on "The Christian Theory of the Christian Life" was also notable for its eloquence. Magee was now so well known throughout the Establishment that his promotion to the bishopric of Peterborough before the close of 1868 excited no surprise. His first speech in the House of Lords was delivered on June 15, 1869, in opposition to the disestablishment of the Irish Church, and his eloquence on this occasion caused many to rank him even higher as a parliamentary orator than as a preacher. In 1876 he made a most effective speech before the Lords in opposition to the bill for absolutely prohibiting vivisection. In March, 1891, he was consecrated Archbishop of York, but died in London on the 5th of the following May. Magee was one of the great orators and controversialists of his time, blending clearness and persuasion with extreme terseness of expression, the keenest wit, and the sharpest sarcasm. His religious views were fairly broad and he had no sympathy with extremists in religious or social matters. In conversation his wit and humor were allowed free play and few were able to worst him in an argument. His writings comprise "Sermons at Saint Saviour's, Bath" (1852); "Sermons at the Octagon Chapel, Bath" (1852); "The Gospel and the Age" (1884); "The Atonement" (1887); "Growth in Grace" (1891); "Christ the Light of All Scripture" (1892); "Addresses and Speeches" (1892).

THE ETHICS OF FORGIVENESS

PREACHED BEFORE THE UNIVERSITY OF OXFORD, 1880

"Forgive us our debts as we forgive our debtors."—Matthew vi, 12.

LET us see what is our Lord's teaching concerning the forgiveness of sin, in the words "Forgive us our debts." What does our Lord here teach us respecting sin? He teaches us that it is something that needs forgiveness. That is to say, that it is not merely a disease to be healed, nor an imperfection to be remedied, but an offence, and an offence entailing a penalty, which cleaves to the offender as a debt until it is paid or remitted cleaves to the debtor. And he further teaches us that for this debt there is a possibility of remission — the forgiveness of sin being analogous to the remitting of a debt.

That is to say, our Lord gives us this as the popular, ordinary, human idea of forgiveness; namely, that it is the letting off to a man of the debt he owes; it is the putting of him by the creditor, as far as he can do so, in the position he would have occupied if he had never contracted that debt.

Briefly then our Lord's statement is this: first, in all sin there is guilt; secondly, a debt of penalty for that guilt; thirdly, the possibility of the remission of that debt; and fourthly, a close analogy between the remission of that debt by God to us and our remission of debt to one another. The question then at once arises for us, How far and under what conditions is it possible for us to forgive our human debtors, those who have offended against us?

Let us study this question first in its simplest form. Let

us suppose an offence committed between two equals, who have no other relation between them than that of their common humanity. Let us suppose that any one of us has been so unfortunate as to have committed some wrong against a fellow man. The instant you do so that man becomes, in spite of you and of himself, your creditor. You are his debtor for two great debts — the debt of penitence, and the debt of reparation. You feel that you ought to be sorry for what you have done and that you ought to make amends for it; and you owe this twofold debt by virtue of a law which either he or you may set in motion, but which neither he nor you can restrain — the law of your own conscience.

There is that within you which, when you have injured another, claims from you at once the double penalty of repentance and restitution. There is within your own breast an advocate of the man you have wronged. There is a voice within you crying against you to the throne of God, the judge of all, and if you cannot agree with this your adversary, it gives you over to the tormentors, remorse and shame, that abide in your own heart and will not depart from it, until you have paid the uttermost farthing of such debt. Such is the nature of the case as it arises instantly and necessarily between your human creditor and you, his debtor. Now it is quite true that your creditor may remit this debt to you and you hold it to be the noblest charity if he does.

He forgives you then, we will suppose, fully, freely, unconditionally, lovingly, nobly if you will — what then? Is all the penalty remitted? Have you escaped all the punishment of your act? He has forgiven you; but have you for that reason forgiven yourself? Nay, is it not the very fulness and freeness of his forgiveness that is heaping coals of fire upon your head, kindled and fanned into a flame by the very breath of his compassion? We know that it is so, and that in all finer and better natures it is ever most keenly so.

Already, then, we have discovered this — that there is, even between equals, no complete remission of penalty for sins possible. Behind the figure of the creditor — even of the forgiving creditor — there already begins to rise up and to project itself upon our path the shadow of law,— which, because it is law, is pitiless, unforgiving and inevitable. Even in this simplest and most rudimentary case of forgiveness, there is therefore no absolute remission.

Now let us take one step further,— let us pass on to the case of social forgiveness. Let us suppose the wrong-doing has had spectators. Let us imagine ourselves spectators of some cruel martyrdom and that we hear the martyr with his dying breath breathing out his forgiveness and blessing on his murderers. They are fully forgiven by him. Would any one of us feel disposed to take up that legacy of forgiveness and to repeat the blessings we had just heard the martyr pronounce upon his tormentors? Should we not rather feel our hearts stirred with the deepest and most righteous indignation, calling, in a very passion of justice, for vengeance upon his murderers?

Should we not feel that the forgiveness he pronounced, though in him it were the highest expression of charity, were in us the lowest and most exquisite baseness? Should we not feel that we could never know rest or peace until we had avenged him of his cruel wrong and that this would not, after all, be revenge, but righteous judgment? But why is it that we could not forgive such a wrong upon another? Just for this reason: It is his wrong and not ours. We are not and cannot be, merely spectators of this crime; we are, by the very fact of our being members of a society to which he and we belong, its judges, and we feel that, as such, we have no right to remit its just and righteous penalty.

But there is another reason why we cannot forgive this offence. The instinct of self-preservation is strong in our hearts, as it is strong in the heart of society. Society cannot afford to suffer martyrdom; still less to court or submit to martyrdom. The myriad interests that are entrusted to its guardianship would be sacrificed if it were to allow of crime with impunity. A society founded upon the basis of pure benevolence and universal forgiveness of offences could not hold together for a single day. Society dare not, cannot forgive its debtors.

You see, we have now advanced a step further; we have still the debtor to be paid, and we have still the law and the person or persons who are to enforce it; but you observe to what small dimensions the personal element in this equation has already shrunk. You see how large already looms the idea of law; you see that the debtor and creditor are already becoming, both together, debtors to a great, inexorable law which binds the creditor to punish and the debtor to suffer. In this aspect then we begin to see that human forgiveness is not such an easy thing. The criminal may have little to fear from the anger of his judge who is enforcing the law, but for that very reason he has nothing to hope from his compassion; for law because it is passionless must also be pitiless.

And now let us take one step, and only one step further. Let us suppose the offender to have paid the penalty for his offence; such penalty at least as he can pay and yet live. He has given, we will suppose, in the way of reparation all that society claimed from him; but is he thereupon freed from all further penalty? Does society that forgives him give him back what it was compelled to take from him? Can it give him back the happy promise of his now wasted life? Can it bring him back the opportunities, the vanished hopes and joys, of the past? Can it restore to him the honor, love, obedience, that once were his? Can it compel men who shrink from his contact as they would from that of a leper,— to give him the honored place, as a guest at life's banquet, which he might once have been entitled to? Can it cut off the consequences of his sin, as it continues to injure others by its example or its consequences, and so goes on multiplying and replenishing the earth with its evil progeny, while the birth of every fresh sin that springs from its parentage multiplies guilt against him? Can it do this? Never.

And thus we see how, by the very condition of things in which we exist, we reach at last a point at which the personal elements of pity, compassion, justice even, seem to vanish altogether, and man is face to face with a stern, impersonal, mechanical, universal law, certain as death, merciless as the grave, which proclaims that for sin in such a constitution of things there is no possibility of remission. So, then, human forgiveness is not quite so simple; the idea of human remission of all penalty for an offence is not quite so natural and easily intelligible as it appears to us when we first hear these words, " Forgive us our debts, as we forgive our debtors."